Alfonso de Liguori

The Incarnation, Birth, and Infancy of Jesus Christ

Or, the Mysteries of the Faith

Alfonso de Liguori

The Incarnation, Birth, and Infancy of Jesus Christ
Or, the Mysteries of the Faith

ISBN/EAN: 9783337022624

Printed in Europe, USA, Canada, Australia, Japan

Cover: Foto ©Lupo / pixelio.de

More available books at **www.hansebooks.com**

The Centenary Edition.

THE COMPLETE WORKS

OF

SAINT ALPHONSUS DE LIGUORI,

DOCTOR OF THE CHURCH,

Bishop of Saint Agatha, and Founder of the Congregation of the Most Holy Redeemer.

TRANSLATED FROM THE ITALIAN.

EDITED BY

REV. EUGENE GRIMM,

Priest of the Congregation of the Most Holy Redeemer.

THE ASCETICAL WORKS.
Volume IV.

THE

INCARNATION, BIRTH AND INFANCY

OF JESUS CHRIST ;

OR,

THE MYSTERIES OF THE FAITH.

Centenary Edition.

THE COMPLETE ASCETICAL WORKS
OF
ST. ALPHONSUS DE LIGUORI

24 vols., Price, per vol., *net*, $1.25.

Each book is complete in itself, and any volume will be sold separately.

Volume I. PREPARATION FOR DEATH ; or, Considerations on the Eternal Truths. Maxims of Eternity—Rule of Life.
" II. WAY OF SALVATION AND OF PERFECTION : Meditations. Pious Reflections. Spiritual Treatises.
" III. GREAT MEANS OF SALVATION AND OF PERFECTION : Prayer. Mental Prayer. The Exercises of a Retreat. Choice of a State of Life, and the Vocation to the Religious State and to the Priesthood.
" IV. THE INCARNATION, BIRTH AND INFANCY OF JESUS CHRIST ; or, The Mysteries of Faith.
" V. THE PASSION AND THE DEATH of JESUS CHRIST.
" VI. THE HOLY EUCHARIST. The Sacrifice, the Sacrament, and the Sacred Heart of Jesus Christ. Practice of Love of Jesus Christ. Novena to the Holy Ghost.
" VII., VIII. GLORIES OF MARY: 1. Explanation of the *Salve Regina*, or Hail, Holy Queen. Discourses on the Feasts of Mary. 2. Her Dolors. Her Virtues. Practices. Examples. Answers to Critics.—Devotion to the Holy Angels. Devotion to St. Joseph. Novena to St. Teresa Novena for the Repose of the Souls in Purgatory.
" IX. VICTORIES OF THE MARTYRS; or, the Lives of the Most Celebrated Martyrs of the Church.
" X., XI. THE TRUE SPOUSE OF JESUS CHRIST : 1. The first sixteen Chapters. 2. The last eight Chapters. Appendix and various small Works. Spiritual Letters.
" XII. DIGNITY AND DUTIES OF THE PRIEST ; or, SELVA, a collection of Material for Ecclesiastical Retreats. Rule of Life and Spiritual Rules.
" XIII. THE HOLY MASS : Sacrifice of Jesus Christ. Ceremonies of the Mass. Preparation and Thanksgiving. The Mass and the Office that are hurriedly said.
" XIV. THE DIVINE OFFICE : Explanation of the Psalms and Canticles.
" XV. PREACHING : The Exercises of the Missions. Various Counsels. Instructions on the Commandments and Sacraments.
" XVI. SERMONS FOR SUNDAYS.
" XVII. MISCELLANY. Historical Sketch of the Congregation of the Most Holy Redeemer. Rules and Constitutions of the Congregation of the Most Holy Redeemer. Instructions about the Religious State. Lives of two Fathers and of a Lay Brother, C.SS.R. Discourses on Calamities. Reflections useful for Bishops. Rules for Seminaries.
" XVIII., XIX., XX., XXI. LETTERS.
" XXII. LETTERS AND GENERAL ALPHABETICAL INDEX.
" XXIII., XXIV. LIFE OF ST. ALPHONSUS DE LIGUORI.

Benziger Brothers, New York. Cincinnati, and Chicago.

The Centenary Edition.

THE INCARNATION, BIRTH AND INFANCY OF JESUS CHRIST;

OR,

THE MYSTERIES OF THE FAITH.

BY
St. ALPHONSUS DE LIGUORI,
Doctor of the Church.

EDITED BY
REV. EUGENE GRIMM,
Priest of the Congregation of the Most Holy Redeemer.
SECOND EDITION.

NEW YORK, CINCINNATI, AND CHICAGO:
BENZIGER BROTHERS,
Printers to the Holy Apostolic See.

R. WASHBOURNE,   M. H. GILL & SON,
18 PATERNOSTER ROW, LONDON.   50 UPPER O'CONNELL STREET, DUBLIN.

APPROBATION.

By virtue of the authority granted me by the Most Rev. Nicholas Mauron, Superior-General of the Congregation of the Most Holy Redeemer, I hereby sanction the publication of the work entitled "The Mysteries of the Faith—The Incarnation," which is Vol. IV. the new and complete edition in English of the works of Saint Alphonsus de Liguori, called "The Centenary Edition."

ELIAS FRED. SCHAUER,

Sup. Prov. Baltimorensis.

BALTIMORE, MD., *September* 8, 1886.

Copyright, 1886, by ELIAS FREDERICK SCHAUER.

CONTENTS.

	PAGE
APPROBATION	6
NOTICE	12

THE MYSTERIES OF THE FAITH.

THE INCARNATION.

DISCOURSES FOR THE NOVENA OF CHRISTMAS.

DISCOURSE
- I. The eternal Word is made man......... 13
- II. The eternal Word being great becomes little.......... 32
- III. The eternal Word from being lord became a servant... 46
- IV. The eternal Word from being innocent becomes as it were guilty...................................... 59
- V. The eternal Word from being strong became weak.... 73
- VI. The eternal Word from being his own has made himself ours... 85
- VII. The eternal Word from being happy made himself afflicted.. 98
- VIII. The eternal Word from being rich made himself poor.. 113
- IX. The eternal Word from being high made himself low.. 126
- Discourse for Christmas night. The birth of Jesus Christ...... 140
- Discourse on the name of Jesus............................. 151
- Examples of the Infant Jesus............................... 164

MEDITATIONS

FOR EVERY DAY OF ADVENT.

MEDITATION
- I. Goodness of God in the work of the redemption....... 172
- II. Grandeur of the mystery of the Incarnation.......... 174
- III. The love of God for men........................... 177
- IV. The Word was made man in the fulness of time....... 179
- V. The abasement of Jesus 182

MEDITATION		PAGE
VI.	Jesus enlightens the world and glorifies God..........	185
VII.	The Son of God was laden with all our iniquities......	187
VIII.	God sends his Son to die in order to restore us to life..	190
IX.	The love that the Son of God has shown us in the redemption..	192
X.	Jesus, the man of sorrows, from the womb of his Mother...	194
XI.	Jesus charged with the sins of the whole world.........	197
XII.	Jesus suffers during his whole life.....................	199
XIII.	Jesus wished to suffer so much to gain our hearts......	201
XIV.	The greatest sorrow of Jesus...........................	204
XV.	The poverty of the Infant Jesus........................	206
XVI.	Jesus is the fountain of grace..........................	208
XVII.	Jesus the charitable physician of our souls.............	210
XVIII.	We should hope all things from the merits of Jesus Christ..	212

MEDITATIONS

For the Novena of Christmas.

I.	God has given us his only Son to save us.............	214
II.	Bitterness of the heart of Jesus in the womb of his mother..	217
III.	Jesus made himself a child to gain our confidence and our love...	219
IV.	The Passion of Jesus lasted during his whole life......	222
V.	Jesus offered himself for our salvation from the beginning...	225
VI.	Jesus a prisoner in the womb of Mary................	227
VII.	The sorrow that the ingratitude of man caused Jesus...	229
VIII.	The love of God manifested to man by the birth of Jesus..	232
IX.	St. Joseph goes to Bethlehem with his holy spouse.....	235

MEDITATIONS

For the Octave of Christmas and the following Days till the Epiphany.

I.	The birth of Jesus....................................	238
II.	Jesus is born an Infant...............................	240
III.	Jesus in swaddling-clothes............................	243

MEDITATION	PAGE
IV. Jesus taking milk	246
V. Jesus lying on the straw	248
VI. Jesus sleeping	251
VII. Jesus weeping	253
VIII. The name of Jesus	255
IX. The solitude of Jesus in the stable	258
X. The occupation of the Infant Jesus in the stable of Bethlehem	261
XI. The poverty of the Infant Jesus	263
XII. The abasement of Jesus	265

FOR THE OCTAVE OF THE EPIPHANY.

I. The adoration of the Magi	268
II. The presentation of Jesus in the Temple	270
III. The flight of Jesus into Egypt	272
IV. The dwelling of Jesus in Egypt	274
V. The return of Jesus from Egypt	277
VI. The dwelling of Jesus at Nazareth	279
VII. The same subject continued	281
VIII. The loss of Jesus in the Temple	283

OTHER MEDITATIONS.

FOR THE FIRST EIGHT DAYS OF ADVENT.

I. The love that God has manifested to us in the incarnation of the Word	286
II. Goodness of God the Father and of God the Son in the work of the redemption	287
III. Motives of confidence that are given to us by the incarnation of the Word	289
IV. Happiness of having been born after the redemption and in the true Church	291
V. Jesus has done and suffered everything to save us	293
VI. The sight of our sins afflicted Jesus from the first moment of his life	294
VII. The desire that Jesus had to suffer for us	296
VIII. Three fountains of grace that we have in Jesus Christ	298

OTHER MEDITATIONS.

FOR THE NOVENA OF CHRISTMAS.

(Chaplet to be recited before every meditation, 300.)

MEDITATION PAGE
I. The love that God has shown to us in becoming man.. 301
II. The love of God in being born an Infant............ 303
III. The life of poverty which Jesus led even from his birth. 305
IV. The life of humility which Jesus led even from his infancy.. 306
V. The life of sorrow which Jesus led even from his birth. 308
VI. The mercy of God in coming down from heaven to save us by his death................................. 309
VII. The journey of the Infant Jesus to Egypt............. 311
VIII. The sojourn of the Infant Jesus in Egypt and in Nazareth.. 312
IX. The birth of the Infant Jesus in the cave of Bethlehem. 314
Another meditation for the feast of the circumcision............ 316
Another meditation for the feast of the Epiphany............... 318
Another meditation for the feast of the Holy Name............. 320
HYMNS.. 322
    Ode on the birth of our Saviour Jesus Christ, 322. The Madonna's Lullaby, 328. St. Joseph addressing the divine child Jesus, 330. To the Infant Jesus in the crib, 331. To the Infant Jesus, 332.
The Way of Bethlehem 334
INDULGENCES attached to the exercises of piety in honor of the Infant Jesus... 347

DARTS OF FIRE;
or,
Proofs that Jesus Christ has given us of his love in the work of the redemption.. 359
HYMN. The soul sighing for Jesus........................ 406
PIOUS SENTIMENTS of a soul that desires to belong entirely to Jesus Christ... 407
    Sentiments of a lively faith, 407; — of confidence, 409; — of penitence, 413; — of purpose of amendment, 415; — of love, 417; — of conformity to the will of God, 421; — Diverse affections, 422.
SIGHS of love towards God.............................. 427

Contents.

ASPIRATIONS of love to Jesus Christ.......................... 434
MAXIMS for attaining perfection in the love of Jesus Christ...... 437
ACTS that the Christian should perform every day.............. 440
MANNER of making mental prayer.............................. 445
EJACULATORY PRAYERS for the twelve greatest solemnities in the year,—seven of our Lord and five of the Blessed Virgin,—which may be used at any other time and on any day, according to each one's devotion................................ 446
HYMN. Aspirations to Jesus................................... 449
NOVENA to the holy name of Jesus............................ 451
HYMN. To the Infant Jesus.................................... 465
INDEX... 466

St. Alphonsus wrote the following little work in 1750; but his infirmities and his many duties did not permit him to publish it till the year 1758.

By a *Novena* we mean the nine days that precede a feast; the first day of the novena of Christmas is, therefore, the 16th of December.

These discourses may serve either for meditation or for spiritual reading. After the discourses will be found novenas of meditations and of prayers. There is also added a list of the indulgences attached to this exercise.—ED.

THE MYSTERIES OF THE FAITH.

THE INCARNATION.

Discourses for the Novena of Christmas.

DISCOURSE I.

The Eternal Word is made Man.

Ignem veni mittere in terram; et quid volo, nisi ut accendatur?

"I am come to cast fire on the earth; and what will I but that it be kindled?"—
Luke, xii. 49.

THE Jews solemnized a day called by them *dies ignis*,[1] the day of fire, in memory of the fire with which Nehemias consumed the sacrifice, upon his return with his countrymen from the captivity of Babylon. Even so, and indeed with more reason, should Christmas-day be called the day of fire, on which a God came as a little child to cast the fire of love into the hearts of men.

I came to cast fire on the earth: so spoke Jesus Christ; and truly so it was. Before the coming of the Messias, who loved God upon earth? Hardly was he known in a nook of the world, that is, in Judea; and even there how very few loved him when he came! As to the rest of the world, some worshipped the sun, some the brutes, some the very stones, and others again even viler creatures still. But after the coming of Jesus Christ, the name of God became everywhere known, and was loved by many. After the Redeemer was born, God was more loved by men in a few years than he had before been in the lapse of four thousand years, since the creation of man.

[1] 2 *Mach.* i. 18.

It is a custom with many Christians to anticipate the arrival of Christmas a considerable time beforehand by fitting up in their homes a crib to represent the birth of Jesus Christ; but few there are who think of preparing their hearts, in order that the Infant Jesus may be born in them, and there find his repose. Among these few, however, we would be reckoned, in order that we too may be made worthy to burn with that happy flame which gives contentment to souls on this earth, and bliss in heaven.

Let us consider on this first day how the Eternal Word had no other end in becoming man than to inflame us with his divine love. Let us ask light of Jesus Christ and of his most holy Mother, and so let us begin.

I.

Adam, our first parent, sins; ungrateful for the great benefits conferred on him, he rebels against God, by a violation of the precept given him not to eat of the forbidden fruit. On this account God is obliged to drive him out of the earthly paradise in this world, and in the world to come to deprive not only Adam, but all the descendants of this rebellious creature, of the heavenly and everlasting paradise which he had prepared for them after this mortal life.

Behold, then, all mankind together condemned to a life of pain and misery, and forever shut out from heaven. But hearken to God, who, as Isaias tells us in his fifty-second chapter, would seem, after our manner of understanding, to give vent to his affliction in lamentations and wailings: *And now what have I here*, saith the Lord, *for My people is taken away gratis*.[1] "And now," says God, "what delight have I left in heaven, now that I have lost men, who were my delight?" *My delights*

---

[1] "Et nunc, quid mihi est hic, dicit Dominus, quoniam ablatus est populus meus gratis?"—*Isai*. lii. 5.

were to be with the children of men.[1] But how is this, O Lord? Thou hast in heaven so many seraphim, so many angels; and canst Thou thus take to heart having lost men? Indeed, what need hast Thou of angels or of men to fill up the sum of Thy happiness? Thou hast always been, and Thou art in Thyself, most happy; what can ever be wanting to Thy bliss, which is infinite? "That is all true," says God; "but" (and these are the words of Cardinal Hugo on the above text of Isaias)—"but, losing man, I deem that I have nothing;[2] I consider that I have lost all, since my delight was to be with men; and now these men I have lost, and, poor hapless creatures, they are doomed to live forever far away from me."

But how can the Lord call men his delight? Yes, indeed, writes St. Thomas, God loves man just as if man were his god, and as if without man he could not be happy; "as if man were the god of God himself, and without him he could not be happy."[3] St. Gregory of Nazianzen adds, moreover, that God, for the love he bears to men, seems beside himself: "we are bold to say it, God is out of himself by reason of his immense love;"[4] so runs the proverb, "Love puts the lover beside himself."

"But no," then said the Lord, "I will not lose man; straightway let there be found a Redeemer who may satisfy my justice in behalf of man, and so rescue him from the hands of his enemies and from the eternal death due to him."

And here St. Bernard, in his contemplations on this subject, imagines a struggle to ensue between the jus-

---

[1] "Deliciæ meæ, esse cum filiis hominum."—*Prov.* viii. 31.
[2] "Non reputo aliquid me habere."
[3] "Quasi homo Dei Deus esset, et sine ipso beatus esse non posset." —*Opusc.* 63, c. 7.
[4] "Audemus dicere quod Deus, præ magnitudine amoris, extra se sit."—*De Div. Nom.* c. 4.

tice and the mercy of God. Justice says: "I no longer exist if Adam be not punished; I perish if Adam die not."[1] Mercy, on the other hand, says: "I am lost if man be not pardoned; I perish if he does not obtain forgiveness."[2] In this contest the Lord decides, that in order to deliver man, who was guilty of death, some innocent one must die: "Let one die who is no debtor to death."[3]

On earth, there was not one innocent. "Since, therefore," says the Eternal Father, "amongst men there is none who can satisfy My justice, let him come forward who will go to redeem man." The angels, the cherubim, the seraphim, all are silent, not one replies; one voice alone is heard, that of the Eternal Word, who says, *Lo, here am I; send Me.*[4] "Father," says the only-begotten Son, "Thy majesty, being infinite, and having been injured by man, cannot be fittingly satisfied by an angel, who is purely a creature; and though Thou mightest accept of the satisfaction of an angel, reflect that, in spite of so great benefits bestowed on man, in spite of so many promises and threats, we have not yet been able to gain his love, because he is not yet aware of the love we bear him. If we would oblige him without fail to love us, what better occasion can we find than that, in order to redeem him, I, Thy Son, should go upon earth, should there assume human flesh, and pay by my death the penalty due by him. In this manner Thy justice is fully satisfied, and at the same time man is thoroughly convinced of our love!" "But think," answered the Heavenly Father—"think, O my Son, that in taking upon Thyself the burden of man's satisfaction, Thou wilt have to lead a life full of sufferings!" "No

[1] "Perii, si Adam non moriatur."
[2] "Perii, nisi misericordiam consequatur."
[3] "Moriatur, qui nihil debeat morti."—*In Annunt. B. M.* s. 1.
[4] "Ecce ego, mitte me."—*Isai.* vi. 8.

The Eternal Word is made Man.

matter," replied the Son: "*Lo, here am I, send Me.*" "Think that Thou wilt have to be born in a cave, the shelter of the beasts of the field; thence Thou must flee into Egypt whilst still an infant, to escape the hands of those very men who, even from Thy tenderest infancy, will seek to take away Thy life." "It matters not: *Lo, here am I, send Me.*" "Think that, on Thy return to Palestine, Thou shalt there lead a life most arduous, most despicable, passing Thy days as a simple boy in a carpenter's shop." "It matters not: *Lo, here am I, send Me.*" "Think that when Thou goest fo.th to preach and to manifest Thyself, Thou wilt have indeed a few, but very few, to follow Thee; the greater part will despise Thee and call Thee impostor, magician, fool, Samaritan; and, finally, they will persecute Thee to such a pass that they will make Thee die shamefully on a gibbet by dint of torments." "No matter: *Lo, here am I, send Me.*"

The decree then being passed that the Divine Son should be made man, and so become the Redeemer of men, the Archangel Gabriel speeds on his way to Mary. Mary accepts him for her Son: *And the Word was made flesh.*[1] And thus behold Jesus in the womb of Mary; having now made his entry into the world in all humility and obedience, he says: "Since, O my Father, men cannot make atonement to Thy offended justice by their works and sacrifices, behold me, Thy Son, now clothed in mortal flesh, behold me ready to give Thee in their stead satisfaction with my sufferings and with my death!" *Wherefore when He cometh into the world He saith: Sacrifice and oblation thou wouldst not; but a body Thou hast fitted to me. . . . Then said I, Behold, I come. . . . It is written of Me that I should do Thy will.*[2]

[1] "Et Verbum caro factum est."—*John,* i. 14.
[2] "Ideo ingrediens mundum dicit: Hostiam et oblationem noluisti; corpus autem aptasti mihi. . . . Tunc dixi: Ecce venio, . . . ut faciam, Deus, voluntatem tuam."—*Heb.* x. 5.

So, then, for us miserable worms, and to captivate our love, has a God deigned to become man? Yes, it is a matter of faith, as the Holy Church teaches us: *For us men, and for our salvation, He came down from heaven . . . and was made man.*[1] Yes, indeed, so much has God done in order to be loved by us.

Alexander the Great, after he had conquered Darius and subdued Persia, wished to gain the affections of that people, and so went about dressed in the Persian costume. In like manner would our God appear to act; in order to draw towards him the affections of men, he clothed himself completely after the human fashion, and appeared made man: *in shape found as a man.*[2] And by this means he wished to make known the depth of the love which he bore to man: *The grace of God our Saviour hath appeared to all men.*[3]

Man does not love me, would God seem to say, because he does not see me. I wish to make myself seen by him and to converse with him, and so make myself loved: *He was seen upon earth, and conversed with men.*[4]

The divine love for man was extreme, and so it had been from all eternity: *I have loved thee with an everlasting love, therefore have I drawn thee, taking pity on thee.*[5] But heretofore it had not appeared how great and inconceivable it was. Then it truly appeared, when the Son of God showed himself a little one in a stable on a bundle of straw: *The goodness and kindness of God our Saviour*

---

[1] "Propter nos homines, et propter nostram salutem, descendit de cœlis. . . . et homo factus est."—*Symb. Nic. et Const.*
[2] "Habitu inventus ut homo."—*Phil.* ii. 7.
[3] "Apparuit gratia Dei Salvatoris nostri omnibus hominibus."—*Tit.* ii. 11.
[4] "In terris visus est, et cum hominibus conversatus est."—*Baruch,* iii. 38.
[5] "In charitate perpetua dilexi te; ideo attraxi te, miserans."—*Jer.* xxxi. 3.

appeared.[1] The Greek text reads: *The singular love of God towards men appeared.* St. Bernard says that from the beginning the world had seen the power of God in the creation, and his wisdom in the government of the world; but only afterwards, in the Incarnation of the Word, was seen how great was his mercy.[2] Before God was seen made man upon earth, men could not conceive an idea of the divine goodness; therefore did he take mortal flesh, that, appearing as man, he might make plain to men the greatness of his benignity.[3]

And in what manner could the Lord better display to thankless man his goodness and his love? Man, by despising God, says St. Fulgentius, put himself aloof from God forever; but as man was unable to return to God, God came in search of him on earth.[4] And St. Augustine had already said as much: "Because we could not go to the Mediator, he condescended to come to us."[5]

I will draw them with the cords of Adam, with the bands of love.[6] Men allow themselves to be drawn by love; the tokens of affection shown to them are a sort of chain which binds them, and in a manner forces them to love those who love them. For this end the Eternal Word chose to become man, to draw to himself by such a pledge

---

[1] "Benignitas et humanitas apparuit Salvatoris nostri Dei."—*Tit.* iii. 4.

[2] "Apparuerat ante potentia in rerum creatione; apparebat sapientia in earum gubernatione; sed benignitas misericordiæ maxime apparuit in humanitate."—*In Nat. D.* s. 1.

[3] "Priusquam appareret humanitas, latebat benignitas. Sed, unde tanta agnosci poterat? Venit in carne, ut, apparente humanitate, benignitas agnosceretur."—*In Epiph.* s. 1.

[4] "Homo, Deum contemnens, a Deo discessit; Deus, hominem diligens, ad homines venit."—*S. de Dupl. Nat. Chr.*

[5] "Quia ad medicum venire non poteramus, ipse ad nos venire dignatus est."—*Serm.* 88, *E. B.*

[6] "In funiculis Adam traham eos, in vinculis charitatis."—*Osee*, xi. 4.

of affection (a stronger than which could not possibly be found) the love of men : "God was made man, that God might be more familiarly loved by man."[1] It seems that our Redeemer wished to signify this very thing to a devout Franciscan called Father Francis of St. James, as is related in the Franciscan Diary for the 15th of December. Jesus frequently appeared to him as a lovely infant : but the holy friar longing in his fervor to hold him in his arms, the sweet child always fled away ; wherefore the servant of God lovingly complained of these departures. One day the divine Child again appeared to him ; but how ? He came with golden chains in his hands, to give him to understand that now he came to make him his prisoner, and to be himself imprisoned by him, nevermore to be separated. Francis, emboldened at this, fastened the chains to the foot of the Infant, and bound him round his heart ; and, in good truth, from that time forward it seemed to him as if he saw the beloved Child in the prison of his heart made a perpetual prisoner. That which Jesus did with this his servant on this occasion, he really has done with all men when he was made man ; he wished with such a prodigy of love to be, as it were, enchained by us, and at the same time to enchain our hearts by obliging them to love him, according to the prophecy of Osee : *I will draw them with the cords of Adam, with the bands of love.*[2]

In divers ways, says St. Leo, had God already benefited man ; but in no way has he more clearly exhibited the excess of his bounty than in sending him a Redeemer to teach him the way of salvation, and to procure for him the life of grace. "The goodness of God has imparted gifts to the human race in various ways ;

---

[1] "Deus homo factus est, ut familiarius ab homine diligeretur."— *Misc.* l. i. tit. 87.

[2] "In funiculis Adam traham eos, in vinculis charitatis."—*Osee*, xi. 4.

but it surpassed the ordinary bounds of its abundant kindness when, in Christ, mercy itself came down to those who were in sin, truth to those wandering out of the way, and life to those who were dead."[1]

St. Thomas asks why the Incarnation of the Word is called the work of the Holy Ghost : *And was incarnate by the Holy Ghost.*[2] It is certain that all God's works, styled by theologians *opera ad extra,* or external works, are the works of all the three divine Persons. And why, therefore, should the Incarnation be attributed solely to the Person of the Holy Ghost ? The chief reason which the Angelic Doctor assigns for it is because all the works of divine love are attributed to the Holy Ghost, who is the substantial love of the Father and of the Son ; and the work of the Incarnation was purely the effect of the surpassing love which God bears to man : " But this proceeded from the very great love of God, that the Son of God should assume flesh to himself in the womb of the Virgin."[3] And this the prophet would signify when he says, *God will come from the south ;*[4] that is, observes the Abbot Rupert, " From the great charity of God, he has shone upon us."[5] For this purpose, again writes St. Augustine, the Eternal Word came upon earth, to make known to man how dearly God loved him.[6] And St. Laurence Justinian : " In no instance has he so clearly

---

[1] "Diversis modis humano generi Bonitas Divina munera impertiit ; sed abundantiam solitæ benignitatis excessit. quando in Christo ipsa ad peccatores Misericodia, ad errantes Veritas, ad mortuos Vita descendit."—*De Nat.* s. 4.

[2] "Et incarnatus est de Spiritu Sancto."

[3] "Hoc autem ex maximo Dei amore provenit, ut Filius Dei carnem sibi assumeret in utero Virginis."—P. 3, q. 32, a. 1.

[4] "Deus ab austro veniet."—*Hab.* iii. 3.

[5] "A magna charitate Dei in nos effulsit."

[6] "Maxime propterea Christus advenit, ut cognosceret homo quantum eum diligat Deus."—*De catech. rud.* c. 4.

manifested his amiable charity to men as when God was made man."[1]

But what still more evinces the depth of the divine love towards the human race is, that the Son of God should come in search of him, whilst man was fleeing away from him. This the Apostle declares in these words, *Nowhere doth He take hold of the angels; but of the seed of Abraham He taketh hold.*[2] On which St. John Chrysostom thus comments: "He says not, he received, but he seized hold of ; from the figure of those who are in pursuit of fugitives, that they may effect their capture."[3] Thus God came from heaven to arrest, as it were, ungrateful man in his flight from him. It is as if he had said, "O man! behold, it is nothing but the love of thee that has brought me on earth to seek after thee. Why wilt thou flee from me? Stay with me, love me; do not avoid me, for I greatly love thee."

God came, then, to seek lost man ; and that man might the more easily comprehend the love of this his God for him, and might surrender his love in return to one who so deeply loved him, he willed, the first time of his appearance under a visible form, to show himself as a tender infant, laid upon straw. "O blessed straw, fairer than roses or lilies," exclaims St. Peter Chrysologus, "what favored land produced you ? Oh, what an enviable lot is yours, to serve as a bed for the King of Heaven ! But, alas !" continues the saint, "alas ! you are but cold for Jesus ; for you know not how to warm him in that damp cavern, where he is now shivering with

---

[1] "In nullo sic amabilem suam hominibus patefecit charitatem, sicut cum Deus homo factus est."—*De Casto Conu.* c. 23.

[2] "Nusquam enim Angelos apprehendit, sed semen Abrahæ apprehendit."—*Heb.* ii. 16.

[3] "Non dixit : Suscepit,—sed : Apprehendit ;—ex metaphora insequentium eos qui aversi sunt, ut fugientes apprehendere valeant."—*In Heb. hom.* 5.

The Eternal Word is made Man. 23

cold ; but you are fire and flames for us, since you supply us with a flame of love which rivers of water shall never quench."[1]

It was not enough, says St. Augustine, for the divine love to have made us to his own image in creating the first man Adam ; but he must also himself be made to our image in redeeming us.[2] Adam partook of the forbidden fruit, beguiled by the serpent, which suggested to Eve that if she ate of that fruit she should become like to God, acquiring the knowledge of good and evil ; and therefore the Lord then said, *Behold, Adam is become one of us*.[3] God said this ironically, and to upbraid Adam for his rash presumption ; but after the Incarnation of the Word we can truly say, " Behold, God is become like one of us."[4]

"Look, then, O man," exclaims St. Augustine, "thy God is made thy brother ;"[5] thy God is made like thee, a son of Adam, as thou art : he has put on thy selfsame flesh, has made himself passible, liable to suffer and to die as thou art. He could have assumed the nature of an angel ; but no, he would take on himself thy very flesh, that thus he might give satisfaction to God with the very same flesh (though sinless) of Adam the sinner. And he even gloried in this, oftentimes styling himself the Son of man ; hence we have every right to call him our brother.

It was an immeasurably greater humiliation for God to become man than if all the princes of the earth, than if

---

[1] "O felices paleas, rosis et liliis pulchriores ! quæ vos genuit tellus ? Non palearum momentaneum, sed perpetuum vos suppeditatis incendium, quod nulla flumina exstinguent."

[2] "In primo homine, fecit nos Deus ad imaginem suam; in hac die, factus est ad imaginem nostram."—*Serm.* 119, *E. B. app.*

[3] "Ecce Adam quasi unus ex nobis factus est "—*Gen.* iii. 22.

[4] "De cætero dicemus veraciter, quia Deus factus est quasi unus ex nobis."—*De Emman.* l. 1, c. 19.

[5] "Deus tuus factus est frater tuus."

all the angels and saints of heaven, with the divine Mother herself, had been turned into a blade of grass, or into a handful of clay ; yes, for grass, clay, princes, angels, saints, are all creatures ; but between the creature and God there is an infinite difference. Ah, exclaims St. Bernard, the more a God has humbled himself for us in becoming man, so much the more has he made his goodness known to us : " The smaller he has become by humility, the greater he has made himself in bounty." [1] But the love which Jesus Christ bears to us, cries out the Apostle, irresistibly urges and impels us to love him : *The charity of Christ presseth us.*[2]

O God ! did not faith assure us of it, who could ever believe that a God, for love for such a worm as man is, should himself become a worm like him ? A devout author says, Suppose, by chance, that, passing on your way, you should have crushed to death a worm in your path; and then some one, observing your compassion for the poor reptile, should say to you, Well, now, if you would restore that dead worm to life, you must first yourself become a worm like it, and then must shed all your blood, and make a bath of it in which to wash the worm, and so it shall revive; what would you reply ? Certainly you would say, And what matters it to me whether the worm be alive or dead, if I should have to purchase its life by my own death ? And much more would you say so if it was not an inoffensive worm, but an ungrateful asp, which, in return for all your benefits, had made an attempt upon your life. But even should your love for that reptile reach so far as to induce you to suffer death in order to restore it to life, what would men say then ? And what would not that serpent do for you, whose death had saved it, supposing it were capable of reason ? But

---

[1] " Quanto minorem se fecit in humilitate, tanto majorem exhibuit in bonitate."—*In Epiph.* s. 1.

[2] " Charitas Christi urget nos."—2 *Cor.* v. 14.

this much has Jesus Christ done for you, most vile worm; and you, with the blackest ingratitude, have tried oftentimes to take away his life; and your sins would have done so, were Jesus liable to die any more. How much viler are you in the sight of God than is a worm in your own sight ! What difference would it make to God had you remained dead and forever reprobate in your sins, as you well deserved ? Nevertheless, this God had such a love for you that, to release you from eternal death, he first became a worm like you; and then, to save you, would lavish upon you his heart's blood, even to the last drop, and endure the death which you had justly deserved.

Yes, all this is of faith: *And the Word was made flesh.*[1] *He hath loved us, and washed us from our sins in His own blood.*[2] The Holy Church declares herself to be filled with terror at the idea of the work of redemption: *I considered Thy work, and was afraid.*[3] And this the prophet said of old: *O Lord, I have heard Thy hearing, and was afraid. . . . Thou wentest forth for the salvation of Thy people; for salvation with Thy Christ.*[4]

Hence St. Thomas terms the mystery of the Incarnation the miracle of miracles;[5] a miracle above all comprehension, in which God showed how powerful was his love towards men, which of God made him man, of Creator a creature.[6] The Creator, says St. Peter Damian, springs from the creature, of Lord it made him servant, of impassible subject to sufferings and to death: *He hath showed might in His arm.*[7] St. Peter of Alcan-

[1] " Et Verbum caro factum est."—*John*, i. 14.
[2] " Dilexit nos, et lavit nos . . . in sanguine suo."—*Apoc.* i. 5.
[3] " Consideravi opera tua, et expavi."—*Off. Circumc. resp.* 6.
[4] " Domine, audivi auditionem tuam, et timui. . . . Egressus es in salutem populi tui, in salutem cum Christo tuo."—*Hab.* iii. 2. 13.
[5] " Miraculum miraculorum."—*De Pot.* q. 6, a. 2, ad 9.
[6] " Creator oritur ex creatura."—*In Nat. B. V.* s. 2.
[7] " Fecit potentiam in brachio suo."—*Luke*, i. 51.

tara, one day hearing the Gospel sung which is appointed for the third Mass on Christmas-night—*In the beginning was the Word*—in reflecting on this mystery became so inflamed with divine love that, in a state of ecstasy, he was borne a considerable space through the air to the foot of the Blessed Sacrament. And St. Augustine says that his soul could feast forever on the contemplation of the exalted goodness of God, manifested to us in the work of human redemption.[1] For this reason it was that the Lord sent this saint, on account of his fervent devotion to this mystery, to inscribe these words on the heart of St. Mary Magdalene of Pazzi: *And the Word was made flesh.*

II.

Whosoever loves, has no other end in loving but to be loved again. God, then, having so dearly loved us, seeks nothing else from us, as St. Bernard remarks, but our love: "When God loves, he desires nothing else than to be loved."[2] Wherefore, he goes on with this admonition to each one of us: "He has made known his love, that he may experience thine."[3] O man, whoever thou art, thou hast witnessed the love which God has borne thee in becoming man, in suffering and dying for thee; how long shall it be before God shall know by experience and by deeds the love thou bearest him? Ah! truly every man at the sight of a God clothed in flesh, and choosing to lead a life of such durance, and to suffer a death of such ignominy, ought to be enkindled with love towards a God so loving. *Oh that Thou wouldst rend the heavens and wouldst come down: the mountains would melt away at Thy presence, . . . the waters would burn with fire.*[4]

---

[1] "Non satiabar considerare altitudinem consilii tui super salutem generis humani."—*Conf.* l. 9, c. 6.
[2] "Cum amat Deus, non aliud vult quam amari."—*In Cant.* s. 83.
[3] "Notam fecit dilectionem suam; experiatur et tuam."—*De Aquæd.*
[4] "Utinam dirumperes cœlos et descenderes! a facie tua montes defluerent . . . aquæ arderent igni."—*Isai.* lxiv. 1.

The Eternal Word is made Man.

Oh that Thou wouldst deign, my God (thus cried out the prophet before the arrival of the Divine Word upon earth), to leave the heavens, and descend here to become man amongst us! Ah, then, on beholding Thee like one of themselves, the mountains would melt away; men would surmount all obstacles, remove all difficulties, in observing Thy laws and Thy counsels; the waters would burn with fire! Oh, surely Thou wouldst enkindle such a furnace in the human heart that even the most frozen souls must catch the flame of Thy blessed love! And, in fact, after the Incarnation of the Son of God, how brilliantly has the fire of divine love shone to many loving souls! And it may be indeed asserted, without fear of contradiction, God was more beloved in one century after the coming of Jesus Christ than in the entire forty preceding centuries. How many youths, how many of the nobly born, and how many monarchs even, have left wealth, honors, and their very kingdoms, to seek the desert or the cloister, that there, in poverty and obscure seclusion, they might the more unreservedly give themselves up to the love of this their Saviour! How many martyrs have gone rejoicing and making merry on their way to torments and to death! How many tender young virgins have refused the proffered hands of the great ones of this world, in order to go and die for Jesus Christ, and so repay in some measure the affection of a God who stooped down to become incarnate and to die for love of them!

Yes, all this is most true; but now comes a tale for tears. Has this been the case with all men? Have all sought thus to correspond with this immense love of Jesus Christ? Alas, my God, the greater part have combined to repay him with nothing but ingratitude! And you also, my brother, tell me, what sort of return have you made up to this time for the love your God has borne you? Have you always shown yourself thankful? Have you ever seriously reflected what those words mean, a God to be made man, and to die for thee?

A certain man, while one day attending Mass without devotion, as too many do, at these concluding words of the last Gospel, *And the Word was made flesh,*[1] made no external act of reverence; at the same instant a devil struck him a severe blow, saying, "Thankless wretch! thou hearest that a God was made man for thee, and dost thou not even deign to bend the knee? Oh, if God had done the like for me, I should be eternally occupied in thanking him!"

Tell me, O Christian! what more could Jesus Christ have done to win thy love? If the Son of God had engaged to rescue from death his own Father, what lower humiliation could he stoop to than to assume human flesh, and lay down his life in sacrifice for his salvation? Nay, I say more; had Jesus Christ been a mere man, instead of one of the divine Persons, and had wished to gain by some token of affection the love of his God, what more could he have done than he has done for thee? If a servant of thine had given for thy love his very life-blood, would he not have riveted thy heart to him, and obliged thee to love him in mere gratitude? And how comes it, then, that Jesus Christ, though he has laid down his life for thee, has still failed to win thy love?

Alas! men hold in contempt the divine love, because they do not, or, rather let us say, because they will not, understand what a treasure it is to enjoy divine grace, which, according to the Wise Man, is an infinite treasure: *An infinite treasure to men, which they that use become the friends of God.*[2] Men appreciate the good graces of a

---

[1] "Et Verbum caro factum est."—*John,* i. 14.

[2] "Infinitus enim thesaurus est hominibus; quo qui usi sunt, participes facti sunt amicitiæ Dei."—*Wisd.* vii. 14.

prince, of a prelate, of a nobleman, of a man of letters, and even of a vile animal; and yet these same persons set no store by the grace of God,—but renounce it for mere smoke, for a brutal gratification, for a handful of earth, for a whim, for nothing.

What sayest thou, my dear brother? Dost thou wish still to be ranked among these ungrateful ones? For, if thou dost not wish for God, says St. Augustine, if thou canst meet with something better than God: "Desire something better, if thou dost deserve something better."[1] Go, find thyself a prince more courteous, a master, a brother, a friend more amiable, and who has shown thee a deeper love. Go, seek for thyself one who is better qualified than God to make thee happy in the present life and in the life to come.

Whoever loves God has nothing to fear, and God cannot help loving in return one who loves him: *I love those who love me*.[2] And what shall he be afraid of who is the beloved of God? *The Lord is my light and my salvation, whom shall I fear?*[3] So said David, and so said the sisters of Lazarus to our Blessed Lord: *He whom thou lovest is sick*.[4] It was enough for them to know that Jesus Christ loved their brother, to convince them that he would do everything for his recovery.

But how, on the contrary, can God love those who despise his love? Come, then, let us once for all make the resolution to give the tribute of our love to a God who has so sincerely loved us. And let us continually beseech him to grant us the precious gift of his holy love. St. Francis de Sales says that this grace of loving God was the grace for which we ought to ask God

---

[1] "Aliud desidera, si melius inveneris."—*In Ps.* 26 *enarr.* 2.
[2] "Ego diligentes me diligo."—*Prov.* viii. 17.
[3] "Dominus illuminatio mea et salus mea; quem timebo?"—*Ps.* xxvi. 1.
[4] "Quem amas, infirmatur."—*John*, xi. 3.

more than for any other; because with divine love all good comes to a soul: *All good things come together with her*.[1] This made St. Augustine say, "Love, and do whatever you like."[2] Whoever loves a person avoids everything that may offend him, and always seeks what may give him most pleasure. Thus is it with one who really loves God; he can never deliberately do anything to offend him, but he studies in every possible manner to please him.

And in order the more quickly and the more surely to obtain this gift of divine love, let us have recourse to the foremost of God's lovers—I mean, to Mary his Mother, who was so inflamed with his holy love that the devils, as St. Bonaventure assures us, had not the boldness even to tempt her: "They were scared away by her burning charity, so that they dared not approach her."[3] And Richard adds that even the seraphim themselves might descend from their lofty throne in heaven to take a lesson in love from the heart of Mary.[4] And because, continues St. Bonaventure, the heart of Mary was a complete furnace of divine love, therefore all who love this Blessed Mother, and address themselves to her, will be inflamed by her with the same love; she will make them resemble herself.[5]

If we wish to add to this discourse some example about the Infant Jesus, we may select one of those related at the end on page 164.

[1] "Venerunt . . . omnia bona pariter cum illa."—*Wisd.* vii. 11.
[2] "Ama, et fac quod vis."
[3] "A sua inflammatissima charitate dæmones pellebantur, in tantum quod non erant ausi illi appropinquare."—*Pro Fest. V. M.* s. 4, a. 3, c. 2.
[4] "Seraphim e cœlo descendere poterant, ut amorem discerent in corde Virginis."
[5] "Quia tota ardens fuit, omnes se amantes eamque tangentes incendit (et sibi assimilat)."—*De B. V. M.* s. 1.

Affections and Prayers.

Let us say with St. Augustine, "O fire, ever burning, inflame me."[1] O Word Incarnate, Thou wert made man to enkindle divine love in our hearts; and how couldst Thou have met with such a want of gratitude in the hearts of men? Thou hast spared nothing to induce them to love Thee; Thou hast even gone so far as to give Thy blood and Thy life for them: and how, then, can men still remain so ungrateful? Do they, perchance, not know it? Yes, they know it, and they believe that for them Thou hast come down from heaven to put on mortal flesh, and to load Thyself with our miseries; they know that for their love Thou hast led a painful life, and embraced an ignominious death; and how, then, can they live forgetful of Thee? They love relatives, friends; they love even animals: if from them they receive any token of good-will, they are anxious to repay it; and yet towards Thee alone are they so loveless and ungrateful. But, alas! in accusing them, I am my own accuser: I who have treated Thee worse than any one else. But Thy goodness encourages me, which I feel has borne with me so long, in order at length to pardon me, and to inflame me with Thy love, provided I will but repent and love Thee. Indeed, my God, I do wish to repent; and I grieve with my whole soul for having offended Thee; I wish to love Thee with my whole heart. I am well aware, my Redeemer, that my heart is no longer worthy of Thy acceptance, since it has forsaken Thee for the love of creatures; but, at the same time, I see that Thou art willing to have it, and with my entire will I dedicate it and present it to Thee. Inflame it, then, wholly with Thy divine love, and grant that from this day forward it may never love any other but Thee, O infinite Goodness! worthy of an infinite love. I love Thee, my Jesus; I love Thee, O sovereign Good! I love Thee, O only Love of my soul!

O Mary my Mother, thou who art the mother of fair love,[2] do thou obtain for me this grace to love my God; I hope it of thee.

[1] "O Ignis qui semper ardes! accende me."—*Solil. an. ad D.* c. 34.
[2] "Mater pulchræ dilectionis."—*Ecclus.* xxiv. 24.

DISCOURSE II.

The Eternal Word being Great becomes Little.

Parvulus natus est nobis, et Filius datus est nobis.
"A child is born to us, and a son is given to us."—*Is.* ix. 6.

Plato said that Love is the loadstone of love.[1] Hence comes the common proverb, as St. John Chrysostom remarks: "If you wish to be loved, love,"[2] for certainly there is no more effectual means to secure for one's self the affections of another than to love him, and to make him aware that he is loved.

But, my Jesus, this rule, this proverb, holds good for others, holds good for all, but not for Thee. Men are grateful to all, but not to Thee. Thou art at a loss what further to do, to show men the love Thou bearest them; Thou hast positively nothing more to do, to allure the affections of men; yet, in point of fact, how many are there among mankind who love Thee? Alas! the greatest number, we may say, nearly all, not only do not love Thee, but they offend Thee and despise Thee.

And shall we stand in the ranks of these heartless wretches? God has not earned this at our hands; that God, so good, so tender of us, who, being great, and of infinite greatness, has thought fit to make himself little in order to be loved by us. Let us seek light from Jesus and Mary.

I.

To compass the idea of the immense love of God to men in becoming himself a man and a feeble child for our love it would be necessary to comprehend his greatness. But what mind of man or angel can conceive the greatness of God, which is indeed infinite?

---

[1] "Magnes amoris, amor."
[2] "Si vis amari, ama."--*Ad pop. Ant. hom.* 13.

St. Ambrose says that to say God is greater than the heavens, than all kings, all saints, all angels, is to do an injury to God; just as it would be an injury to a prince to say that he was greater than a blade of grass, or a small fly. God is greatness itself, and all greatness together is but the smallest atom of the greatness of God.

David, contemplating the divine greatness, and seeing that he could not and never would be able to comprehend it, could only say, *O Lord, who is like to Thee?*[1] O Lord, what greatness shall ever be found like to Thine? And how in truth should David ever be able to comprehend it, since his understanding was but finite, and God's greatness infinite? *Great is the Lord, and greatly to be praised; and of His greatness there is no end.*[2] *Do I not fill heaven and earth, saith the Lord.*[3] Thus all of us, according to our mode of understanding, are nothing but so many miserable little fishes, living in this immense ocean of the essence of God: *In Him we live, move, and be.*[4]

What are we, then, in respect to God? And what are all men, all monarchs of earth, and even all saints and all angels of heaven, confronted with the infinite greatness of God? We are all like or even smaller than a grain of sand in comparison with the rest of the earth: *Behold,* says the prophet Isaias, *the Gentiles are as a drop of a bucket, and are counted as the smallest grain of a balance; behold, the islands are as little dust. . . . All nations are before Him as if they had no being at all.*[5]

Now this God, so great, has become a little infant; and

---

[1] "Domine, quis similis tibi?"—*Ps.* xxxiv. 10.
[2] "Magnus Dominus, et laudabilis nimis; et magnitudinis ejus non est finis."—*Ps.* cxliv. 3.
[3] "Numquid non cœlum et terram ego impleo?"—*Jer.* xxiii. 24.
[4] "In ipso enim vivimus, et movemur, et sumus."—*Acts,* xvii. 28.
[5] "Ecce gentes quasi stilla situlæ, et quasi momentum stateræ, reputatæ sunt; ecce insulæ quasi pulvis exiguus. Omnes gentes, quasi non sint, sic sunt coram eo."—*Isa.* xl. 15-17.

for whom? A child is born to us:[1] for us he is born. And wherefore? St. Ambrose gives us the answer: "He is a little one, that you might be a perfect man; he is bound in swaddling-clothes, that you might be unbound from the fetters of death; he is on earth, that you might be in heaven."[2]

Behold, then, the Immensity become an infant, whom the heavens cannot contain: see him imprisoned in poor rags, and laid in a narrow vile manger on a bundle of straw, which was at once his only bed and pillow. "See," says St. Bernard—"see power is ruled, wisdom instructed, virtue sustained. God taking milk and weeping, but comforting the afflicted!"[3] A God Almighty so tightly wrapped in swathing-bands that he cannot stir! A God who knows all things, made mute and speechless! A God who rules heaven and earth needing to be carried in the arms! A God who feeds all men and animals, himself having need of a little milk to support him! A God who consoles the afflicted, and is the joy of paradise, himself weeps and moans and has to be comforted by another!

In fine, St. Paul says *that the Son of God, coming on earth, emptied Himself*.[4] He annihilated himself, so to say. And why? To save man and to be loved by man. "Where Thou didst empty Thyself," says St. Bernard, "there did mercy, there did charity, more brilliantly appear."[5] Yes, my dear Redeemer, in proportion as Thy

---

[1] "Parvulus natus est nobis."

[2] "Ille parvulus, ut vir possis esse perfectus; ille involutus pannis, ut tu mortis laqueis absolutus sis; ille in terris, ut tu in coelis."—*In. Luc.* 2.

[3] "Videas potentiam regi, sapientiam instrui, virtutem sustentari; Deum lactentem et vagientem, sed miseros consolantem."—*De Laud. V. M. hom.* 2.

[4] "Semetipsum exinanivit."—*Phil.* ii. 7.

[5] "Ubi te exinanivisti, ibi pietas magis emicuit, ibi charitas plus effulsit."—*In Cant.* s. 45.

The Eternal Word becomes Little. 35

abasement was great in becoming man and in being born an infant, so were Thy mercy and love shown to be greater towards us, and this with a view to win over our hearts to Thyself.

The Jews, although by so many signs and wonders they had a certain knowledge of the true God, were not, however, satisfied; they wished to behold him face to face. God found means to comply even with this desire of men; he became man, to make himself visible to them. "Knowing," says St. Peter Chrysologus, "that mortals felt an anguish of desire to see him, God chose this method of making himself visible to them."[1] And to render himself still more attractive in our eyes, he would make his first appearance as a little child, that in this guise he might be the more charming and irresistible; he showed himself an infant, that he might make himself the more acceptable in our eyes, says the same St. Chrysologus.[2] "Yes," adds St. Cyril of Alexandria, "he abased himself to the humble condition of a little child in order to make himself more agreeable to our hearts." "For our advantage was this emptying made."[3] For this indeed was the form most suitable to win our love.

The prophet Ezechiel rightly exclaimed that the time of Thy coming on earth, O Incarnate Word, should be a time of love, the season of lovers: *Behold, Thy time was the time of lovers*.[4] And what object had God in loving us thus ardently, and in giving us so clear proofs of his love, other than that we might love him? "God loves only in order to be loved,"[5] says St. Bernard. God himself had already said as much: *And now, O Israel, what*

---
[1] "Sciens Deus visendi se desiderio cruciari mortales, unde se visibilem faceret, hoc elegit."—*Serm.* 147.
[2] "Se parvulum exhibuit, ut seipsum faceret gratum."
[3] "Exinanitio facta ad usum nostrum."
[4] "Ecce tempus tuum, tempus amantium."—*Ezech*. xvi. 8.
[5] "Non ad aliud amat Deus, nisi ut ametur."—*In Cant.* s. 83.

does the Lord thy God require of thee, but that thou fear and love Him?[1]

In order to force us to love him God would not commission others, but chose to come himself in person to be made man and to redeem us. St. John Chrysostom makes a beautiful reflection on these words of the apostle: *For nowhere doth He take hold of the angels, but of the seed of Abraham He taketh hold.*[2] Why, asks the saint, did he not say *received*, but rather *apprehended?*[3] Why did not St. Paul simply say that God assumed human flesh? Why would he affirm with marked emphasis that he took it, as it were, by force, according to the strict meaning of the word *apprehend?* He answers that he spoke thus, making use of the metaphor of those who give chase to the flying.[4] By this he would convey the idea that God already longed to be loved by man, but man turned his back upon him, and cared not even to know of his love; therefore God came from heaven, and took human flesh, to make himself known in this way, and to make himself loved, as it were, by force by ungrateful man, who fled from him.

For this, then, did the Eternal Word become man; for this he, moreover, became an infant. He could, indeed, have appeared upon this earth a full-grown man, as the first man Adam appeared. No, the Son of God wished to present himself under the form of a sweet little child, that thus he might the more readily and the more forcibly draw to himself the love of man. Little children of themselves are loved at once, and to see them and to love them is the same thing. With this view, says St.

---

[1] "Et nunc, Israel! quid Dominus Deus tuus petit a te, nisi ut timeas . . . et diligas eum?"—*Deut.* x. 12.

[2] "Nusquam enim Angelos apprehendit, sed semen Abrahæ apprehendit."—*Heb.* ii. 16.

[3] "Quare non dixit: Suscepit;—sed: Apprehendit?"

[4] "Ex metaphora insequentium eos qui aversi sunt."

Francis de Sales, the Eternal Word chose first to be seen among men as an infant, to conciliate to himself the love of all mankind.

St. Peter Chrysologus writes: "How should our Lord come, who wishes to drive away fear, to seek love? What breast so savage as not to soften before such a childhood? what hardness which it will not subdue, what love does it not claim? Thus, therefore, he would be born who willed to be loved and not feared."[1] The saint would say that if our Redeemer had come to be feared and respected by men, he would have come as a full-grown man and with royal dignity; but because he came to gain our love, he chose to come and to show himself as an infant, and the poorest of infants, born in a cold stable between two animals, laid in a manger on straw, without clothing or fire to warm his shivering little limbs: "thus would he be born, who willed to be loved and not feared."[2] Ah, my Lord! who was it that drew Thee from heaven to be born in a stable? It was love, the love Thou bearest toward men. Who took Thee from the right hand of Thy Father, where Thou sittest, and placed Thee in a manger? Who snatched Thee from Thy throne above the stars, and put Thee to lie on a little straw? Who changed Thy position from the midst of angels, to be placed betwixt a pair of beasts? It was all the work of love; Thou inflamest the seraphim, and dost Thou not shiver with cold? Thou supportest the heavens, and must Thou be now carried in the arms? Thou providest food for men and beasts, and now dost Thou crave a little milk to sustain Thy life? Thou makest the seraphim happy, and now dost Thou weep and moan?

---

[1] "Et qualiter venire debuit, qui voluit timorem pellere, quærere charitatem? Infantia hæc, quam barbariem non vincit? quam duritiem non resolvit? Quid non amoris expostulat? Sic ergo nasci voluit, qui amari voluit, non timeri."—*Serm.* 158.

[2] "Sic nasci voluit, qui amari voluit, non timeri."

Who has reduced Thee to such misery? Love has done it: "Thus would he be born who willed to be loved and not feared."

Love then, love, O souls, exclaims St. Bernard, love now this little Child, for he is exceedingly to be loved "Great is the Lord, and exceedingly to be praised. The Lord is a little one, and exceedingly to be loved."[1] Yes, says the saint, this God was already existing from eternity, as he is now worthy of all praise and reverence for his greatness, as David has sung: *Great is the Lord and exceedingly to be praised.*[2] But now that we behold him become a little infant, needing milk, and unable to stir himself, trembling with cold, moaning and weeping, looking for some one to take and warm and comfort him; ah, now indeed does he become the most cherished one of our hearts! "The Lord is a little one, and exceedingly to be loved!"

We ought to adore him as our God, but our love ought to keep pace with our reverence towards a God so amiable, so loving.

St. Bonaventure reminds us that "a child finds its delight with other children, with flowers, and to be in the arms."[3] The saint's meaning is, that if we would please this divine Infant, we too must become children, simple and humble; we must carry to him flowers of virtue, of meekness, of mortification, of charity; we must clasp him in the arms of our love.

And, O man, adds St. Bernard, what more do you wait to see before you will give yourself wholly to God? See with what labor, with what ardent love, your Jesus has

---

[1] "Magnus Dominus, et laudabilis nimis; parvus Dominus, et amabilis nimis."—*In Cant.* s. 48.

[2] "Magnus Dominus, et laudabilis nimis."—*Ps.* cxliv. 3.

[3] "Puer cum pueris, cum floribus, cum brachiis libenter esse solet."
—*Dom. infra oct. Nat.* s. 4.

The Eternal Word becomes Little. 39

come down from heaven to seek you.[1] Hearken, he goes on to say, how, scarcely yet born, his wailings call to you, as if he would say, O soul of mine, it is thee I am seeking; for thee, and to obtain thy love, I am come from heaven to earth. "Having scarcely quitted the Virgin's womb, he calls thy beloved soul after the manner of infants, Ah, ah, my soul, my soul! I am seeking you; for you am I making this pilgrimage."[2]

O God, even the very brutes, if we do them a kindness, if we give them some trifle, are so grateful for it; they come near us, they do our bidding after their own fashion, and they show symptoms of gladness at our approach. And how comes it, then, that we are so ungrateful towards God, the same God who has bestowed his whole self upon us, who has descended from heaven to earth, has become an infant to save us and to be loved by us? Come, then, let us love the Babe of Bethlehem, is the enraptured cry of St. Francis; let us love Jesus Christ, who has sought in the midst of such sufferings to attach our hearts to him.

II.

And for love of Jesus Christ, we ought to love our neighbors, even those who have offended us. The Messias is called by Isaias, *Father of the world to come.*[3] now, in order to be the sons of this Father, Jesus admonishes us that we must love our enemies, and do good to those who injure us: *Love your enemies, do good to them that hate you, . . . that you may be the children of your Father*

---

[1] "Oh! quanto labore et quam ferventi amore quæsivit animam tuam amorosus Jesus!"

[2] "Virginis uterum vix egressus, dilectam animam tuam more infantium vocat: A, a, anima mea, anima mea! te quæro, pro te hanc peregrinationem assumo."—*T. II.* s. 51, a. 2, c. 2.

[3] "Pater futuri sæculi."—*Isa.* ix. 6.

who is in heaven.[1] And of this he himself set us the example on the cross, praying his Eternal Father to forgive those who were crucifying him.

"He who pardons his enemy," says St. John Chrysostom, "cannot but obtain God's pardon for himself;"[2] and we have the divine assurance of it: *Forgive, and you shall be forgiven.*[3] There was a certain religious, who otherwise had not led a very exemplary life, at the hour of death bewailed his sins, not without great confidence and joy, because, said he, "I have never avenged an injury done me;"[4] as much as to say: It is true that I have offended the Lord, but he has engaged to pardon him who pardons his enemies; I have pardoned all who offended me, so then I am confident God will likewise pardon me.

But to speak with reference to all persons in general; how can we, sinners as we are, despair of pardon, when we think of Jesus Christ? For this very object the Eternal Word humbled himself so far as to take human flesh, that we might procure our pardon from God: *I am come, not to call the just, but sinners.*[5] Hence we may address him in the words of St. Bernard: "Where Thou didst empty Thyself, there Thy mercy, there Thy charity, shone forth the more."[6] And St. Thomas of Villanova gives us excellent encouragement, saying: "What art thou afraid of, O poor sinner? How shall He condemn thee, if thou be penitent, who died expressly that thou mightest not be condemned? How shall he reject thee, if thou

---

[1] "Diligite inimicos vestros, benefacite his qui oderunt vos, . . . ut sitis filii Patris vestri."—*Matt.* v. 44.

[2] "Non est possibile quod homo qui dimiserit proximo, non recipiat remissionem a Domino."—*In Act. hom.* 36.

[3] "Dimittite, et dimittemini."—*Luke*, vi. 37.

[4] "Nunquam injurias vindicavi."

[5] "Non enim veni vocare justos, sed peccatores."—*Matt.* ix. 13.

[6] "Ubi te exinanivisti, ibi pietas magis emicuit, ibi charitas plus effulsit."

desirest to retain him who came down from heaven to seek thee?"[1]

Let not, then, the sinner be afraid, provided he will be no more a sinner, but will love Jesus Christ; let him not be dismayed, but have a full trust; if he abhor sin, and seek after God, let him not be sad, but full of joy: *Let the heart of them rejoice that seek the Lord.*[2] The Lord has sworn to forget all injuries done to him, if the sinner is sorry for them: *If the wicked do penance . . . I will not remember all his iniquities.*[3] And that we might have every motive for confidence, our Saviour became an infant: "Who is afraid to approach a child?"[4] asks the same St. Thomas of Villanova.

"Children do not inspire terror or aversion, but attachment and love,"[5] says St. Peter Chrysologus. It seems that children know not how to be angry; and if perchance at odd times they should be irritated, they are easily soothed; one has only to give them a fruit, a flower, or bestow on them a caress, or utter a kind word to them, and they have already forgiven and forgotten every offence.

A tear of repentance, one act of heart-felt contrition, is enough to appease the Infant Jesus. "You know the tempers of children," pursues St. Thomas of Villanova; "a single tear pacifies them, the offence is forgotten. Approach, then, to Him while he is a little one, while he would seem to have forgotten his majesty."[6] He has

[1] "Quid times, peccator? Quomodo te damnabit pœnitentem, qui moritur ne damneris? Quomodo te abjiciet redeuntem, qui de cœlo venit quærere te?"—*Tr. de Adv. D.*

[2] "Lætetur cor quærentium Dominum."—*Ps.* civ. 3.

[3] "Si autem impius egerit pœnitentiam . . . omnium iniquitatum ejus . . . non recordabor."—*Ezech.* xviii. 21.

[4] "Ad parvulum accedere quis formidet?"—*In Nat. D. conc.* 4.

[5] "Puer nescit irasci, et. si irascitur, facile placatur."

[6] "Parvulorum mores agnoscitis; una lacrymula placatur offensus, injuriam non recordatur. Accedite ergo ad eum, dum parvulus est, dum majestatis videtur oblitus."

put off his divine majesty, and appears as a child to inspire us with more courage to approach his feet.

" He is born an Infant," says St. Bonaventure, " that neither his justice nor his power might intimidate you."[1] In order to exempt us from every feeling of distrust, which the idea of his power and of his justice might cause in us, he comes before us as a little babe, full of sweetness and mercy. "O God !" says Gerson, " Thou hast hidden Thy wisdom under a childish age, that it might not accuse us."[2] O God of mercy, lest Thy divine wisdom might reproach us with our offences against Thee, Thou hast hidden it under an infant's form : " Thy justice under humility, lest it should condemn."[3] Thou hast concealed Thy justice under the most profound abasement, that it might not condemn us : Thy power under weakness, lest it should torment."[4] Thou hast disguised Thy power in feebleness, that it might not visit us with chastisement.

St. Bernard makes this reflection: "Adam, after his sin, on hearing the voice of God, *Adam, where art thou ?*"[5] was filled with dismay: *I heard Thy voice, and was afraid.*[6] But, continues the saint, now, the Incarnate Word being made man upon earth, has laid aside all semblance of terror :[7] " Do not fear; he seeks thee, not to punish, but to save thee.[8] Behold, he is a child, and voiceless ; for the voice of a child will excite compassion rather than fear. The Virgin Mother wraps his delicate limbs in swaddling-clothes : and art thou still in alarm ?"[9] That

[1] " Nascitur parvulus, ut non formides potentiam, non justitiam."
[2] " Celasti, Deus, sapientiam in infantuli ætate, ne accuset."
[3] " Justitiam in humilitate, ne condemnet."
[4] " Potentiam in infirmitate, ne cruciet."
[5] " Adam . . . . ubi es ?"
[6] " Vocem tuam audivi . . . et timui."—*Gen.* iii. 9.
[7] " Homo natus, terrorem deposuit."
[8] " Noli timere; non puniendum, sed salvandum requirit."
[9] " Ecce infans est, et sine voce ; nam vagientis vox magis miseranda est, quam tremenda. Tenera membra Virgo Mater pannis alligat, et adhuc trepidas ?"—*In Nat. D.* s. 1.

God, who should punish thee, is born an infant, and has lost all accents to affright thee, since the accents of a child, being cries of weeping, move us sooner to pity than to fear; thou canst not apprehend that Jesus Christ will stretch out his hands to chastise thee, since his Mother is occupied in swathing them in linen bands.

"Be of good cheer, then, O sinners," says St. Leo, "the birthday of the Lord is the birthday of peace and joy."[1] "The Prince of Peace"[2] was he called by Isaias. Jesus Christ is a Prince, not of vengeance on sinners, but of mercy and of peace, constituting himself the mediator betwixt God and sinners. "If our sins," says St. Augustine, "are too much for us, God does not despise his blood."[3] If we cannot ourselves make due atonement to the justice of God, at least the Eternal Father knows not how to disregard the blood of Jesus Christ, who makes payment for us.

A certain knight, called Don Alphonsus Albuquerque, making once a sea voyage, and the vessel being driven among the rocks by a violent tempest, already gave himself up for lost; but at that moment espying near him a little child, crying bitterly, what did he do? He seized him in his arms, and so lifting him towards heaven, "O Lord," said he," though I myself be unworthy to be heard, give ear at least to the cries of this innocent child, and save us." At the same instant the storm abated, and he remained in safety. Let us miserable sinners do in like manner. We have offended God; already has sentence of everlasting death been passed upon us; divine justice requires satisfaction, and with right. What have we to do? To despair? God forbid! let us offer up to God this Infant, who is his own

---

[1] "Natalis Domini, natalis est pacis."—*In Nat. D.* s. 6.
[2] "Princeps pacis."—*Isa.* ix. 6.
[3] "Si peccata nostra superant nos, pretium suum non contemnit Deus."—*Serm.* 22, *Ed. B.*

Son, and let us address him with confidence : O Lord, if we cannot of ourselves render Thee satisfaction for our offences against Thee, behold this Child, who weeps and moans, who is benumbed with cold on his bed of straw in this cavern; he is here to make atonement for us, and he pleads for Thy mercy on us. Be it that we are undeserving of pardon, the tears and sufferings of this Thy guiltless Son merit it for us, and he entreats Thee to pardon us.

This is what St. Anselm advises us to do ; he says that Jesus Christ himself, from his earnest desire not to have us perish, animates each one of us who finds himself guilty before God with these words : O sinner, do not lose heart ; if by thy sins thou hast unhappily become the slave of hell, and hast not the means to free thyself, act thus : take me, offer me for thyself to the Eternal Father, and so thou shalt escape death, thou shalt be in safety. "What can be conceived more full of mercy than what the Son says to us : Take me, and redeem thyself."[1] This was, moreover, exactly what the divine Mother taught Sister Frances Farnese. She gave the Infant Jesus into her arms, and said to her : "Here is my Son for you ; be careful to make your profit of him by frequently offering him to his heavenly Father."

And if we would still have another means to secure our forgiveness, let us obtain the intercession of this same divine Mother in our behalf ; she is all-powerful with her blessed Son to promote the interests of repentant sinners, as St. John Damascene assures us. Yes, for the prayers of Mary, adds St. Antoninus, have the force of commands with her Son, in consideration of the love he bears her : " The prayer of the Mother of God has the force of a command."[2] Hence, wrote St. Peter

---

[1] " Quid misericordius intelligi valet, quam cum Filius dicit: Tolle me, et redime te ?"—*Cur. D. II.* l. 2, c. 20.

[2] " Oratio Deiparæ habet rationem imperii."—P. 4, tit. 15, c. 17, § 4.

Damian, when Mary goes to entreat Jesus Christ in favor of one who is devout to her, "she appears to command (in a certain sense), not to ask, as a mistress, not a handmaid ; for the Son honors her by denying her nothing."[1] For this reason St. Germanus adds that the most holy Virgin, by the authority of mother which she exercises, or, rather, which she did exercise for a time over her Son upon earth, can obtain the pardon of the most abandoned sinner. "Thou, by the power of thy maternal authority, gainest even for the most enormous sinners the exceeding grace of pardon."[2]

Affections and Prayers.

O my sweet, amiable, and holy Child ! Thou art at a loss what more to do to make Thyself beloved by men. It is enough to say that from being the Son of God Thou wert made the Son of man, and that Thou chosest to be born among men like the rest of infants, only poorer and more meanly lodged than the rest, selecting a stable for Thy abode, a manger for Thy cradle, and a little straw for Thy couch. Thou didst desire thus to make Thy first appearance before us in the semblance of a poor child, that even from Thy very birth Thou mightest lose no time in attracting our hearts towards Thee ; and so Thou didst go on through the remainder of Thy life, ever showing us fresh and more striking tokens of Thy love, so that at length Thou didst will to shed the last drop of Thy blood and die overwhelmed with shame upon the infamous tree of the cross. And how is it that Thou couldst have encountered such ingratitude from the majority of mankind ; for I see few indeed that know Thee, and fewer still that love Thee ? Ah, my dear Jesus, I too desire to be reckoned among this small number ! In time past, it is true, I have not known Thee ; but, heedless of Thy love, I have only sought my own gratifications, making no account what-

[1] " Accedis, non solum rogans, sed imperans; Domina, non ancilla; nam Filius nihil negans honorat te."—*In Nat. B. V.* s. 1.

[2] " Tu autem, materna auctoritate pollens, etiam iis qui enormiter peccant, eximiam remissionis gratiam concilias."—*In Deip. Dorm.* s. 2.

ever of Thee and of Thy friendship. But now I am conscious of the wrong I have done; I am sorry for it, I grieve over it with my whole heart. O my sweet Child and my God, forgive me for the sake of Thy infancy. I love Thee, and that so dearly, O my Jesus, that even if I knew that all mankind were about to rebel against Thee and to forsake Thee, yet I promise never to leave Thee, though it should cost me my life a thousand times. I am well aware that I am indebted to Thee for this light and this good resolution. I thank Thee for it, O my love! and I beseech Thee to preserve it to me by Thy grace. But Thou knowest my weakness, Thou knowest my past treasons; for pity's sake do not abandon me, or I shall fall away even worse than before. Accept of my poor heart to love Thee; there was a time when it cared not for Thee, but now it is enamoured of Thy goodness, O divine Infant! O Mary! O great Mother of the Incarnate Word! neither do Thou abandon me; for Thou art the mother of perseverance, and the stewardess of divine grace. Help me, then, and help me always; with thy aid, O my hope! I trust to be faithful to my God till death.

DISCOURSE III.

The Eternal Word from being Lord became a Servant.

Semetipsum exinanivit, formam servi accipiens.

"He humbled himself, taking the form of a servant."—*Phil.* ii. 7, 8.

On considering the immense mercy of our God in the work of the human redemption, St. Zachary had good reason to exclaim, *Blessed be the Lord God of Israel, because He hath visited and wrought the redemption of His people.*[1] Blessed forever be God, who vouchsafed to come down upon earth and to be made man in order to redeem mankind. *That being delivered from the hands of our enemies, we may serve Him without fear.*[2] In order that, loosened from the shackles of sin and of death, wherein our ene-

[1] "Benedictus Dominus Deus Israel, quia visitavit, et fecit redemptionem plebis suæ."

[2] "Ut sine timore, de manu inimicorum nostrorum liberati, serviamus illi."—*Luke*, i. 68–74.

The Eternal Word became a Servant. 47

mies held us fast bound and enthralled, we might fearlessly, and with the freedom of the children of God, love him and serve him during this life, and afterwards go and possess and enjoy him face to face in the kingdom of the blessed,—in that kingdom closed against us indeed, heretofore, but now thrown open to us by our divine Saviour.

We were, in fact, all heretofore the slaves of hell; but what has the Eternal Word, our sovereign Lord, done to free us from that slavery? From being Lord he became a servant. Let us consider what a mercy and what an excessive love this has been; but first let us beg light of Jesus and Mary.

I.

Almighty God is Lord of all that is, or that can be in the world: *In Thy power are all things; for Thou hast created all.*[1] Who can ever deny God the sovereign dominion over all things, if he be the Creator and Preserver of all? *And He hath on His garment and on His thigh written King of kings and Lord of lords.*[2] Maldonatus explains the words "on his thigh," to mean here, "by his own very nature;" and the drift of it is, that to the monarchs of earth outward majesty is annexed by gift and favor of the supreme King, that is God; but God himself is King by his very nature; so that he cannot possibly be otherwise than King and Lord of all.

But this sovereign King, though he bore sway over the angels in heaven, and ruled all creatures, yet he did not rule over the hearts of mankind; mankind was groaning under the miserable tyranny of the devil. Yes, before the coming of Jesus Christ this tyrant was lord,

---

[1] "In ditione enim tua cuncta sunt posita. . . . Tu fecisti cœlum et terram."—*Esth.* xiii. 9.

[2] "Et habet in vestimento et in femore suo scriptum: **Rex regum et Dominus dominantium.**—*Apoc.* xix. 16.

and even made himself worshipped as God, with incense and sacrifices, not only of their animals, but even of their own children and of their own lives; and he, their enemy and tyrant, what return did he make them?—how did he treat them? He tortured their bodies with the most barbarous cruelty, he blinded their minds, and by a path of pain and misery conducted them down to everlasting torments. It was this tyrant that the divine Word came on purpose to overthrow, and to release mankind from his wretched thraldom, in order that the unfortunate creatures, freed from the darkness of death, rescued from the bondage of this savage monster, and enlightened to know what was the true way of salvation, might serve their real and lawful Master, who loved them as a Father, and from slaves of Satan wished to make them his own beloved children: *That being delivered from the hands of our enemies, we might serve Him without fear.* The prophet Isaias had long ago foretold that our Redeemer should destroy the empire which Satan held over mankind: *And the sceptre of their oppressor Thou hast overcome.*[1] And why did the prophet call him oppressor? Because, says St. Cyril,[2] this heartless master exacts from the poor sinners who become his slaves heavy tribute, in the shape of passions, hatreds, disorderly affections, by means of which he binds them in a still faster servitude, while at the same time he scourges them. Our Saviour came, then, to release us from the slavery of this deadly foe; but how?—in what manner did he release us?—Let us learn from St. Paul what he did: *Who being in the form of God, thought it not robbery to be equal to God, but emptied himself, taking the form of a servant, being made in the likeness of men.*[3] He was already, says the Apostle, the only-

[1] "Sceptrum exactoris ejus superasti."—*Isa.* ix. 4.

[2] "*In Is. l.* 1, or. 5.

[3] "Cum in forma Dei esset, non rapinam arbitratus est esse se æqualem Deo; sed semetipsum exinanivit, formam servi accipiens, in similitudinem hominum factus."—*Phil.* ii. 6.

The Eternal Word became a Servant. 49

begotten Son of God, equal to his Father, eternal as his Father, almighty as his Father, immense, most wise, most happy, and sovereign Lord of heaven and earth, of angels and of men, no less than his Father; but for the love of man he stooped to take the lowly form of a servant, by clothing himself in human flesh, and likening himself to men; and since sin had made them vassals of the devil, he came in the form of man to redeem them, offering his sufferings and death in satisfaction to the divine justice for the punishment due to them. Ah! who would have believed it, if holy faith did not assure us of it? Who could ever have hoped for it?—who could ever have conceived it? But faith tells us and assures us that this supreme and sovereign Lord *emptied himself, taking the form of a servant.*

From his tenderest childhood, the Redeemer, by becoming a servant, was eager to begin and wrench from the devil that dominion which he had over man, according to the prophecy of Isaias: *Call his name, hasten to take away the spoils: Make haste to take away the prey.*[1] "That is," as St. Jerome explains it, "suffer the devil to reign no longer."[2] Behold Jesus, scarcely born, says the Venerable Bede, before he assumes the form and office of a servant, in order to gain us freedom from the slavery of hell, he causes himself to be enrolled as a subject of Cæsar, and pays him the tribute: "Scarcely born, he is registered in the census of Cæsar, and for our liberation he himself is inscribed in the list of servitude."[3] Observe how, in token of his servitude, he begins to pay off our debts by his sufferings; how he allows himself to be wrapped in swaddling-clothes (a type of the cords which

---

[1] "Voca nomen ejus: Accelera spolia detrahere, Festina prædari." *Isa.* viii. 3.

[2] "Hoc est: Ne ultra patiatur regnare diabolum."

[3] "Mox natus, censu Cæsaris adscribitur, atque ob nostri liberationem ipse servitio subditur."—*In Luc.* 2.

should bind him at a later day, to be led to death by cruel executioners). "God suffers himself," says a certain author, "to be bound up in swaddling-bands, because he had come to unbind the world from its debts."[1] Behold him during the whole course of his after-life obeying with ready submission a simple Virgin and a man: *He was subject to them.*"[2] Look at him as a servant in the poor cottage at Nazareth, employed by Mary and Joseph at one time in smoothing the wood to be worked upon by Joseph in his trade; at another time in collecting the scattered shavings for fuel; then in sweeping the house, in fetching water from the well, in opening or in closing the shop; in fine, says St. Basil, as Mary and Joseph were poor, and obliged to earn a livelihood by the work of their hands, Jesus Christ, in order to practise obedience, and to show towards them that reverence which as to Superiors he owed them, endeavored to render them all the services which lay in his power as man. "In his early age Jesus was subject to his parents, and obediently underwent every kind of bodily fatigue; for, as they were poor, they necessarily were obliged to labor. But Jesus showed his obedience by his submission to them, by undergoing every kind of labor."[3] What! a God to serve! a God to sweep the house! a God to work! Ah, how the mere thought of this should inflame us all, and make us burn with love!

Subsequently, when our Saviour went forth to preach, he made himself the servant of all, declaring that he had come not to be served, but to serve all others: *The*

---

[1] "Patitur Deus se pannis alligari, qui totius mundi debita venerat soluturus."—*De Nat. Chr.* s. 3.

[2] "Erat subditus illis."—*Luke*, ii. 51.

[3] "In prima ætate, subditus parentibus, omnem laborem corporalem obedienter sustinuit. Cum illi enim essent pauperes, merito laboribus dediti erant. Jesus autem, his subditus, omnium etiam simul perferendo labores, obedientiam declarabat."—*Const. mon.* c. 4.

Son of Man is not come to be ministered unto, but to minister.[1] As much as to say, according to the commentary of Cornelius à Lapide, "I have conducted myself, and still conduct myself, so as to show how I would willingly minister to all as the servant of all."[2]

Hence Jesus Christ, says St. Bernard, at the close of his life, was not content to take the form of a simple servant, in order to be at the command of others, but even of a wicked servant, in order to be punished as such, and so to pay off that punishment which was due to us as the servants of hell in chastisement of our sins. "Taking not only the form of a servant, that he might obey, but of a wicked servant that he might be chastised, and so pay the penalty of the servant's sin."[3]

Behold, finally, says St. Gregory of Nyssa, how the Lord of all submits as an obedient subject to the unjust sentence of Pilate, and to the hands of his executioners, who barbarously torture and crucify him. "The Lord of all is obedient to the sentence of the judge, the king of all does not disdain to feel the hand of the executioners."[4] St. Peter had said as much before: *He delivered Himself to him that judged Him unjustly.*[5] And, like a servant, he is resigned to punishment, as if he had well deserved it: *When He was reviled, He did not revile; and when He suffered, He threatened not.*[6] Thus did our God

[1] "Filius hominis non venit ministrari, sed ministrare."—*Matt.* xx. 28.
[2] "Ita me gessi et gero, ut velim omnibus ministrare, quasi omnium servus."
[3] "Non solum formam servi accepit, ut subesset; sed etiam mali servi, ut vapularet; et servi peccati, ut pœnam solveret."—*Serm. de Pass.*
[4] "Omnium Dominus judicis sententiæ subjicitur; omnium Rex carnificum manu exerceri non gravatur."—*De Beatit. or.* 1.
[5] "Tradebat autem judicanti se injuste."—1 *Peter*, ii. 23.
[6] "Cum malediceretur, non maledicebat; cum pateretur, non comminabatur."—*Ib.* ii. 23.

love us to such a pass, that for our love he chose to obey as a servant even unto death, and a death of such extreme bitterness and ignominy as the death of the cross: *Becoming obedient unto death, even to the death of the cross.*[1] He obeyed, indeed, not as God, but as man, and as a servant, as he had made himself: *Taking the form of a servant, and being made in the likeness of men.*[2]

The world stood in admiration of that grand act of charity, which St. Paulinus performed in consenting to become a slave for the ransom of the son of a poor widow. But what comparison does this bear with the charity of our Redeemer, who being God, and in order to rescue us from the slavery of the devil and from death, our just due, chose to become a servant, to be fast bound with cords, to be nailed to the cross, and there in the end to lay down his life in a sea of sorrow and ignominy? In order, says St. Augustine, that the servant might become lord, God chose to become a servant.[3]

"O amazing condescension of Thy bounty towards us! O inestimable tenderness of Thy charity!"[4] exclaims the Holy Church. "That Thou mightest redeem the servant, Thou hast delivered up the Son."[5] Thou, then, O God of boundless majesty, hast been so fascinated with love for men, that to redeem these Thy rebellious servants Thou hast consented to condemn Thy only Son to death. But, O Lord, replies the holy man Job: *What is a man, that Thou shouldst magnify him? or why dost Thou*

---

[1] "Factus obediens usque ad mortem, mortem autem crucis."—*Phil.* ii. 8.
[2] "Formam servi accipiens, in similitudinem hominum factus."—*Phil.* ii. 7.
[3] "Ut servus in dominum verteretur, formam servi Dominus accepit."—*Serm.* 371, *E. B.*
[4] "O mira circa nos tuæ pietatis dignatio! O inæstimabilis dilectio charitatis."—*In Sabb. S.*
[5] "Ut servum redimeres, Filium tradidisti."

The Eternal Word became a Servant. 53

set Thy heart upon him?[1] What is man, who is so vile, and has proved so ungrateful to Thee, that Thou shouldst make him so great, by honoring and loving him to such an excess? Tell me (he goes on to say), why are the salvation and happiness of man of so much importance to Thee? Tell me why Thou lovest him so much, that it would seem as if Thy heart was set on nothing else but to love and to make man happy?

II.

Speed on, then, with gladness, O ye souls that love God and hope in God, speed on your way with gladness! What if Adam's sin, and still more our own sins, have wrought sad ruin on us? let us understand that Jesus Christ, by the Redemption, has infinitely more than repaired our ruin: *Where sin abounded, grace did more abound.*[2] Greater (says St. Leo) has been the acquisition which we have made by the grace of our Redeemer, than was the loss which we had suffered by the malice of the devil.[3] Isaias had long ago prophesied that by means of Jesus Christ man should receive graces from God far surpassing the chastisement merited by his sins: *He hath received of the hand of the Lord double for all his sins.*[4] It is in this sense that Adam the commentator explains this text, as we find in Cornelius à Lapide: "God hath so given remission of sins to the Church through Christ, that she hath received double (that is manifold blessings) instead of the punishments of sin

---

[1] "Quid est homo, quia magnificas eum? aut quid apponis erga eum cor tuum?"—*Job*, vii. 17.

[2] "Ubi autem abundavit delictum, superabundavit gratia."—*Rom.* v. 20.

[3] "Ampliora adepti sumus per Christi gratiam, quam per diaboli amiseramus invidiam."—*De Asc. D.* s. 1.

[4] "Suscepit de manu Domini duplicia pro omnibus peccatis suis." —*Isa.* xl. 2.

which she deserved." The Lord said: *I am come that they may have life, and may have it more abundantly.*[1] I am come to give life to man, and a more abundant measure of life than what they had lost by sin. *Not as the offence, so also the gift.*[2] Great had been the sin of man; but greater, says the Apostle, has been the gift of redemption, which has not only just sufficed for a remedy, but superabundantly: *and with Him plentiful redemption.*[3] St. Anselm says, that the sacrifice of the life of Jesus Christ surpassed all the debts of sinners: "The life of that Man surpasses every debt which sinners owe."[4] For this reason the Church styles the fault of Adam a happy one: "O happy fault, which deserved to have so great a Redeemer."[5] It is true that sin has clouded the mind to the knowledge of eternal truths, and has introduced into the soul the concupiscence of sensible goods, forbidden by the divine command; yes, but what helps and means has not Jesus Christ obtained for us by his merits, in order to procure us light and strength to vanquish all our enemies, and to advance in virtue? The holy sacraments, the Sacrifice of Mass, prayer to God through the merits of Jesus Christ,—ah! these are indeed arms and means sufficient, not only to gain the victory over all temptation and concupiscence, but even to run forward and fly in the way of perfection. It is certain that by these very means given to us, all the saints of the new law have become saints. Ours, then, is the fault, if we do not avail ourselves of them.

Oh, how much more are we bound to thank Almighty

[1] "Ego veni ut vitam habeant, et abundantius habeant."—*John.* x. 10.

[2] "Non sicut delictum, ita et donum."—*Rom.* v. 15.

[3] "Et copiosa apud eum redemptio."—*Ps.* cxxix. 7.

[4] "Vita Hominis illius superat omne debitum quod debent peccatores."—*Med. de Red. hum.*

[5] "O felix culpa, quæ talem ac tantum meruit habere Redemptorem!"—*In Sabb. S.*

God for having brought us into life after the coming of the Messias! How much greater blessings have we received after the accomplishment of redemption by Jesus Christ! How did Abraham desire; how did the prophets and patriarchs of the Old Testament long to see the Redeemer born! But they saw him not. They deafened the heavens, so to speak, with their groans of desire and with their ardent prayers: *Drop down dew, ye heavens from above, and let the clouds rain the just,*[1] was their incessant exclamation. Rain down, O heavens, and send us the Just One, to appease the wrath of that God whom we ourselves cannot appease, because we are all sinners: *Send forth, O Lord, the Lamb, the Ruler of the earth.*[2] Send, O Lord, the Lamb, who by sacrificing himself shall satisfy Thy justice for us, and so shall reign in the hearts of men, who are living on this earth the unhappy slaves of the devil: *Show us, O Lord, Thy mercy, and grant us Thy salvation.*[3] Hasten and show us, O God of mercies, that greatest mercy which Thou hast already promised us, namely, our Saviour. Such were the aspirations and longing exclamations of the saints. But for all that, during the space of four thousand years, they had not the happy lot to see the Messias born: we, however, have had this happiness. But what are we doing? What knowledge have we, to take advantage of it? Do we know how to love this amiable Redeemer who is come at last, who has already ransomed us from the hands of our foes, has freed us by his own death from the eternal death which we had deserved, has thrown open Paradise for us, has provided us with so many sacraments, and with so many aids to serve him and love him in peace during this life, that we might go and

---

[1] "Rorate, cœli, desuper, et nubes pluant Justum."—*Isa.* xlv. 8.
[2] "Emitte Agnum, Domine, dominatorem terræ."—*Ibid.* xvi. 1.
[3] "Ostende nobis, Domine, misericordiam tuam, et salutare tuum da nobis."—*Ps.* lxxxiv. 8.

enjoy him forever in the life to come? "He was," says St. Ambrose, "wrapped up in swaddling-clothes, that you might be loosed from snares; his poverty is my patrimony; the feebleness of the Lord is my strength; his tears have washed away my guilt."[1] Very great would be your ingratitude to your God, O Christian soul, if you were not to love him, after he has been pleased to be bound in swaddling-clothes, that you might be released from the chains of hell; after he has become poor, that you might be made partaker of his riches; after he has made himself weak, to give you power over your enemies; after he has chosen to suffer and to weep, that by his tears your sins might be washed away.

But, O God! how few there are who show themselves grateful for so immense a love by faithfully loving this their Redeemer! Alas! the greater part of men, after so incomparable a benefit, after so many great mercies and so much love, still say to God: Lord, we will not serve Thee; we would rather be slaves of the devil and condemned to hell than be Thy servants. Listen how God upbraids such thankless wretches: *Thou hast burs My bands, and thou saidst: I will not serve.*[2] What say you, my brother? have you too been one of these? But tell me, whilst living far from God and the slave of the devil, tell me, have you felt happy? Have you been at peace? Ah, no, the divine words can never fail: *Because thou didst not serve the Lord thy God with joy and gladness of heart, thou shalt serve thy enemy in hunger and thirst, and nakedness, and in want of all things.*[3] Since thou hast

[1] "Fuit ille involutus in pannis, ut tu mortis laqueis absolutus sis; meum paupertas illius patrimonium est, et infirmitas Domini mea virtus est, mea lacrymæ illæ delicta lavarunt."—*In Luc.* 2.

[2] "Rupisti vincula mea, et dixisti: Non serviam."—*Jer.* ii. 20.

[3] "Eo quod non servieris Domino Deo tuo in gaudio . . , servies inimico tuo . . . in fame, et siti, et nuditate, et omni penuria."—*Deut.* xxviii. 47.

preferred to serve thy enemy rather than to serve thy God, behold how that tyrant has treated thee. He has made thee groan as a slave in chains, poor, afflicted, and deprived of every interior consolation. But come, rise up ; God speaks to thee whilst thou mayest still be freed from the fetters of death which bind thee : *Loose the bonds from off thy neck, O captive daughter of Sion.*[1] Make haste while time is left, unbind thyself, poor soul, who hast become the voluntary slave of hell, strike off these cursed chains that hold thee fast as a prey for hell, and bind thyself instead with my chains of gold, chains of love, chains of peace, chains of salvation : *her bands are a healthful binding.*[2] But in what manner are souls bound to God? By love : *Have charity, which is the bond of perfection.*[3] A soul that always walks by the single way of the fear of punishment, and from this single motive avoids sin, is always in great danger of making a relapse before long into sin ; but he that attaches himself to God by love is sure not to lose him as long as he loves him ; and for this reason we must continually beg God to grant us the gift of his holy love, always praying and saying : O Lord, keep me united with Thee, never suffer me to be separated from Thee and from Thy love. The fear which we ought rather to desire and beg of God is a filial fear, the fear of ever displeasing this our good Lord and Father. Let us also always have recourse to most holy Mary, our Mother, that she may obtain for us the grace to love nothing else but God, and that she would so closely unite us by love to her Blessed Son, that we may never more see ourselves separated from him by sin.

[1] "Solve vincula colli tui, captiva filia Sion."—*Isa.* lii. 2.
[2] "Vincula illius, alligatura salutaris."—*Ecclus.* vi. 31.
[3] "Charitatem habete, quod est vinculum perfectionis."—*Coloss.* iii. 14.

Affections and Prayers.

O my Jesus! Thou hast been pleased to become a servant for love of me, and in order to release me from the chains of hell; and not only the servant of Thy Father, but of men and of executioners, even to the laying down of Thy life; and I, for the love of some wretched and poisonous pleasure, have so often forsaken Thy service, and have become the slave of the devil. A thousand times over I curse those moments in which, by a wicked abuse of my free-will, I despised Thy grace, O infinite Majesty! In pity pardon me, and bind me to Thyself with those delightful chains of love with which Thou keepest Thy chosen souls in closest union with Thee. I love Thee, O Incarnate Word; I love Thee, O my sovereign Good! I have now no other desire but to love Thee; and I have only one fear, that of seeing myself deprived of Thy love. O never suffer me to be separated from Thee again. I beseech Thee, O my Jesus! by all the sufferings of Thy life and of Thy death, do not suffer me ever more to leave Thee: " Suffer me not to be separated from Thee, suffer me not to be separated from Thee."[1] Ah, my God, after all the favors Thou hast shown me, after pardoning me so repeatedly, and when now Thou dost enlighten me with so clear a knowledge, and invitest me to love Thee with so tender an affection, if I should ever be so wretched as again to turn my back upon Thee, how could I presume ever to receive pardon afresh? and not rather be afraid that in that same instant Thou would cast me headlong into hell? Ah, never permit it; let me say again: " Suffer me not to be separated from Thee."

O Mary, my refuge, thou hast hitherto been my sweet advocate; for it was thou that didst prevail on God still to wait for me and to pardon me with so much mercy; help me at present, obtain for me the grace to die, and to die a thousand times, sooner than ever again to lose the grace of my God.

[1] " Ne permittas me separari a te ; ne permittas me separari a te."

DISCOURSE IV.

The Eternal Word from being Innocent becomes as it were Guilty.

Consolamini, consolamini, popule meus, dicit Deus vester.
" Be comforted, be comforted, my people, saith your God."—*Is.* xl. 1.

Previous to the coming of our Redeemer, the whole unhappy race of mankind groaned in misery upon this earth ; all were children of wrath, nor was there one who could appease God, justly indignant at their sins : *Behold, Thou art angry, and we have sinned : . . . there is none that riseth up, and taketh hold of Thee.*[1] Yes, because it is God himself who has been offended by man : man, being nothing but a miserable creature, was unable, by whatever extent of chastisement, to make atonement for the injury offered to an infinite majesty : there was need of another god to satisfy the divine justice. But such a god did not exist, neither could there be found any besides the one God alone : on the other hand, the person offended could not make satisfaction to himself ; so that ours was a desperate case.

But take comfort, take comfort, O men, saith the Lord by the mouth of Isaias : *Be comforted, be comforted, my people, saith your God ; for her evil is come to an end.*[2] And the reason is, because God himself hath discovered a way of saving man, while at the same time his justice and his mercy shall both be satisfied : *Justice and peace have kissed.*[3] The Son of God has himself become man, has taken the form of a sinner, and loading his own shoulders with the burden of satisfying for mankind, he has made full compensation to the divine justice for the

---
[1] " Ecce tu iratus es. . . . Non est qui. . . . consurgat, et teneat te."—*Isa.* lxiv. 5.
[2] " Consolamini, consolamini, popule meus, dicit Deus vester. . . . . quia completa est malitia."—*Isa.* xl. 1.
[3] " Justitia et Pax osculatæ sunt."—*Ps.* lxxxiv. 11.

penalty merited by men, by the sufferings of his life and of his death ; and thus the opposite claims of justice and of mercy have been paid.

Has Jesus Christ, then, from being innocent become guilty, to free men from eternal death? that is to say, has he chosen to pass for a sinner? Yes, the love which he bears to mankind has brought him even to this pass. Let us consider him in this state ; but let us first beg light of Jesus and Mary to profit by it.

I.

What was Jesus Christ? He was, answers St. Paul, *holy, innocent, undefiled.*[1] He was, to speak more correctly, sanctity itself, innocence itself, purity itself, since he was true Son of God, true God as his Father ; and so dear to that Father, that the Father there on the banks of the Jordan declared, that in that Son he found all his complacency. But this Son being bent upon freeing mankind from their sins and from the death incurred by them, what did he do ? *He appeared to take away our sins*, says St. John.[2] He presented himself before his heavenly Father, and offered himself to pay for mankind ; and then the Father, as the Apostle tells us, sent him on earth to be clothed in human flesh, to take the appearance of sinful man, and to be made in all things like to sinners : *God sending His own Son in the likeness of sinful flesh.*[3] And then St. Paul adds : *And of sin hath condemned sin in the flesh.*[4] And by this he means, according to the explanation of St. John Chrysostom and Theodoret, that the Father sentenced sin to be dethroned from the tyranny which it exercised over mankind, by dooming

[1] "Sanctus, innocens, impollutus."—*Heb.* vii. 26.
[2] "Apparuit ut peccata nostra tolleret."—1 *John*, iii. 5.
[3] "Deus Filium suum mittens in similitudinem carnis peccati."—*Rom.* viii. 3.
[4] ' Et de peccato damnavit peccatum in carne."

The Eternal Word becomes as it were Guilty. 61

to death his own divine Son, who, though he assumed flesh that was to all seeming contaminated with sin, was nevertheless holy and innocent.

God, therefore, in order to save mankind, and at the same time to answer the claims of his justice, was pleased to condemn his own Son to a painful life and to a shameful death. And can this ever be true? It is of faith, and St. Paul assures us of it: *He spared not even His own Son; but delivered Him up for us all.*[1] Jesus Christ himself affirms it to us: *God so loved the world, as to give his only-begotten Son.*[2] Celius Rodiginus relates, that there was a certain man, called Dœotarus, who had several sons, but loved one of them more than all the rest; insomuch that in order to leave him his whole fortune, he had the monstrous cruelty to murder all the others. But God has done quite the reverse; he has slain his well-beloved Son, his only Son, in order to give salvation to us vile and ungrateful worms: *God so loved the world, as to give His only-begotten Son.*

Let us weigh these words: *God so loved the world.* What? a God condescends to love men, miserable worms, that have been rebellious and ungrateful towards him, and to love them to such an extent ("the word *so* signifies the vehemence of love," says St. John Chrysostom), so as to give his only-begotten Son! that he chose to give them his very Son, and that only-begotten one whom he loved as much as himself! Not a servant, not an angel, not an archangel did he give, but his own Son,[3] subjoins the same holy Doctor. But in what manner did he choose to give him? He gave him to us lowly, hum-

---

[1] "Proprio Filio suo non pepercit, sed pro nobis omnibus tradidit illum."—*Rom.* viii. 32.

[2] "Sic enim Deus dilexit mundum, ut Filium suum unigenitum daret."—*John*, iii. 16.

[3] "Non servum, non Angelum, non Archangelum dedit, sed Filium suum!"—*In Jo. nom.* 27.

bled, poor, despised; he gave him into the hands of slaves to be treated as a miscreant, and even to be put to death, covered with shame, on an infamous gibbet. O grace! O force of the love of a God! exclaims St. Bernard: "O grace! O the strength of love!"[1] O God, who would not be touched to hear of such an instance, that a monarch, to release his slave, was compelled to put his only son to death,—that son who was all the love of his father, and was beloved by him as his very self? Had not God done this, says St. John Chrysostom, who could ever have imagined it or hoped for it? "What things the human mind could never have conceived, could never have hoped for, these things he has bestowed on us."[2]

But, O Lord, it seems like an injustice to sentence an innocent son to die for the purpose of saving a slave who has offended Thee. "According to all human reasoning," says Salvian, "one would certainly accuse that man of outrageous injustice who should kill an innocent son in order to free his servants from the death which they had deserved."[3] Yet no, with God this has not passed for injustice, because the Son made the spontaneous offering of himself to the Father to satisfy for men: *He was offered, because it was His own will.*[4] Behold, then, how Jesus voluntarily sacrifices himself as a victim of love for us; behold him, how as a mute lamb he puts himself into the hands of the shearer, and although innocent, he comes to suffer from men the greatest ignominies and torments, without even opening his mouth: *He shall be dumb as a lamb before His shearer, and He shall not open His*

---

[1] "O gratiam! O amoris vim!"

[2] "Quæ nunquam humanus animus aut cogitare aut sperare potuit, hæc nobis largitus est."—*In* 1 *Tim. hom.* 4.

[3] "Quantum ad rationem humanam pertinet, injustam rem homo quilibet faceret, si pro pessimis servis filium bonum occideret."—*De Gub. D.* l. 4.

[4] "Oblatus est, quia ipse voluit."—*Isa.* liii. 7.

mouth.¹ Behold, in fine, our loving Redeemer, who to save us chose to suffer death and the punishment deserved by us: *Surely He hath borne our infirmities, and carried our sorrows.*² St. Gregory Nazianzen says, "He refused not to suffer as guilty, provided only that men might obtain salvation."³

Who has done this? asks St. Bernard. What has been the cause of this immense prodigy? A God to die for his creatures! Who has done this? Charity has done this.⁴ This has been wrought by the love which God bears to man. The saint pursues his meditation on the time when our amiable Redeemer was seized by the soldiers in the garden of Gethsemani, as is related by St. John: *And they bound Him.*⁵ And then he says to our Lord: "What hast Thou to do with chains?"⁶ My Lord, he says, I behold Thee bound by this vile rabble as if Thou wert a criminal, and they are about to drag Thee to an unjust death. But, O God, what have cords and chains to do with Thee? such things belong to evil-doers, but not to Thee, who art innocent, who art the Son of God, innocence itself, holiness itself. St. Laurence Justinian replies that the bonds which dragged Jesus Christ to death were not those that were fastened on him by the soldiers, but the love he bore towards men; and hereupon he exclaims: "O charity, how strong are thy bonds, by which even a God could be bound!"⁷

¹ "Et quasi agnus coram tondente se, obmutescet, et non aperiet os suum."—*Isai.* liii. 7.
² "Vere languores nostros ipse tulit, et dolores nostros ipse portavit."—*Ibid* liii. 4.
³ "Tanquam impius pati non recusat, modo homines salutem consequantur."
⁴ "Quis hoc fecit? Fecit amor."
⁵ "Comprehenderunt Jesum, et ligaverunt eum."—*John*, xviii. 12.
⁶ "Quid tibi et vinculis!"—*De Pass. D.* c. 4.
⁷ "O charitas! quam magnum est vinculum tuum, quo Deus ligari potuit!"—*Lign. v. de Char.* c. 6.

The same St. Bernard goes on to consider the iniquitous sentence of Pilate, who condemned Jesus to the cross, after several times having declared him innocent; and then, turning himself to Jesus, he thus bewails himself before him: "What hast Thou done, O most innocent Saviour, that Thou receivest such a judgment?"[1] Ah, my Lord, I hear this wicked judge condemning Thee to die upon the cross; and what evil hast Thou done? what crime hast Thou ever perpetrated to deserve such a death of torture and shame?—a death awarded to none but to the most guilty wretches? But he then resumes by replying: Ah, I now comprehend, O my Jesus! what crime it is of which Thou art guilty? It is of having loved mankind too dearly: "Thy love is Thy crime."[2] Yes, it is this love, more than Pilate, that condemns Thee to death; because it is to pay off the penalties due from mankind that Thou hast willed to suffer death.

As the time of the Passion of our Blessed Redeemer drew near, he besought his Father that he would hasten to glorify him, by permitting him to offer to him the sacrifice of his life: *Father, glorify Thy Son.*[3] At this, St. John Chrysostom asks, in astonishment, "What sayest Thou? Dost thou call these things glory?"[4] A Passion and a death accompanied with such sufferings and shame, dost Thou call this Thy glory? And the saint then replies to his own question for Jesus Christ: "Yes, since it is for my beloved ones, I esteem it a glory."[5] Yes, so immense is the love I entertain for mankind that it makes me regard it my glory to suffer and to die for their sake.

[1] "Quid fecisti, O innocentissime Salvator! quod sic condemnaveris?"
[2] "Amor tuus, peccatum tuum."
[3] "Et nunc clarifica me tu, Pater."—*John*, xvii. 5.
[4] "Quid dicis? hæc gloriam appellas?"
[5] "Ita, pro dilectis hæc gloriam existimo."—*In Eph. hom.* 8.

II.

Say to the faint-hearted, Take courage, and fear not: behold your God will bring the revenge of recompense; God Himself will come and will save you.[1] Fear not, then, says the prophet; be no more in despair, O poor sinners! What fear can you have not to be pardoned, when the Son of God comes down from heaven to save you? Has not he himself made compensation to God by the sacrifice of his life for that just vengeance which our sins demanded? If you cannot by your own works appease an offended God, behold one that can appease him; this very infant which you now see reposing on straw, trembling with cold, and weeping, he, with his tears, propitiates him.

You have no grounds for being any more sad, says St. Leo, on account of the sentence of death fulminated against you, now that life itself is born for you; "nor is there any lawful room for sadness, when it is the birthday of life."[2] And St. Augustine: "O sweet day for penitents, to-day sin is taken away, and shall the sinner despair?"[3] If you are unable to render due satisfaction to the divine justice, look on Jesus who does penance for you; already does he commence to do it in this little cave; he will persevere in doing penance all his life, and finally bring it to a conclusion on the cross, to which (according to the saying of St. Paul) he will affix the decree of your condemnation, cancelling it with his own blood: *Blotting out the handwriting of the decree that was*

---

[1] "Dicite pusillanimis: Confortamini, et nolite timere; ecce Deus vester ultione.n adducet retributionis; Deus ipse veniet, et salvabit vos."—*Isa.* xxxv. 4.

[2] "Neque fas est locum esse tristitiæ, ubi natalis est Vitæ."—*In Nat. D.* s. 1.

[3] "Dulcis dies pœnitentibus; hodie peccatum tollitur, et peccator desperat."—*S.* 117, *E. B. app.*

5

against us, which was contrary to us. And He hath taken the same out of the way, fastening it to the cross.[1]

The same apostle says that Jesus Christ, by dying for us, was made our justification: *He is made unto us wisdom, and justice, and sanctification, and redemption.*[2] "Justice," comments St. Bernard, "in the washing-away of sins."[3] Yes; for God, accepting on our behalf the torments and death of Jesus Christ, is obliged to pardon us by virtue of the compact made: *Him that knew no sin, for us He hath made sin, that we might be made the justice of God in Him.*[4] The innocent one was made a victim for our sins, in order that forgiveness through his merits might of right belong to us. For this reason David prays God to save him, not only for his mercy's sake, but likewise for the sake of his justice: *Deliver me in Thy justice.*[5]

The eagerness of God to save sinners was always immense. This eagerness led him to approach them with that cry: *Return, ye transgressors, to the heart.*[6] Sinners, enter once more into your own hearts; think of the benefits you have received from me, on the love I have borne you, and offend me no more. *Turn ye to Me, and I will turn to you.*[7] Turn back to me, and I will receive you in my embraces: *Why will you die, O house of Israel? Return ye and live.*[8] My children, why will you destroy

---

[1] "Delens quod adversus nos erat chirographum decreti, quod erat contrarium nobis, et ipsum tulit de medio, affigens illud cruci."— *Coloss.* ii. 14.

[2] "Factus est nobis sapientia a Deo, et justitia, et sanctificatio, et redemptio."—1 *Cor.* i. 30.

[3] "In ablutione peccatorum."—*In Cant.* s. 22.

[4] "Eum, qui non noverat peccatum, pro nobis peccatum fecit, ut nos efficeremur justitia Dei in ipso."—2 *Cor.* v. 21.

[5] "In justitia tua libera mea."—*Ps.* xxx. 2.

[6] "Redite, prævaricatores, ad cor."—*Isa.* xlvi. 8.

[7] "Convertimini ad me . . . et convertar ad vos."—*Zach.* i. 3.

[8] "Quare moriemini, domus Israel? . . . revertimini, et vivite."— *Ezech.* xviii. 31.

yourselves, and of your own free-will condemn yourselves to everlasting death? Return to me and you shall live.

In a word, his infinite mercy induced him to descend from heaven to earth to come and free us from eternal death: *Through the bowels of the mercy of our God, in which the Orient from on high hath visited us.*[1] But here we must be mindful of what St. Paul says: previously to God becoming man he reserved mercy for us; but he could not feel compassion for our miseries, because compassion implies some suffering, and God is incapable of suffering. Now, says the apostle, in order to be moved also with compassion for us the Eternal Word willed to become man, capable of suffering, and similar to other men who are afflicted with compassion, so that he might be able not only to save us, but also to compassionate us: *For we have not a High Priest who cannot have compassion on our infirmities, but one tempted in all things like as we are, without sin.*[2] And in another passage: *It behoved Him in all things to be made like unto His brethren, that He might become merciful.*

Oh, what a tender compassion has Jesus Christ for poor sinners! This makes him say, that he is that shepherd who goes about seeking the lost sheep, and on finding it he arranges a festival, saying: *Rejoice with Me, because I have found My sheep that was lost. And He lays it upon His shoulders rejoicing*;[3] and thus he carefully keeps possession of it in his fond embraces for fear he should again lose it. This, too, caused him to say that he is that loving Father who, whenever a prodigal son that

[1] "Per viscera misericordiæ Dei nostri, in quibus visitavit nos Oriens ex alto."—*Luke*, i. 73.

[2] "Non enim habemus pontificem qui non possit compati infirmitatibus nostris, tentatum autem per omnia pro similitudine absque peccato. Debuit per omnia fratribus similari, ut misericors fieret."—*Heb*. iv. 15; ii. 17.

[3] "Congratulamini mihi, quia inveni ovem meam quæ perierat. Imponit in humeros suos gaudens."—*Luke*, xv. 4-6.

has left him returns to his feet, does not thrust him away, but embraces him, kisses him, and as it were faints away for the consolation and fondness which he feels in beholding his repentance: *And running to him, He fell upon his neck and kissed him.*[1] This causes him to say, *I stand at the gate and knock;*[2] that is, that, although driven away from the soul by sin, he does not abandon her, but he places himself outside the door of her heart and knocks by his calls to gain readmittance. This made him say to his disciples, who with an indiscreet zeal would have called down vengeance on those who repulsed them: *You know not of what spirit you are.*[3] You see that I have so much compassion on sinners; and do you desire vengeance on them? Go, go away, for you are not of my spirit. Finally, this compassion made him say: *Come to me, all you that labor and are burdened, and I will refresh you.*[4] Come to me, all you that are afflicted and tormented with the weight of your sins, and I will give you ease.

And, in fact, with what tenderness did our amiable Redeemer, the moment she repented, forgive Magdalene, and change her into a saint! With what kindness did he forgive the paralytic, and at the same moment restore him to bodily health! And with what sweet gentleness, above all, did he treat the woman taken in adultery! The priests brought that sinner before him, that he might condemn her; but Jesus turning towards her said: *Hath no man condemned thee? Neither will I condemn thee.* As if he would thereby say: None of those who conducted thee hither hath condemned thee, and how, then, shall I

---

[1] "Accurrens cecidit super collum ejus, et osculatus est eum."—*Luke*, xv. 20.

[2] "Ecce sto ad ostium, et pulso."—*Apoc.* iii. 20.

[3] "Nescitis cujus spiritus estis."—*Luke*, ix. 55.

[4] "Venite ad me omnes, qui laboratis et onerati estis, et ego reficiam vos."—*Matt.* xi. 28.

condemn thee, I who came to save sinners? *Go in peace, and sin no more.*[1]

Oh no, let us not be afraid of Jesus Christ; but let us be afraid of our own obstinacy, if after offending him we will not listen to his voice, inviting us to be reconciled. *Who is he that shall condemn?* says the apostle: *Christ Jesus that died; who also maketh intercession for us.*[2] If we persist in our obstinacy, Jesus Christ will be constrained to condemn us; but if we repent of the evil we have done, what fear need we have of Jesus Christ? Who has to pronounce on us sentence? Think (says St. Paul) that the self-same Redeemer has to sentence thee who died just that he might not condemn thee; that self-same one who, that he might pardon thee, hath given himself no pardon: "In order to redeem the servant, He hath not spared himself,"[3] says St. Bernard.

Go, then, O sinner, go to the stable of Bethlehem, and thank the Infant Jesus, all shivering with cold for thy sake in that cave, moaning and weeping for thee on a bundle of straw; give thanks to this thy Redeemer, who has come down from heaven to call thee to himself and to save thee. If thou art desirous of pardon, he is waiting thee in that manger to pardon thee. Go quickly, then, and obtain thy pardon; and afterwards do not forget the excessive love which Jesus Christ has borne thee: *Forget not the kindness of thy surety.*[4] Forget not (says the prophet) that high favor he has done thee by making himself surety for thy debts to God, in taking on himself the chastisement deserved by thee; do not forget it,

---

[1] " Nemo te condemnavit? . . . Nec ego te condemnabo. Vade, et jam amplius noli peccare."—*John.* viii. 10, 11.

[2] " Quis est qui condemnet? Christus Jesus, qui mortuus est, . . . qui etiam interpellat pro nobis."—*Rom.* viii. 34.

[3] "Ut servum redimeret, sibi Filius ipse non pepercit."—*Serm. de Pass.*

[4] " Gratiam fidejussoris ne obliviscaris."—*Ecclus.* xxix. 20.

and love him for it. And know further, that shouldst thou love him, thy past sins will not stand in the way of thy receiving from God those specially great and choice graces which he is wont to bestow on his most beloved souls: *All things work together unto good.*[1] "Even sins," subjoins the gloss. Yes, even the remembrance of the sins we have committed contributes to the advantage of the sinner who bewails and detests them, because this very thing will conquer to make him more humble and more pleasing to God, when he sees how God has welcomed him into the arms of his loving mercies: *There shall be joy in heaven upon one sinner that doth penance, more than upon ninety-nine just.*[2]

But of what sinner it is to be understood that he gives more joy to heaven than a whole multitude of just ones? It is to be understood of that sinner who, out of gratitude to the divine goodness, devotes himself wholly and fervently to the love of God, after the example of a St. Paul, a St. Mary Magdalene, a St. Mary of Egypt, a St. Augustine, and a St. Margaret of Cortona. To this last saint in particular, who had formerly spent several years in sin, God revealed the place prepared for her in heaven, amongst the Seraphim; and even during her life he showed her many signal favors, insomuch that, beholding herself so favored, she one day said to God, "O Lord, how is it that Thou lavishest so many graces on me? Hast Thou, then, forgotten the sins I have committed against Thee?" And God thus answered her: "And do you not know what I have before told you, that when a soul repents of its faults I no longer remember all the outrages it has been guilty of towards me?" This same thing he had long ago announced by his Prophet Eze-

[1] "Omnia cooperantur in bonum."—*Rom.* viii. 28.
[2] "Ita gaudium erit in cœlo super uno peccatore pœnitentiam agente, quam super nonaginta novem justis."—*Luke*, xv. 7.

chiel: *If the wicked do penance . . . I will not remember all his iniquities.*[1]

Let us conclude. Our sins, then, do not prevent us from becoming saints; God offers us readily every assistance if we only desire it and ask it. What more remains? It remains for us to give ourselves entirely to God, and to devote to his love at least the remainder of our days in this life. Come, then, let us bestir ourselves; what are we doing? If we fail, we fail through ourselves, and not through God. Let us never be so unhappy as to turn all these mercies and loving calls of God into subjects of remorse and despair upon our death-bed, at that last moment when no more time is left to do anything; then the night sets in: *The night cometh, when no man can work.*[2]

Let us recommend ourselves to the most holy Mary, who, as St. Germanus says, makes it her glory to turn the most abandoned sinners into saints, by procuring for them the grace of conversion, not in an ordinary, but in an extraordinary degree; and this she is well able to do, because what she asks of Jesus Christ she asks as a Mother: "But thou, powerful with God by thy maternal authority, obtainest a wonderful grace of reconciliation for sinners, even for those who have sinned enormously;"[3] and she herself encourages us in those words put into her mouth by the Holy Church: *With me are riches . . . that I may enrich them that love me;*[4] and elsewhere· *In me is all grace of the way and of the truth, in me is all hope of*

---

[1] "Si impius egerit pœnitentiam . . . omnium iniquitatum ejus . . . non recordabor."—*Ezech.* xviii. 21.

[2] "Venit nox, quando nemo potest operari."—*John*, ix. 4.

[3] "Tu autem, materna in Deum auctoritate pollens, etiam iis qui enormiter peccant, eximiam remissionis gratiam concilias."—*In Deip. Dorm.* s. 2.

[4] "Mecum sunt divitiæ, . . . ut ditem diligentes me."—*Prov.* viii. 18.

life and of virtue.[1] Come to me all, she says, because you shall find with me every hope of saving yourselves, and of saving yourselves as saints.

Affections and Prayers.

O my Redeemer and God! and who am I, that Thou shouldst have loved me, and still continuest to love me, so much? What hast Thou ever received from me that has obliged Thee so to love me? what, except slights and provocations, which were a reason for Thee to abandon me, and to banish me forever from Thy face? But, O Lord! I accept of every penalty except this. If Thou dost forsake me, and deprive me of Thy grace, I can nevermore love Thee. I have not the pretensions to escape punishment; but I wish to love Thee, and to love Thee exceedingly. I wish to love Thee as a sinner is bound to love Thee, who, after so many special favors, and so many marks of love received from Thee, has, in spite of all, so frequently turned his back upon Thee; who, for the sake of wretched momentary and poisonous gratifications, has renounced Thy grace and Thy love. Pardon me, O my beloved Infant, for I am sorry with my whole heart for every single displeasure I have given Thee. But know that I shall not be content with a simple pardon; I desire also the grace to love Thee ardently; I wish to make compensation by my love as much as possible for the past ingratitude which I have shown Thee. An innocent soul loves Thee as innocent, and thanks Thee for having preserved it from the death of sin. I must love Thee as a sinner; that is, as one who has rebelled against Thee, as one condemned to hell, as often as I deserved it; and then so often graciously received back by Thee and re established in the way of salvation, and over and above enriched with lights, with helps, with invitations to become a saint. O Redeemer, and Redeemer again and again of my soul! my soul is now enamoured of Thee, and loves Thee. Thou hast loved me above measure, so that, overcome by Thy love, I could no longer resist its winning appeals, and at last I now surrender myself, and fix all my love on Thee. I love Thee, then, O infinite Goodness! I love Thee, O most lovable God!

[1] " In me gratia omnis viæ et veritatis, in me omnis spes vitæ et virtutis; transite ad me omnes."—*Eccles.* xxiv. 25.

Do Thou never cease to enkindle more and more in my heart the flames and fiery darts of love. For Thy own glory cause Thyself to be greatly loved by one who has greatly offended Thee. Mary, my Mother, thou art the hope, the refuge of sinners; assist a sinner who desires to prove faithful to his God; help me to love him, and to love him exceedingly.

DISCOURSE V.

The Eternal Word from being Strong became Weak.

Dicite pusillanimis: Confortamini, et nolite timere: . . . Deus ipse veniet, et salvabit vos.

" Say to the faint-hearted : Take courage, and fear not : God Himself will come and will save you."—*Isa.* xxxv. 4.

Isaias, speaking of the coming of the Redeemer, made this prediction: *The land that was desolate and impassable shall be glad, and the wilderness shall rejoice and shall flourish like the lily.*[1] The Prophet had been speaking of the pagans (among whom were our unfortunate ancestors), who were living in heathendom, as in a desert land, void of a single man that knew and worshipped the true God, but peopled only with those who were slaves of the devil: a desert land and impassable, because there was no path of salvation known to these wretched people. And he foretold that the land, though so miserable then, would afterwards rejoice at the coming of the Messias, and would see itself filled with followers of the true God, strengthened by his grace against all the enemies of their salvation; and that it would blossom as the lily, by purity of morals and by the sweet odor of all holy virtues. Wherefore Isaias proceeds to say: *Say to the faint-hearted, Take courage, and fear not: God Himself will come and save you.*[2] This very event, foretold by Isaias, has

---

[1] "Lætabitur deserta et invia, et exsultabit solitudo, et florebit quasi lilium."—*Isa.* xxxv. 1.

[2] " Dicite pusillanimis: Confortamini, et nolite timere; . . . Deus ipse veniet, et salvabit vos."

already happened. Let me, then, exclaim with gladness: Go on joyfully, O children of Adam! go on joyfully, be no more faint-hearted. Even though you perceive yourselves weak, and unable to stand against so many enemies, "Fear not; God himself will come and save you."[1] God himself has come on earth, and has redeemed us, by imparting to you strength sufficient to combat and to vanquish every enemy of your salvation.

How did our Redeemer procure for us this strength? From being *strong* and omnipotent, he has become *weak*. He has taken on himself our weakness, and by so doing has communicated to us his strength. Let us see the truth of this. But let us first seek light of Jesus and Mary.

I.

God is that strong one who alone can be called strong, because he is strength itself; and whoever is strong derives strength from him: *Strength is Mine, and by Me kings reign*,[2] saith the Lord. God is that mighty one who can do whatsoever he will; and he can do this with ease; he has merely to wish it: *Behold, Thou hast made heaven and earth by Thy great power, and no word shall be hard to Thee*.[3] By a nod he created heaven and earth out of nothing: *He spoke, and they were made*.[4] And did he choose to do so, he could destroy the immense machinery of the universe by a single nod, as he created it: *At a beck He can utterly destroy the whole world*.[5] We know already how, when it pleased him, he burnt five entire cities with a deluge of fire. We know how, previously to that, he

[1] "Nolite timere; . . . Deus ipse veniet, et salvabit vos."
[2] "Mea est fortitudo; per me reges regnant."—*Prov.* viii. 14.
[3] "Ecce tu fecisti cœlum et terram in fortitudine tua; . . . non erit tibi difficile omne verbum."—*Jer.* xxxii. 17.
[4] "Ipse dixit et facta sunt."—*Ps.* cxlviii. 5.
[5] "Potest. . . . universum mundum uno nutu delere."—2 *Mach.* viii. 18.

The Eternal Word became Weak.

inundated the whole earth with a deluge of waters, to the destruction of all mankind, with the sole exception of eight persons. *O Lord*, says the wise man: *who can ever resist the strength of your arm ?*[1]

Hence we may see the rashness of the sinner who wrestles against God, and carries his audacity so far as even to lift up his hand against the Almighty: *He hath stretched out his hand against God, and hath strengthened himself against the Almighty.*[2] Suppose we should see an ant make an assault upon a soldier, would we not think it rashness? But how much more rash is it for a man who makes an assault on the Creator himself, who scorns his precepts, disregards his threats, despises his grace, and declares himself his enemy!

But these rash and ungrateful men are the very men whom the Son of God has come to save, by making himself man, and by taking on himself the chastisement deserved by them, in order to obtain pardon for them. And then, seeing that man from the wounds inflicted by sin continued very weak and powerless to resist the strength of his enemies, what did he do? From strong and almighty as he was, he became weak, and assumed to himself the bodily infirmities of man, in order to procure for man by His merits the strength of soul requisite to subdue the attacks of the flesh and of hell. And so, behold him made a little child, in need of milk to sustain his life, and so feeble that he cannot feed himself, that he cannot move himself.

The Eternal Word, in coming to be made man, wished to conceal his strength: *God will come from the south; there is His strength hid.*[3] We find (says St. Augustine)

---

[1] " Virtuti brachii tui quis resistet?"—*Wis.* xi. 22.
[2] " Tetendit enim adversus Deum manum suam, et contra Omnipotentem roboratus est."—*Job.* xv. 25.
[3] " Deus ab austro veniet . . . ; ibi abscondita est fortitudo ejus." —*Hab.* iii. 3, 4.

Jesus Christ strong and feeble,—strong, since he created all things; feeble, since we behold him made man like us: "We find Jesus strong and weak, strong, by whom all things were made without labor. Would you see him weak? The Word was made flesh."[1] Now this strong one has chosen to become weak, says the saint, to repair by his weakness our infirmity, and so to obtain our salvation: *He hath built us up by His strength, He hath sought us by His infirmity.*[2] For this reason he likens himself to the hen, when he speaks with Jerusalem: *How often would I have gathered together thy children, as the hen doth gather her chickens under her wings! and thou wouldst not.*[3] St. Augustine remarks that the hen in rearing her chickens grows weak, and by this mark is known to be a mother; so was it with our loving Redeemer, by becoming infirm and weak, he made himself known for the father and mother of us poor weak creatures.

Behold him who governs the heavens (says St. Cyril) swathed in rags, and unable even to stretch forth his little arms.[4] Behold him in that journey which by his Father's will he had to make into Egypt; he wished already to obey, but he cannot walk; Mary and Joseph are obliged to take turns in carrying him in their arms. And in their return from Egypt, as St. Bonaventure contemplates, they have frequently to stop and rest, because the divine child was now so much grown that he was too large to be carried in the arms; whilst, on the other hand, he was too small and feeble to make a long jour-

---

[1] "Invenimus fortem et infirmum Jesum: fortem, per quem sine labore facta sunt omnia; infirmum vis nosse? Verbum caro factum est."

[2] "Condidit nos fortitudine sua; quæsivit nos infirmitate sua."—*In Jo.* tr. 15.

[3] "Quoties volui congregare filios tuos, quemadmodum gallina congregat pullos suos sub alas, et noluisti!"—*Matt.* xxiii. 37.

[4] "Qui cœlum regit, fasciis involvitur."

ney: "He is so large that he cannot be carried, and so small that he cannot walk alone."[1]

Look at him afterwards in the shop at Nazareth, growing towards manhood, how busily he toils and labors in helping Joseph at his trade of carpenter! Who can ever attentively consider Jesus, that beautiful youth, fatiguing and exhausting himself to bring into form some rough-hewn piece of wood, and not exclaim: But, most sweet youth, art Thou not that God, who by a mere nod didst create the world out of nothing? And how comes it that Thou hast labored now for a whole day, and bathed in sweat, to fashion this piece of wood; and even still Thy work remains unfinished? Who has reduced Thee to such a state of weakness? O holy faith! O divine love! O God! O God! how such a thought as this, if once well penetrated, would suffice, not only to inflame us, but to reduce us, so to speak, into ashes with the fire of love! Has a God, then, come to such a pass as this? and wherefore? To make himself loved by men!

Observe him, again, at the close of his life bound with cords in the garden, from which he cannot loose himself; tied in the prætorium to a pillar to undergo the scourging; see him with the cross on his shoulders, but too feeble to carry it, and therefore he frequently falls upon the road; see him fixed to the cross with nails, from which he can find no escape; behold him, finally, how, for very exhaustion and weakness, he is already in his agony, draws near his end, and expires.

II.

And for what reason did Jesus Christ become so weak? He made himself weak, as we said above, that so he might communicate his strength to us, and by this

---

[1] "Sic magnus est, quod portari non prævalet; et sic parvus, quod per se ire non potest."—*Med. vit. Chr.* c. 13.

means conquer and subdue the powers of hell: *The lion of the tribe of Juda hath prevailed.*[1] David says that the will to save us and to free us from death is a part and property of God's divine nature. Our God is the God of salvation: *And of the Lord, of the Lord are the issues from death.*[2] On which passage Bellarmine makes this commentary: " This is proper to him, this is his very nature ; our God is a saving God , and of our God are the issues of death—that is, the delivery from death."[3] Are we indeed weak ? let us put our trust in Jesus Christ, and we shall be capable of all things: *I can do all things in Him who strengtheneth me,*[4] said the Apostle. I am able for all things, not by my own strength, but by the strength which my Redeemer has obtained for me through his merits: *Have confidence, I have overcome the world.*[5] Take courage, my children, Jesus Christ says to us ; if you are unable to resist your enemies, *I have overcome the world;* and know that I have overcome it for you. My conquest was to give you the spoils ; avail yourselves now of the arms which I leave you to defend yourselves, for you are sure to triumph.

What are the arms which Jesus Christ has left us ? They are two, the use of the sacraments and prayer.

Everybody knows that by means of the sacraments, especially of penance and the Holy Eucharist, are imparted to us the graces which our Saviour has merited for us ; and experience shows us every day that those who frequent the sacraments easily keep themselves in the grace of God. And, especially, how is he that often

[1] " Vicit Leo de tribu Juda."—*Apoc.* v 5.
[2] " Deus noster, Deus salvos faciendi ; et Domini, Domini exitus mortis."—*Ps.* lxvii. 21.
[3] " Hoc est illi proprium. hæc est ejus natura: ipse Deus noster est Deus salvans, et Dei nostri sunt exitus mortis, id est liberatio a morte."
[4] " Omnia possum in eo qui me confortat."—*Phil.* iv. 13.
[5] " Confidite ; ego vici mundum."—*John,* xvi. 33.

The Eternal Word became Weak. 79

communicates strengthened in a wonderful manner to vanquish temptations! The Holy Eucharist is called bread, the heavenly bread, that we may understand how the Communion preserves the life of the soul, which is divine grace, just as earthly bread preserves the life of the body. For the same reason the Council of Trent calls Holy Communion a remedy which relieves us from venial and preserves us from mortal sins: "An antidote by which we are freed from daily faults, and are preserved from mortal sins.[1] St. Thomas, speaking of the Holy Eucharist, says that the wound left by sin would remain incurable, were it not for this remedy which is given to us. "It would be incurable, were it not the medicine of God applied to cure us."[2] Moreover, Innocent III. says that the Passion of Jesus Christ delivers us from the chains of sin, and the Holy Communion delivers us from the will to sin: "The mystery of the Cross delivers us from the power of sin; the mystery of the Eucharist, from the will to sin."[3]

The other grand means of overcoming temptations is prayer offered to God through the merits of Jesus Christ: *Amen, Amen, I say to you* (said our Redeemer), *if you ask the Father anything in My name, He will give it you.*[4] Whatsoever, then, we ask of God in the name of Jesus Christ, that is, through his merits, we shall certainly obtain it. And this, we see, happens continually; all those who are tempted and have recourse to God, and invoke him through Jesus Christ, invariably come off victori-

[1] "Antidotum quo liberemur a cûlpis quotidianis, et a peccatis mortalibus præservemur."—*Sess.* 13, *cap.* 2.
[2] "Esset incurabilis, nisi subveniretur medicina Dei."—*De Sacr. alt.* c. 1.
[3] "Per crucis mysterium, eripuit nos a potestate peccati; per Eucharistiæ sacramentum, liberat nos a voluntate peccandi."—*De Alt. Myst.* l. 4, c. 44.
[4] "Amen, amen dico vobis: si quid petieritis Patrem in nomine meo, dabit vobis."—*John*, xvi 23.

ous; and, on the contrary, those who in temptation (especially of impurity) neglect to recommend themselves to God, fall miserably and perish. And then they excuse themselves by saying they are but of flesh, and are very weak. But how can they reasonably allege their weakness as an excuse, when they are able to acquire strength by having recourse to Jesus Christ (for it is enough to call with confidence on his Most Holy Name), and they will not do so? What excuse, I say, would that man have for having been vanquished by his enemy, who, when the requisite arms for his defence were presented him, had despised and refused them? Were such a man to allege his weakness, who would not instantly condemn him with these words,—And you, knowing as you did your own weakness, why did you not avail yourself of the arms that were offered you?

St. Augustine says that the devil was put in chains by Jesus Christ; he can bark, but he cannot bite any one, except those who wish to be bitten. That man is really a fool (continues the saint) who allows himself to be bitten by a dog chained up: " Christ came and chained the devil. He is bound in chains like a dog. Foolish is the man whom a dog in chains bites. He can bark, he can make attempts; he can only bite him who wills so; for he does not extort our consent from us, but seeks it."[1] And in another passage he says that the Redeemer has given us every remedy to effect our cure; he that will not observe the laws and is put to death, dies because he wishes his own death. " As far as the physician is concerned, he came to heal; he destroys himself who will not observe the laws."[2] He that takes

[1] "Venit Christus, et alligavit diabolum. Alligatus est tamquam innexus canis catenis. Stultus homo ille est, quem canis in catena positus mordet. Ille latrare potest, sollicitare potest ; mordere non potest, nisi volentem: non enim extorquet a nobis consensum, sed petit."—*S.* 37, *E. B. app.*

[2] " Quantum in medico est, sanare venit ægrotum ; ipse se interimit, qui præcepta medici observare non vult."—*In Jo. tr.* 12.

The Eternal Word became Weak. 81

advantage of Jesus Christ is not weak; no, but he waxes strong on the strength of Jesus Christ. Jesus it is who, as St. Augustine says, not only cheers us on to the combat, but affords us help; if we fail, he is ready to succor us; and of his immense goodness he himself crowns us in the end: "He encourages you to fight, and helps you to conquer, and supports you if you languish, and crowns you victorious."[1] Isaias prophesied, *Then shall the lame man leap as a hart;*[2] that is, by the merits of the Redeemer, he who could not stir one step should skip over the hills as a swift hart: *And that which was dry land shall become a pool, and the thirsty land springs of water;*[3] he foretells that the most parched-up soil should teem with virtues: *In the dens where dragons dwelt before shall rise up the verdure of the reed and the bulrush*;[4] and that in those souls in which devils formerly abode should be propagated the vigor of the reed,—namely, of humility, because, according to the commentary of Cornelius à Lapide, "the humble man is empty in his own eyes;"[5] and of the bulrush,—namely, of charity, because, as the same commentator says, in certain places they use it for wicks to burn in lamps.

In a word, we find in Jesus Christ all grace, all strength, all help, whenever we have recourse to him: *In all things you are made rich in Him, so that nothing is wanting to you in any grace.*[6] For this very end he was made man, and

---

[1] "Hortatur ut pugnes, et adjuvat ut vincas, et deficientem sublevat, et vincentem coronat."—*In Ps.* xxxii. *en.* 2.

[2] "Tunc saliet, sicut cervus, claudus."

[3] "Et quæ erat arida, erit in stagnum, et sitiens in fontes aquarum."

[4] "In cubilibus, in quibus prius dracones habitabant, orietur viror calami et junci."—*Isa.* xxxv. 6-7.

[5] "Quia humilis est vacuus in oculis suis."

[6] "In omnibus divites facti estis in illo . . . , ita ut nihil vobis desit in ulla gratia."—1 *Cor.* i. 5.

emptied himself: "*He emptied Himself.*"[1] "He, as it were, reduced himself to nothing," says a certain author; "He made himself empty of majesty, of glory, of strength."[2] In a manner, he lowered himself to nothing; he put off his majesty, glory, and power, and took on himself ignominies and infirmities, to make over to us his worth and his virtues, that so he might be our light, our justice, our satisfaction, and our ransom: *Who is made unto us wisdom, and justice, and sanctification, and redemption.*[3] And he remains ready at any moment to give health and strength to every one that asks him.

I saw one girt about the paps with a golden girdle.[4] St. John saw the Lord with his breasts full of milk (that is, full of graces), and bound about with a girdle of gold; this signifies that Jesus Christ is, as it were, hemmed round and compressed with the love he bears to man; and as the mother, whose breast is oversupplied with milk, seeks for children who may imbibe the nourishment and relieve her of the burden, so does he yearn for us to come and seek graces of him, and the necessary help to conquer our enemies, who strive to rob us of his friendship and of eternal salvation.

Oh, how bounteous and liberal is God with a soul that sincerely and resolutely seeks him! *The Lord is good to the soul that seeketh Him.*[5] Wherefore, if we do not become saints, the failure rests with us, because we do not resolve to wish for God alone: *The sluggard willeth and willeth not.*[6] The lukewarm will and will not; and there-

---

[1] "Semetipsum exinanivit."—*Phil.* ii. 7.

[2] "Quasi ad nihilum se redegit; se evacuavit majestate, gloria, et robore."

[3] "Factus est nobis sapientia a Deo, et justitia, et sanctificatio, et redemptio."—1 *Cor.* i. 30.

[4] "Vidi . . . præcinctum ad mamillas zona aurea."—*Apoc.* i. 12.

[5] "Bonus est Dominus . . . animæ quærenti illum."—*Lam.* iii. 25.

[6] "Vult et non vult piger."—*Prov.* xiii. 4.

fore they remain defeated, because they want the resolute will to please God alone. A resolute will overcomes everything; for when once a soul determines really to give itself wholly to God, God immediately gives it the hand and the strength to surmount all difficulties that may occur in the way of perfection. This was the splendid promise which Isaias signified to us in these words: *O, that Thou wouldst rend the heavens and wouldst come down; the mountains would melt away at Thy presence.*[1] *The crooked shall become straight, and the rough ways plain.*[2] At the coming of the Redeemer he will endow our souls with such a strength of good-will that they will find levelled down the mountains of all the carnal appetites; and they will find the crooked ways made straight, and the rough ways plain; that is, the contempts and labors which formerly were so difficult and hard for men to bear will, by means of the grace given by Jesus Christ, and of the divine love which he enkindles in their hearts, be afterwards all made sweet and easy. Thus was it that St. John of God rejoiced at being beaten as a fool in a hospital; thus St. Lidwine was glad to find herself during so many years tied down to her bed by a body full of wounds and sores; thus St. Laurence exulted and mocked the tyrant, while scorching on a gridiron, and giving his life for Jesus Christ. And so likewise do so many souls enamoured of God find peace and contentment, not, indeed, in the pleasures and honors of the world, but in sufferings and insults.

Ah! let us beg Jesus Christ to impart to us that fire which he came on earth to enkindle; that so we may no longer find it difficult to despise goods of dirt, and to undertake great things for God. "He that loves, labors

---

[1] "Utinam dirumperes cœlos, et descenderes! a facie tua montes defluerent."—*Isa.* lxiv. 1.

[2] " Erunt prava in directa, et aspera in vias planas."—*Isa.* xl. 4.

not,"[1] says St. Augustine; the soul that loves God only finds it neither irksome nor painful to suffer, to pray, to mortify itself, to humble itself, and to detach itself from the pleasures of earth. The more it works and suffers, the more it is eager to do and to suffer: *Jealousy is hard as hell; the lamps thereof are fire and flames.*[2] The flames of divine love are like the flames of hell, which never say it is enough. Nothing whatever satisfies a soul that loves God. As for hell no fire is sufficient, so for the loving soul its ardor is never satisfied.

Let us ask this great gift through the intercession of Mary, by whose hands (as was revealed to St. Mary Magdalene of Pazzi) divine love is bestowed upon souls. She is God's treasure, the treasurer of all graces (especially of divine love), as she was called by the Idiota, " The treasure and the treasurer of graces."[3]

Affections and Prayers.

My sovereign God and Redeemer, I was lost; Thou hast ransomed me from hell. But, unhappy me! I have often afterwards lost myself anew, and Thou hast as often released me from eternal death: " I am Thine, save me."[4] Since, as I hope, I am now Thine, suffer me never more to cast myself away by rebelling against Thee, I am resolved to suffer death, and a thousand deaths, rather than see myself ever again Thy enemy and the slave of the devil. But Thou knowest my weakness, Thou knowest my past treacheries. Thou must give me strength to resist the assaults which hell will make upon me. I know that I shall be assisted by Thee in temptation whenever I shall have recourse to Thee, since I have Thy promise for it : *Ask, and you shall receive.*[5] *Every one that asketh receiveth.*[6] But

---

[1] "Qui amat, non laborat."—*In Jo. tr.* 48.
[2] " Dura sicut infernus æmulatio; lampades ejus, lampades ignis atque flammarum."—*Cant.* viii. 6.
[3] " Thesaurus et Thesauraria gratiarum."—*Cont. de V. M. in prol.*
[4] " Tuus sum ego; salvum me fac."—*Ps.* cxviii. 94.
[5] " Petite et accipietis."—*John,* xvi. 24.
[6] "Omnis enim qui petit, accipit."—*Matt.* vii. 8.

my fear is, lest in the moment of trial I should fail to recommend myself to Thee, and so be miserably overcome. This, therefore, is the grace which I most earnestly implore of Thee: grant me light and strength on all occasions to have recourse to Thee, and to invoke Thee whenever I am tempted ; and, moreover, I entreat Thee to grant me Thy help, that I may always ask Thee for this grace. Grant it me by the merits of Thy Precious Blood. And thou, O Mary, obtain it for me by the love which thou bearest to Jesus Christ.

DISCOURSE VI.
The Eternal Word from being His Own has made Himself Ours.

Parvulus natus est nobis, et Filius datus est nobis.
" A child is born to us, and a Son is given to us."—*Is.* xi. 6.

Tell me, cruel Herod, why dost thou command so many innocent babes to be murdered and sacrificed to thy ambition of reigning ? Art thou perchance afraid that the Messias lately born may rob thee of thy kingdom ? " Why art thou so troubled, Herod ?" asks St. Fulgentius. " This King who is born came not to vanquish kings by fighting, but to subdue them by dying." [1] This King, of whom thou art in such terror, is not come to conquer the monarchs of the earth by force of arms, but he is come to reign in the hearts of men by suffering and dying for their love. " He came, therefore" (concludes St. Fulgentius), " not that he might combat alive, but that he might triumph slain." [2] Our amiable Redeemer did not come to carry on war during his life, but to triumph over the love of men, when he should have laid down his life on the gibbet of the cross, as he himself said: *When I shall be lifted up, I will draw all things to Myself.*[3]

[1] " Quid est quod sic turbaris, Herodes ? Rex iste qui natus est, non venit reges pugnando superare, sed moriendo subjugare."
[2] " Venit ergo non ut pugnet vivus, sed ut triumphet occisus."—*S. de Epiph. et Inn. nece.*
[3] " Si exaltatus fuero a terra, omnia traham ad meipsum."—*John*, xii. 52.

But let us leave Herod aside, O devout souls, and let us come to ourselves. Why, then, did the Son of God come upon earth? was it to give himself to us? Yes, Isaias assures us of it: *A Child is born to us, and a Son is given to us.*[1] The love which this loving Saviour bears us, and the desire which he has to be loved by us, has induced him to do this. Being his own, he has become ours. Let us see it; but let us first ask light from the Most Holy Sacrament and from the divine Mother.

I.

The greatest privilege of God, nay, the whole of God, is to be his own, that is, to exist of himself, and to depend on no one. All creatures, however grand and excellent they may be, are nothing in reality, because whatsoever they have, they have from God, who has created them and preserves them; and this in such a manner that if God were for a single moment to cease from preserving them, they would instantly lose their being and return to nothing. God, on the contrary, because he exists of himself, cannot fail; nor can there be any one to destroy him, or to diminish his greatness, his power, or his happiness. But St. Paul says that the Eternal Father has given the Son to us: *He delivered Him up for us all.*[2] And that the Son has given himself for us: *Christ also hath loved, us and hath delivered Himself for us.*[3] Has God, then, in giving himself for us, made himself ours? Yes, replies St. Bernard: "He is born, who belonged to himself;"[4] he who wholly appertained to himself chose to be born for us and to become ours; love triumphs over God.[5] This God, over whom none besides can rule, has,

[1] "Parvulus natus est nobis, et Filius datus est nobis."
[2] "Pro nobis omnibus tradidit illum!"—*Rom.* viii. 32.
[3] "Dilexit nos, et tradidit semetipsum pro nobis!"—*Eph.* v. 2.
[4] "Natus est nobis, qui sibi erat."
[5] "Triumphat de Deo amor."

so to speak, yielded himself captive to love; love has gained the victory over him, and from being his own has reduced him into our possession: *God so loved the world, as to give His only-begotten Son.*[1] God has so loved men, says Jesus Christ, that he has even given them his only-begotten Son. And the Son himself, also through love, was pleased to give himself to men to be loved by them.

In divers ways had God already striven to win the hearts of men, at one time with benefits, at another with threats, and again with promises; but he had still fallen short of his aim. His infinite love, says St. Augustine, made him devise the plan of giving himself entirely to us by the Incarnation of the Word, in order thus to oblige us to love him with our whole hearts. "Then love found out the plan of delivering up itself."[2] He could have sent an angel, a seraph, to redeem man; but, aware that man, had he been redeemed by a seraph, would have had to divide his heart, by partly loving his Creator and partly his redeemer, God, who would possess the entire heart and the entire love of man, "wished therefore to be" (says a pious author) "both our Creator and Redeemer;"[3] as he was our Creator, so he would likewise become our Redeemer.

And behold him already arrived from heaven in a stable; as a child, born for us and given to us: *A Child is born to us, and a Son is given to us.*[4] This was precisely what the angel signified when addressing the shepherds: *To-day is born to you a Saviour.*[5] As much as to say: O ye men, go to the cave of Bethlehem; there adore the Infant, which you will find laid on the straw, in a manger,

---

[1] "Sic enim Deus dilexit mundum, ut Filium suum unigenitum daret."—*John*, iii. 16.
[2] "Modum tunc, ut se proderet, invenit amor."
[3] "Voluit esse nobis Creator et Redemptor."
[4] "Parvulus natus est nobis, et Filius datus est nobis."
[5] "Natus est vobis hodie Salvator."—*Luke*, ii. 11.

and shivering with cold; know that he is your God, who would not consent to send any one else to save you, but would come himself, that he might gain for himself all your love.

Yes, it was with the purpose of making himself loved that the Eternal Word came upon earth to converse among men: *He conversed with men.*[1] If a king speaks a confidential word to one of his vassals, if he smiles upon him, or presents him with a flower, oh, how honored and happy does that vassal consider himself! How much more so, should the king seek his friendship; should he request his company every day at table; should he desire him to take up his residence in his own palace, and to abide always near him! Ah! my Great King, my beloved Jesus, as before the Redemption Thou couldst not assume man into heaven, whose gates remained closed by sin, Thou camest down upon earth to converse with men as their brothers, and to give Thyself wholly to them, from the excess of the love Thou bearest them! *He loved us and delivered Himself up for us.*[2] Yes, exclaims St. Augustine, this most loving and most merciful God, through his love to man, chose to give him not only his goods, but even his very self. " The most merciful God, through his love of man, poured out upon him not only his goods, but his whole self."[3]

Well, then, the affection which this sovereign Lord entertains towards us miserable worms is so immense that it induced him to give himself wholly to us, being born for us, living for us, and even offering up his life and all his blood for us, in order to prepare us a bath of salvation, and to wash us from all our sins: *He hath loved us and washed us in His own blood.*[4] But, Lord (remon-

[1] " Cum hominibus conversatus est."—*Bar.* iii. 38.
[2] " Dilexit nos, et tradidit semetipsum pro nobis !"
[3] " Deus piissimus, præ amore hominis, non solum sua, verum seipsum impendit."—*Man.* c. 26.
[4] " Dilexit nos, et lavit nos in sanguine suo."—*Apoc.* i. 5.

strates the Abbot Guerric), this appears an extreme prodigality of Thyself, coming from the great anxiety Thou hast to be loved by mankind. "O God! if we may dare say so, prodigal of Himself through desire of man!"[1] "And is it not so?" he continues: "how otherwise can we style this God than prodigal of himself who, in order to recover lost man, not only gives whatever he has, but even his own self?"[2]

St. Augustine says that God, in order to captivate the love of men, has cast several darts of love into their hearts: "God knows how to take aim at love; he draws the arrow that he may make a lover."[3] What are these arrows? They are all the creatures that we see around us; for God has created them all for man, that man might love him; hence the same saint says, "Heaven and earth and all things tell me to love Thee."[4] It seemed to the saint that the sun, the moon, the stars, the mountains, the plains, the seas, and the rivers spoke to him and said, Augustine, love God, because God has created us for thee, that thou mightest love him. When St. Mary Magdalene of Pazzi held in her hand a beautiful fruit or flower, she declared that that fruit or flower was as a dart to her heart, which wounded her with the love of God; thinking as she did how from all eternity God had designed to create that flower that she might discover his love, and love him in return. St. Teresa, moreover, said that all the fair things which we see,—the lakes, the rivers, the flowers, the fruits, the birds,—all upbraid us with our ingratitude to God, for all are tokens

---

[1] "O Deum, si fas est dici, prodigum sui præ desiderio hominis!"
[2] "An non prodigum sui, qui, non solum sua, sed seipsum impendit, ut hominem recuperaret?"—*In Pent.* s. 1.
[3] "Novit Dominus sagittare ad amorem; sagittat, ut faciat amantem."—*In Ps.* cxix.
[4] "Cœlum et terra et omnia mihi dicunt ut te amem."—*Conf.* l. 10, c. 6.

of the love God bears us. It is related likewise of a pious hermit, that, walking in the country, and beholding the herbs and the flowers, he fancied they reproached him with his ingratitude; so that, as he went along, he struck them gently with his staff, saying to them: Hush, be silent, I understand you, no more! you upbraid me with my ingratitude, because God has created you in such beauty for my sake, that I might love him, and I love him not; oh, be silent, I hear you, enough, enough! And thus the good man pursued his way, giving vent to the ardors of love which he felt consuming his heart for God at the sight of those fair creatures.

Thus, then, all these creatures were so many darts of love to the heart of man; but God was not satisfied with these darts only; they were not enough to gain him the love of men: *He hath made me as a chosen arrow; in his quiver he hath hidden me.*[1] On this passage Cardinal Hugo remarks, that as the sportsman keeps in reserve the best arrow for the last shot, in order to secure his prey; so did God among all his gifts keep Jesus in reserve till the fulness of time should come, and then he sent him as a last dart to wound with love the hearts of men: "The choicest arrow is reserved; so Christ was reserved in the bosom of the Father, until the fulness of time should come, and he was sent to wound the hearts of the faithful."[2] Jesus, then, was the choice and reserved arrow, at the discharge of which, according as David had long ago foretold, entire nations should fall vanquished: *Thy arrows are sharp; under Thee shall people fall.*[3] Oh, how many stricken hearts do I behold burning with love before the manger of Bethlehem!

[1] "Posuit me sicut sagittam electam; in pharetra sua abscondit me."—*Isa.* xlix. 2.

[2] "Sagitta electa reservatur; ita Christus quasi reservatus est in sinu Patris, donec venit plenitudo temporis, et tunc missus est ad vulnerandum corda fidelium."

[3] "Sagittæ tuæ acutæ; populi sub te cadent."—*Ps.* xliv. 6.

The Eternal Word has made Himself Ours. 91

how many at the foot of the cross in Calvary ! how many before the Holy Presence of the Blessed Sacrament on our altars !

St. Peter Chrysologus says that our Redeemer took many various forms to attract the love of man: "For our sake he showed himself under different forms, who remains in the one form of his majesty."[1] That God, who is unchangeable, would appear now as a child in a stable, now as a boy in a workshop, now as a criminal on a scaffold, and now as bread upon the altar. In these varying guises Jesus chose to exhibit himself to us; but whatever character he assumed, it was always the character of a lover. Ah, my Lord, tell me, is there anything else left for Thee to devise in order to make Thyself loved? *Make known his inventions,* cried out Isaias.[2] Go, O redeemed souls, said the prophet, go and publish everywhere the loving devices of this loving God, which he has thought out and executed to make himself loved by man; for after lavishing so many of his gifts upon them, he was pleased to bestow himself, and to bestow himself in so many ways: "If thou desirest a cure for thy wound" (says St. Ambrose), "he is a Physician;"[3] if thou art infirm and wouldst be healed, behold Jesus, who heals thee by his Blood: "If thou be parched up with fever, he is a fountain;"[4] if the impure flames of worldly affections trouble thee, behold the fountain to refresh thee with his consolations. "Dost thou fear death, he is life; dost thou long for heaven, he is the way; in fine, if thou dost not wish to die, he is the life; if thou wishest heaven, he is the way."[5]

[1] "Propter te varias monstratur in formas, qui manet unica suæ majestatis in forma."—*Serm.* 23.
[2] "Notas facite in populis adinventiones ejus."—*Isa.* xii. 4.
[3] "Si vulnus curare desideras, medicus est."
[4] "Si febribus æstuas, fons est."
[5] "Si mortem times, vita est; si cœlum desideras, via est."—*De Virg.* l. 3.

And not only has Jesus Christ given himself to all men in general, but he wished, moreover, to give himself to each one in particular. This was what caused St. Paul to say, *He loved me and delivered Himself for me.*[1] St. John Chrysostom says that God has the same love for each one of us as he has for all men together.[2] So that, my dear brother, if there had been no others in the world beside yourself, the Redeemer would have come for the sake of you alone, and would have given his blood and his life for you. And who can ever express or conceive (says St. Laurence Justinian) the love which God bears to each man? "Nor is it possible to express with what affection God is moved towards each one."[3] This led St. Bernard to say also, in speaking of Jesus Christ, "Given wholly to me, and spent wholly for my interests."[4] This caused St. John Chrysostom also to say, "He gave himself entirely to us, he reserved nothing for himself."[5] He gave us his blood, his life, himself in the Blessed Sacrament; there remains nothing more to give us. In fine, says St. Thomas, after God has bestowed himself on us, what else remains for him to give us? "God had no room to extend himself further."[6] Wherefore after the work of the redemption, God has nothing more to give us, nothing more that he can do for the love of man.

II.

So that every man should say, with St. Bernard, "I owe myself for myself; what can I return the Lord for

[1] "Dilexit me, et tradidit semetipsum pro me."—*Gal.* ii. 20.
[2] "Adeo singulum quemquam hominem diligit, quo diligit orbem universum."—*In Gal.* ii.
[3] "Neque valet explicari quo circa unumquemque Deus moveatur affectu."—*De Tr. Chr. Ag.* c. 5.
[4] "Totus mihi datus, totus in meos usus expensus est."—*In Circumc.* s. 3.
[5] "Totum nobis dedit, nihil sibi reliquit."
[6] "Deus ultra quo se extenderet, non habet."—*De Beatit.* c. 2.

himself?"[1] I belong to God, and to God I must give back myself, for having created me and given me my being; but after I have given myself, what return shall I make to God for having given himself to me? We have, however, no need to disturb ourselves any longer; it is enough if we give our love to God, and God is satisfied. The kings of the earth glory in the possession of kingdoms and of wealth, Jesus Christ rests content with the sovereignty of our hearts; this he considers his principality; and this principality he sought to obtain by dying on the cross: *And the government is upon his shoulder.*[2] By these words, "the government is upon his shoulder,"[3] several interpreters, with St. Basil, St. Cyril, St. Augustine, and others, understand the cross which our Redeemer carried on his shoulders. This heavenly King, says Cornelius à Lapide, is a very different master from the devil: the devil burdens the backs of his subjects with heavy loads; Jesus, on the contrary, takes on his own shoulders the burdens of his kingdom, embracing the cross, on which he will die, in order to gain the mastery of our hearts: "The devil lays burdens on the shoulders of his subjects, Christ will bear the weight of his government on his shoulders; for he will carry the sceptre of his kingdom—that is, the cross—on his own shoulders, and will reign from the tree."[4] It is the remark of Tertullian that while earthly monarchs bear the sceptre and crown as symbols of royalty, Jesus Christ bore the Cross, which was the throne which he mounted to rule over our love: "Every king bears the symbol of

---

[1] "Me pro me debeo; quid Deo retribuam pro se?"—*De dil. D.* c. 5.
[2] "Et factus est principatus super humerum ejus."—*Isa.* ix. 6.
[3] "Principatus super humerum ejus."
[4] "Diabolus onera imponit humeris subditorum; Christus suis humeris sustinebit onus sui principatus; quia Christus sceptrum imperii sui, puta Crucem, humeris suis bajulabit, atque regnabit a ligno."

his power on his shoulder, and a diadem on his head, or a sceptre in his hand. The King Jesus Christ alone bore his power on his shoulder, namely, the cross, that from it he might rule."[1]

Hence, Origen says, if it be that Jesus Christ has given himself to each one, what great thing will a man do if he give himself wholly to Jesus Christ? "If Christ gave himself, will man do much in giving himself to God, who was the first to give himself to man?"[2] Let us, then, with a good will give our heart and our love to this God, who, in order to gain it, has had to give his blood, his life, and his whole self: *If thou didst know the gift of God, and who He is that saith to thee, Give Me to drink.*[3] Oh, if thou didst but know (said Jesus to the Samaritan woman) the grace which thou receivest from God, and who it is that asks of thee to drink! Oh, did the soul but understand what a favor it is when God requests us to love him in those words: *Thou shalt love the Lord thy God.*[4] Should a subject hear his prince command him to love him, the bare mention of such a request would be enough to captivate him. And does not a God captivate us when he requires our heart? saying: *My son, give Me thy heart.*[5]

But this heart he will not have divided, he will have it whole and entire; he wishes us to love him with our whole heart: *Thou shalt love the Lord thy God with thy whole heart,*[6] otherwise he is not content. For this end

[1] "Quis regnum insigne potestatis suæ humero præfert, et non aut capite diadema, aut in manu sceptrum? Solus Rex Christus Jesus potestatem suam in humero extulit, Crucem scilicet, ut exinde regnaret."—*Adv. Jud.*
[2] "Christus semetipsum dedit; quid ergo magnum faciet homo, si semetipsum offerat Deo, cui ipse se prior obtulit Deus?"
[3] " Si scires donum Dei, et quis est qui dicit tibi: Da mihi bibere."—*John*, iv. 10.
[4] " Diliges Dominum Deum tuum."—*Matt.* xxii. 57.
[5] " Præbe, fili mi, cor tuum mihi."—*Prov.* xxiii. 26.
[6] " Diliges Dominum Deum tuum ex toto corde tuo."

he has given us all his blood, his whole life, his whole self, in order that we may give our entire selves to him, and be wholly his. And let us understand that then we shall give our whole heart to God when we shall give him our will entirely, not wishing anything henceforward but what God wishes,—and he certainly only wishes our welfare and our happiness: *To this end Christ died and rose again, that he might be the Lord both of the dead and of the living. Therefore whether we live or whether we die, we are the Lord's.*[1] Jesus was pleased to die for us; more than this he could not have done to win all our love, and to be the sole Lord of our heart: so that from this day forward we are bound to make known to heaven and to earth, in life and in death, that we are no longer our own, but that we belong solely and entirely to God.

Oh, how God longs to see, and how dearly he loves a heart that is wholly his! Oh, what delicate and loving caresses does God show, what good things, what delights, what glory does God prepare in Paradise for a heart that is wholly his!

The Venerable Father John Leonard of Lettera, a Dominican, one day beheld Jesus Christ under the appearance of a hunter, and traversing the forest of this earth with an arrow in his hand. The servant of God asked him what he was thus engaged about. Jesus answered that he was hunting after hearts. Who knows, I say, whether in this Novena the Infant Redeemer will have the success to hit and to make a prize of some hearts which he has been hunting after for a long time, and hitherto has been unable to wound and to capture!

Devout souls, if Jesus gain us, we shall also gain Jesus. The advantage of such an exchange is all on our side. "Teresa" (said the Lord one day to this saint),

[1] " In hoc enim Christus mortuus est et resurrexit, ut et mortuorum et vivorum dominetur.—Sive ergo vivimus, sive morimur, Domini sumus."—*Rom.* xiv. 8.

"up to this time you have not been all mine; now that you are all mine, be assured that I am all yours." St. Augustine calls love "a bond which binds the lover with the loved one."[1] God has every wish to clasp us and unite us to himself; but it is also necessary for us to strive and unite ourselves to God. If we wish God to give himself entirely to us, it is likewise necessary for us to give ourselves entirely to him.

Affections and Prayers.

Oh! happy me, if, from this day forward, I shall be able always to say with the sacred spouse, *My Beloved to me and I to Him.*[2] My God, my Beloved has given himself all to me; it is but reasonable for me to give myself all to my God, and to say, *What have I in heaven? and besides Thee what do I desire upon earth?*[3]

Oh, my beloved Infant, my dear Redeemer, since Thou hast come down from heaven to give Thyself to me, what else shall I go about seeking in heaven or on earth besides Thee, who art my sovereign Good, my only treasure, the Paradise of souls? Be Thou, then, the sole Lord of my heart, do thou possess it wholly. May my heart obey Thee alone, and seek to please Thee alone! May my soul love Thee alone, and mayest Thou alone be its portion! Let others strive after and enjoy (if enjoyment can ever be found out of Thee) the goods and fortunes of this world; Thee alone do I desire, who art my fortune, my riches, my peace, my hope in this life and in eternity. Behold, then, my heart; I give it wholly to Thee; it is no longer mine own, but Thine. In the same manner as at Thy entrance into the world Thou didst offer to the Eternal Father, and present to him Thine entire will, as David has taught: *In the head of the book it is written of Me, that I should do Thy will; O my God, I have desired it;*[4] so do I on this day offer to Thee, my Saviour,

[1] "Vitta copulans amantem et quod amatur."—*De Trin.* l. 8, c. 10.
[2] "Dilectus meus mihi, et ego illi."—*Cant.* ii. 16.
[3] "Quid enim mihi est in cœlo? et a te quid volui super terram?... Deus cordis mei, et pars mea, Deus, in æternum."—*Ps.* lxxii. 25.
[4] "In capite libri scriptum est de me, ut facerem voluntatem tuam; Deus meus, volui."—*Ps.* xxxix. 8.

The Eternal Word has made Himself Ours. 97

my entire will. At one time it was rebellious against Thee, and with it I offended Thee; but for all the wicked consent by which I have miserably forfeited Thy friendship I am now heartily sorry, and I consecrate my entire will to Thee. *Lord, what wilt Thou have me to do?*[1] tell me what Thou desirest of me, for I am willing to do all. Dispose of me and of my affairs as Thou wilt, for I accept of all, and in everything I resign myself to Thee. I know well that Thou willest what is best for me, and therefore I abandon my soul fully into Thy hands: *Into Thy hands I commend my spirit.*[2] For pity's sake, help it and preserve it! and grant that it may be always and entirely Thine own, since Thou hast redeemed it with the last drop of Thy blood: *Thou hast redeemed me, O Lord, the God of truth.*[3]

O happy thou, most holy Virgin Mary! thou wert wholly and always God's own,—all fair, all pure, and without spot: *Thou art all beautiful, and there is no stain in thee.*[4] Thou alone, among all souls, wert styled by thy Spouse his dove, his perfect one: *One is My dove, My perfect one.*[5] Thou art the garden closed against every imperfection and fault, and all laden with the flowers and fruits of virtue. Ah, my Queen and my Mother, thou who art so lovely in the eyes of thy God, take pity on my soul, which has become so deformed by sin. But if for the past I have not belonged to God, now I wish to be his, and his entirely. I wish to spend the remainder of my life solely in loving my Redeemer, who hast loved me so much; suffice it to say, who has given his entire self to me. O my hope, procure me strength to be grateful and faithful to him till death! Amen. This is my hope, so may it be!

[1] "Domine, quid me vis facere?"—*Acts*, ix. 6.
[2] "In manus tuas commendo spiritum meum."
[3] "Redemisti me, Domine Deus veritatis."—*Ps.* xxx. 6.
[4] "Tota pulchra es, Amica mea, et macula non est in te."—*Cant.* iv. 7.
[5] "Una est columba mea, perfecta mea."—*Cant.* vi. 8.

DISCOURSE VII.

The Eternal Word from being Happy made Himself Afflicted.

Et erunt oculi tui videntes Præceptorem tuum.
" And thy eyes shall see thy teacher."—*Isa.* xxx. 20.

St. John says, *All that is in the world is the concupiscence of the flesh, and the concupiscence of the eyes, and the pride of life.*[1] Behold the three sinful loves which held dominion over man after the sin of Adam,—the love of pleasures, the love of riches, the love of honors, which generate human pride. The divine Word, to teach us, by his example, the mortification of the senses, by which the love of pleasures is subdued, from being happy became afflicted ; to teach us detachment from the goods of this earth, from rich he became poor ; and, finally, to teach us humility, which overcomes the love of honors, from being exalted he became humble. We will speak on these three points during these three last days of the Novena ; to-day let us speak of the first.

Our Redeemer came, then, to teach us the love of the mortification of the senses more by the example of his life than by the doctrines which he preached; and, therefore, from happy, as he is and had always been from all eternity, he became afflicted. Let us see it, and let us ask light of Jesus and Mary.

I.

The Apostle, speaking of the divine beatitude, calls God the only one happy and powerful : *The blessed and only mighty.*[2] And with reason, because all the happiness which can be enjoyed by us his creatures is nothing

---
[1] " Omne quod est in mundo, concupiscentia carnis est, et concupiscentia oculorum, et superbia vitæ."—1 *John,* ii. 16.
[2] " Beatus et solus potens."—1 *Tim* vi. 15.

The Eternal Word made Himself Afflicted. 99

more than the smallest participation of the infinite happiness of God. The blessed in heaven find therein their happiness; that is, in entering into the immense ocean of the happiness of God: *Enter Thou into the joy of thy Lord.*[1] This is the paradise which God bestows on the soul at the moment when it enters into possession of his eternal kingdom.

God, in creating man at the beginning, did not place him on earth to suffer, but put him into *the paradise of pleasure.*[2] He put him in a place of delight, in order that he might pass thence to heaven, where he should enjoy for all eternity the glory of the blessed. But by sin unhappy man made himself unworthy of the earthly, and closed against himself the gates of the heavenly paradise, wilfully condemning himself to death and to everlasting misery. But the Son of God, in order to rescue man from such a state of ruin, what did he do? From blessed and most happy as he was, he chose to become afflicted and tormented. Our Redeemer could, indeed, have rescued us from the hands of our enemies without suffering. He could have come on earth and continued in his happiness, leading here below a pleasant life, receiving the honor justly due to him as King and Lord of all. It was enough, as far as regarded the redemption, that he should have offered to God one drop of blood, one single tear, to redeem the world and an infinity of worlds: "the least degree of the suffering of Christ" (says the Angelic Doctor) "would have sufficed for redemption, on account of the infinite dignity of his Person."[3] But no: "*Having joy set before Him, He endured the Cross.*[4] He renounced all honors and pleasures

[1] "Intra in gaudium Domini tui."—*Matt.* xxv. 21.
[2] "Posuit eum in paradiso voluptatis."—*Gen.* ii. 15.
[3] "Quælibet passio Christi suffecisset ad redemptionem, propter infinitam dignitatem personæ."—*Quodlib.* 2, a. 2.
[4] "Proposito sibi gaudio, sustinuit crucem."—*Heb.* xii. 2.

and made choice on earth of a life all full of toils and ignominies. Yes, says St. John Chrysostom, any action whatever of the Incarnate Word sufficed for redemption; but it did not suffice for the love which he bore to man. "What was sufficient for redemption was not sufficient for love."[1] And whereas he that loves desires to see himself loved in return, Jesus Christ, in order to be loved by man, was pleased to suffer exceedingly, and to choose for himself a life of continual suffering, to put man under an obligation of loving him. Our Lord revealed to St. Margaret of Cortona that in his whole life he never experienced the smallest degree of sensible consolation: *Great as the sea is Thy destruction.*[2] The life of Jesus Christ was bitter as the sea, which is thoroughly bitter and salt, and contains not one drop of water that is sweet. And therefore Isaias justly calls Jesus Christ a *Man of sorrows*,[3] as though he had been capable on this earth of nothing but anguish and sorrows. St. Thomas says that the Redeemer did not simply take on himself sorrows, but that "He endured sorrow in its highest degree;"[4] whereby he would signify that he chose to be the most afflicted man that had ever been upon earth, or should ever be hereafter.

Yes, because this Man was born on purpose to suffer, therefore he assumed a body particularly adapted for suffering. On entering the womb of Mary, as the Apostle tells us, he said to his Eternal Father, when he cometh into the world he saith, *Sacrifice and oblation Thou wouldst not; but a body Thou hast fitted to Me.*[5] My Father, Thou hast rejected the sacrifices of men, because they were not

[1] "Quod sufficiebat redemptioni, non sufficiebat amori."
[2] "Magna est enim velut mare contritio tua."—*Lam.* ii. 13.
[3] "Virum dolorum."—*Isa.* liii. 3.
[4] "Assumpsit dolorem in summo."
[5] "Hostiam et oblationem noluisti, corpus autem aptasti mihi."— *Heb.* x. 5.

able to satisfy Thy divine justice for the offences committed against Thee : Thou hast given me a body, as I requested of Thee ; a body delicate, sensitive, and made purposely for suffering ; I gladly accept of this body, and I offer it to Thee ; because by enduring in this body all the pains which will accompany me through my life, and shall finally cause my death upon the cross, I purpose to propitiate Thee towards the human race, and thus to gain for myself the love of mankind.

And behold him scarcely entered into the world, when he already begins his sacrifice by beginning to suffer ; but in a manner far different from that in which men suffer. Other children, while remaining in the womb of their mothers, do not suffer, because they are only in their natural place ; and if they do suffer in some slight degree, at least they are unconscious of what they feel, since they are deprived of understanding ; but Jesus, while an infant, endures for nine months the darkness of that prison, endures the pain of not being able to move, and is perfectly alive to what he endures. It is for this reason that Jeremias said, *A woman shall compass a man.*[1] He foretold that a woman, which was Mary, should bear enclosed in her womb, not a child indeed, but a man ; a child truly as to age ; but a perfect man as to the use of reason, since Jesus Christ was full of wisdom from the first instance in his life : *In whom are hid all the treasures of wisdom and knowledge.*[2] Whence St. Bernard said, "Jesus was a man while not yet as born, but in wisdom, not in age."[3] And St. Augustine, "The unspeakably Wise was in his wisdom a speechless Infant."[4]

[1] "Femina circumdabit virum."—*Jer.* xxxi. 22.
[2] "In quo sunt omnes thesauri sapientiæ et scientiæ absconditi."—*Col.* ii. 3.
[3] "Vir erat Jesus necdum etiam natus, sed sapientia, non ætate."—*De Laud. V. M. hom.* 2.
[4] "Erat ineffabiliter sapiens, sapienter infans."—*Serm.* 187, *F. B.*

He comes forth, then, from the prison of his mother's womb, but for what? is it perhaps to enjoy himself? He comes forth to fresh suffering, for he chooseth to be born in the depth of winter, in a cavern, where beasts find stabling, and at the hour of midnight; and he is born in such poverty that he has no fire to warm him, nor clothes enough to screen him from the cold. "A grand pulpit is that manger,"[1] says St. Thomas of Villanova. Oh, how well does Jesus teach us the love of suffering in the grotto of Bethlehem! "In the stable" (adds Salmeron) "all is vile to the sight, unpleasant to the hearing, offensive to the smell, hard and revolting to the touch."[2] Everything in the stable is painful: everything is painful to the sight, for one sees nothing but rugged and dark rocks; everything is painful to the hearing, for he hears only the cries of brute beasts; everything is painful to the smell, from the stench of the litter that is scattered around; and everything is painful to the touch, for his cradle is only a narrow manger, and his bed only a handful of straw. Look on this Infant God, how he lies bound up in swaddling-clothes, so that he cannot stir: "God endures," said St. Zeno, "to be bound in swaddling-clothes, because he had come to pay the debts of the whole world."[3] And hereupon St. Augustine remarks, "O Blessed rags, with which we wipe away the filth of sins!"[4] Observe him how he trembles with cold; how he weeps, to let us know that he suffers, and offers to the Eternal Father those first tears to release us from that endless wailing which we had deserved! "Blessed

---

[1] "Magna cathedra, præsepium illud."—*In Nat. D. conc.* 1.

[2] "In præsepe, omnia sunt vilia visui, ingrata auditui, olfactui molesta, tactui dura et aspera."—*T.* ii. tr. 33.

[3] "Patitur Deus se pannis alligari, qui totius mundi debita venerat soluturus."—*De Nat. Chr.* s. 3.

[4] "O felices panni, quibus peccatorum sordes extersimus!"—*S.* 119, *E. B. app.*

tears," says St. Thomas of Villanova, "which blot out our iniquities?"[1] O tears for us most blessed, since they obtain for us the pardon of our sins!

And thus did the life of Jesus Christ continue always in affliction and sorrow. But a short time after he was born he was obliged to fly as an exile, and wander into Egypt to escape out of the hands of Herod. Then, in that barbarous country he passed many years of his childhood poor and unknown. Nor was the life which he led on his return from Egypt, dwelling at Nazareth, very different up to the time when he received death from the hands of the executioner on the cross in a sea of sorrows and infamy.

But, besides, we must also well understand here that the pains which Jesus Christ endured in his Passion, the scourging, the crowning with thorns, the crucifixion, his agony, death, and all the other torments, and ignominies which he suffered at the end of his life, he also suffered at the beginning; because from the beginning he had always before his eyes the sad scene of all the torments which he would have to suffer when about to leave this earth, as he predicted by the mouth of David : *My sorrow is continually before me.*[2] We hide from the sick man the knife or the fire with which he is to be cut or cauterized in order to regain his health ; but Jesus would not have the instruments of his Passion, by which he was to lose his life, that he might gain for us eternal life, hidden from his sight ; he desired always to have before his eyes the scourge, the thorns, the nails, the cross, which were to drain all the blood from his veins, till he died of pure grief, deprived of all consolation.

One day Jesus Christ appeared to Sister Magdalene Orsini, who had been suffering a heavy affliction for a long

---

[1] " Felices lacrymæ, quibus nostra abluuntur crimina."—*In Nat. D. conc.* I.

[2] " Dolor meus in conspectu meo semper."—*Ps.* xxxvii. 18.

time, under the form of a crucifix, to comfort her by the remembrance of his Passion, and to animate her to bear her cross with patience. She said to him : " But Thou, my Lord, wast only three hours on the cross, while I have suffered this pain for many years." Then our Lord from the cross replied : " Ignorant creature that Thou art ! from the first moment that I was in the womb of Mary I suffered all that I had afterwards to suffer in my death." " Christ," says Novarinus, " even in the womb of his mother, had the impression of the cross on his mind ; so that no sooner was he born than he might be said to have the principality on his shoulders."[1] So, then, My Redeemer, throughout Thy whole life I shall find Thee nowhere but on the cross : " Lord, I find Thee nowhere but on the cross," said Dragone Ostiense. Yes, for the cross on which Jesus Christ died was ever in his mind to torment him. Even whilst sleeping, says Bellarmine, the sight of the cross was present to the heart of Jesus : " Christ had his cross always before his eyes. When he slept, his heart watched ; nor was it ever free from the sight of the cross."

But it was not so much the sorrows of his Passion which saddened and embittered the life of our Redeemer, as the sight of all the sins which men would commit after his death. These were the cruel executioners which made him live in continual agony, oppressed by such an overwhelming grief that pain alone would have been enough to make him die of pure sorrow. Father Lessius says that the sight alone of the ingratitude of mankind would have been sufficient to make Jesus Christ die of grief a thousand times.

The scourges, the cross, death itself, were not hateful objects to him, but most dear, chosen, and desired by

[1] " Christus crucem etiam in ventre Matris menti impressam habuit, adeo ut vix natus principatum super humerum (*Isa.* ix. 6) habere dicatur."—*Umb. Virg.* c. 11, *exc.* 38.

himself. He had offered himself spontaneously to suffer them: *He was offered because it was His own will.*[1] He did not give his life against his will, but by his own election, as he tells us by St. John: *I lay down My life for My sheep.*[2] This was indeed the chief desire of his whole life, that the time of his Passion should arrive, that the redemption of mankind might be completed; for this reason he said on the night preceding his death: *With desire I have desired to eat this pasch with you before I suffer.*[3] And before this time arrived he seemed to console himself by saying, *I have a baptism, wherewith I am to be baptized; and how am I straitened until it be accomplished!*[4] I must be baptized with the baptism of my own blood; not indeed to wash my own soul, but those of my sheep, from the stains of their sin; and how ardently do I desire the arrival of the hour when I shall be bleeding and dead on the cross! St. Ambrose says that the Redeemer was not afflicted by the fear of death, but by the delay of our redemption: "Not from the fear of his death, but from the delay of our redemption."[5]

In a sermon on the Passion, St. Zeno describes Jesus Christ choosing for himself the trade of a carpenter in this world; for as such was he known and called: *Is not this the carpenter, and the son of a carpenter?*[6] Because carpenters are always handling wood and nails, it would seem that Jesus exercising this trade took pleasure in such things, seeing that they represented to him better than anything else the nails and the cross by which he willed

---

[1] "Oblatus est, quia ipse voluit."—*Isa.* liii. 7.
[2] "Animam meam pono pro ovibus meis."—*John*, x. 15.
[3] "Desiderio desideravi hoc Pascha manducare vobiscum."—*Luke*, xxii. 15.
[4] "Baptismo autem habeo baptizari; et quomodo coarctor usque dum perficiatur!"—*Luke*, xii. 50
[5] "Non ex metu mortis suæ, sed ex mora nostræ redemptionis."—*In Luc.* xii.
[6] "Nonne hic est faber,—fabri filius?"—*Mark*, vi. 3; *Matt.* xiii. 55.

to suffer: "The Son of God took delight in this work, in which the wood and the nails continually reminded him of the cross that awaited him."[1]

Thus (to return to the point) we see it was not so much the thought of his Passion that afflicted the heart of our Redeemer, as the ingratitude with which mankind would repay his love. It was this ingratitude which made him weep in the stable of Bethlehem; which caused him to sweat blood in his deadly agony in the garden of Gethsemane; which filled him with such sorrow that he says even that it alone was sufficient to make him die: *My soul is sorrowful, even to death;*[2] and, finally, this ingratitude it was which caused him to die in desolation and deprived of all consolation on the cross; for, says F. Suarez, Jesus Christ wished rather to satisfy for the pain of loss due to man than for the pain of sense.[3] Therefore the pains which our Lord suffered in his soul were much greater than all those he suffered in his body.

II.

We then, also, by our sins contributed to make the whole life of our Saviour embittered and afflicted. But let us thank his goodness in giving us time to remedy the evil which has been done.

How, then, are we to remedy it? By bearing patiently all the crosses which he sends us for our good. And he himself tells us how we can bear these troubles with patience: *Put me as a seal upon thy heart.*[4] Put upon thy heart the image of me crucified; which means to say, consider my example and the pains which I have suffered for thee, and so shalt thou bear all crosses in peace.

[1] "Dei Filius illis delectabatur operibus, quibus lignorum segmentis et clavis sibi sæpe futuræ crucis imago præformabatur."
[2] "Tristis est anima mea usque ad mortem."—*Matt.* xxvi. 38.
[3] "Principalius Christus satisfecit pro pœna damni, quam sensus."
[4] "Pone me ut signaculum super cor tuum."—*Cant.* viii. 6.

St. Augustine says that this heavenly physician made himself weak, that he might heal our weakness by his own infirmity: "Wondrous medicine! the physician deigns to become sick, to heal his patient by his own infirmity,"[1] according to that which Isaias says, *By His bruises we are healed.*[2] To heal our souls, which are weakened by sin, this medicine of suffering was the only one necessary; and Jesus Christ desired to be the first to taste it, that we who are the true sinners should not refuse to take it also: "The physician drinks first, that the sick man may not hesitate to drink also."[3]

Believing this, says St. Epiphanius, as true followers of Jesus Christ, we ought to thank him when he sends us crosses: "It is a virtue peculiar to a Christian to give thanks when in adversity."[4] And this is reasonable, because by sending us crosses he makes us like to himself. St. John Chrysostom makes an observation which is very consoling; he says that when we thank God for his benefits, we do but give him that which we owe him; but that when we suffer some pain with patience for his love, then God in a certain way becomes our debtor: "If you thank God for good things, you pay a debt; if you thank him for evil things, you make him your debtor."[5]

If thou wouldst render love to Jesus Christ, says St. Bernard, learn from him how thou must love him: "Learn from Christ how to love Christ."[6] Be happy

[1] "Mirabile genus medicinæ! Medicus voluit ægrotare, et ægrotos sua infirmitate sanare."—*Serm.* 247. E. B. *app.*
[2] "Et livore ejus sanati sumus."—*Isa.* liii. 5.
[3] "Prior bibit Medicus sanus, ut bibere non dubitaret ægrotus."—*Serm.* 88, E. B.
[4] "Christianorum propria virtus est, etiam in adversis, referre gratias."
[5] "In bonis gratias agens, reddidisti debitum; in malis, Deum reddidisti debitorem."—*In Ps.* ix.
[6] "Disce a Christo, quemadmodum diligas Christum."—*In Cant.* s. 20.

to suffer something for that God who has suffered so much for thee. The desire of pleasing Jesus Christ, and of making known to him the love they bore him, was that which rendered the saints hungry and thirsty, not for honors and pleasures, but for sufferings and contempt. This made the Apostle say, *God forbid that I should glory, save in the cross of our Lord Jesus Christ.*[1] Being a happy companion of his crucified God, he desired no other glory than that of seeing himself on the cross. This was also what made St. Teresa say, "Either to suffer or to die;"[2] as if she had said, My Spouse, if it is Thy will to draw me to Thyself by death, behold I am ready to come, and I thank Thee for it; but if Thou wilt leave me any longer on this earth, I cannot trust myself to remain without suffering: "Either to suffer or to die." It was this that made St. Mary Magdalene of Pazzi go still farther: "To suffer, and not to die;" by which she meant, My Jesus, I desire to be in heaven, that I may love Thee more; but I desire still more to suffer, that I may repay in part the love which Thou hast shown towards me by suffering so much for me. And the Venerable Sister Mary of Jesus Crucified, a Sicilian nun, was so enamoured of sufferings that she went so far as to say, "Truly Paradise is beautiful; but one thing is wanting, because there there is no suffering." For the same reason also St. John of the Cross, when Jesus appeared to him with his cross on his shoulders, and said to him, John, ask what thou wilt of me, would ask for nothing but sufferings and contempt: "Lord, that I may suffer and be despised for Thy sake."

If, then, we have not the strength to desire and seek for sufferings, let us at least try to accept with patience those tribulations which God sends us for our good:

---

[1] "Mihi autem absit gloriari, nisi in cruce Domini nostri Jesu Christi."—*Gal.* vi. 14.

[2] "Domine! pati et contemni pro te."

"Where there is patience, there is God,"[1] says Tertullian. Where is God? Give me a soul that suffers with resignation, there assuredly is God: *The Lord is nigh unto them that are of a contrite heart.*[2] The Lord takes delight in being near to those that are in affliction. But what kind of afflicted people? it must be those who suffer in peace, and are resigned to the divine will. To such as these God gives true peace, which consists, as St. Leo says, in uniting our will to the will of God: "True Christian peace consists in not being separated from the will of God."[3] St. Bonaventure tells us that the divine will is like honey, which makes even bitter things sweet and pleasant. The reason is this, that he who obtains all that he wishes has nothing left to desire: "Blessed is he who has everything he desires,"[4] says St. Augustine. Therefore he who wills nothing but what God wills is always happy; for, as everything happens by the will of God, the soul has always that which it wills.

And when God sends us crosses, not only let us be resigned, but let us also thank him, since it is a sign that he means to pardon our sins, and save us from hell, which we have deserved. He who has offended God must be punished; and therefore we ought always to beg of him to chastise us in this world, and not in the next. That sinner is to be pitied who does not receive his chastisement in this life, but, on the contrary, is prosperous. May God preserve us from that mercy of which Isaias speaks: *Let us have pity on the wicked.*[5] "I do not want this mercy," says St. Bernard; "such pity is worse

---

[1] "Ubi Deus, ibidem et patientia."—*De Patient.*
[2] "Juxta est Dominus iis qui tribulato sunt corde."—*Ps.* xxxiii. 19.
[3] "Christiano vera pax est a Dei voluntate non dividi."—*In Nat. D.* s. 9.
[4] "Beatus est, qui habet omnia quæ vult, et nihil vult male."—*De Trin.* l. 13, c. 5.
[5] "Misereamur impio!"—*Isa.* xxvi. 10.

than any anger."[1] The prayer of the saint was, Lord, I desire not this mercy: for it is more terrible than any chastisement. When God does not punish a sinner in this life, it is a sign that he waits to punish him in eternity, where the punishment will have no end. St. Laurence Justinian says:

"From the price thy Redeemer had to pay, learn the value of his gifts and the gravity of thy sin."[2] When we see a God dead on the cross, we ought to consider the great gift which he has made us in giving us his blood to redeem us from hell, and at the same time to understand the malice of sin, which made the death of a God necessary to obtain pardon for us: "Nothing," says Dragone, "frightens me away from sin so strongly as the sight of Thy Son suffering so exceedingly cruel a death as its penalty."[3] O eternal God! nothing terrifies me more than to see Thy Son punished by so cruel a death on account of sin.

Let us therefore be comforted, when we see ourselves afflicted by God for our sins in this world; for it is a sign that he will show mercy to us in the next. The thought alone of having displeased so good a God, if we love him, ought to be of more consolation to us when we see ourselves chastised and afflicted, than if we were prosperous, and filled with the consolations of this world. St. John Chrysostom says, "If a man loves God, he will have more consolation in being punished for having offended so merciful a Lord than if he were to escape unpunished."[4] Any one who loves another (continues the

[1] "Misericordiam hanc nolo; super omnem iram miseratio ista."— *In Cant.* s. 42.

[2] "De pretio erogato, Redemptoris tui agnosce munus tuæque prævaricationis pondus."

[3] "Nihil ita me deterret, sicut videre Filium tuum propter peccatum crudelissima morte mulctatum."

[4] "Major consolatio erit ei qui punitur, si amet Dominum, postquam exacerbavit tam misericordem, quam ei qui non punitur."

saint) is more punished in thinking that he has grieved the person whom he loves than at the punishment he receives for his crime.

Let us, then, be consoled when we are suffering; and if these reflections are not sufficient to console us, let us go to Jesus Christ, and he will console us, as he has promised to all: *Come to Me, all you that labor and are burdened, and I will refresh you.*[1] When we have recourse to our Lord, he will either deliver us from our affliction, or will give us strength to bear it patiently. And this is a greater grace than the former; because the tribulations which we bear with resignation, not only enable us to satisfy in this life for our debts, but also merit for us greater glory eternally in Paradise.

Let us also, when we are afflicted and in sorrow, go and seek Mary, who is called the Mother of mercy, the cause of our joy, the comfort of the afflicted. Let us go to this good Lady, who, as Lanspergius says, never lets any one depart from her unconsoled and in sadness: "She holds the bosom of her compassion open to all; she permits no one to depart from her in sorrow."[2] St. Bonaventure says that it is her office to compassionate those who are in trouble: "To thee is the office of mercy committed."[3] Whence Richard of St. Laurence subjoins that he who invokes her will always find her ready to assist him.[4] "And who has ever sought thy aid in vain? Who, O blessed one, ever asked thy assistance and was neglected?"[5]

[1] "Venite ad me omnes, qui laboratis et onerati estis, et ego reficiam vos."—*Matt.* xi. 28.
[2] "Omnibus pietatis sinum apertum tenet, neminem a se redire tristem sinit "—*Alloq.* l. 1, can. 12.
[3] "Tibi miserendi est officium commissum."—*Stim. div. am.* p. 3, c. 19.
[4] "Inveniet semper paratam auxiliari."—*De Laud. B. M.* l. 2, p. 1.
[5] "Quis, O Domina ! tuam rogavit opem, et fuit unquam derelictus ?'—*Vit. S. Theoph. ap. Sur.* 4 *febr.*

Affections and Prayers.

St. Mary Magdalene of Pazzi ordered two nuns, over whom she was Superior, to remain at the feet of the Holy Infant during the time of the Nativity, and there to imitate the service done to him by the animals in the stable; that is, that they should cherish the poor shivering Infant by the warmth of their praises, their thanksgivings and sighs of love which they were to pour out from their burning hearts. O my dear Redeemer, would that I also could fulfil that office! Yes, I praise Thee, my Jesus, I praise Thine infinite mercy, I praise Thine infinite charity, which makes Thee glorious both in heaven and earth; and I unite my voice to that of the Angel: *Glory to God in the highest.*[1] I thank Thee in the name of all mankind; but I thank Thee especially for myself, a miserable sinner. What would have become of me, what hope could I have of pardon and salvation, if Thou, my Saviour, hadst not come down from heaven to save me? I praise Thee, then, I thank Thee, and I love Thee. I love Thee above all things, I love Thee more than myself, I love Thee with all my soul, and I give myself all to Thee. Receive, O Sacred Infant, these acts of love; if they are but cold, because coming from a frozen heart, do Thou inflame this poor heart of mine; a heart that has offended Thee, but is now penitent. Yes, my Lord, I repent above all things for having despised Thee who hast loved me so much. Now I desire nothing but to love Thee; and this only do I beg of Thee: give me Thy love, and do with me what Thou wilt. I was once a slave of hell; but now that I am free from those unhappy chains, I consecrate myself entirely to Thee; I give Thee my body, my goods, my life, my soul, my will, and my whole liberty. I desire no longer to belong to myself, but only to Thee, my only good. Ah, bind my heart to Thy feet, that it may no more stray from Thee. O most holy Mary! obtain for me the grace of living always bound to thy Son by the blessed chains of love. Tell him to accept me as the slave of his love. He grants all that you ask. Pray to him, pray to him, for me. This is my hope.

[1] "Gloria in altissimis Deo!"—*Luke,* ii. 14.

DISCOURSE VIII.

The Eternal Word from being Rich made Himself Poor.

Excutere de pulvere, consurge, sede, Jerusalem.
"Shake thyself from the dust; arise, sit up, O Jerusalem."—*Is.* lii. 2.

Arise, Christian soul, says the Prophet, shake off the dust of earthly affections: *Shake thyself from the dust;*[1] *arise;*[2] arise from the mire in which thou art lying in misery, and sit up: *Sit up, O Jerusalem,*[3] sit as a queen, and rule over those passions which would deprive thee of eternal glory, and which expose thee to the danger of everlasting destruction.

But to attain this, what must the soul do? It must study and consider well the life of Jesus Christ, who, from being rich, as possessing all the riches of heaven and earth, made himself poor, despising all the goods of the world. It is impossible for any one to think of Jesus having become poor for his sake, and not at the same time to be moved to despise all for the love of him. Let us so consider him, and for this let us implore Jesus and Mary to enlighten us.

I.

Everything that is in heaven and on earth is God's. *The world is mine, and the fulness thereof.*[4] But even this is little; heaven and earth are but the least portion of the riches of God. The riches of God are infinite, and can never fail, because his riches do not depend on others, but he, who is the Infinite Good, possesses them himself. Therefore it was that David said: *Thou art my*

---
[1] "Excutere de pulvere."
[2] "Consurge."
[3] "Sede, Jerusalem."
[4] "Meus est enim orbis terræ, et plenitudo ejus."—*Ps.* xlix. 12.

God, for Thou hast no need of my goods.[1] Now this God, who is so rich, made himself poor by becoming man, that he might thereby make us poor sinners rich: *Being rich, He became poor for your sakes; that through his poverty you might be rich.*[2]

What! a God become poor? And why? Let us understand the reason. The riches of this world can be nothing but dust and mire; but it is mire that so completely blinds men that they can no longer see which are the true riches. Before the coming of Jesus Christ, the world was full of darkness, because it was full of sin: *All flesh had corrupted its way upon the earth.*[3] Mankind had corrupted the law and reason, so that, living like brutes, intent only on acquiring the riches and pleasures of this world, they cared no more for the riches of eternity. But the divine mercy ordained that the very Son of God himself should come down to enlighten these blind creatures: *To them that dwelt in the region of the shadow of death light is risen.*[4]

Jesus was called the Light of the Gentiles: *A Light for the revelation of the Gentiles.*[5] *The light shineth in darkness.*[6] Thus did the Lord from the first promise to be himself our Master, and a Master who should be seen by us; who should teach us the way of salvation, which consists in the practice of all the virtues, and especially that of holy poverty: *And thy eyes shall see thy Teacher.*[7]

---

[1] "Deus meus es tu, quoniam bonorum meorum non eges."—*Ps.* xv. 2.

[2] "Egenus factus est, cum esset dives, ut illius inopia vos divites essetis."—2 *Cor.* viii. 9.

[3] "Omnis quippe caro corruperat viam suam."—*Gen.* vi. 12.

[4] "Habitantibus in regione umbræ mortis, lux orta est eis."—*Isa.* ix. 2.

[5] "Lumen ad revelationem gentium."—*Luke*, ii. 32.

[6] "Lux in tenebris lucet, . . . quæ illuminat omnem hominem."—*John*, i. 5.

[7] "Et erunt ocu'i tui videntes Præceptorem tuum."—*Isa.* xxx. 20.

Moreover, this Master was not only to teach us by his words; but still more by the example of his life.

St. Bernard says that poverty was not to be found in heaven, it existed only on earth; but that man, not knowing its value, did not seek after it. Therefore the Son of God came down from heaven to this earth, and chose it for his companion throughout his whole life, that by his example he might also render it precious and desirable to us: "Poverty was not found in heaven, but she was well known on earth, and men knew not her excellence. So the Son of God loved her, and came down from heaven to take her to himself, that we might learn to value her when we see how he regards her."[1] And behold our Redeemer as an Infant, who at the very beginning of his life made himself a teacher of poverty in the cave of Bethlehem; which is expressly called by the same St. Bernard, "the School of Christ,"[2] and by St. Augustine "the Grotto of Doctrine."[3]

For this end was it decreed by God that the edict of Cæsar should come forth; namely, that his Son should not only be born poor, but the poorest of men, causing him to be born away from his own house, in a cave which was inhabited only by animals. Other poor people, who are born in their own houses, have certainly more comforts in the way of clothes, of fire, and the assistance of persons who lend their aid, even if it is out of compassion. What son of a poor person was ever born in a stable? In a stable only beasts are born. St. Luke relates how it happened. The time being come that Mary was to be delivered, Joseph goes to seek

---

[1] "Paupertas non inveniebatur in cœlis ; porro in terris abundabat, et nesciebat homo pretium ejus. Hanc itaque Dei Filius concupiscens descendit, ut eam eligat sibi, et nobis sua æstimatione faciat pretiosam."—*In Vig. Nat.* s. 1.

[2] "Schola Christi."

[3] "Spelunca magistra."

some lodging for her in Bethlehem. He goes about and inquires at every house, and he finds none. He tries to find one in an inn, but neither there does he find any: *There was no room for them in the inn.*[1] So that Mary was obliged to take shelter and bring forth her Son in that cave where, notwithstanding all the concourse of people, there was no one; there were only two animals. When the sons of princes are born, they have warm rooms prepared for them, adorned with hangings, silver cradles, the finest clothes, and they are waited on by the highest nobles and ladies of the kingdom. The King of heaven, instead of a warm and beautiful room, has nothing but a cold grotto, whose only ornament is the grass that grows there; instead of a bed of feathers, he has nothing but a little hard sharp straw; instead of fine garments, he has but a few poor rough cold and damp rags: "The Creator of Angels" (writes St. Peter Damian) "is not said to have been clad in purple, but to have been wrapped in rags. Let worldly pride blush at the resplendent humility of the Saviour."[2] Instead of a fire, and of the attendance of great people, he has but the warm breath and the company of two animals; finally, in place of the silver cradle, he must lie in a vile manger. What is this, said St. Gregory of Nyssa, the King of kings, who fills heaven and earth with his presence, finds no better place to be born in than a stable for beasts? "He who encompasses all things in his embrace is laid in the manger of brute cattle."[3] Yes, for this King of kings for our sake wished to be poor, and the poorest of all. Even the children of the poor have milk enough

[1] "Non erat eis locus in diversorio."—*Luke*, ii. 7.
[2] "Conditor Angelorum, non ostro obsitus, sed vilibus legitur panniculis obvolutus: erubescat terrena superbia, ubi coruscat humilitas Redemptoris!"—*De Vest. eccl.* c. 2.
[3] "Qui complexu suo ambit omnia, in brutorum præsepe reclinaur!"—*De Beatit. or.* 1.

provided for them, but Jesus Christ wished to be poor even in this; for the milk of Mary was miraculous, and she received it not naturally, but from heaven, as the holy Church teaches us: "The Virgin gave him milk from a breast filled from heaven."[1] And God, in order to comply with the desire of his Son, who wished to be poor in everything, did not provide Mary with milk in abundance, but only with as much as would barely suffice to sustain the life of his Son; whence the same holy Church says: "He was was fed on a little milk."[2]

And Jesus Christ, as he was born poor, so did he also continue in poverty all his life. Not only was he poor, but a beggar; for the word *egenus*, used by St. Paul, signifies in the Greek text a beggar; so that Cornelius à Lapide says, "It is evident that Christ was not only poor, but also a beggar."[3] Our Redeemer, after being born in such poverty, was obliged to fly from his own country into Egypt. In this journey, St. Bonaventure goes on to consider and compassionate the poverty of Mary and Joseph, who, travelling like poor people on so long a journey, and carrying the Holy Infant, must have suffered very much on account of their poverty: "What did they do for food?" (says the saint). "Where did they repose at night? how were they lodged?"[4] What could they have had to eat except a little hard bread? Where could they have slept at night, in that desert, if not on the ground, in the open air, or under some tree? Who that met these three great pilgrims on their way would ever have taken them for anything else than three poor beggars?

[1] " Virgo lactabat ubere de cœlo pleno."—*In Circ. resp.* 8.
[2] " Lacte modico pastus est."—*In Nativ. ad L.*
[3] "Patet Christum, non tantum pauperem fuisse, sed et vere mendicum."
[4] " Quomodo faciebant de victu? ubi nocte quiescebant? quomodo hospitabantur?"—*Med. vit. Chr.* c. 12.

They arrive in Egypt; and any one may imagine how great must have been the poverty which for seven years they had to endure, being as they were without relatives and without friends. St. Basil says that they had scarcely enough to subsist on, procuring their food by the work of their hands: "They worked hard, in the sweat of their brow, to gain for themselves by such means the necessaries of life."[1] Ludolph of Saxony tells us that sometimes the Infant Jesus, constrained by hunger, went to ask Mary for a little bread, and that Mary sent him away, saying that there was not any: "Sometimes the Son asked for bread to satisfy his hunger, but the Mother had it not to give."[2]

From Egypt they returned into Palestine to live again in Nazareth, and there Jesus continues his life of poverty. Here the house is poor and the furniture is poor: "A poor cottage scantily furnished; such was the dwelling which the Creator of the world chose for himself," says St. Cyprian.[3] In this cottage he lives as a poor man, gaining his livelihood by the sweat of his brow, in the same manner that all workmen and their children do; so that he was called and was believed by the Jews to be a simple workman: "Is not this the carpenter? Is not this the carpenter's son!"[4]

Finally, then, the Redeemer comes forth to preach, and in these three last years of his life he changes not his fortune or his condition; but he lives in even greater poverty than before, living on alms. Therefore he said to a certain man, who wished to follow him, in order to

---

[1] "Sudores frequentabant, necessaria vitæ inde sibi quærentes.' —*Const. mon.* c. 5.

[2] "Aliquando Filius, famem patiens, panem petiit, nec unde daret Mater habuit."—*Vit. Chr.* p. 1, c. 13.

[3] "Domus paupercula, supellex exigua: tale elegit Fabricator mundi hospitium."—*Lib. de Nativ.*

[4] "Nonne hic est faber,—fabri filius?"—*Mark*, vi. 3; *Matt.* xiii. 55.

lead an easier life: *The foxes have holes, and the birds of the air nests; but the Son of Man hath not where to lay His head.*¹ He meant to say: Man, if thou hopest to better thy condition by becoming my follower, thou dost err, for I came on earth to teach poverty; and therefore have I made myself poorer than the foxes or the birds of the air, which have their holes and their nests; while I have not even a foot of ground belonging to me on this earth, where I may rest my head; and so would I have all my disciples to be: "Dost thou hope" (is the comment of Cornelius à Lapide on this text) "that in following me thou wilt increase thy riches? Thou art in error, for I, as the master of perfection, am poor, and such I wish my disciples to be."² For it follows, says St. Jerome, that "the servant of Christ has nothing but Christ."³ The true servants of Christ neither have, nor desire to have, anything but Christ. In a word, Christ lived poor, and he at last died poor; for St. Joseph of Arimathea was obliged to give him a burial-place; and others, out of charity, provided the sheet in which to wrap his dead body.

II.

Cardinal Hugo, meditating on the poverty, the contempt, and the pains to which it pleased our Redeemer to submit, says, "He made himself, as it were, a fool, and condescended to our miseries."⁴ God seems to have gone on to madness in his love for men, being willing to embrace so many miseries to obtain for them the riches of divine grace and eternal glory. And whoever says

¹ "Vulpes foveas habent, et volucres cœli nidos; Filius autem hominis non habet ubi caput reclinet."—*Matt.* viii. 20.
² "Speras te in mei sequela posse rem tuam augere; sed erras: quia ego, velut perfectionis Magister, pauper sum, talesque volo esse meos discipulos."
³ "Servus Christi nihil præter Christum habet."—*Ep. ad Heliod.*
⁴ "Quasi insanus factus, ad miserias nostras descendit."

the same author, would have believed, if Christ had not done it, that while he was the master of all riches, he would have made himself so poor ! that being Lord of all, he should have become a servant ! that being the King of heaven, he should have chosen to be so despised ! that being blessed, he should choose so many sufferings ! "Who could believe that the possessor of all things would condescend to poverty,—the Lord to slavery, the King to ignominy, the ever-blessed to suffering!"[1]

There are, it is true, many princes in this world who delight in employing their riches for the relief of the poor ; but where shall we find a king who, to alleviate the poverty of the poor, has made himself poor like them, as Jesus Christ did ? It is related as a prodigious example of charity that the holy King Edward, seeing a beggar on the road, who was unable to move, and was there remaining utterly abandoned, took him up on his shoulders with great tenderness, and carried him to the church. Yes, this was so great an act of charity that all the people were astonished at it ; but Edward did not for this cease to be king, and he remained as rich as he was before. But the Son of God, the King of heaven and earth, to save the lost sheep, which was man, not only descended from heaven to seek him, not only put him on his shoulders, but laid aside his own majesty, his riches, and honors ; he made himself poor, even the poorest among men: "He hid his purple under miserable garments," says St. Peter Damian ;[2] he hid the purple, that is, the divine Majesty, beneath the clothes of a wretched carpenter's boy: "He who enriches others" (says St. Gregory Nazianzen) " has no riches him-

[1] " Quis crederet divitem ad paupertatem descendere, dominum ad servitutem, regem ad ignominiam, deliciosum ad austeritatem ?"

[2] " Abscondit purpuram sub miseriæ vestimentis."—*Serm. in Nat. Salv.*

self; he undergoes the poverty of my carnal nature, that I may obtain the wealth of his divine nature."[1] He who provides riches for the rich chose himself to be poor, that he might merit for us, not indeed earthly, miserable, and perishable riches, but divine riches, which are infinite and eternal, thus endeavoring by his example to detach us from the affection of all earthly things, which brings us often into great danger of everlasting destruction. It is mentioned in the life of St. John Francis Regis, that his ordinary meditation was on the poverty of Jesus Christ.

Albertus Magnus tells us that Jesus Christ chose to be born in a stable, open to the public road, for two reasons: one, that we might understand more fully that we are all pilgrims in this world, and that we are only here in passing. "Thou art a stranger, look and pass by,"[2] says St. Augustine. Any one who is lodging in a temporary place would not certainly bestow any affection on it, thinking that in a short time he will have to leave it. Oh! if men would always remember that they are but travellers in this world, and on their way to eternity, who would be found to attach himself to earthly riches, and, so doing, to run the risk of losing the riches of eternity? The other reason was, says Albertus Magnus, "to teach us to despise the world;"[3] that by this example we might learn to despise the world, whose riches cannot satisfy our hearts. The world teaches its followers that happiness consists in the possession of riches, pleasures, and honors; but this deceitful world was condemned by the Son of God when he became man. *Now is the judgment of the world.*[4] And this con-

---

[1] "Qui alios ditat, paupertate afficitur; carnis meæ paupertatem subit, ut ego divinitatis opes consequar."—*In Pasch. or.* 2.
[2] "Hospes es, vides, et transis."
[3] "Ut mundum contemnere doceret."
[4] "Nunc judicium est mundi."—*John*, xii. 31.

demnation of the world began (according to St. Anselm and St. Bernard) in the stable of Bethlehem. Jesus Christ wished to be born there in poverty, "that through his poverty we might become rich;" that from his divine example we should pluck out of our hearts all affection to the things we possess here, and should give it to virtue and holy love. "Christ," says Cassian, "began a new way; he loved that which the world hated, namely, poverty." [1]

Therefore the saints, after the example of the Saviour, have always sought to despoil themselves of everything, and to follow, like poor people, Jesus Christ, who was himself poor. St. Bernard says, "The poverty of Christ is richer than all the treasures of the world." [2] The poverty of Christ brings us greater riches than all worldly treasures; because it excites us in acquiring the riches of heaven and in despising those of the world. Hear what St. Paul said: *I count all things but as dung, that I may gain Christ.*[3] When compared with the grace of Jesus Christ, the Apostle esteemed everything else as dung and filth. Look at St. Benedict, who, in the flower of his youth, left the riches and comfort of his father's house, and went to live in a cave, and received a little bread as an alms from a monk called Romanus, who supported him in this way out of charity. See how St. Francis Borgia abandons all his riches, and goes to live like a poor man in the Society of Jesus. St. Anthony, abbot, sells his rich patrimony, distributes it to the poor, and then goes to dwell in a desert. Behold St. Francis of Assisi giving back even his shirt to his father, that he may live as a beggar all his life.

[1] "Initiavit Christus viam novam: dilexit, quam mundus odio habuit, paupertatem."

[2] "Ditior Christi paupertas cunctis thesauris."—*In Vig. Nat.* s. 4.

[3] "Omnia detrimentum feci et arbitror ut stercora, ut Christum lucrifaciam."—*Phil.* iii. 8.

He who covets possessions, said St. Philip Neri, will never become a saint. And so it is; for the heart that is full of this world has no room for divine love: "Dost thou bring an empty heart?"[1] This was what the monks of old chiefly required, in accepting those who came to join themselves to their company. And when they asked them, dost thou bring a heart void of all earthly affection? they meant to say, If thou dost not do so, thou canst never belong entirely to God: *For where thy treasure is, there is thy heart also.*[2] The treasure of each one is anything that he loves and prizes. Once, when a certain rich man died, who was damned, St. Anthony of Padua published his damnation from the pulpit; and, as a sign of the truth of what he said, he told the people to go to the place where he had kept his money, and that they should find the heart of that wretched man in the midst of his money. And they did actually go, and they found his heart still warm in the midst of his money.

God cannot be the treasure of any one who retains affection for the goods of this life; therefore David prayed: *Create a clean heart in me, O God.*[3] Lord, cleanse my heart from earthly affections, that I may be able to say that thou art the God of my heart, and my eternal riches: *The God of my heart, and my portion forever.*[4] He, then, who really wishes to become a saint must drive away from his heart everything that is not God. What are treasures? what possessions? what riches? what is the use of these goods, if they do not satisfy the heart, and we must leave them so soon? *Lay not up to*

---

[1] "Affersne cor vacuum?"
[2] "Ubi enim est thesaurus tuus, ibi est et cor tuum."—*Matt.* vi. 21.
[3] "Cor mundum crea in me, Deus."—*Ps.* l. 12.
[4] "Deus cordis mei, et pars mea, Deus, in æternum."—*Ps.* lxxii. 26.

yourselves treasures on earth, where the rust and moth consume . . ., but lay up to yourselves treasures in heaven.[1]

O what great happiness is prepared by God in heaven for those who love him ! O what a treasure is the grace of God and divine love to those know it ! *That I may enrich them that love me.*[2] God contains in himself and brings with him riches and the reward : *Behold His reward is with Him,*[3] says Isaias. It is God alone who is the reward of the blessed in heaven ; he alone is sufficient to make them happy : *I am thy reward exceeding great.*[4]

But he who would love God exceedingly in heaven must first love him very much on earth. According to the degree of love which we bear towards God when we finish the journey of life, will be the degree of love with which we shall continue to love God for all eternity. And if we wish to be certain of nevermore being separated from our Sovereign Good in this life, let us always bind ourselves more closely to him by the chains of love, and say with the sacred spouse : *I found Him whom my soul loveth; I held Him; and I will not let Him go.*[5] How did the spouse hold her beloved ? " With the arms of love," replies the Abbot William. " Yes," says St. Ambrose, " God is held with the chains of love."[6] God allows himself to be bound by us with chains of love. Happy, then, is the man who can say with St. Paulinus : " Let the rich enjoy their riches, kings their kingdoms ;

---

[1] " Nolite thesaurizare vobis thesauros in terra, ubi ærugo et tinea demolitur . . .; thesaurizate autem vobis thesauros in cœlo."—*Matt.* vi. 19.

[2] " Mecum sunt divitiæ . . . ut ditem diligentes me."—*Prov.* viii. 18.

[3] " Ecce merces ejus cum eo."—*Isa.* lxii. 11.

[4] " Ego . . . merces tua magna nimis."—*Gen.* xv. 1.

[5] " Inveni quem diligit anima mea; tenui eum, nec dimittam."— *Cant.* iii. 4.

[6] " Christus tenetur vinculis charitatis."—*De Virginib.* l. 3.

but let Christ be my riches and my kingdom."[1] And with St. Ignatius: "Give me only Thy love and Thy grace, and I am rich enough."[2] Lord, give me Thy grace and Thy holy love; may I love Thee, and be loved by Thee; and I am sufficiently rich: I desire nothing more; nor is there anything else that I could desire. "No one," says St. Leo, "need fear want who possesses all things in the Lord."[3] Let us also never fail to have recourse to the divine Mother, and to love her, after God, above all things; for she herself assures us (in the words of the Holy Church) that she enriches with graces all those who love her: "With me are riches . . . that I may enrich them that love me."[4]

Affections and Prayers.

My dear Jesus, inflame me with Thy holy love; since for this end Thou didst come upon this earth. It is true that I am so wretched as to have often offended Thee, after the many special lights and graces which have been bestowed on me; I am no longer worthy to be consumed in those blessed flames with which the saints are inflamed, I ought rather to burn in the fire of hell; but now, being free from that prison which I have deserved, I feel that Thou dost also turn towards me notwithstanding my ingratitude, and say, *Thou shalt love the Lord thy God with all thy heart.*[5] I thank Thee, my God, that Thou dost again give me this sweet precept; and as Thou dost command me to love Thee, I will obey Thee, and will love Thee with my whole heart. Lord, I have hitherto been ungrateful

---

[1] "Sibi habeant divitias suas divites, sibi regna sua reges; nobis gloria et possessio et regnum Christus est."—*Ep. ad Aprum.*

[2] "Amorem tui solum cum gratia tua mihi dones, et dives sum satis."

[3] "Non pavet indigentia laborare, cui donatum est in Domino omnia possidere."—*In Quadr.* s. 4.

[4] "Mecum sunt divitiæ . . ., ut ditem diligentes me."—*Prov.* viii. 18.

[5] "Diliges Dominum Deum tuum ex toto corde tuo."—*Matt.* xxii. 37.

and blind, because I have not been mindful of the love Thou hast borne me. But now Thou dost enlighten me again, and dost make me understand how much Thou hast done for my sake : now that I think that Thou didst become man for me, that Thou didst take upon Thee my miseries ; now that I see Thee trembling with cold on the straw, crying and weeping for me,—O my infant God, how can I live without loving Thee? Ah, my Love, pardon me for all the displeasure I have caused Thee. O God, how could I, knowing as I did by faith how much Thou hast suffered for me, how could I have offended Thee so much? But this straw that torments Thee, that vile manger in which Thou art lying, those tender cries which Thou dost put forth, those loving tears which Thou dost shed,—these all make me firmly hope for pardon and grace to love Thee for the rest of my life. I love Thee, O Incarnate Word; I love Thee, O Divine Child ; and I give myself all to Thee. For the sake of those pains which Thou didst suffer in the stable of Bethlehem, accept, O my Jesus ! this miserable sinner, who desires to love Thee. Help me, give me perseverance ; I hope for all things from Thee. O Mary ! great Mother of this great Son, and most beloved by him, pray to him for me.

DISCOURSE IX.

The Eternal Word from being High made Himself Low.

Discite a me, quia mitis sum et humilis corde.

" Learn of Me, because I am meek and humble of heart."—*St. Matt.* xi. 29.

Pride was the chief cause of the fall of our first parents, who, not being willing to submit themselves to the obedience of God, thereby caused their own ruin, and that of all the human race. But the mercy of God as a remedy against such destruction, decreed that his only-begotten Son should humble himself to take upon himself our flesh ; and by the example of his life should induce men to love humility, and to detest pride, which renders them hateful in the sight of God and man. For this end is it that St. Bernard now invites us to visit the cave of Bethlehem, saying, " Let us go even to Bethlehem: there we have what to admire, what to love, and what to imitate."[1]

Yes; in that cave we have first of all cause to wonder.[2] What! a God in a stable! a God on straw! that God who sits on the highest throne of the majesty of heaven: *I saw the Lord sitting upon a throne high and elevated*,[3] says Isaias; and then where do we see him? In a manger, unknown and abandoned, with none around him save a few poor shepherds and two animals!

"We have what to love;" we shall easily find one in whom to place our affection, seeing there a God, who is the Infinite Good, and who has chosen to debase himself by appearing to the world as a poor Infant, thereby to make himself more endearing and pleasing in our eyes. As St. Bernard says again, "The more degraded he appears to me, the more dear is he to me."[4]

We shall lastly find what to imitate: "We have what to imitate."[5] We find the Supreme Being, the King of heaven, become an humble poor little Infant, desirous in this way, from his very infancy, of teaching us by his example that which he was afterwards to tell us by word of mouth: " He proclaims by his example (says the same holy Abbot) what he is afterwards to teach by his mouth: learn of Me, for I am gentle and humble of heart."[6] Let us ask for light of Jesus and Mary.

[1] "Habemus quod amemus et admiremur, habemus etiam quod imitemur."—*De Circ.* s. 3.
[2] "Quod admiremur."
[3] "Vidi Dominum sedentem super solium excelsum et elevatum."—*Isa.* vi. 1.
[4] " Quanto pro me vilior, tanto mihi carior."—*In Epiph. D.* s. 1.
[5] "Quod imitemur."
[6] " Clamat exemplo quod postmodum prædicaturus est verbo: Discite a me, quia mitis sum et humilis corde."—*In Nat. D.* s. i.

I.

Who does not know that God is the first, the highest in nobility, and the source whence all nobility proceeds? He is of an infinite greatness. He is independent; for he has not received his greatness from any other, but has always possessed it in himself. He is the Lord of all, whom all creatures obey: *The winds and the sea obey Him.*[1] Truly, therefore, does the Apostle say, that to God alone belong honor and glory: *To the only God be honor and glory.*[2] But the Eternal Word, to provide a remedy for man's disgrace, which was brought about by his pride, having made himself an example of poverty (as we considered in the last discourse), to detach man from worldly goods, desired also to make himself an example of humility, to free him from the vice of pride.

And in doing this, the first and greatest example of humility which he gave was making himself a man, and clothing himself with our miseries: *In habit found as a man.*[3] Cassian says that any one who puts on the dress of another man hides himself under it; in like manner God hid his divine nature under the lowly dress of human flesh. "He who is clothed is hidden under his clothes; so the divine nature concealed itself beneath the clothing of flesh."[4] And St. Bernard: "The divine Majesty became small, in order that it might join itself to our earthly nature; and that God and clay, majesty and weakness, the most extreme abasement and the highest grandeur, might be united in one person."[5] A

[1] "Venti et mare obediunt ei."—*Matt.* viii. 27.
[2] "Soli Deo honor et gloria."—1 *Tim.* i. 17.
[3] "Habitu inventus ut homo."—*Phil.* ii. 7.
[4] "Qui vestitur, sub veste absconditur; sic natura divina sub carnis veste delituit."
[5] "Contraxit se Majestas, ut seipsam limo nostro conjungeret, et in persona una unirentur Deus et limus, majestas et infirmitas, tanta vilitas et sublimitas tanta."—*In Vig. Nat.* s. 3.

God to unite himself to dust ! greatness to misery ! sublimity to wretchedness ! But that which must make us wonder still more is, that not only did God choose to appear as a creature, but as a sinful creature, putting on sinful flesh: *God sending his own Son in the likeness of sinful flesh.*[1]

But the Son of God was not even contented to appear as a man, and as a sinful man: he desired further to choose the most lowly and humble life among men; so that Isaias called him the last, the most humble of men: *Despised and the most abject of men.*[2] Jeremias said that he should be covered with ignominy: *He shall be filled with reproaches.*[3] And David, that he should be made the scorn of men, and the outcast of the people: *The reproach of men, and the outcast of the people.*[4] For such an end Jesus Christ wished to be born in the most abject way that could be imagined. What an ignominy for a man, even though he is poor, to be born in a stable! Who is there that is born in a stable? The poor are born in their huts, at least on beds of straw; stables are fit only for beasts and worms; and the Son of God chose to be born on this earth like a worm: *I am a worm, and no man.*[5] Yes, says St. Augustine, in such humility did the King of the universe choose to be born, in order to show us his majesty and power in his very humility, by which he could through his example make those men who are born full of pride love humility: "Such was the will of the Most High, who is also so humble, to show forth his majesty by very humility."[6]

[1] "Deus Filium suum mittens in similitudinem carnis peccati."—*Rom.* viii. 3.
[2] "Novissimum virorum."—*Isa.* liii. 3.
[3] "Saturabitur opprobriis."—*Lam.* iii. 30.
[4] "Opprobrium hominum et abjectio plebis."—*Ps.* xxi. 7.
[5] "Ego autem sum vermis, et non homo."—*Ibid.*
[6] "Sic voluit nasci excelsus humilis, ut in ipsa humilitate ostenderet majestatem."—*De Symb. ad cat.* l. 2, c. 5.

An angel announced to the shepherds the birth of the Messias; and the signs which he gave them by which they might find him and recognize him were all signs of humility. When you shall find a child (said he) in a stable, wrapped up in rags, and lying in a manger on the straw, know that it is your Saviour: *And this shall be a sign unto you; you shall find the infant wrapped in swaddling-clothes, and laid in a manger.*[1] In such a state is it that we find a God who is coming to this earth to destroy pride.

Then the life which Jesus Christ led in Egypt, where he was in exile, was in conformity with his birth. During the years he remained there, he lived as a stranger, unknown, and in poverty, in the midst of those barbarians. Who knew him there? who made any account of him?

He returned to Judea, and continued to live the same sort of a life he had led in Egypt. He lived for thirty years in a shop, supposed by all to be the son of a common workman, doing the work of a serving-boy, poor, unseen, and despised. In that holy family there were no servants. "Joseph and Mary," writes St. Peter Chrysologus, "have neither servant nor servant-maid: themselves are at once master and servant."[2] There was but one servant in that family, and he was the Son of God, who wished to become the Son of Man, that is, of Mary, that he might be an humble servant, and obey a man and a woman as their servant: *And He was subject to them.*[3]

After thirty years of hidden life, finally the time came that our Saviour was to appear in public to preach his heavenly doctrines, which he had come from heaven to

---

[1] "Et hoc vobis signum: invenietis infantem pannis involutum, et positum in præsepio."—*Luke*, ii. 12.

[2] "Joseph et Maria non habent famulum, non ancillam; ipsi domin et famuli."—*Hom. de Nat. Dom.*

[3] "Et erat subditus illis."—*Luke*, ii. 51.

teach us; and therefore it was necessary that he should make himself known as the true Son of God. But, O my God! how many were there that acknowledged and honored him as he deserved? Besides the few disciples who followed him, all the rest, instead of honoring him, despised him as a vile man and an impostor. Ah, then was verified in the fullest manner the prophecy of Simeon: *This child is set for a sign which shall be contradicted.*[1] Jesus Christ was contradicted and despised by all: he was despised in his doctrine; for when he declared that he was the only-begotten Son of God, he was called a blasphemer, and as such was condemned to death; as the wicked Caiphas said, *He hath blasphemed; He is guilty of death.*[2] He was despised in his wisdom; for he was esteemed a fool without sense: *He is mad: why hear you Him?*[3] His morals were reproached as being scandalous,—they called him a glutton, a drunkard, and the friend of wicked people: *Behold a man that is a glutton, and a drinker of wine, a friend of publicans and sinners.*[4] He was accused of being a sorcerer, and of having commerce with devils: *By the prince of the devils He casteth out devils.*[5] He was called a heretic, and one possessed by the devil: *Do we not say well, that Thou art a Samaritan, and hast a devil?*[6] A deceiver: *For that deceiver said*, etc.[7] In fine, Jesus Christ was considered by all the people so wicked a man that there was no need of a tribunal to

[1] "Positus est hic . . . in signum cui contradicetur."—*Luke*, ii. 34.
[2] "Blasphemavit . . . Reus est mortis."—*Matt.* xxvi. 65.
[3] "Insanit; quid eum auditis?"—*John*, x. 20.
[4] "Ecce homo devorator et bibens vinum, amicus publicanorum et peccatorum."—*Luke*, vii. 34.
[5] "In principe dæmoniorum ejicit dæmones."—*Matt.* ix. 34.
[6] "Nonne bene dicimus nos, quia Samaritanus es tu et dæmonium habes?"—*John*, viii. 48.
[7] "Seductor ille."—*Matt.* xxvii. 63.

condemn him to be crucified: *If He were not a malefactor, we would not have delivered Him up to thee.*[1]

At last the Saviour came to the end of his life and to his Passion; and, O God, what contempt and ill-treatment did he not receive in his Passion! He was betrayed and sold by one of his own disciples for thirty pieces of money, a less price than would be given for a beast. By another disciple he was denied. He was dragged through the streets of Jerusalem bound like a thief, abandoned by all, even by his few remaining disciples. He was treated shamefully as a slave, when he was scourged. He was struck on the face in public. He was treated as a fool, when Herod had a white garment put on him, that he might be thought a foolish person without any sense: "He despised him as ignorant," says St. Bonaventure, " because he did not answer a word; as foolish, because He did not defend himself."[2] He was treated as a mock-king, when they put into his hand a piece of reed instead of a sceptre, a tattered red garment upon his shoulders instead of the purple, and a chaplet of thorns on his head for a crown; after thus deriding him, they saluted him: *Hail, King of the Jews!*[3] and then they covered him with spitting and blows, *and spitting upon Him;*[4] *and they gave Him blows.*[5]

Finally, Jesus Christ willed to die; but by what death? by the most ignominious death, which was the death of the cross: *He humbled Himself, becoming obedient unto*

---

[1] "Si non esset hic malefactor, non tibi tradidissemus eum."—*John,* xviii. 30.

[2] "Sprevit illum . . . tamquam ignorantem, quia verbum non respondit; tamquam stolidum, quia se non defensavit."—*In Luc.* xxiii.

[3] "Ave, Rex Judæorum."

[4] "Et expuentes in eum."—*Matt.* xxvii. 30.

[5] "Dabant ei alapas."—*John,* xix. 3.

death, even to the death of the cross.[1] Any one who suffered the death of the cross at that time was considered the vilest and most wicked of criminals: *Cursed is every one that hangeth on a tree.*[2] Therefore, the names of those who were crucified were always held as cursed and infamous; so that the Apostle wrote: *Christ is made a curse for us.*[3] St. Athanasius, commenting on this passage, says: "He is called a curse, because he bore the curse for us."[4] Jesus took upon himself this curse, that he might save us from eternal malediction. But where, Lord, exclaims St. Thomas of Villanova, where is Thy beauty, where is Thy majesty in the midst of so much ignominy? "Where, O God, is Thy glory, where Thy majesty?"[5] And he answers: "Ask not, God has gone out of Himself."[6] And the saint's meaning was this: that we should not seek for glory and majesty in Jesus Christ, since he had come to give us an example of humility, and manifest the love that he bears towards men; and that this love had made him, as it were, go out of himself.

II.

In the fables of the pagans, it is related that the god Hercules, for the love which he bore to the king Augea, undertook to tame his horses; and that the god Apollo, out of love for Admetus, kept his flocks for him. These are inventions of imagination; but it is of faith that Jesus Christ, the true Son of God, for the love of men, humbled himself to be born in a stable, and to lead a

---

[1] "Humiliavit semetipsum, factus obediens usque ad mortem, mortem autem crucis."—*Phil.* ii. 8.
[2] "Maledictus omnis qui pendet in ligno."—*Gal.* iii. 13.
[3] "Factus pro nobis maledictum."—*Ibid.*
[4] "Dicitur maledictum, quod pro nobis maledictum suscepit."
[5] "Ubi est, Deus, gloria tua, majestas tua?"
[6] "Noli quærere; extasim passus est Deus."—*Serm. de Transfig.*

contemptible life, and in the end to die by the hands of executioners on an infamous gibbet. "O grace! O power of love!" exclaims St. Bernard, "didst Thou, the Most High, become the lowest of all!"[1] O the strength of divine love! the greatest of all has made himself the lowest of all! "Who did this?" rejoins St. Bernard, "it was love, regardless of its dignity.[2] Love triumphs over God."[3] Love does not consider dignity, when there is question of gaining for itself the person it loves. God, who can never be conquered by any one, has been conquered by love; for it was that love that compelled him to make himself man, and to sacrifice himself for the love of man in an ocean of sorrows and contempt. "He emptied Himself," concludes the holy abbot, "that thou mayest know that it was through love that the Highest made himself equal to thee."[4] The divine Word, who is majesty itself, humbled himself so far as to annihilate himself, that mankind might know how much he loved them.

Yes, says St. Gregory Nazianzen, because in no other way could he better show forth the divine love than by abasing himself, and taking upon himself the greatest misery and ignominy that men even suffer on this earth. "God could not otherwise declare his love for us than by descending for our sakes to what was most low."[5] Richard of St. Victor adds that man having had the boldness to offend the majesty of God, in order to expiate his guilt, the intervention of the most excessive humiliation

---

[1] "O gratiam, O amoris vim! itane summus omnium imus factus est omnium!"

[2] "Fecit amor, dignitatis nescius."

[3] "Triumphat de Deo amor."

[4] "Semetipsum exinanivit, ut scias amoris fuisse, quod altitudo adæquata est."—*In Cant.* s. 64.

[5] "Non aliter Dei amor erga nos declarari poterat, quam quod nostra causa ad deteriorem partem se dejecerit."

The Eternal Word made Himself Low. 135

was necessary: "For the expiation of the sin, the humiliation of the highest to the lowest was necessary."[1] St. Bernard goes on to say, the more our God abased himself, so much the more did he show forth his goodness and love: "The lower he showed himself to be in human nature, the greater did he declare himself in goodness."[2]

Now, after a God has suffered so much for the love of man, will man have a repugnance to humble himself for the love of God? *Let this mind be in you, which was also in Christ Jesus.*[3] He who is not humble, and who does not seek to imitate the humility of Jesus Christ, is not worthy of the name of Christian; for Jesus Christ, as St. Augustine says, came into the world in an humble way to put down pride. The pride of man was the disease which drew from heaven this divine physician, which loaded him with ignominies, and caused him to die on the cross Let the proud man, then, at least be ashamed when he sees that a God so humbled himself in order to cure him of pride: "Because of this very vice of pride, God came in humility. This disease drew him down from heaven, humbled him even to the form of a servant, overwhelmed with calumnies, hung him upon the cross. Blush, then, O man, to be proud, for whom God has become humble."[4] And St. Peter Damian writes: "To raise us, he lowered himself."[5] He chose to abase himself, that he might raise us out of the mire of our sins, and might place us in the company of the angels in

[1] "Oportuit ut, ad expiationis remedium, fieret humiliatio de summo ad imum."—*De Verbo inc.* c. 8.

[2] "Quanto minorem se fecit in humanitate, tanto majorem exhibuit in bonitate."—*In Epiph. D.* s. 1.

[3] "Hoc enim sentite in vobis, quod et in Christo Jesu."—*Phil.* ii. 5.

[4] "Propter hoc vitium superbiæ Deus humilis venit. Iste morbus Medicum de cœlo deduxit, usque ad formam servi humiliavit, contumeliis egit, ligno suspendit. Erubescat homo esse superbus, propter quem factus est humilis Deus."—*In Ps.* xviii. *en.* 2.

[5] "Ut nos erigeret, se inclinavit."—*Hom. in Nat. D.*

heaven: *Lifting up the poor out of the dunghill, that He may place him with the princes of His people.*[1] " His abasement in our exaltation."[2] O the greatness of divine love! exclaims St. Augustine. For the sake of man, a God takes upon himself contempt, that he may share his honor with man. He makes himself familiar with grief and pain, that man may have salvation: he even suffers death, to obtain life for man. "O wondrous condescension! He comes to receive contempt, that he may confer honors; he comes to be satiated with grief, that he may give salvation; he comes to undergo death, that he may give life."[3]

Jesus Christ, by choosing for himself so humble a birth, so despicable a life, and so ignominious a death, has ennobled and taken away all bitterness from contempt and opprobrium. It is for this that the saints in this world were always so fond and even desirous of being despised; they seemed not to be able to desire or seek for anything but to be despised and trodden underfoot for the love of Jesus Christ. When the divine Wo d. came upon this earth, well was that prophecy of Isaias fulfilled: *In the dens where dragons dwelt before shall rise up the verdure of the reed and the bulrush.*[4] That where the demons, the spirits of pride, dwelt, there, at the sight of the humility of Jesus Christ, should arise the spirit of humility. "The verdure of the reed signifies humility,"[5] says St. Ugo, commenting on this passage ; the humble man is empty

[1] "De stercore erigens pauperem, ut collocet eum cum principibus, cum principibus populi sui."—*Ps.* cxii. 7.

[2] "Humilitas ejus nostra nobilitas est."—*De Trin.* l. 2.

[3] "Mira commutatio: venit accipere contumelias, dare honores, venit haurire dolorem, dare salutem, venit subire mortem, dare vitam."—*In Ps.* xxx. *en.* 2.

[4] "In cubilibus in quibus prius dracones habitabant, orietur viror calami."—*Isa.* xxxv. 7.

[5] "'Calami,' id est, humilitatis, quia humilis est vacuus in oculis suis."

in his own eyes ; the humble are not full of themselves, as the proud are, but empty, considering what is the truth, that all they have is the gift of God.

From this we may well understand that an humble soul is as dear to God as the proud heart is odious in his eyes. But is it possible, says St. Bernard, for people to be proud after seeing the life of Jesus Christ? "Though the divine majesty annihilates itself, a worm lifts itself up in pride!"[1] Is it possible that a mere worm, loaded with sins, should be proud, when he sees the God of infinite majesty and purity humble himself so much, in order to teach us to be humble!

But let it be known that proud people do not get on with God. St. Augustine thus warns us: "Lift yourself up, and God will depart from you; humble yourself, and God will come to you."[2] The Lord flies from the proud; but, on the contrary, God cannot despise a heart that humbles itself, even though it should be a sinful one: *A contrite and humble heart, O God, Thou wilt not despise.*[3] God has promised to hear all who pray to him: *Ask, and it shall be given you. . . . For every one that asketh receiveth.*[4] But he has declared that he will not listen to the proud, as St. James tells us: *God resisteth the proud, and giveth grace to the humble.*[5] He resists the prayers of the proud, and does not listen to them; but he cannot deny any grace to the humble, whatever they may ask. In fact, St. Teresa said that the greatest graces she had ever received were those which were granted her when she

[1] "Ubi sese exinanivit Majestas, vermiculus intumescit?"—*In Nat. D.* s. 1.

[2] "Erigis te, Deus fugit a te ; humilias te, Deus descendit ad te."—*Serm.* 117, *E. B. app.*

[3] "Cor contritum et humiliatum, Deus, non despicies."—*Ps.* l. 19.

[4] "Petite, et dabitur vobis . . . ; omnis enim qui petit, accipit."—*Matt.* vii. 7.

[5] "Deus superbis resistit, humilibus autem dat gratiam."—*James*, iv. 6.

more particularly humbled herself in the presence of God. The prayer of the humble penetrates into heaven by its own efficacy, without needing any one to present it; and it does not depart without obtaining from God that which it desires: *The prayer of him that humbleth himself shall pierce the clouds;* . . . *and he will not depart till the Most High beholds.*[1]

Affections and Prayers.

O my despised Jesus! by Thy example Thou hast done too much to render reproaches and contempt sweet in the eyes of those that love Thee. But how is it, then, that instead of embracing them, as Thou hast done, when I received some little contempt from men, I behaved with so much pride, and took occasion from it to offend Thy infinite majesty, sinner and proud that I was? Ah, Lord, I see why it is; I did not know how to bear an affront patiently, because I did not know how to love Thee. If I had loved Thee truly, it would have been sweet and pleasing to me. But since Thou dost promise pardon to him who repents, I repent with all my heart of all the excesses of my life,—a life so unlike Thine. But I desire to amend; and therefore I promise Thee to be willing to suffer patiently from this day forward all the contempt to which I shall be subject, for Thy love, O my Jesus! who wast so much despised for the love of me. I understand that humiliations are precious mines by which Thou dost enrich souls with eternal treasures. I deserve other humiliations and other reproaches for having despised Thy grace; I deserve to be trampled on by the devils. But Thy merits are my hope. I will change my life, and will no longer displease Thee; henceforth I will seek for nothing but Thy divine pleasure. I have deserved many times to be sent to burn in hell-fire; Thou hast waited for me till now, and, as I hope, hast pardoned me; grant, therefore, that instead of burning in that unhappy flame, I may be inflamed with the blessed fire of Thy holy love. No, I will no longer live without loving Thee. Help me; let me not live any more ungrateful to Thee, as I have hitherto done. For the future I

---

[1] "Oratio humiliantis se nubes penetrabit . . .; et non discedet, donec Altissimus aspiciat."—*Ecclus.* xxxv. 21.

will love Thee only; I desire that my heart should belong to Thee alone. Ah, take possession of it, and keep it forever, that I may be always Thine, and Thou mayest be always mine; that I may love Thee; and Thou mayst love me forever. Yes, this is my hope, O my God! that I shall always love Thee, and that Thou wilt always love me. I believe in Thee, Infinite Goodness; I hope in Thee, Infinite Goodness; I love Thee, Infinite Goodness; I love Thee, and I will say always I love Thee, I love Thee, I love Thee, and because I love Thee, I will do all I can to please Thee. Dispose of me as Thou wilt. All I ask is, that Thou wouldst give me grace to love Thee, and then do with me as Thou pleasest. Thy love is, and always shall be, my only treasure, my only desire, my only good, my only love. Mary, my hope, Mother of beautiful love, do thou help me in loving the God of love with all my heart and forever.

Discourse for Christmas Night—The Birth of Jesus Christ.

Evangelizo vobis gaudium magnum . . . quia natus est vobis hodie Salvator.

"I bring you good tidings of great joy, ... for this day is born to you a Saviour."—*St Luke* ii. 10, 11.

I bring you good tidings of great joy.[1] Thus said the angel to the shepherds, and thus do I say to you, O devout souls! on this night. I bring you tidings of great joy. And what tidings could be a greater joy to a nation of poor exiles, condemned to death, than for them to be told that their Saviour had come, not only to deliver them from death, but also to obtain for them permission to return to their country? And this is what I announce to you this night : *A Saviour is born to you.*[2] Jesus Christ is born ; and he is born for you, to deliver you from everlasting death, and to open to you heaven, which is our country, and from which we had been banished in punishment for our sins.

But in order that you should show your gratitude from this time forth, by loving your new-born Redeemer, allow me to set him before your eyes ; let me show you where he was born, and where he may be found on this night, that you may go to him and thank him for so great a favor, and for his great love. Let us ask for light from Jesus and Mary.

I.

Let me, then, briefly relate to you the history of the birth of this King of the world, who came down from heaven for your salvation.

[1] " Evangelizo vobis gaudium magnum."
[2] " Natus est vobis hodie Salvator."

Discourse for Christmas Night. 141

Octavius Augustus, the Emperor of Rome, wishing to know the strength of his empire, decreed that there be a general numbering of all his subjects; and for this purpose he ordered all the governors of the provinces—and, among the rest, Cyrinus, governor of Judea— to make every one come to enroll himself, and at the same time pay a certain tribute as a sign of vassalage : *There went out a decree . . . that the whole world should be enrolled.*[1] As soon as this decree was promulgated, Joseph obeys immediately ; he does not even wait till his holy spouse should be delivered, though she was near her time. I say he obeyed immediately, and set out on his journey with Mary, then pregnant with the divine Word, to go and enroll himself in the city of Bethlehem: *to be enrolled with Mary his espoused wife, who was with child.*[2] The journey was a long one—for, according to some authors, it was ninety leagues ; that is to say, four days—long and difficult, for they had to traverse mountains and steep paths, through the wind, the rain, and the cold.

When a king makes his first entry into a city of his kingdom, what honors are not prepared for him! what preparations are not made, and triumphal arches erected! Do thou then, O happy Bethlehem! prepare thyself to receive thy King with honor; for the prophet Micheas has told thee that he is coming to thee, and that he is Lord not only of all Judea, but of the whole world. And know, says the prophet, thou, out of all the cities of the earth, art the fortunate one that has been chosen by the King of heaven for his birthplace, that he may afterwards reign, not indeed in Judea, but in the hearts of men who live in Judea and in all the rest of the world: *And thou, Bethlehem Ephrata, art a little one among the thou-*

---

[1] "Exiit edictum a Cæsare Augusto ut describeretur universus orbis."—*Luke*, ii. 1.

[2] "Ut profiteretur cum Maria desponsata sibi uxore prægnante." —*Luke*, ii. 5.

sands of *Judea: out of thee shall He come forth that is to be ruler in Israel.*[1] But behold these two illustrious pilgrims, Joseph and Mary, who bears within her womb the Saviour of the world, are about to enter into Bethlehem. They enter and go to the house of the imperial minister to pay the tribute, and to enroll themselves in the book as subjects of Cæsar, where they also inscribed the offspring of Mary, namely, Jesus Christ, who was the Lord of Cæsar and of all the princes of the earth. But who acknowledges them? Who goes before them to show them honor? who salutes them, and who receives them? *He came unto His own, and His own received Him not.*[2] They travel like poor people, and as such they are despised; they are treated even worse than the other poor, and are driven away. Yes; for *it came to pass when they were there her days were accomplished that she should be delivered.*[3] Mary knew that the time of her delivery was come, and that it was here, and on that night, that the Incarnate Word willed to be born, and to manifest himself to the world. She therefore told Joseph, and he hastened to procure some lodging in the houses of the townspeople, so as not to take his spouse to the inn to be delivered, as it was not a decent place for her to be in; besides which, it was then full of people. But he found not any one to listen to him; and very likely he was insulted, and called a fool by some of them, for taking his wife about at that time of night, and in such a crowd of people, when she was near her delivery; so that at last he was obliged, unless he would remain all night in the street, to take her to the public inn, where there were many other poor people lodging that night. He

---

[1] "Et tu, Bethlehem Ephrata, parvulus es in millibus Juda; ex te mihi egredietur, qui sit Dominator in Israel."—*Mich.* v. 2.

[2] "In propria venit, et sui eum non receperunt."—*John,* i. 11.

[3] "Factum est autem, cum essent ibi, impleti sunt dies ut pareret." —*Luke,* ii. 6.

went there; but they were refused admittance even there, and they were told that there was no room for them: *There was no room for them in the inn.*[1] There was room for all, even for the lowest, but not for Jesus Christ.

That inn was a figure of those ungrateful hearts where many find room for miserable creatures, but not for God. How many love their relatives, their friends, even animals, but do not love Jesus Christ, and care neither for his grace nor his love! But the ever-blessed Mary said once to a devout soul: "It was the dispensation of God that neither I nor my Son should find a lodging amongst men, that those souls who love Jesus might offer themselves as a lodging-place, and might affectionately invite him to come into their hearts."

But let us go on with the history. These poor travellers, then seeing themselves repulsed on every side, leave the city to try and find some place of refuge without its walls. They walk on in the dark; they go round about and examine, till at last they see a grotto, which was cut out of stone in the mountain under the city. Barradas, Bede, and Brocardus say that the place where Jesus Christ was born was a rock that had been excavated under the walls of Bethlehem, divided off from the city, and like a cavern, and which served as a stable for cattle. When they came to it, Mary said to Joseph: "There is no occasion to go any farther; let us go into this cave and remain there." "What!" replied Joseph; "my spouse, dost thou not see that this cave is quite exposed; that it is cold and damp, and that water is running down on all sides? Dost thou not see that it is no lodging for men, but it is a shed for beasts? How can you stop here all night, and be delivered here?" Then Mary said, "It is nevertheless true that this stable is the regal palace in which the Eternal Son of God desires to be born on earth."

[1] "Non erat eis locus in diversorio."—*Luke*, ii. 7.

Oh, what must the angels have said when they saw the divine Mother enter into this cave to bring forth her Son! The sons of princes are born in rooms adorned with gold; they have cradles enriched with precious stones, fine clothes, a retinue of the first lords of the kingdom; and has the King of heaven nothing but a cold stable without a fire to be born in, some poor swaddling-clothes to cover him, a little straw for his bed, and a vile manger to lie in? "Where is the palace," asks St. Bernard, "where is the throne?"[1] Where, says the saint, is the court, where is the royal palace for this King of heaven? for I see nothing but two animals to keep him company, and a manger for cattle, where he must be laid. O happy grotto, that witnessed the birth of the divine Word! Happy manger, to have had the honor of receiving the Lord of heaven! Happy straw, which served as a bed to him who sits on the shoulders of the seraphim! Ah, when we think of the birth of Jesus Christ, and of the manner in which it took place, we ought all to be inflamed with love; and when we hear the names of cave, manger, straw, milk, tears, in reference to the birth of the Redeemer, these names ought to be so many incitements to our love, and arrows to wound our hearts. Yes, happy was that grotto, that crib, that straw; but still happier are those souls who love this amiable Lord with fervor and tenderness, and who receive him in the Holy Communion into hearts burning with love. Oh, with what desire and pleasure does Jesus Christ enter into and repose in a heart that loves him!

II.

No sooner had Mary entered into the cavern than she began immediately to pray; and the hour of her delivery being come, she loosened her hair, out of reverence,

[1] "Ubi aula? ubi thronus?"

spreading it over her shoulders; and behold she sees a great light, she feels in her heart a heavenly joy! She casts down her eyes; and, O God! what does she see? She sees on the ground an infant, so tender and beautiful that he fills her with love; but he trembles, he cries, and stretches out his arms to show that he desires she should take him into her bosom: "I stretched forth my arms to seek the caresses of my mother,"[1] according to the revelation of St. Bridget. Mary calls Joseph. "Come, Joseph," she said, "come and see; for the Son of God is now born." Joseph comes; and when he sees Jesus already born, he adores him in the midst of a torrent of sweet tears: "The old man entered, and, prostrating himself, wept for joy."[2] Then the Blessed Virgin reverently took her beloved Son in her arms, and placed him in her bosom. She tried to warm him by the heat of her cheeks and of her bosom: "Pressing him to her cheeks and bosom, she warmed him with all the joy and tenderness of a mother's love."[3]

Consider the devotion, the tenderness, the love which Mary felt at seeing in her arms and on her breast the Lord of the world, the Son of the Eternal Father, who had deigned even to become her Son, choosing her from amongst all women to be his Mother. Mary, now holding him to her bosom, adores him as God, kissing his feet as her king, and then his face as her Son. Then she hastily seeks to cover him, and wraps him up in swaddling-clothes. But, O God! how hard and rough are those clothes; for they are clothes of the poor, and they are cold and damp, and in that cave there is no fire to warm them by!

Come, ye monarchs and emperors, come, all ye princes

[1] "Extendebat membra, quærens Matris favorem."
[2] "Intravit senex, et, prosternens se, plorabat præ gaudio."
[3] "Maxilla et pectore calefaciebat eum cum lætitia et tenera compassione materna."—*Rev.* l. 7, c. 21.

of the world, come and adore your highest King, who for your love is now born; and born in such poverty in a cave. But who appears? No one. *He came unto His own, and His own received Him not.*[1] Ah! the Son of God has indeed come into the world; but the world will not know him.

But if men do not come, the angels draw near to adore their Lord. Thus did the Eternal Father ordain for the honor of his Son: *And let all the angels of God adore Him.*[2] They come in great numbers and praise their God, singing with great joy, *Glory to God in the highest; and on earth peace to men of good-will.*[3] Glory to the divine mercy, which, instead of chastising rebellious men, causes this same God to take upon himself their punishment, and so to save them. Glory to the divine wisdom, which has devised a means of satisfying his justice, and at the same time of delivering man from the death he had deserved. Glory to the divine power, destroying in so signal a manner the powers of hell, by the divine Word coming in poverty to suffer pains, contempt, and death; and thus to draw the hearts of men to himself, and to leave everything for his sake,—honors, riches, and life; as so many virgins and young men have done, and even nobles and princes, to show their gratitude for the love of this God. Finally, glory to the divine love, which induced God to become a little child, poor and lowly, to live a hard life, and to die a cruel death, in order to show man the love which he bears him, to gain his love in return. "In the stable we see power reduced to impotence, and wisdom become mad through excess of love."[4]

[1] "In mundo erat..., et mundus eum non cognovit."—*John*, i. 10.

[2] "Et adorent eum omnes Angeli Dei."—*Heb.* i. 6.

[3] "Gloria in altissimis Deo, et in terra pax hominibus bonæ voluntatis."—*Luke*, ii. 14.

[4] "Agnoscimus in stabulo exinanitam Majestatem, Sapientiam amoris nimietate infatuatam."—*Serm. in Nat. D.*

Discourse for Christmas Night. 147

We see, in this stable, says St. Laurence Justinian, the power of God, as it were, annihilated; we see God, who is wisdom itself, become as it were a fool through the excess of love which he bears to men.

III.

Arise, all ye nobles and peasants; Mary invites all, rich and poor, just and sinners, to enter the cave of Bethlehem, to adore and to kiss the feet of her new-born Son. Go in, then, all ye devout souls; go and see the Creator of heaven and earth on a little hay, under the form of a little Infant; but so beautiful that he sheds all around rays of light. Now that he is born and is lying on the straw, the cave is no longer horrible, but is become a paradise. Let us enter; let us not be afraid.

Jesus is born; he is born for all, for each one who desires him: *I am the Flower of the field* (as he tells us in the Canticles) *and the Lily of the valley*.[1] He calls himself the lily of the valley to show us that as he was born in so great humility, so it is only the humble who find him; therefore the angel did not go and announce the birth of Jesus Christ to Cæsar or to Herod, but to poor humble shepherds. He also calls himself the flower of the field, because he shows himself forth so as to be seen by all: *I am the Flower of the field*;[2] upon which Cardinal Hugo commenting says, "Because I allow myself to be found by all." Flowers in gardens are shut up and enclosed between walls, nor is every one permitted to come and gather them; whereas the flowers of the field are open to all, and any one who likes may take them; and so does Jesus Christ desire to be accessible to all who desire him.

Let us arise and enter, the door is open; "There are no satellites," says St. Peter Chrysologus, "to say that

[1] "Ego Flos campi et Lilium convallium."—*Cant.* ii. 1.
[2] "Ego Flos campi quia palam me exhibeo omnibus ad inveniendum."

this is not the time."[1] Monarchs are shut up in their palaces, and the palaces are surrounded with soldiers; it is not easy to have audiences with princes; those who would speak to them must expect to have their patience tried; they will often be sent away and told to come again,—that this is not the hour of audience. Jesus Christ does not do so; he remains in that cave; and he is there as a little child, attracting all who come to seek him; and the cave is open without guards and without doors; so that all may go in when they please to seek him and speak to him; and even to embrace this Infant King, if they love him and desire him.

Let every soul, then, enter. Behold and see that tender Infant, who is weeping as he lies in the manger on that miserable straw. See how beautiful he is; look at the light which he sends forth, and the love which he breathes; those eyes send out arrows which wound the hearts that desire him; the very stable, the very straw, cry out,[2] says St. Bernard, and tell you to love him who loves you; to love God, who is infinite love; and who came down from heaven, and made himself a little child, and became poor, to make you understand the love he bears you, and to gain your love by his sufferings.

Come and say to him: " Ah, beautiful Infant! tell me whose child art Thou?" He replies: "My Mother is this pure and lovely Virgin who is standing by me." And who is thy Father? "My Father," he says, "is God." How is this? Thou art the Son of God, and art so poor; and why? Who will acknowledge Thee in such a condition? Who will respect Thee? "No," replies Jesus, "holy faith will make known who I am, and will make me loved by those souls whom I came to redeem and to inflame with my love." I am not come, says he, to make myself feared, but to make myself loved; and therefore I

---

[1] "Non est satelles qui dicat: Non est hora."—*In Ps.* iv.
[2] "Clamat stabulum, clamat præsepe."—*In Nat. D.* s. 5.

wished to show myself to you for the first time as a poor and humble Infant, that, seeing to what my love for you has reduced me, you might love me the more. But tell me, my sweet Infant, why dost Thou turn Thine eyes on every side? What art Thou looking for? I hear Thee sigh; tell me wherefore are these sighs? O God! I hear Thee weep; tell me wherefore dost Thou weep? Yes, replies Jesus, I turn my eyes around; for I am seeking for some soul that desires me. I sigh out of desire to see myself near to a heart that burns for me, as I burn with love for it. But I weep; and it is because I do not see, or I see but few souls, who seek me and wish to love me.

Exhortation during the Kissing of the Feet of the Holy Infant, which is a Practice observed in some Churches.

Now then, O all ye devout souls, does Jesus invite you to come and kiss his feet this night. The shepherds who came to visit him in the stable of Bethlehem brought their gifts; you must also bring your gifts. What will you bring him? Listen to me; the most acceptable present you can bring him is that of a contrite and loving heart. Let each one then say to him before he comes:

Affections and Prayers.

Lord, I should not have dared to approach Thee, seeing myself so deformed by my sins; but since Thou, my Jesus, dost invite me so courteously, and dost call me so lovingly, I will not refuse. After having so many times turned my back upon Thee, I will not add this fresh insult, namely, that of refusing this affectionate, this loving invitation, out of distrust. Say to him, Thou must know that I am poor, and that I have nothing to give Thee. I have nothing but this heart; this I now offer to Thee. It is true that this my heart offended Thee at one time; but now it is penitent, and I bring it to Thee penitent. Yes, O Infant! I repent of having offended Thee. I confess that I have been a traitor, cruel and ungrateful; that it is I who have caused

Thee to suffer so much, and who have made Thee shed so many tears in the stable of Bethlehem; but Thy tears are my hope. I am a sinner, it is true, and I do not deserve to be pardoned; but I come before Thee, who, being God, hast become a little child to obtain pardon for me. Eternal Father, if I merit hell, look at the tears of Thy innocent Son; they invoke Thy pardon in my behalf. Thou dost deny nothing to the prayers of Thy Son. Listen to him, then, now that he asks Thee to pardon me on this night,—the night of joy, the night of salvation, the night of pardon. Ah, my Infant Jesus, I hope for pardon from Thee; but the forgiveness of my sins alone is not sufficient for me. On this night Thou dost grant great spiritual graces; I also desire that Thou shouldst bestow a great grace on me,—it is, the grace to love Thee. Now that I am about to approach Thy feet, inflame me wholly with Thy holy love, and bind me to Thee; but bind me so effectually that I may nevermore be separated from Thee. I love Thee, O my God, who didst become a little child for my sake; but I love Thee very little; I desire to love Thee very much, and thou hast to enable me to do it. I come, then, to kiss Thy feet, and I offer Thee my heart; I leave it in Thy hands; I will have it no longer; do Thou change it, and keep it forever; do not give it back to me again; for if Thou dost, I fear lest it should betray Thee afresh.

Most holy Mary, thou who art the Mother of this great Son, but who art also my Mother, it is to thee that I consecrate my poor heart; present it to Jesus; and he will not refuse to receive it, when presented by thee. Do thou, then, present it, and beg him to accept it.

Discourse on the Name of Jesus.

Vocatum est nomen ejus Jesus.
" His Name was called Jesus."—*St. Luke*, ii. 21.

This great name of Jesus was not given by man, but by God himself ; " The name of Jesus," says St. Bernard, " was first preordained by God."[1] It was a new name : *A new Name, which the mouth of the Lord shall name.*[2] A new name, which God alone could give to him whom he destined for the Saviour of the world. A new and an eternal name; because, as our salvation was decreed from all eternity, so from all eternity was this name given to the Redeemer. Nevertheless this name was only bestowed on Jesus Christ in this world on the day of his circumcision: *And after eight days were accomplished that the child should be circumcised, His name was called Jesus.*[3] The Eternal Father wished at that time to reward the humility of his Son by giving him so honorable a name. Yes, while Jesus humbles himself, submitting in his circumcision to be branded with the mark of a sinner, it is just that his Father should honor him by giving him a name that exceeds the dignity and sublimity of any other name: *God hath given Him a Name which is above all names.*[4] And he commands that this name should be adored by the angels, by men, and by devils : *That in the Name of Jesus every knee should bow of those that are in heaven, on earth, and under the earth.*[5] If, then, all creatures are to adore this

[1] "Nomen Jesus primo fuit a Patre prænominatum."—*T.* ii. s. 49.
[2] "Nomen novum, quod os Domini nominabit."—*Isa.* lxii. 2.
[3] " Et postquam consummati sunt dies octo, ut circumcideretur puer, vocatum est nomen ejus Jesus."
[4] " Donavit illi nomen quod est super omne nomen."—*Phil.* ii. 9.
[5] " Ut in nomine Jesu omne genu flectatur, cœlestium, terrestrium, et infernorum."—*Phil.* ii. 10.

great name, still more ought we sinners to adore it, since it was in our behalf that this name of Jesus, which signifies Saviour, was given to him; and for this end also he came down from heaven, namely, to save sinners: "For us men and for our salvation he came down from heaven, and was made man."[1] We ought to adore him, and at the same time to thank God who has given him this name for our good; for it is this name that consoles us, defends us, and makes us burn with love. This will form the three points of our discourse. Let us consider them; but first let us beg for light from Jesus and Mary.

I.

In the first place, the name of Jesus consoles us; for when we invoke Jesus, we find relief in all our afflictions. When we have recourse to Jesus, he wishes to console us, because he loves us; and he can do so, because he is not only man, but he is also the Omnipotent God; otherwise he could not properly have this great name of Saviour. The name of Jesus signifies that the bearer of it is of an infinite power, infinite wisdom, and infinite love; so that if Jesus Christ had not united in himself all these perfections, he could not have saved us: "If any one of these," says St. Bernard, "had been wanting, Thou couldst not call Thyself Saviour."[2] Thus, when speaking of the circumcision, the saint says: "He was circumcised as being the Son of Abraham, he was called Jesus as being the Son of God."[3] He is branded as man with the mark of sin, having taken upon himself the burden of atoning for sinners; and from his very infancy he be-

---

[1] "Propter nos homines, et propter nostram salutem, descendit de cœlis . . ., et homo factus est."—*Symb. Nic.*

[2] "Nec omnino aut vocari posset aut esse Salvator, si forte quippiam horum defuisset."—*In Circ.* s. 2.

[3] "Circumciditur tamquam Filius Abrahæ; Jesus vocatur tamquam Filius Dei."—*In Circ.* s. 1.

Discourse on the Name of Jesus. 153

gan, to satisfy for their crimes, by suffering and shedding his blood; but he is called Jesus, he is called the Saviour, inasmuch as he is the Son of God, because to God alone does the office of salvation belong.

The name of Jesus is said by the Holy Spirit to be like oil poured out: *Thy name is as oil poured out.*[1] And so indeed it is, says St. Bernard; for as oil serves for light, for food, and for medicine, so especially the name of Jesus is light: "it is a light when preached."[2] And how was it, says the saint, that the light of faith shone forth so suddenly in the world so that in a short time so many Gentile nations knew the true God, and became his followers, if it was not through hearing the name of Jesus preached? "Whence, think you, shone forth in the whole world, so bright and so sudden, the light of faith, except from the preaching of the name of Jesus?"[3] Through this name we have been happily made sons of the true light, that is, sons of the Holy Curch; since we were so fortunate as to be born in the bosom of the Roman Church, in Christian and Catholic kingdoms,— a grace which has not been granted to the greater part of men, who are born amongst idolaters, Mahometans, or heretics. Further, the name of Jesus is a food that nourishes our souls. "The thought of it is nourishment." This name gives strength to find peace and consolation even in the midst of the miseries and persecutions of this world. The holy Apostles rejoiced when they were ill treated and reviled, being comforted by the name of Jesus: *They went from the presence of the council rejoicing that they were counted worthy to suffer for the name of Jesus.*[4] It is light, it is food, and it is also

[1] "Oleum effusum nomen tuum."—*Cant.* i. 2.
[2] "Lucet prædicatum."
[3] "Unde putas in toto orbe tanta et tam subita fidei lux, nisi de prædicato nomine Jesu?"
[4] "Ibant gaudentes a conspectu Concilii, quoniam digni habiti sunt pro nomine Jesu contumeliam pati."—*Acts*, v. 41.

medicine to those who invoke it: "When pronounced, it soothes and anoints."[1] The holy Abbot says: "At the rising of the light of this name, the clouds disperse, the calm returns."[2] If the soul of any one is afflicted and in trouble, let him pronounce the name of Jesus, and immediately the tempest will cease and peace will return. Does any one fall into sin? Does he run in despair into the snares of death? Let him invoke the name of Life, and will he not at once return to life?[3] If any one has been so wretched as to fall into sin, and feels diffident of pardon, let him invoke this name of Life, and he shall immediately be encouraged to hope for pardon, by calling on Jesus, who for this end was destined by the Father to be our Saviour,—namely, to obtain pardon for sinners. Euthymius says that if when Judas was tempted to despair, he had invoked the name of Jesus, he would not have given way to the temptation: "If he had invoked that name, he would not have perished."[4] Therefore, he adds, no sinner can perish through desperation, however lost he may be, who invokes his Holy Name, which is one of hope and salvation: "Despair is far off where this name is invoked."[5]

But sinners leave off invoking this saving name, because they do not wish to be cured of their infirmities. Jesus Christ is ready to heal all our wounds; but if people cherish their wounds, and will not be healed, how can Jesus Christ heal them? The Venerable Sister Mary of Jesus Crucified, a Sicilian nun, once saw the Saviour, as it seemed, in a hospital, going round with medicines in

[1] "Invocatum lenit et ungit."
[2] "Ad exortum nominis lumen, nubilum diffugit, redit serenum."
[3] "Labitur quis in crimen; currit ad laqueum mortis desperando; nonne, si invocet nomen vitæ, confestim respirabit ad vitam?"—*In Cant.* s. 15.
[4] "Si illud nomen invocasset, non periisset."
[5] "Longe est desperatio, ubi est hujus nominis invocatio."

his hand, to cure the sick people who were there; but these miserable people, instead of thanking him and begging him to come to them, drove him away. In like manner do many sinners, after they have of their own free-will poisoned their souls with sins, refuse the gifts of health, that is, the grace offered them by Jesus Christ, and thus remain lost through their infirmities.

But, on the other hand, what fear can that sinner have who has recourse to Jesus Christ, since Jesus offers himself to obtain our pardon from his Father, he having paid the penalty due from us by his death? St. Laurence Justinian says: "He who had been offended, appointed himself as intercessor, and himself paid what was owing to him."[1] Therefore, adds the saint, "if thou art bound down by sickness, if sorrows weary thee, if thou art trembling with fear, invoke the name of Jesus."[2] O poor man, whoever thou art, if thou art weighed down by infirmity or by grief and fear, call on Jesus, and he will console thee. It is enough that we pray to the Father in his name, and all we ask will be granted to us. This is the promise of Jesus himself, which he repeated many times, and which cannot fail: *If you ask the Father anything in My name, He will give it you:*[3] . . . *that whatsoever you shall ask of the Father in My name, He may give it you.*[4]

II.

In the second place, we said tnat the name of Jesus defends us. Yes, it defends us against all the deceits

[1] "Qui offensus fuerat, ipse se intercessorem destinavit; quod illi debebatur, exsolvit."—*Serm. in Nat. D.*

[2] "Si configeris ægritudine, si doloribus fatigaris, si concuteris formidine, Jesu nomen edicito."—*Serm. in Circ. D.*

[3] "Si quid petieritis Patrem in nomine meo, dabit vobis."—*John*, xvi. 23.

[4] "Quodcumque petieritis Patrem in nomine meo, hoc faciam."—*John*, xiv. 13.

and assaults of our enemies. For this reason the Messias was called *the Mighty God;*[1] and his name was called by the wise man a strong tower: *The name of the Lord is a strong tower;*[2] that we may know that he who avails himself of this powerful name will not fear all the assaults of hell. St. Paul writes thus: *Christ humbled Himself, becoming obedient unto death, even to the death of the cross.*[3] Jesus Christ during his life humbled himself in obeying his Father, even to die on the cross; which is as much as to say, as St. Anselm remarks, he humbled himself so much that he could humble himself no more;[4] and therefore his divine Father, as a reward for this humility and obedience of his Son, raised him to such a sublime dignity that he could have no higher: *For which cause God hath given Him a name which is above all names; that every knee should bow, of those that are in heaven, on earth, and under the earth.*[5] He has given him a name which is so great and powerful that it is venerated in heaven, on earth, and in hell. A name powerful in heaven, because it can obtain all graces for us; powerful on earth, because it can save all who invoke it with devotion; powerful in hell, because this name makes all the devils tremble. These rebel angles tremble at the sound of that most sacred name, because they remember that Jesus Christ was the Mighty One who destroyed the dominion and power they had before over man. They tremble, says St. Peter Chrysologus, because at that name they have to adore the whole majesty of God:

[1] "Fortis."—*Isa.* ix. 6.
[2] "Turris fortissima, nomen Domini."—*Prov.* xviii. 10.
[3] "Humiliavit semetipsum, factus obediens usque ad mortem, mortem autem crucis; propter quod et Deus exaltavit illum."—*Phil.* ii. 8.
[4] "Ipse se tantum humiliavit, ut ultra non posset; propter quod Deus tantum exaltavit, ut ultra non posset."
[5] "Et donavit illi nomen quod est super omne nomen, ut in nomine Jesu omne genu flectatur cœlestium, terrestrium, et infernorum."

Discourse on the Name of Jesus. 157

'In this name the whole majesty of God is adored."[1] Our Saviour himself said, that through this powerful name his disciples should cast out devils: *In My name they shall cast out devils.*[2] And, in fact, the Church in her exorcisms always makes use of this name in driving out the infernal spirits from those who are possessed. And priests who are assisting dying persons call to their aid the name of Jesus, to deliver them from the assaults of hell, which at that last moment are so terrible.

If we read the life of St. Bernardine of Sienna, we shall see how many sinners the saint converted, how many abuses he put an end to, and how many cities he sanctified, by trying when he preached to induce the people to invoke the name of Jesus. St. Peter says that there is no other name given to us by which we can find salvation but this ever-blessed name of Jesus: *For there is no other name under heaven given to men whereby we must be saved.*[3] Jesus is he who has not only saved us once for all, but he continually preserves us from the danger of sin, by his merits, each time we invoke him with confidence: *Whatsoever you shall ask the Father in My name, that will I do.*[4]

In temptations, then, I repeat with St. Laurence Justinian, "whether you are tempted by the devil, or are attacked by men, invoke the name of Jesus."[5] If the devils and men torment you and urge you to sin, call on Jesus, and you will be delivered; and if temptations do not cease to persecute you, continue to invoke Jesus,

---

[1] "In hoc nomine, Deitatis tota adoratur majestas."—*Serm.* 144.
[2] "In nomine meo dæmonia ejicient."—*Mark*, xvi. 17.
[3] "Nec enim aliud nomen est sub cœlo datum hominibus, in quo oporteat nos salvos fieri."—*Acts.* iv. 12.
[4] "Quodcumque petieritis Patrem in nomine meo, hoc faciam."—*John*, xiv. 13.
[5] "Si tentaris a diabolo, si ab hominibus opprimeris, Jesu nomen edicito."—*Serm. in Circ. D.*

and you will never fall. Those who practise this devotion have experienced that they keep themselves safe, and that they always come off victorious.

Let us always add also the name of Mary, which is likewise terrible to hell, and we shall always be secure. "This short prayer—Jesus and Mary—is easy to remember," says Thomas à Kempis, "and powerful to protect; is strong enough to deliver us from all the assaults of our enemies."[1]

III.

In the third place, the name of Jesus not only consoles us and preserves us from all evil, but it also inflames with holy love all those who pronounce it with devotion. The name of Jesus, that is, of Saviour, is a name which expresses in itself love, for it recalls to us how much Jesus Christ has done and suffered to save us. "The name of Jesus," says St. Bernard, "places before thee all that God has done for the salvation of the human race."[2] So that a pious author said, with all the affection of his heart "O my Jesus, how much did it cost Thee to be Jesus, that is, my Saviour!"[3]

St. Matthew writes, when speaking of the crucifixion of Jesus Christ, *And they put over His head His cause written: This is Jesus the King of the Jews.*[4] The eternal Father then so ordained that on the Cross on which our Redeemer died should be written, This is Jesus, the Saviour of the world. Pilate wrote this, not that he had judged him guilty because Jesus Christ took to himself the title of King; for Pilate made no account of this

[1] "Hæc sancta oratio, Jesu et Maria, brevis ad legendum, facilis ad tenendum, fortis ad protegendum."—*Vall. lil.* c. 13.

[2] "Omnia quæcumque Deus pro salute hominum ordinavit, in Jesu nomine comprehenduntur."—*T.* ii. s. 49.

[3] "O Jesu! quanti tibi constitit esse Jesum, Salvatorem meum!"

[4] "Et imposuerunt super caput ejus causam ipsius scriptam : 'Hic est Jesus, Rex Judæorum.'"

accusation: and at the same time that he condemned him he declared him innocent, and protested that he had no part in his death: *I am innocent of the blood of this just man.*[1] Why, then, did he give him the title of king? He wrote it by the will of God, who thereby wished to say to us men, Do you know why my innocent Son is dying? He is dying because he is your Saviour; this divine pastor dies on this infamous tree in order to save you, his sheep. Therefore it was said in the sacred Canticles, *His name is as oil poured out.*[2] St. Bernard explains this, saying, "that is, the effusion of the divinity."[3] In the redemption God himself, out of the love which he bore us, gave himself and communicated himself entirely to us: *He hath loved us, and hath delivered Himself for us.*[4] And, that he might be able to communicate himself to us, he took upon himself the burden of suffering the pains due by us. *He hath borne our infirmities, and carried our sorrows.*[5] By this title, says St. Cyril of Alexandria, he desired to cancel the original decree of condemnation which had already been passed against us poor sinners: "By this title affixed to his cross he blotted out the decree issued against the human race."[6] According to the word of the apostle, *Blotting out the handwriting of the decree that was against us.*[7] Our loving Redeemer wished to deliver us from the malediction we had deserved, by making himself the object of the divine curse in taking all our sins upon

---

[1] "Innocens ego sum a sanguine justi hujus."—*Matt.* xxvii. 24.
[2] "Oleum effusum nomen tuum."
[3] "Nempe effusio divinitatis."
[4] "Dilexit nos, et tradidit semetipsum pro nobis."—*Eph.* v. 2.
[5] "Languores nostros ipse tulit, et dolores nostros ipse portavit."—*Isa.* liii. 4.
[6] "Hoc adversus genus nostrum chirographum titulo in cruce confixo delevit."—*In Jo.* l. 12. c. 29.
[7] "Delens quod adversus nos erat chirographum decreti."—*Col.* ii. 14.

him : *Christ hath redeemed us from the curse of the law, being made a curse for us.*[1]

Therefore it is not possible for a soul that is faithful to pronounce the name of Jesus, and to remember all that he has done to save us, and not to be inflamed with love towards one who has loved us so much. " When I utter the name of Jesus," says St. Bernard, "I see before me a man of meekness, humility, kindness, and mercy, who at the same time is the Almighty God, who heals and strengthens me."[2] When we say Jesus, we should imagine to ourselves that we see a man, meek, benignant, kind, and full of all virtues ; and then we must think that he is our God, who, to cure our wounds, chose to be despised, wounded, and even to die of pure grief on a cross. St Anselm, therefore, exhorts all who call themselves Christians to cherish the beautiful name of Jesus, to have it always in their hearts, that it may be their only food, their only consolation. "Let Jesus be ever in thy heart. Let him be thy food, thy delight, thy consolation."[3] Ah, says St. Bernard, it is he alone who experiences it, that can know what sweetness, what a paradise even in this valley of tears, it is truly to love Jesus.[4]

" The love of Jesus, what it is,
None but his lov'd ones know."

Well did St. Rose of Lima know this happiness, from whose mouth came out such a burning flame of love,

[1] "Christus nos redemit de maledicto legis, factus pro nobis maledictum."—*Gal.* iii. 13.

[2] "Cum nomino Jesum, hominem mihi propono mitem, humilem, benignum, misericordem, omni sanctitate conspicuum eumdemque Deum omnipotentem, qui me sanet et roboret."—*In Cant.* s. 15.

[3] "Sit tibi Jesus semper in corde ; hic sit cibus, dulcedo et consolatio tua !"

[4] "Expertus potest credere quid sit Jesum diligere."—*Jub. de nom. Jesu.*

after she had received Holy Communion, that it burned the hands of those that gave her water (as was the custom) to drink after Communion. As also did St. Mary Magdalene of Pazzi, who, with a crucifix in her hand, cried out, burning with love, "O God of love! O God of love! even mad with love." And St. Philip Neri, whose ribs were forced out to give room for his heart, which was burning with divine love, to beat more freely. St. Stanislaus Kostka, who was obliged to have his breast bathed with cold water to mitigate the great ardor with which he was burning for the love of Jesus. St. Francis Xavier, who for the same cause unclosed his bosom, saying, " Lord, it is enough ; no more," in this way declaring himself unable to bear the great flame that was burning in his heart.

Let us also try as much as we can to keep Jesus in our hearts by loving him, and to keep him on our lips by often calling on him. St. Paul says that the name of Jesus cannot be pronounced (that is, with devotion) except by the operation of the Holy Spirit: *And no man can say the Lord Jesus but by the Holy Ghost.*[1] So that the Holy Spirit communicates himself to all those who devoutly pronounce the name of Jesus.

The name of Jesus is strange to some, and why is it ? Because they love not Jesus. The saints have always on their lips this name of salvation and love. There is not a page in all the epistles of St. Paul in which he does not name Jesus many times. St. John also names him often. The blessed Henry Suso, the more to increase his love for this holy name, one day, with a sharp iron, engraved the name of Jesus on his bosom over his heart ; and being all bathed in his blood, he said, Lord, I desire to write Thy name on my heart itself, but I cannot ; Thou who canst do everything, imprint, I pray Thee, Thy sweet

[1] "Nemo potest dicere : Dominus Jesus—nisi in Spiritu Sancto."
—1 *Cor.* xii. 3.

name on my heart, so that neither Thy name nor Thy love may ever be effaced from it. St. Jane of Chantal imprinted the name of Jesus on her heart with a hot iron.

Jesus Christ does not expect so much from us; he is satisfied if we keep him in our hearts by love, and if we often invoke him with affection. And as whatever he did and said during his life, he did it all for us, so it is but just that whatever we do, we should do it in the name of Jesus Christ, and for his love, as St. Paul exhorts us : *All whatsoever you do, in word or in work, all things do ye in the name of the Lord Jesus Christ.*[1] And if Jesus has died for us, we ought to be ready willingly to give our lives for the name of Jesus Christ, as the same apostle declared he was ready to do: *For I am ready, not only to be bound, but to die also in Jerusalem, for the name of the Lord Jesus.*[2]

Let us now come to the conclusion. If we are in affliction, let us invoke Jesus, and he will console us. If we are tempted, let us invoke Jesus, and he will give us strength to withstand all our enemies. If, lastly, we are in aridity, and are cold in divine love, let us invoke Jesus, and he will inflame our hearts. Happy are they who have this most tender and holy name always on their lips ! A name of peace, a name of hope, a name of salvation, and a name of love. And oh! happy shall we be if we are fortunate enough to die pronouncing the name of Jesus ! But if we desire to breathe out our last sigh with this sweet name on our tongue, we must accustom ourselves to repeat it often during our life.

Let us also always add the beautiful name of Mary, which is also a name given from heaven, and is a powerful name which makes hell tremble ; and is besides a

---

[1] "Omne quodcumque facitis in verbo aut in opere, omnia in nomine Domini Jesu Christi."—*Col.* iii. 17.

[2] " Ego enim, non solum alligari, sed et mori . . . paratus sum, propter nomen Domini Jesu."—*Acts*, xxi. 13.

Discourse on the Name of Jesus.

sweet name, in that it reminds us of that Queen who, being the Mother of God, is also our Mother, the Mother of mercy, the Mother of love.

Affections and Prayers.

Since, then, O my Jesus! Thou art the Saviour who hast given Thy blood and Thy life for me, I pray Thee to write Thy adorable name on my poor heart; so that having it always imprinted in my heart by love, I may also have it ever on my lips, by invoking it in all my necessities. If the devil tempts me, Thy name will give me strength to resist him; if I lose confidence, Thy name will animate me to hope; if I am in affliction, Thy name will comfort me, by reminding me of all Thou hast endured for me. If I find myself cold in Thy love, Thy name will inflame me by reminding me of the love Thou hast shown me. Hitherto I have fallen into so many sins, because I did not call on Thee; from henceforth Thy name shall be my defence, my refuge, my hope, my only consolation, my only love. Thus do I hope to live, and so do I hope to die, having Thy name always on my lips.

Most holy Virgin, obtain for me the grace of invoking the name of thy Son Jesus in all my necessities, together with thine own, my Mother Mary; but let me invoke them always with confidence and love, so that I may be able also to say to thee as did the devout Alphonsus Rodriguez: " Jesus and Mary, may I suffer for you; may I die for you; may I be wholly yours, and in nothing my own!"[1] O my beloved Jesus! O Mary, my beloved Lady! give me the grace to suffer and to die for your love. I will be no longer mine own, but altogether yours; yours in life, and yours in death, when I hope by your help to expire saying, Jesus and Mary, help me! Jesus and Mary, I recommend myself to you; Jesus and Mary, I love you, and I give and deliver up to you my whole soul.

[1] "Jesu et Maria! pro vobis patiar, pro vobis moriar; sim totus vester, sim nihil meus."

Examples of the Infant Jesus.

EXAMPLE I.

It is related in the *Flowery Meadow* that a devout lady wished to know what souls were the dearest to Jesus. One day, whilst she was hearing Mass, at the elevation of the Sacred Host, she saw the Infant Jesus on the altar, and with him three young virgins. Jesus took the first, and caressed her very much. He went to the second, and, having taken her veil off her face, he struck her severely on the cheek, and turned his back upon her; but soon after, seeing the child looking sorrowful, he comforted her with all sorts of kindness. At last he approached the third; he seized her by the arm as if he were angry, struck her, and drove her away from him; but the more she saw herself ill-used and driven off, the more the little virgin humbled herself and followed him: and thus the vision ended. This devout woman, remaining in the church with great desire to know what was the meaning of the vision, Jesus appeared to her again, and told her that there are on the earth three sorts of souls that love him. Some love him; but their love is so weak that if they are not coaxed by spiritual pleasures they become uneasy, and are in danger of turning their backs upon him; and of these the first virgin was a figure. The second represented those souls who love him with a less feeble love, but who require to be comforted from time to time. The third was a figure of those more courageous souls who, although constantly desolate, and deprived of spiritual consolations, do not cease doing all they can to please their Lord; and these,

Examples of the Infant Jesus. 165

he said, were the souls in which he took the greatest delight.

EXAMPLE II.

Father Cagnolio relates, from Father Patrignani, that after having committed a great many sins, a certain nun arrived at such an excess of crime that having one day communicated, she drew from her mouth the sacred particle, placed it in a handkerchief, and afterwards, having shut herself up in a cell, she threw the Blessed Sacrament on the ground, and began to trample it under her feet. But lo! she casts her eyes down, and what does she see? She sees the Sacred Host changed into the form of a beautiful Infant, but all bruised and covered with blood, who said to her, "And what have I done to thee, that thou treatest me so ill?" Upon which the wretched creature, full of contrition and repentance, threw herself on her knees in tears, and said to him, "O my God, dost Thou ask me what Thou hast done to me? Thou hast loved me too much." The vision disappeared, and the nun changed her whole life, and became a model of penance.

EXAMPLE III.

It is related in the chronicles of the Cistercians that a certain monk of Brabant, who was travelling on Christmas-night, as he passed through a forest, heard a cry as it were of a new-born infant. He approached the place whence he heard the cries, and saw a beautiful infant in the middle of the snow, who was crying and trembling with the cold. Moved to compassion, the monk immediately dismounted from his horse, and, approaching the infant, said: "O my child, how is it that thou art thus abandoned to weep and die in the midst of this snow?" And he heard a voice answer him: "Alas! how can I help crying, whilst I see myself thus abandoned by all, and that no one receives me or has compassion upon me?" And having said this, he disappeared, giving us to understand that he was our Redeemer, who by this vision meant to reprove the ingratitude of men, who, having seen him born for their sake in a stable, leave him to cry there without even pitying him.

EXAMPLE IV.

It is related by Bollandus that the most holy Mary appeared one day to the Blessed Coletta, whilst she was praying to her to intercede for sinners, and that she showed her her Infant Son all torn and cut to pieces, "My daughter," she said, "have compassion me and on my Son; behold how sinners treat him."

EXAMPLE V.

Pelbart relates that a certain soldier was full of vices; but he had a devout wife, who, not being able to reform him, recommended him at least not to omit saying every day a Hail Mary before some image of our Lady. One day, as he was going to commit sin, he passed by a church, which, by chance, he entered; and seeing an image of our Blessed Lady, he knelt down and said a Hail Mary; and what did he then see? he saw the Infant Jesus in the arms of Mary all covered with bleeding wounds. Upon which he said, "O God, what barbarian has thus ill-treated this innocent babe?" "It is you, sinner," answered Mary: "it is you who thus ill-use my Son." Then, full of contrition, he begged her to obtain for him pardon, calling her Mother of Mercy. She replied, "You sinners call me Mother of Mercy, but you do not cease to make me a mother of sorrows and of misery." But the penitent did not lose courage, and continued to pray to Mary to intercede for him. The Blessed Virgin turned to her Son, and asked him to

Examples of the Infant Jesus. 167

pardon this sinner. Her Son seemed reluctant to do so; but then Mary said to him, "O my Son, I will not leave Thy feet if Thou dost not forgive this afflicted man, who has recommended himself to me." Then Jesus said to her: "O my Mother, I never have refused you anything; do you desire the pardon of this sinner? let him be pardoned; and in token of the pardon which I grant him, I desire that he should come and kiss my wounds." The sinner went up to the image, drew near, and whilst he was kissing them, the wounds were closed. Immediately on leaving the church, he asks pardon of his wife, and with mutual consent they both left the world, and became religious in two monasteries at the same time, and ended their lives by a holy death.

EXAMPLE VI.

It is mentioned in the life of Brother Benedict Lopez that while he remained in the army he led a life stained with sins. One day he entered a church in Travancor, and saw an image of Mary with the Infant Jesus. Our Lord placed before his eyes his abandoned life. At the sight of his sins he almost despaired of pardon; but turning to Mary, with tears in his eyes, he commended himself to her; and he then perceived that the Holy Infant also was weeping, and that his tears were falling on the altar; so much so that it was observed by others, who hastened to collect them in a cloth. Soon after this, Benedict, full of contrition, forsook the world, and became a lay-brother in the Society of Jesus, in which he lived and died with the greatest devotion to the Sacred Infancy of Jesus Christ.

EXAMPLE VII.

Father Patrignani relates that there was in Messina a youth of noble birth called Dominic Ansalone, who was in the habit of going often to a certain church to visit an

Examples of the Infant Jesus.

image of Mary holding in her arms the Infant Jesus, of which he became quite enamoured. Now, it happened that when Dominic lay at the point of death he implored his parents with great earnestness to bring the image of the beloved Child into his room. His wishes were satisfied; full of delight, he placed it on his bed, and looking at it in the most loving manner, and now and then turning to the Infant, he said, " My Jesus, have pity on me !" then turning to the bystanders, " Behold," he said, "behold how beautiful is my little Saviour !" On the last night of his life he called his parents, and in their presence he first said to the Holy Infant, " My Jesus, I leave Thee my heir !" And then he begged his father and mother to employ a certain small sum of money which he had, in having nine Masses celebrated after his death, and with the rest to make a handsome robe for his Infant heir. Before he died, he raised his eyes to heaven with a look of joy, and said, "Oh, how beautiful !—how beautiful is my Lord !" and saying this, he expired.

EXAMPLE VIII.

It is related in the *Mirror of Examples* of a certain devout English boy, named Edmund,* that being one day

* This happy young man is no other than St. Edmund, Archbishop of Canterbury, as we may see in his life by Surius, November 16.

We may here add a more recent example, which we read in the Life of the Venerable Brother Gerard Majella, of the Congregation of the Most Holy Redeemer, by Father Tannoia. Animated with fervent piety already in his infancy, he loved to visit a church in which was honored the mother of God holding the Infant Jesus in her arms. While Gerard was one day entering the church the divine Infant came to meet him and offered him a piece of white bread—a symbol of the gift that he was soon to give him in the most adorable sacrament of the Eucharist. Gerard, attracted by the sweet charms of the Infant Saviour, went often to the same church, and Jesus very frequently bestowed upon him the same favor.

Later on he entered the service of a master who was extremely

Examples of the Infant Jesus. 169

in the country with other children, as he was fond of prayer and solitude, he separated himself from them, and walked alone in a meadow, entertaining himself in devout aspirations and affections towards Jesus Christ. Behold, a beautiful Infant appeared to him, and saluted him with, "God bless you, My dear Edmund!" And then he asked him whether he knew who he was? Edmund answered that he did not. "What dost thou mean by not knowing me?" replied the heavenly Infant, "when I am always at thy side. If, then, thou desirest to know me, look at my forehead." Edmund looked and read on his forehead these words: "Jesus of Nazareth, the King of the Jews." The Child then added, "This is my name; and I desire that in remembrance of the love I bear thee, thou shouldst every night sign thy forehead with this name, and it shall deliver thee from sudden death; as it will also deliver every one who shall do the same." Edmund ever after signed himself with the name of Jesus. On one occasion the devil seized his hands, in order to prevent him from doing so; but he conquered him by prayer, and then constrained him to tell him what was the weapon which he most feared; the devil replied that it was those words with which he signed his forehead.

EXAMPLE IX.

Father Nadasi relates that the devotion of sending about the image of the Infant Jesus to the nuns, each

harsh and who omitted no opportunity to try Gerard's heroic patience. A key was one day accidentally dropped into a well. Foreseeing the trouble and the irritation that this accident would cause his master, and the sins that would be the result, Gerard, full of confidence, took a small statue of the Infant Jesus, lowered it into the well by means of a cord, and said, "You must see to it that my master does not become impatient." When he had drawn up the statue in the presence of a large number of people, it was holding the key in its hands.—ED.

one having it one day, having been introduced into a monastery, one of these virgins whose turn it was, after having spent a long time in prayer, at the close of evening took the image and shut it up in a little closet. But she had hardly lain down to sleep when she heard the Holy Infant knocking at the door of the closet; she therefore got out of bed, and, having replaced the image on her little altar, she prayed again for a very long time. She then shut it up again, but the Infant again knocked; again she took it out and prayed. At last, weary with sleep, she went and rested herself on the bed, and slept till daybreak; and on awakening she blessed this night that had been passed in holy conversation with her Beloved.

EXAMPLE X.

It is related in the *Dominican Diary* for the 7th October, that when St Dominic was preaching at Rome there was there a sinner called the beautiful Catharine. She received a Rosary from the hands of the saint, and began to recite it; but she did not leave off her wicked course of life. One day Jesus appeared to her; first, in the shape of a young man, and afterwards the figure changed itself into that of a beautiful Infant, but with a crown of thorns upon his head and a cross on his shoulders, tears flowing from his eyes and blood from his body. He then said to her, It is enough; no more, Catharine; it is enough, do not offend me any more: see how much thou hast cost me since I began as an Infant to suffer for thee, and never left off suffering till my death. Catharine thereupon went immediately in search of St. Dominic, confessed to him, and, instructed by him, after having given all she had to the poor, and having shut herself up in a narrow cell, led a life of such fervor, and received such graces from the Lord, that the saint was struck with admiration. And at last, having been visited by most holy Mary, she died a most happy death.

EXAMPLE XI.

The Venerable Sister Jane of Jesus and Mary, a Franciscan, whilst she was one day meditating on the Infant Jesus being persecuted by Herod, heard a great noise as of armed men pursuing some one, and then saw before her a beautiful boy looking much distressed, who seemed to be running away, and who said to her: "O Jane, help me and save me; I am Jesus of Nazareth; I am flying from sinners, who want to take my life away, and persecute me worse than Herod; do you save me."

EXAMPLE XII.

It is related in the life of Father Zucchi of the Society of Jesus, who was most devout to the Infant Jesus, and whose image he used in order to gain many souls to God, that one day he gave one of these little images to a lady, who, though perfectly innocent and good in her habits, yet was very far from having the idea of becoming a nun. The young lady accepted the gift; but smiling she said to him, What have I to do with this Infant? He answered, Nothing, but to put it on the spinet, on which you so frequently play. She did so; and having constantly this image before her eyes, she could not avoid often looking at it, and from looking at it she began to feel a small touch of devotion. Then she was inflamed with a desire to become better; so that the spinet was rather an occasion to her of prayer than of amusement. At last she resolved to leave the world and become a religious. Then, full of joy, she went and related to Father Zucchi that the Infant had drawn her to his love; and, disengaging her affections from earthly things, had taken entire possession of them himself. She became a religious, and gave herself up to a life of perfection.

Meditations for Every Day of Advent.

MEDITATION I.

FIRST SUNDAY.

Goodness of God in the Work of the Redemption.

Et incarnatus est de Spiritu Sancto. . . . Et homo factus est

"And was incarnate of the Holy Ghost, and was made man."—*Symbol. Const.*

Consider that God, having created the first man, in order that he might serve him and love him in this life, and be conducted afterwards to reign with him forever in Paradise, enriched him for this end with knowledge and grace. But ungrateful man rebelled against God, refusing him the obedience which he owed him in justice and gratitude; and thus, miserable sinner, was he left with all his posterity as a rebel, deprived of divine grace, and forever excluded from paradise. Behold, then, after this ruin, caused by sin, all men lost! All were living in blindness, or in the darkness of the shadow of death. The devil had dominion over them, and hell destroyed innumerable victims amongst them.

But God, seeing men reduced to this miserable state, was moved with pity, and resolved to save them. And how? He did not send an angel, a seraph; but to show to the world the immense love that he bore to these ungrateful worms, *He sent His own Son in the likeness of sinful flesh.*[1] He sent his own Son to become man, and to clothe himself with the same flesh as sinful men, in order

---

[1] "Deus Filium suum mittens in similitudinem carnis peccati."— *Rom.* viii. 3.

that, by his suffering and death, he might satisfy the divine justice for their crimes, and thus deliver them from eternal death; and, reconciling them with his divine Father, might obtain for them divine grace, and might render them worthy to enter into life eternal.

Consider, on the one hand, the immense ruin that sin brings upon souls, as it deprives them of the friendship of God and of Paradise, and condemns them to an eternity of pain. And, on the other hand, consider the infinite love which God showed in this great work of the incarnation of the Word, causing his only-begotten Son to sacrifice his divine life by the hands of executioners on a cross, in a sea of sorrows and of infamy, to obtain for us pardon and life eternal. Oh, in contemplating this great mystery and this excess of divine love, how can we do otherwise than exclaim: O infinite goodness! O infinite mercy! O infinite love! for a God to become man, and to die for me!

Affections and Prayers.

But how is it my Jesus, that after Thou hast repaired this ruin of sin by Thy own death, I have so often wilfully renewed it again by the many offences I have committed against Thee? Thou hast saved me at so great a cost, and I have so often chosen to damn myself, in losing Thee, O infinite Good! But what Thou hast said gives me confidence that when the sinner who has turned his back upon Thee is converted to Thee, Thou wilt not refuse to embrace him: *Turn ye to Me, and I will turn to you.*[1] Thou hast also said, *If any man shall . . . open to Me the door, I will come in to him.*[2] Behold, Lord, I am one of these rebels, an ungrateful traitor, who have often turned my back upon Thee, and driven Thee from my soul; but now I repent with all my heart for having thus ill-used Thee and despised Thy grace; I repent of it, and love Thee above every-

[1] "Convertimini ad me . . . , et convertar ad vos."—*Zach.* i. 3.
[2] "Si quis . . . aperuerit mihi januam, introibo ad illum."—*Apoc.* iii. 20.

thing. Behold, the door of my heart is already open; enter Thou, but enter never to leave it again. I know well that Thou wilt never leave me, if I do not again drive Thee away; but this is my fear, and this is the grace which I ask of Thee, and which I hope always to ask; let me die rather than be guilty of this fresh and still greater ingratitude. My dearest Redeemer, I do not deserve to love Thee, after all the offences that I have committed against Thee; but for Thy own merits' sake I ask of Thee the gift of Thy holy love, and therefore I beseech Thee make me know the great good Thou art, the love Thou hast borne me, and how much Thou hast done to oblige me to love Thee. Ah, my God and Saviour, let me no longer live ungrateful to Thy great goodness. My Jesus, I will never leave Thee again; I have already offended Thee enough. It is only right that I should employ the remaining years of my life in loving Thee and pleasing Thee. My Jesus, my Jesus, help me; help a sinner that wishes to love Thee. O Mary, my Mother, thou hast all power with Jesus, seeing thou art his Mother; beg of him to forgive me; beg of him to enchain me with his holy love. Thou art my hope; in thee do I confide.

MEDITATION II.

FIRST MONDAY.

Grandeur of the Mystery of Incarnation.

Et verbum caro factum est.

"And the Word was made flesh."—*St. John*, i. 14.

Our Lord sent St. Augustine to write upon the heart of St. Mary Magdalene of Pazzi the words, *And the Word was made flesh.* Oh, let us also pray the Lord to enlighten our minds, and to make us understand what an excess and what a miracle of love this is, that the eternal Word, the Son of God, should have become man for the love of us.

The holy Church is struck with awe at the contemplation of this great mystery: *I considered Thy works and was*

First Monday of Advent.

afraid.[1] If God had created a thousand other worlds, a thousand times greater and more beautiful than the present, it is certain that this work would be infinitely less grand than the incarnation of the Word: *He hath showed might in His arm.*[2] To execute the great work of the Incarnation, it required all the omnipotence and infinite wisdom of God, in order to unite human nature to a divine person, and that a divine person should so humble himself as to take upon him human nature. Thus God became man, and man became God; and hence, the divinity of the Word being united to the soul and body of Jesus Christ, all the actions of this Man-God became divine: his prayers were divine, his sufferings divine, his infant cries divine, his tears divine, his steps divine, his members divine, his very blood divine, which became, as it were, a fountain of health to wash out all our sins, and a sacrifice of infinite value to appease the justice of the Father, who was justly offended with men.

And who, then, are these men? Miserable, ungrateful, and rebellious creatures. And yet for these God becomes man; subjects himself to human miseries; suffers and dies to save these unworthy sinners: *He humbled Himself, becoming obedient unto death, even to the death of the cross.*[3] O holy faith! If faith did not assure us of it, who would believe that a God of infinite majesty should abase himself so far as to become a worm like us, in order to save us at the cost of so much suffering and disgrace, and of so cruel and shameful a death?

"O grace! O power of love!"[4] cries St. Bernard. O grace, which men could not even have imagined, if God himself had not thought of granting it to us! O divine

---

[1] "Consideravi opera tua et expavi."—*In Circ. Dom. resp.* 6.
[2] "Fecit potentiam in brachio suo."
[3] "Humiliavit semetipsum, factus obediens usque ad mortem, mortem autem crucis!"—*Phil.* ii. 8.
[4] "O gratiam, O amoris vim!"

love, which can never be fathomed! O mercy! O infinite charity, worthy only of an infinite bounty!

Affections and Prayers.

O soul, O body, O blood of my Jesus! I adore you and thank you; you are my hope; you are the price paid to save me from hell, which I have so often merited. O my God! what a miserable and hopeless life would await me in eternity, if Thou, my Redeemer, hadst not thought of saving me by Thy sufferings and death! But how is it that souls, redeemed by Thee with so much love, knowing all this, can live without loving Thee, and can despise the grace which Thou hast acquired for them with so much suffering? And did not I also know all this? How, then, could I offend Thee, and offend Thee so often? But, I repeat it, Thy blood is my hope. I acknowledge, my Saviour, the great injuries that I have done to Thee. Oh that I had rather died a thousand times! Oh that I had always loved Thee! But I thank Thee that Thou yet givest me time to do so. I hope in the time that remains to me in this life, and for all eternity, to sing forever Thy praises for the mercies Thou hast shown me. I have deserved, on account of my sins, to be more and more in darkness; but Thou hast given me more and more light. I deserved that Thou shouldst abandon me; but Thou, with calls still more loving, didst come to me and seek me. I deserved that my soul should remain more hardened; but Thou hast softened and touched it with compunction, so that by Thy grace I now feel great sorrow for the offences that I have committed against Thee; I feel within me an ardent desire of loving Thee; I feel fully resolved to lose everything rather than Thy friendship; I feel a love towards Thee that makes me abhor everything that displeases Thee. And this sorrow, this desire, this resolution, and this love, who is it that gives them to me? It is Thou, O Lord, in Thy great mercy. Therefore, my Jesus, this is a proof that Thou hast pardoned me; it is a proof that Thou now lovest me, and that Thou willest me at all costs to be saved; Thou willest that I should be saved, and I will save myself principally to give Thee pleasure. Thou lovest me, and I also love Thee; but my love is but little. Oh, give me more love; Thou deservest more love from me, for I have received from Thee more special favors than others; I pray Thee, do Thou increase the flames of my love. Most holy Mary, obtain for me that the love of Jesus may consume and destroy in me every affection that has not God for its object. Thou dost listen to the prayers of all that call on thee; listen to me also, obtain for me love and perseverance.

MEDITATION III.

FIRST TUESDAY.

The Love of God for Men.

Sic Deus dilexit mundum, ut Filium suum unigenitum daret.
" God so loved the world as to give His only-begotten Son."—*St. John*, iii. 16.

Consider that the eternal Father, in giving us his Son for a Redeemer, for victim and price of our ransom, could not have given us stronger motives for hope and love, to inspire us with confidence, and to oblige us to love him. In giving us his Son (says St. Augustine), he could give us nothing more. He desires that we should avail ourselves of this immense gift in order to gain for ourselves eternal salvation, and every grace that we want; whilst in Jesus we find all that we can desire ; we find light, strength, peace, confidence, love, and eternal glory; for Jesus Christ is a gift which contains all the gifts that we can seek for or desire.

How hath He not also, with Him, given us all things?[1] God having given us his beloved only-begotten Son, who is the fountain and treasure of all good, who need fear that he should deny us any favor that we ask of him? *Christ Jesus is of God made unto us wisdom, and justice, and sanctification, and redemption.*[2] God hath given him to us in order that he might be to us ignorant and blind crea-

[1] "Quomodo non etiam cum illo omnia nobis donavit?"—*Rom.* viii. 32.
[2] "Qui factus est nobis sapientia a Deo, et justitia, et sanctificatio et redemptio,"—1 *Cor.* i. 30.

tures light and wisdom, wherewith to walk in the way of salvation; in order that to us who are deserving of hell he might be justice, enabling us to aspire to paradise; that to us sinners he might be sanctification, to obtain for us holiness; that, finally, to us slaves of the devil he might be a ransom to purchase for us the liberty of the sons of God. In short, the Apostle says that with Jesus Christ we have been enriched with every good gift and every grace, if we ask it through his merits: *In all things you are made rich in Him, . . . so that nothing is wanting to you in any grace.*[1]

And this gift which God has made us of his Son is a gift to each one of us; for he hath given him entirely to each of us, as if he had given him to each one alone, so that every one of us may say: Jesus is all mine; his body is mine; his blood is mine; his life is mine; his sorrows, his death, his merits, are all mine. Wherefore St. Paul said, *He loved me and delivered Himself for me.*[2] And every one may say the same thing: "My Redeemer has loved me; and for the love that he bore me he hath given himself entirely to me."

Affections and Prayers.

O eternal God! who could ever have given us this treasure of infinite value, but Thou, who art a God of infinite love? O my Creator, what more couldst Thou have done to give us confidence in Thy mercy, and to put us under an obligation of loving Thee? O Lord, I have repaid Thee with ingratitude; but Thou hast said, *To them that love God all things work together unto good.*[3] Therefore, notwithstanding the great number and the enormity of my sins, I will not despair of Thy bounty; rather let my transgressions serve to humble me the more whenever I meet with any insult; other insults and humi-

[1] "In omnibus divites facti estis in illo . . . ita ut nihil vobis desit in ulla gratia."—1 *Cor.* i. 5.
[2] "Dilexit me, et tradidit semetipsum pro me."—*Gal.* ii. 20.
[3] "Diligentibus Deum omnia cooperantur in bonum."—*Rom.* viii. 28.

liations does he deserve who has had the temerity to offend Thy divine majesty. I wish that my sins may serve to reconcile me the more to the crosses which Thou shalt send me, that I may be more diligent to serve and honor Thee, in order to compensate for the injuries I have committed against Thee. O my God! I will always remember the displeasure I have caused Thee, in order that I may the more exalt Thy mercy, and be inflamed with love for Thee, who hast brought me back when I was flying from Thee, and who hast done me so much good after I had behaved so ill to Thee. I trust, O Lord! that Thou hast already forgiven me. I repent, and will always repent, of the outrages I have committed against Thee. I will endeavor to please Thee by making compensation by my love for the ingratitude I have shown Thee; but I depend upon Thee to help me; from Thee I hope to obtain the grace to fulfil this my desire. O my God! for Thy Glory's sake, vouchsafe to grant that, as I have offended Thee much, I may also love Thee much. My God, my God, how can I ever leave off loving Thee, and separate myself again from Thy love! O Mary, my queen! do thou assist me; thou knowest my weakness; grant that I may have recourse to thee whenever the devil tries to separate me from God. My Mother, my hope, do thou help me.

MEDITATION IV.

FIRST WEDNESDAY.

The Word was made Man in the Fulness of Time.

Ubi venit plenitudo temporis misit Deus Filium suum.
" When the fulness of time was come, God sent His Son."—*Gal.* iv. 4.

Consider that God allowed four thousand years to pass, after the transgression of Adam, before he sent his Son upon earth to redeem the world. And in the mean time, oh, what fatal darkness reigned upon the earth! The true God was not known or adored, except in one small corner of the world. Idolatry reigned everywhere; so that devils and beasts and stones were adored as gods.

But let us admire in this the divine Wisdom : he deferred the coming of the Redeemer in order to render his advent more welcome to man, in order that the malice of sin might be better known, as well as the necessity of a remedy and the grace of the Saviour. If Jesus Christ had come into the world immediately after the fall of Adam, the greatness of this favor would have been but slightly appreciated. Let us therefore thank the goodness of God for having sent us into the world after the great work of redemption was accomplished. Behold, the happy time is come which was called the fulness of time : *When the fulness of time was come, God sent his Son, . . . that he might redeem them that were under the law.*[1]

It is called *fulness*, on account of the fulness of grace which the Son of God came to communicate to men by the redemption of the world. Behold the angel who is sent as ambassador into the town of Nazareth to announce to the Virgin Mary the coming of the Word, who desires to become incarnate in her womb. The angel salutes her, calls her full of grace and blessed among women. The humble Virgin, chosen to be the Mother of the Son of God, is troubled at these praises on account of her great humility : but the angel encourages her, and tells her that she has found grace with God; that is to say, that grace which brought peace between God and man, and the reparation of the ruin caused by sin. He then tells her that she must give her Son the name of Saviour : *Thou shalt call his name Jesus;*[2]—and that this her Son is the very Son of God, who is to redeem the world, and thus to reign over the hearts of men. Behold, at last Mary consents to be the Mother of such a Son : *Be it unto me according to Thy word.*[3] And the

[1] "Ubi venit plenitudo temporis, misit Deus Filium suum . . ut eos, qui sub lege erant, redimeret."
[2] "Vocabis nomen ejus Jesum."—*Luke*, i. 31.
[3] " Fiat mihi secundum verbum tuum."

First Wednesday of Advent.

eternal Word takes flesh and becomes man : *And the Word was made flesh.*[1]

Let us thank this Son, and let us also thank his Mother, who, in consenting to be the mother of such a Son, consented also to be the Mother of our salvation, and Mother also of sorrows, accepting at that time the deep abyss of sorrows that it would cost her to be the Mother of a Son who was to come into the world to suffer and die for man.

Affections and Prayers.

O divine Word, become man for me, though I behold Thee thus humbled and become a little infant in the womb of Mary, yet I confess and acknowledge Thee for my Lord and King, but a king of love. My dearest Saviour, since Thou hast come down upon earth and clothed Thyself with our miserable flesh, in order to reign over our hearts, I beseech Thee come and establish Thy reign in my heart also, which was once, alas, ruled over by Thine enemies, but is now, I hope, Thine, as I desire that it may be always Thine, and that from this day forth Thou mayest be its only Lord : *Rule Thou in the midst of Thy enemies.*[2] Other kings reign by the strength of arms, but Thou comest to reign by the power of love ; and therefore Thou dost not come with regal pomp, nor clothed in purple and gold, nor adorned with sceptre and crown, nor surrounded by armies of soldiers. Thou comest into the world to be born in a stable,—poor, forsaken, placed in a manger on a little straw, because thus Thou wouldst begin to reign in our hearts. Ah, my infant King, how could I so often rebel against Thee, and live so long Thy enemy, deprived of Thy grace, when, to oblige me to love Thee, Thou hast put off Thy divine majesty, and hast humbled Thyself even to appearing, first, as a babe in a cave ; then as a servant in a shop ; then as a criminal on a cross ? Oh, happy me, if, now that I have been freed (as I hope) from the slavery of Satan, I allow myself forever to be governed by Thee and by Thy love ! O Jesus, my King, who art so amiable and so loving to our

---

[1] " Et Verbum caro factum est."
[2] " Dominare in medio inimicorum tuorum."—*Ps.* cix. 2.

souls, take possession, I pray Thee, of mine; I give it entirely to Thee; accept it, that it may serve Thee forever, but serve Thee only for love. Thy majesty deserves to be feared, but Thy goodness still more deserves to be loved. Thou art my King, and shalt be always the only object of my love; and the only fear I shall have will be the fear of displeasing Thee. This is what I hope. Do Thou help me with Thy grace. O Mary, our dear Lady! it is for thee to obtain for me that I may be faithful to this beloved King of my soul.

MEDITATION V.

First Thursday.

The Abasement of Jesus.

Formam servi accipiens.

" Taking the form of a servant."—*Phil.* ii. 7.

The eternal Word descends on earth to save man; and whence does he descend ? *His going out is from the end of heaven.*[1] He descends from the bosom of his divine Father, where from eternity he was begotten in the brightness of the saints. And where does he descend ? He descends into the womb of a Virgin, a child of Adam, which in comparison with the bosom of God is an object of horror; wherefore the Church sings, " Thou didst not abhor the Virgin's womb."[2] Yes, because the Word being in the bosom of the Father is God like the Father, —is immense, omnipotent, most blessed and supreme Lord, and equal in everything to the Father. But in the womb of Mary he is a creature, small, weak, afflicted, a servant inferior to the Father, *taking the form of a servant.*[3]

It is related as a great prodigy of humility in St Alexis that, although he was the son of a Roman gentle-

---

[1] " A summo cœlo egressio ejus."—*Ps.* xviii. 7.
[2] " Non horruisti virginis uterum."
[3] " Formam servi accipiens."—*Phil.* ii. 7.

man, he chose to live as a servant in his father's house. But how is the humility of this saint to be compared with the humility of Jesus Christ? Between the son and the servant of the father of St. Alexis there was, it is true, some difference; but between God and the servant of God there is an infinite difference. Besides, this Son of God having become the servant of his Father, in obedience to him, made himself also the servant of his creatures, that is to say, of Mary and Joseph: *And he was subject to them.*[1] Moreover, he made himself even a servant of Pilate, who condemned him to death, and he was obedient to him and accepted it; he became a servant to the executioners, who scourged him, crowned him with thorns, and crucified him; and he humbly obeyed them all, and yielded himself into their hands.

O God! and shall we, after this, refuse to submit ourselves to the service of so loving a Saviour, who, to save us, has subjected himself to such painful and degrading slavery? And rather than be the servants of this great and so loving a Lord, shall we be content to be slaves of the devil, who does not love his servants, but hates them and treats them like a tyrant, making them miserable and wretched in this world and in the next? But if we have been guilty of this great folly, why do we not quickly give up this unhappy servitude? Courage, then, since we have been delivered by Jesus Christ from the slavery of hell; let us now embrace and bind around us with love those sweet chains, which will render us servants and lovers of Jesus Christ, and hereafter obtain for us the crown of the eternal kingdom amongst the blessed in Paradise.

Affections and Prayers.

My beloved Jesus, Thou art the Sovereign of heaven and earth; but for the love of me Thou hast made Thyself a servant

---

[1] "Et erat subditus illis."—*Luke* ii. 51.

even of the executioners who tore Thy flesh, pierced Thy head, and finally left Thee nailed on the cross to die of sorrow. I adore Thee as my God and Lord, and I am ashamed to appear before Thee, when I remember how often, for the sake of some miserable pleasure, I have broken Thy holy bonds, and have told Thee to Thy face that I would not serve Thee. Ah, Thou mayst justly reproach me: *Thou hast burst my bands, and thou saidst: I will not serve.*[1] But still, O my Saviour, Thy merits and Thy goodness, which cannot despise a heart that repents and humbles itself, give me courage to hope for pardon: *A contrite and humble heart, O God, Thou wilt not despise.*[2] I confess, my Jesus, that I have offended Thee greatly; I confess that I deserve a thousand hells for the sins I have committed against Thee; chasten me as Thou seest fit, but do not deprive me of Thy grace and love. I repent above every other evil of having despised Thee. I love Thee with my whole heart. I propose from this day forth to desire to serve Thee and love Thee alone. I pray Thee bind me by Thy merits with the chains of Thy holy love, and never suffer that I see myself released from them again. I love Thee above everything, O my deliverer; and I would prefer being Thy servant to being master of the whole world. And of what avail would all the world be to him who lives deprived of Thy grace? "My sweetest Jesus, permit me not to separate myself from Thee, permit me not to separate myself from Thee."[3] This grace I ask of Thee, and I intend always to ask it; and I beg of Thee to grant me this day the grace to repeat continually to the end of my life this prayer: My Jesus, grant that I may never again separate myself from Thy love. I ask this favor of thee also, O Mary, my Mother: help me by thy intercession, that I may never separate myself again from my God.

[1] " Rupisti vincula mea, et dixisti : Non serviam."—*Jer.* ii. 20.
[2] " Cor contritum et humiliatum, Deus, non despicies."—*Isa.* l. 19.
[3] " Jesu dulcissime! ne permittas me seperari a te ; ne permittas me seperari a te."

MEDITATION VI.

FIRST FRIDAY.

Jesus enlightens the World and glorifies God.

Creavit Dominus novum super terram.
" The Lord hath created a new thing upon the earth."—*Jer.* xxxi. 22.

Before the coming of the Messias the world was buried in a dark night of ignorance and sins. The true God was hardly known, save in one single corner of the earth, that is to say, in Judea alone: *In Judea God is known.*[1] But everywhere else men adored as gods devils, beasts, and stones. Everywhere there reigned the night of sin, which blinds souls, and fills them with vices, and hides from them the sight of the miserable state in which they are living, as enemies of God and condemned to hell: *Thou hast appointed darkness, and it is night; in it shall all the beasts of the wood go about.*[2]

From this darkness Jesus came to deliver the world: *To them that dwelt in the region of the shadow of death, light is risen.*[3] He delivered it from idolatry by making known to them the light of the true God; and he delivered them from sin by the light of his doctrine and of his divine example: *For this purpose the Son of God appeared that He might destroy the works of the devil.*[4] The prophet Jeremias foretold that God should create a new child to be the Redeemer of men: *The Lord hath created a new thing upon the earth.*[5] This new child was Jesus Christ. He is

---

[1] "Notus in Judæa Deus."—*Ps.* lxxv. 2.

[2] "Posuisti tenebras et facta est nox ; in ipsa pertransibunt omnes bestiæ silvæ."—*Ps.* ciii. 20.

[3] "Habitantibus in regione umbræ mortis, lux orta est eis."—*Isa.* ix. 2.

[4] "In hoc apparuit Filius Dei, ut dissolvat opera diaboli."—1 *John,* iii. 8.

[5] "Creavit Dominus novum super terram.'

the Son of God, who is the object of the love of all the saints in paradise, and is the love of the Father himself, who thus speaks of him: *This is my beloved Son, in whom I am well pleased.*[1] And this Son is he who made himself man. A new child, because he has given more glory and honor to God in the first moment of his creation than all the angels and saints together have given him, or shall give him for all eternity. And therefore did the angels at the birth of Jesus sing, *Glory to God in the highest.*[2] The child Jesus has rendered more glory to God than all the sins of men have deprived him of.

Let us therefore, poor sinners, take courage ; let us offer to the eternal Father this Infant; let us present to him the tears, the obedience, the humility, the death, and the merits of Jesus Christ, and we shall make compensation to God for all the dishonor that we have caused him by our offences.

Affections and Prayers.

My eternal God, I have dishonored Thee by so often preferring my will to Thine, and my vile and miserable pleasures to Thy holy grace. What hope of pardon would there be for me, if Thou hadst not given me Jesus Christ on purpose that he might be the hope of us miserable sinners ? *He is a propitiation for our sins.*[3] Yes ; for Jesus Christ, in sacrificing his life in satisfaction for the injuries we have done Thee, has given Thee more honor than we have dishonor by our sins. Receive me, therefore, O my Father, for the love of Jesus Christ. I repent, O infinite Goodness, of having outraged Thee: *Father, I have sinned against heaven, and before Thee: I am not worthy to be called Thy son.*[4] I am not worthy of forgiveness; but Jesus

---

[1] " Hic est Filius meus dilectus, in quo mihi bene complacui."— *Matt.* xvii. 5.

[2] " Gloria in altissimis Deo."—*Luke*, ii. 14.

[3] " Ipse est propitiatio pro peccatis nostris."—1 *John*, ii. 2.

[4] "Pater ! peccavi in cœlum et coram te; jam non sum dignus vocari filius tuus."—*Luke*, xv. 21.

Christ is worthy to be heard favorably by Thee. He prayed once for me on the cross, *Father, forgive*;[1] and even now in heaven he is constantly begging Thee to receive me as a son: *We have an advocate, Jesus Christ, who ever intercedes for us.*[2] Receive an ungrateful son, who once forsook Thee, but now returns, resolved to desire to love Thee. Yes, my Father, I love Thee, and will always love Thee. O my Father, now that I know the love that Thou hast borne me, and the patience Thou hast shown me for for so many years, I trust no longer to live without loving Thee. Give me a great love, that may make me constantly lament the displeasure I have given Thee, who art so good a Father; cause me ever to burn with love towards Thee, who art so loving a Father. My Father, I love Thee, I love Thee, I love Thee! O Mary! God is my Father, and thou art my mother. Thou canst do all things with God; help me; obtain for me holy perseverance and his holy love.

MEDITATION VII.

FIRST SATURDAY.

The Son of God was laden with all our Iniquities.

Deus Filium suum mittens in similitudinem carnis peccati, et de peccato damnavit peccatum in carne.

" God sending His own Son, in the likeness of sinful flesh, even of sin, condemned sin in the flesh."--*Rom.* viii. 3.

Consider the humble state to which the Son of God chose to abase himself; he not only vouchsafed to take upon him the form of a servant, but that of a sinful servant: *In the likeness of sinful flesh.*[3] Therefore St. Bernard writes: "He not only assumed the form of a servant, that he might be under subjection, but even that of a wicked servant, that he might be beaten."[4] He not only would assume the condition of a servant to be subject

---

[1] "Pater! dimitte illis."—*Luke,* xxiii. 34.
[2] "Interpellat pro nobis."—*Rom.* viii. 34.
[3] " In similitudinem carnis peccati."
[4] "Non solum formam servi accepit, ut subesset, sed etiam mali servi, ut vapularet."—*Serm. de Pass.*

to others, he who was Lord of all; but even the appearance of a criminal servant, to be punished as a malefactor, he who was the Saint of all saints. For this end he clothed himself with the same flesh of Adam which had been infected by sin. And although he did not contract the stain of sin, nevertheless he took upon himself all the miseries which human nature had contracted as a penalty for sin.

Our Redeemer, in order to obtain for us salvation, offered himself voluntarily to his Father to make satisfaction for our sins : *He was offered because it was His own will.*[1] And his Father loaded him with all our crimes: *He hath laid on Him the iniquity of us all.*[2] And thus behold the divine Word, innocent, most pure, and holy, behold him even from his infancy charged with all the blasphemies, with all the unsightliness, with all the sacrileges, and with all the crimes of men; become for the love of us the object of the divine malediction, on account of the sins for which he had bound himself to satisfy the divine justice. So that Jesus charged himself with as many maledictions as there have ever been, or ever shall be, mortal sins committed by all mankind. And thus he presented himself to his Father, when he came into the world, even from his birth, as a criminal and a debtor, guilty of all our sins, and as such was condemned by his Father to die as a malefactor accursed on a cross : *And of sin hath condemned sin in the flesh.*[3]

Oh, if the eternal Father were capable of feeling sorrow, what anguish of mind would he not have felt at being obliged to treat as a criminal, and as the most villanous criminal in the world, this innocent Son, his beloved one, who was worthy of all his love! *Behold the*

---

[1] "Oblatus est, quia ipse voluit."—*Isa.* liii. 7.

[2] "Et posuit Dominus in eo iniquitatem omnium nostrum."—*Isa.* liii. 6.

[3] "Et de peccato damnavit peccatum in carne."

First Saturday of Advent.

Man,[1] said Pilate, when he showed him to the Jews covered with stripes, in order to move them to compassion towards this innocent one who had been thus ill-treated. *Behold the Man*, the eternal Father seems to say to us all, showing him to us in the stable of Bethlehem. This poor child (he says) whom you behold, laid on a manger for beasts, and stretched on straw, is my beloved Son, who is come into the world to take upon himself your sins and your sorrows; love him, therefore, because he is infinitely worthy of your love, and you are under infinite obligations to love him.

Affections and Prayers.

O my innocent Saviour, mirror without spot, love of the eternal Father, chastisements and maledictions did not belong to Thee, but to me, a miserable sinner; but Thou wouldst show to the world the excess of love Thou didst bear us by sacrificing Thy life to obtain for us pardon and salvation, and paying by Thy sufferings the penalties which we had incurred by our sins. May all creatures praise and bless Thy mercy and Thy infinite bounty! I thank Thee on behalf of all men, but especially for myself: because as I have offended Thee more than others, so Thou hast hast suffered the pains which Thou didst endure more for me than for others, Accursed a thousand times be all those sinful pleasures which I have delighted in, and which have cost Thee so much sorrow! But since Thou hast paid the price of my ransom, I beseech Thee let not the blood which Thou has spilled for love of me be lost to me. I am sorry that I have despised Thee, O my love; but oh, grant me more sorrow; make me know the evil I have committed in offending Thee, my Redeemer and my God, who hast suffered so much to oblige me to love Thee! I love Thee, O infinite Bounty, but I desire to love Thee more; I desire to love Thee as much as Thou deservest to be loved. O my Jesus, do Thou cause Thyself to be loved both by me and by all men; for Thou dost indeed deserve to be loved. I pray Thee, enlighten the minds of those sinners who will not know Thee or will not love Thee; make them

---
[1] "Ecce homo."

understand what Thou hast done for the love of them, and the ardent desire Thou hast for their salvation. Most holy Mary, pray to Jesus for me, and for all sinners; obtain for us light and grace to love thy Son, who has loved us so much.

MEDITATION VIII.

Second Sunday.

God Sends His Son to die in order to restore us to Life.

Deus autem, qui dives est in misericordia, propter nimiam charitatem suam qua dilexit nos, et cum essemus mortui peccatis, convivificavit nos in Christo.

" But God (who is rich in mercy) for His exceeding charity wherewith He loved us, even when we were dead in sins, hath quickened us together in Christ.—*Eph.* ii. 4, 5.

Consider that sin is the death of the soul; because this enemy of God deprives us of divine grace, which is the life of the soul. We, therefore, miserable sinners, were already by our sins dead and condemned to hell. God, through the immense love which he bears to our souls, determined to restore us to life; and how did he do so? He sent his only-begotten Son into the world to die, in order that by his death he might restore us to life.

With reason therefore does the Apostle call this work of love *exceeding charity;*[1] too much love; yes, indeed, for man could never have hoped to receive life in such a loving manner if God had not found this means of redeeming him: *Having obtained eternal redemption.*[2] All men were therefore dead—there was no remedy for them. But the Son of God, through the bowels of his mercy, hath come down from heaven, *the Orient from on high,* and has given us life. Justly, therefore, does the Apostle call Jesus Christ our life: *When Christ shall appear, who is your life.*[3] Behold our Redeemer, clothed with flesh and

[1] "Nimiam charitatem."
[2] "Æterna redemptione inventa."—*Heb.* ix. 12.
[3] "Cum Christus apparuerit, vita vestra."—*Col.* iii. 4.

Second Sunday of Advent. 191

become an infant, says to us: *I am come that they may have life, and may have it more abundantly.*[1] For this end he accepted death, that he might give us life. It is but reasonable, therefore, that we should live only to God, who has condescended to die for us: *Christ died, that they who live may not live to themselves, but unto Him who died for them.*[2] It is reasonable that Jesus Christ should be the only sovereign of our heart since he has spent his blood and his life to gain it to himself: *To this end Christ died and rose again, that He might be Lord both of the dead and of the living.*[3] O my God! who would be so ungrateful a wretch as to believe as an article of faith that God died to secure his love, and yet refuse to love him, and, renouncing his friendship, choose voluntarily to make himself a slave of hell?

Affections and Prayers.

O my Jesus! if Thou hadst not accepted and suffered death for me, I should have remained dead in my sins, without hope of salvation and without the power of ever loving Thee. But after Thou hast obtained life for me by Thy death, I have again many times voluntarily forfeited it by returning to sin. Thou didst die to gain my heart to Thyself, and I by my rebellion have made it a slave of the devil. I lost all reverence for Thee, and I said that I would no longer have Thee for my master. All this is true; but it is also true that Thou desirest not the death of the sinner, but that he should be converted and live; and therefore didst Thou die to give us life. I repent of having offended Thee, my dearest Redeemer; and do Thou pardon me through the merits of Thy Passion; give me Thy grace; give me that life which Thou hast purchased for me by Thy death, and henceforth mayest Thou have entire dominion over my

---

[1] "Ego veni ut vitam habeant, et abundantius habeant."—*John,* x. 10.

[2] "Mortuus est Christus, ut, et qui vivunt, jam non sibi vivant, sed ei qui pro ipsis mortuus est."—2 *Cor.* v. 15.

[3] "In hoc enim Christus mortuus est et resurrexit, ut et mortuorum et vivorum dominetur."—*Rom.* xiv. 9.

heart. Never let the devil have possession of it again; he is not my God, he does not love me, and has not suffered anything for me. In past times he was not the true sovereign, but the robber of my soul; Thou alone, my Jesus, art my true Lord, who hast created and redeemed me with Thy blood; Thou alone hast loved me, and oh, how much! It is therefore only just that I should be Thine alone during the life that remains to me. Tell me what Thou wouldst have me to do; for I will do it all. Chastise me as Thou wilt; I accept everything Thou sendest me; only spare me the chastisement of living without Thy love; make me love Thee, and then dispose of me as Thou wilt. Most holy Mary, my refuge and consolation, recommend me to thy Son: his death and thy intercession are all my hope.

MEDITATION IX.

SECOND MONDAY.

The Love that the Son of God has shown us in the Redemption.

Dilexit nos, et tradidit semetipsum pro nobis.
" He hath loved us, and hath delivered Himself for us."—*Eph.* v. 2.

Consider that the eternal Word is that God who is so infinitely happy in himself that his happiness cannot be greater than it is, nor could the salvation of all mankind have added anything to it or have diminished it; and yet he has done and suffered so much to save us miserable worms that if his beatitude (as St. Thomas says) had depended on that of man, he could not have done or suffered more: "As if without him He could not be happy;"[1] and, indeed, if Jesus Christ could not have been happy without redeeming us, how could he have humbled himself more than he has done, in taking upon himself our infirmities, the miseries of infancy, the troubles of human life, and a death so barbarous and ignominious?

None but God was capable of loving to such an excess

[1] "Quasi sine ipso beatus esse non posset."—*Opusc.* 63, c. 7.

so wretched sinners as we are, and who were so unworthy of being loved. A devout author says : If Jesus Christ had permitted us to ask of him to give us the greatest proof of his love, who would have ventured to ask of him that he should become a child like unto us, that he should clothe himself with all our miseries, and make himself of all men the most poor, the most despised, and the most ill-treated, even to being put to death by the hands of executioners, and in the greatest torments upon an infamous gibbet, cursed and forsaken by all, even by his own Father, who abandoned his Son that he might not abandon us in our ruin ?

But that which we should not have had the boldness even to think of, the Son of God has thought of and accomplished. Even from his childhood he has sacrificed himself for us to sufferings, to opprobrium, and to death; *He hath loved us, and hath delivered Himself for us.*[1] He hath loved us, and out of love hath given us himself, in order that we, by offering him as a victim to the Father, in satisfaction for our debts, might through his merits obtain from the divine goodness all the graces that we desire ; a victim dearer to the Father than if we had offered him the lives of all men and of all the angels. Let us therefore continually offer to God the merits of Jesus Christ, and through them let us seek and hope for every good.

Affections and Prayers.

My Jesus, I should indeed do great injustice to Thy mercy and Thy love, if, after Thou hast given me so many proofs of the love Thou bearest me, and the desire Thou hast to save me, I should still distrust Thy mercy and Thy love. My beloved Redeemer, I am a poor sinner; but Thou hast said that Thou didst come to seek sinners : *I am not come to call the just, but sinners.*[2] I am a poor infirm creature,—Thou camest to cure

[1] " Dilexit nos et tradidit semetipsum pro nobis."
[2] " Non enim veni vocare justos, sed peccatores."—*Matt.* ix. 13.

the infirm, and Thou didst say, *They that are whole need not the physician, but they that are sick.*[1] I was lost through my sins; but Thou didst come to save the lost: *The Son of man is come to save that which was lost.*[2] What, then, can I fear, if I am willing to amend my life and to become Thine? I have only myself and my own weakness to fear; but my own weakness and poverty ought to increase my confidence in Thee, who hast declared Thyself to be the refuge of the destitute: *The Lord is become a refuge for the poor.*[3] And Thou hast promised to grant their desires: *The Lord hath heard the desire of the poor.*[4] Therefore I implore this favor of Thee, O my Jesus! give me confidence in Thy merits, and grant that I may always recommend myself to God through Thy merits. Eternal Father, save me from hell, and first from sin, for the love of Jesus Christ; for the merits of this Thy Son enlighten my mind to obey Thy will; give me strength against temptations; grant me the gift of Thy holy love; and, above all, I beseech Thee to give me the grace to pray to Thee to help me, for the love of Jesus Christ, who hast promised that Thou wilt grant to him who prays in his name whatever he asks of Thee. If I continue to pray to Thee in this way, I shall certainly be saved; but if I neglect it, I shall certainly be lost. Most holy Mary, obtain for me this great gift of prayer, and that I may persevere in recommending myself constantly to God, and also to thee, who dost obtain from God whatever thou willest.

MEDITATION X.

SECOND TUESDAY.

Jesus, the Man of Sorrows, from the Womb of His Mother.

Virum dolorum et scientem infirmitatem.
"A man of sorrows, acquainted with infirmity."—*Isa.* liii. 3.

Thus does the prophet Isaias designate our Lord Jesus Christ "the man of sorrows;" yes, because this man was

[1] "Non egent qui sani sunt medico, sed qui male habent."—*Luke*, v. 31.
[2] "Venit enim Filius hominis salvare quod perierat."—*Matt.* xviii. 11.
[3] "Factus est Dominus refugium pauperi."—*Ps.* ix. 10.
[4] "Desiderium pauperum exaudivit Dominus."—*Ps.* x. 17.

created on purpose to suffer, and from his infancy began to endure the greatest sorrows that any man ever suffered. The first man, Adam, enjoyed for some time upon this earth the delights of the earthly paradise; but the second Adam, Jesus Christ, did not pass a moment of his life without sorrows and anguish; for even from a child he was afflicted by the foresight of all the sufferings and ignominy that he would have to endure during his life, and especially at his death, when he was to close that life immersed in a tempest of sorrow and opprobrium, as David had predicted: *I am come into the depth of the sea, and a tempest hath overwhelmed me.*[1]

Even from the womb of Mary, Jesus Christ accepted obediently the sacrifice which his Father had desired him to make, even his Passion and death: *Becoming obedient unto death.*[2] So that even from the womb of Mary he foresaw the scourges and presented to them his flesh; he foresaw the thorns, and presented to them his head; he foresaw the blows, and presented to them his cheeks; he foresaw the nails, and presented to them his hands and his feet; he foresaw the cross, and offered his life. Hence it is true that even from his earliest infancy our blessed Redeemer every moment of his life suffered a continual martyrdom; and he offered it every moment for us to his eternal Father.

But what afflicted him most was the sight of the sins which men would commit even after this painful redemption. By his divine light he well knew the malice of every sin, and therefore did he come into the world to do away with all sins; but when he saw the immense number which would be committed, the sorrow that the Heart of Jesus felt was greater than all the sorrows that all men ever suffered or ever will suffer upon earth.

[1] "Veni in altitudinem maris, et tempestas demersit me."—*Ps.* lxviii. 3.
[2] " Factus obediens usque ad mortem."—*Phil.* ii. 8.

Affections and Prayers.

My sweetest Redeemer, when shall I begin to be grateful to Thy infinite goodness? When shall I begin to acknowledge the love that Thou hast borne me, and the sorrows Thou hast endured for me? Hitherto, instead of love and gratitude, I have returned Thee offences and contempt; shall I then continue to live always ungrateful to Thee, my God, who hast spared nothing to acquire my love? No, my Jesus, it shall not be so. During the days that may yet remain to me I will be grateful to Thee; and Thou wilt, I trust, help me to be so. If I have offended Thee, Thy sufferings and Thy death are my hope. Thou hast promised to forgive the penitent. I repent with my whole soul of having despised Thee. Fulfil, therefore, Thy promise, my Beloved, and forgive me. O dearest Infant, I behold Thee in the manger already nailed to Thy cross, which is constantly present to Thee, and which Thou dost already accept for me. O my crucified Infant! I thank Thee for it, and I love Thee. Stretched upon this straw, suffering already for me, and preparing Thyself even now to die for this love of me, Thou dost command and invite me to love Thee: *Love the Lord thy God.*[1] And I desire nothing more than to love Thee. Since, therefore, Thou willest that I should love Thee, give me all that love that Thou requirest of me; love for Thee is Thy gift, and the greatest gift that Thou canst make to a soul. Accept, O my Jesus! for Thy lover a sinner who has so greatly offended Thee. Thou didst come from heaven to seek the lost sheep; do Thou, therefore, seek me, and I will seek none other but Thee. Thou desirest my soul, and my soul desires nothing but Thee. Thou lovest him that loves Thee, and sayest, *Those that love Me I love.*[2] I love Thee, do Thou also love me; and if Thou lovest me, bind me to Thy love; but bind me so that I may never again be able to disengage myself from Thee. Mary, my Mother, do thou help me. Let it be thy glory also to see thy Son loved by a miserable sinner, who has hitherto so greatly offended him.

[1] "Diliges Dominum Deum tuum."
[2] "Ego diligentes me diligo."—*Prov.* viii. 17.

MEDITATION XI.

SECOND WEDNESDAY.

Jesus charged with the Sins of the Whole World.

Iniquitates eorum ipse portabit.
"He bore their iniquities."—*Is.* liii. 11.

Consider that the divine Word, in becoming man, chose not only to take the form of a sinner, but also to bear all the sins of men, and to satisfy for them as if they were his own: *He bore their iniquities.*[1] Father Cornelius adds, "as if he had committed them himself."[2] Let us here reflect what an oppression and anguish the heart of the Infant Jesus must have felt, who had already charged himself with the sins of the whole world, in finding that the divine justice insisted on his making a full satisfaction for them.

Well did our Lord know the malice of every sin, whilst, through the divine light which accompanied him, he knew immeasurably more than all men and angels the infinite goodness of his Father, and how infinitely deserving he is of being revered and loved. And then he saw drawn up in array before him an innumerable number of transgressions which were to be committed by men and for which he was to suffer and die. Our Lord once showed to St. Catharine of Sienna the hideousness of one single venial sin; and such was the dread and sorrow of the saint that she fell senseless to the ground. What, then, must have been the sufferings of the Infant Jesus when, on his entrance into the world, he saw before him the immense array of all the crimes of men for which he was to make satisfaction!

And then he knew in particular every sin of each one

[1] "Iniquitates eorum ipse portabit."
[2] "Ac si ipse ea patrasset."

of us: "He had regard to every particular sin,"[1] says St. Bernard of Sienna. And Cardinal Hugo says that the executioners "caused him exterior pain by crucifying him, but we interior pain by sinning against him."[2] He means that each one of our sins afflicted the soul of Jesus Christ more than crucifixion and death afflicted his body. Such is the beautiful recompense which has been rendered to our divine Saviour for his love by every one who remembers to have offended him by mortal sin.

Affections and Prayers.

My Beloved Jesus, I, who have offended Thee, am not worthy of Thy favors, but through the merit of that pain which Thou didst suffer, and which Thou didst offer up to God at the sight of my sins, and to satisfy divine justice for them, give me a share in that light by which Thou didst see their malice, and in that hatred with which Thou didst then abominate them. Can it then be true, my amiable Saviour, that ever since Thou wert an infant, and in every moment of Thy life, I have been a murderer of Thy sacred heart, and a murderer more cruel than all those who crucified Thee? And I have renewed and increased this suffering every time I have repeated my offences against Thee? O Lord! Thou hast indeed died to save me; but Thy death will not save me, if I do not on my part detest every evil, and have true sorrow for the sins I have committed against Thee. But even this sorrow must be given me by Thee. Thou givest it to him that asks it of Thee. I ask it of Thee through the merits of all the sufferings Thou didst endure on this earth; give me sorrow for my sins, but a sorrow that will correspond to my transgressions. Help me, O Lord! to make that act of contrition which I now intend to do. O eternal God, supreme and infinite Good! I, a miserable worm, have dared to lose respect for Thee, and to despise Thy grace, I detest above every evil and abhor the injuries I have committed against Thee; I repent

---

[1] "Ad quamlibet culpam singularem habuit aspectum."—*T.* il. s. 56, a. 1, c. 1.

[2] "Fecerunt eum dolore extrinsecus crucifigendo, sed nos peccando intrinsecus."

of them with my whole heart, not so much on account of hell, which I have deserved, as because I have offended Thy infinite goodness. I hope for pardon from Thee through the merits of Jesus Christ: and I hope also to obtain, together with Thy pardon the grace of loving Thee. I love Thee, O God, who art worthy of infinite love, and I will always repeat to Thee, I love Thee, I love Thee, I love Thee; and as Thy beloved St. Catharine of Genoa said to Thee, while she stood in spirit at Thy feet, O Thou crucified one, so will I also say to Thee now that I am standing also at Thy feet, My Lord, no more sins, no more sins! No, for Thou indeed dost not deserve to be offended, O my Jesus, but Thou only deservest to be loved. My blessed Redeemer, help me. My mother Mary, assist me, I pray thee; I only ask of thee to obtain for me that I may love God during the time that is left me in this life.

MEDITATION XII.

SECOND THURSDAY.

Jesus suffers during His Whole Life.

Dolor meus in conspectu meo semper.

" My sorrow is continually before me."—*Ps.* xxxvii. 18.

Consider that all the sufferings and ignominy that Jesus endured in his life and death, all were present to him from the first moment of his life: *My sorrow is continually before me;*[1] and even from his childhood he began to offer them in satisfaction for our sins, beginning even then to fulfil his office of Redeemer. He revealed to one of his servants that from the commencement of his life even until his death, he suffered continually; and suffered so much for each of our sins that if he had had as many lives as there are men, he would as many times have died of sorrow, if God had not preserved his life that he might suffer more.

Oh, what a martyrdom did the loving heart of Jesus constantly endure in beholding all the sins of men!

[1] " Dolor meus in conspectu meo semper."

Meditation XII.

He beheld every single fault.[1] Even whilst he was in the womb of Mary every particular sin passed in review before Jesus, and each sin afflicted him immeasurably. St. Thomas says that this sorrow which Jesus Christ felt at the knowledge of the injury done to his Father, and of the evil that sin would occasion to the souls that he loved, surpassed the sorrows of all the contrite sinners that ever existed, even of those who died of pure sorrow; because no sinner ever loved God and his own soul as much as Jesus loved his Father and our souls. Wherefore that agony which our Redeemer suffered in the garden at the sight of our sins was endured by him even from his mother's womb: *I am poor, and in labors from my youth.*[2] Thus through the mouth of David did our Saviour prophesy of himself, that all his life should be a continual suffering. From this St. John Chrysostom deduces that we ought not to afflict ourselves for anything but for sin alone; and that since Jesus was afflicted all his life long on account of our sins, so we who have committed them ought to feel a continual sorrow for them, remembering that we have offended God who has loved us so much. St. Margaret of Cortona never ceased to shed tears for her sins: one day her confessor said to her, "Margaret, no more tears; it is enough, our Lord has already forgiven thee." "What," answered the saint, "how can my tears and my sorrows suffice for the sins for which my Jesus was afflicted all his life long!"

Affections and Prayers.

Behold, my Jesus, at Thy feet the ungrateful sinner, the persecutor who kept Thee in continual affliction during all Thy life. But I will say to Thee with Isaias: *But Thou hast delivered my soul that it should not perish ; Thou hast cast all my sins*

---

[1] "Ad quamlibet culpam singularem habuit aspectum."
[2] "Pauper sum ego et in laboribus a juventute mea."—*Ps.* lxxxvii. 16.

behind Thy back.[1] I have offended Thee, I have pierced Thee through with all my sins ; but Thou hast not refused to bear on Thy shoulders all my sins ; I have voluntarily cast my soul into the fire of hell every time that I have consented to offend Thee gravely; and Thou, at the cost of Thy own blood, hast continually liberated me and prevented me from being entirely lost. My beloved Redeemer, I thank Thee. I could wish to die of sorrow when I think how I have abused Thy infinite goodness ; forgive me, my Love, and come and take entire possession of my heart. Thou hast said that Thou wouldst not disdain to enter into the abode of him that opens to Thee, and to remain in his company : *If any man shall open to Me the door, I will come in to him, and will sup with him.*[2] If I have hitherto driven Thee away from me. I now love Thee, and desire nothing but Thy favor. Behold, the door is open, enter Thou into my heart, but enter never to depart from it again. I am poor ; but if Thou enter Thou wilt make me rich. I shall always be rich as long as I possess Thee, the sovereign good. O Queen of Heaven, sorrowful Mother of this suffering Son, I have also been a cause of sorrow to thee, because thou hast participated, in great part, in the sufferings of Jesus: my Mother, do thou also forgive me, and obtain for me the grace to be faithful to thee, now that I hope my Jesus has returned into my soul.

MEDITATION XIII.

SECOND FRIDAY.

Jesus wished to suffer so much in order to gain our Hearts.

Baptismo habeo baptizari; et quomodo coarctor usque dum perficiatur!

"I have a baptism wherewith I am to be baptized; and how am I straitened until it be accomplished !"—*St. Luke*, xii. 50.

Consider that Jesus suffered, even from the first moment of his life, and all for the love of us. During the whole of his life he had no other object in view, after

[1] "Tu autem eruisti animam meam, ut non periret; projecisti post tergum tuum omnia peccata mea."—*Isa.* xxxviii. 17.

[2] "Si quis . . . aperuerit mihi januam, intrabo ad illum, et cœnabo cum illo."—*Apoc.* iii. 20.

the glory of God, than our salvation. He, as the Son of God, had no need to suffer in order to deserve Paradise ; but whatever he suffered of pain, of poverty, of ignominy, he applied it all towards meriting for us eternal salvation. And even although he could have saved us without suffering, yet he chose to embrace a life of nothing but sufferings, poor, despised, and deprived of every comfort, with a death the most desolate and bitter that was ever endured by any martyr or penitent, only to make us understand the greatness of the love he bore us, and to gain our affections.

He lived thirty-three years, and he lived sighing after the hour in which he was to sacrifice his life, which he desired to offer up to obtain for us divine grace and eternal glory, in order that he might have us with him forever in paradise. It was this desire which made him say, *I have a baptism wherewith I am to be baptized; and how am I straitened until it be accomplished!* [1] He desired to be baptized with his own blood, not to wash out his own sins, since he was innocent and holy, but the sins of men whom he loved so much: *He loved us, and washed us in his own blood.*[2] Oh, excess of the love of God, which all the men and angels that ever existed will never arrive at understanding or praising as it deserves.

St. Bonaventure complains on considering the great ingratitude of men for so great love: "It is wonderful that the hearts of men do not break for love of Thee."[3] It is a wonder, says the saint, to see a God endure such sufferings, shedding tears in a stable, poor in a workshop, languishing on a cross ; in short, afflicted and troubled

---

[1] "Baptismo habeo baptizari; et quomodo coarctor usque dum perficiatur !"

[2] "Dilexit nos, et lavit nos a peccatis nostris in sanguine suo."—*Apoc.* i. 5.

[3] "Mirum est quomodo pro tuo amore corda hominum non scinduntur."—*Stim. div. am.* p. 2, c. 2.

the whole of his life for the love of men ; and then to see these men, who not only do not burn with love towards such a loving God, but even have the boldness to despise his love and his grace. O Lord, how is it possible to know that a God should have given himself up to so much suffering for men, and yet that there should be men who can offend, and not love this merciful God!

Affections and Prayers.

My beloved Redeemer, I am also one of those ungrateful wretches who have repaid Thy immense love, Thy sorrows, and Thy death, with offences and contempt. O my dearest Jesus! how is it possible that, seeing as Thou didst the ingratitude that I should show Thee for all Thy mercies, Thou couldst yet love me so much, and resolve to endure so much contempt and suffering for me! But I will not despair. The evil is already done. Give me, therefore, O my Saviour, that sorrow which Thou hast merited for me by Thy tears; but let it be a sorrow equal to my iniquities. O loving heart of my Saviour, once so afflicted and desolate for my sake, and now all burning with love for me, I beseech Thee, change my heart, give me a heart that will make reparation for the offences I have committed against Thee, give me a love that will equal my ingratitude!

But I already feel a great desire of loving Thee. I give Thee thanks, my Saviour, because I see that Thy mercy has already changed my heart. I hate, above every evil, the insults I have offered Thee; I detest them, I abhor them. I now esteem Thy friendship above all the riches and kingdoms of the world. I desire to please Thee as much as is possible to me; I love Thee, who art infinitely amiable; but I see that this my love is too small. Do Thou increase the flame, give me more love. Thy love for me ought to be responded to by a greater degree of love by me, who have so much offended Thee, and who, instead of chastisement, have received so many special favors from Thee. O sovereign Good, permit me not to be any longer ungrateful for all the favors that Thou hast bestowed upon me: " I will die with love of the love of Thee," I will say with St. Francis, " who hast deigned to die for love of the love of me."[1] Mary, my hope, help me ; pray to Jesus for me !

[1] "Moriar amore amoris tui, qui amore amoris mei dignatus es mori!"

MEDITATION XIV.*

SECOND SATURDAY.

The Greatest Sorrow of Jesus.

Quæ utilitas in sanguine meo, dum descendo in corruptionem?
" What profit is there in my blood, whilst I go down to corruption ?"—*Ps.* xxix. 10.

Jesus Christ revealed to the Venerable Agatha of the Cross that whilst he was in his Mother's womb, that which afflicted him more than any other sorrow was the hardness of the hearts of men, who should, after his Redemption, despise the graces which he came into the world to diffuse. And he had expressed this sentiment before, by the mouth of David, in the words just quoted, which are generally thus understood by the holy Fathers: *What profit is there in my blood, whilst I go down to corrupton?*[1] St. Isidore explains *whilst I descend into corruption*, " whilst I descend to take the nature of man, so corrupted by vices and sins;" as if he had said, " O my Father, I am indeed going to clothe myself with human flesh, in order to shed my blood for men; but *what profit is there in my blood?*"—the greater part of the world will set no value on my blood, and will go on offending me, as if I had done nothing for the love of them."

This sorrow was the bitter chalice which Jesus begged the Eternal Father to remove from him, saying: *Let this chalice pass from Me.*"[2] What chalice? The sight of the contempt with which his love was treated. This made him exclaim again on the cross: *My God, my God, why hast thou forsaken Me?*[3] Our Lord revealed to St. Catharine

---

[1] " Quæ utilitas in sanguine meo, dum descendo in corruptionem?"
[2] " Transeat a me calix iste !"—*Matt.* xxvi. 39.
[3] " Deus meus ! Deus meus ! ut quid dereliquisti me?"—*Matt.* xxvii. 46.

---

* On December 16 we begin the Novena, page 214.

of Sienna, that this was the abandonment of which he complained—the knowledge, namely, that his Father would have to suffer that his Passion and his love should be despised by so many men for whom he died.

And this same sorrow tormented the Infant Jesus in the womb of Mary, the foresight of such a prodigality of sorrows, of ignominy, of blood-shedding, and of so cruel and ignominious a death, and all to so little purpose. The holy Child saw, even there, what the Apostle says, that many (indeed the greater number) should trample under foot his blood, and despise his grace, which this blood would obtain for them: *Treading under foot the Son of God, and offering an affront to the Spirit of grace.*[1] But if we have been of the number of these ungrateful men, let us not despair; Jesus, at his birth, came to offer peace to men of good-will, as he made the angels sing : *And on earth peace to men of good-will.*[2] Let us, then, change our will, repent of our sins, and resolve to love this good God, and we shall find peace, that is, the divine friendship.

Affections and Prayers.

O my most amiable Jesus, how much have I too caused Thee to suffer during Thy lifetime! Thou hast shed Thy blood for me with so much sorrow and love, and what fruit hast Thou hitherto drawn from me but contempt, offences, and insults? But, my Redeemer, I will no longer afflict Thee ; I hope that in future Thy Passion will produce fruit in me by Thy grace, which I feel is already assisting me. I will love Thee above every other good ; and to please Thee, I am ready to give my life a thousand times. Eternal Father, I should not have the boldness to appear before Thee to implore either pardon or graces, but Thy Son has told me, that whatever grace I ask of Thee in his name Thou wilt grant it to me : *If ye shall ask any-*

---

[1] " Filium Dei conculcaverit . . . , et spiritui gratiæ contumeliam fecerit !"—*Heb.* x. 29.

[2] " Et in terra pax hominibus bonæ voluntatis."—*Luke*, ii. 14.

thing of the Father in my name, he will give it you.[1] I offer Thee, therefore, the merits of Jesus Christ, and in his name I ask of Thee first a general pardon of all my sins; I ask holy perseverance even unto death; I ask of Thee, above all, the gift of Thy holy love, that it may make me always live according to Thy divine will. As to my own will, I am resolved to choose a thousand deaths sooner than offend Thee, and to love Thee with my whole heart, and to do everything that I possibly can to please Thee. But in order to do all this, I beg of Thee, and hope to receive from Thee, grace to execute what I purpose. My Mother Mary, if thou wilt pray for me, I am safe. Oh, pray for me, pray; and cease not to pray till thou seest that I am changed, and made what God wishes me to be.

MEDITATION XV.

SECOND SUNDAY.

The Poverty of the Infant Jesus.

Invenientes infantem . . . positum in præsepio.
"You shall find the infant laid in a manger."—*St. Luke*, ii. 16.

The Holy Church, in contemplating this great mystery and prodigy of a God being born in a stable, exclaims, full of admiration, "O great mystery! O wonderful sacrament! for animals to behold the Lord lying in a manger."[2]

In order to contemplate with tenderness and love the birth of Jesus, we must pray the Lord to give us a lively faith. If without faith we enter into the grotto of Bethlehem, we shall have nothing but a feeling of compassion at seeing an infant reduced to such a state of poverty that, being born in the depth of winter, he is laid in a manger of beasts, without fire, and in the midst of a cold cavern. But if we enter with faith, and consider what

[1] "Si quid petieritis Patrem in nomine meo, dabit vobis."—*John*, xvi. 23.

[2] "O magnum mysterium et admirabile sacramentum, ut animalia viderent Dominum natum, jacentem in præsepio!"—*Off. Nat. resp.* 4.

an excess of bounty and love it was in a God to humble himself to appear like a little child, wrapped in swaddling-clothes, placed on straw, crying and shivering with cold, unable to move, depending for subsistence on his mother's milk, how is it possible that we should not feel ourselves gently constrained to give all our affections to this Infant God, who has reduced himself to this state to make us love him! St. Luke says that the shepherds, after having visited Jesus in the manger, *returned glorifying and praising God for all the things they had heard and seen.*[1] And yet what had they seen? Nothing more than a poor child trembling with cold on a little straw; but, being enlightened by faith, they recognized in this child the excess of divine love; and inflamed by this love they went on their way glorifying God, that they had the happiness to behold a God *who had emptied himself*[2] and annihilated himself for the love of men.

Affections and Prayers.

O my amiable and sweet Infant! although I behold Thee so poor and lying on straw, yet I confess and adore Thee as my Lord and Creator. I know what it was that reduced Thee to so miserable a state: it was the love that Thou didst bear me. But when I remember, O my Jesus! how I have treated Thee in times past, the injuries I have committed against Thee, I wonder in myself how Thou hast borne with me. Accursed sins, oh, what have you done! You have made me cause bitterness to the heart of my beloved Saviour. Oh, my dearest Redeemer, for the sake of the sufferings Thou didst endure and the tears Thou didst shed in the stable of Bethlehem, give me tears, give me a great sorrow, that may make me all my life long lament the displeasure I have caused Thee. Grant me a love for Thee, but such a love as may compensate for the offences I have committed against Thee. I love Thee, my Infant Saviour; I love Thee, my Infant God; I love Thee, my love, my life, my all. I

---

[1] "Reversi sunt pastores glorificantes et laudantes Deum in omnibus quæ audierant et viderant."—*Luke*, ii. 20.

[2] "Semetipsum exinanivit!"—*Phil.* ii. 7.

promise Thee from this day forth to love none but Thee. Do Thou help me by Thy grace, without which I can do nothing. Mary, my hope, thou dost obtain whatever thou willest from thy Son, obtain for me his holy love ; my Mother, hear me !

MEDITATION XVI.

THIRD MONDAY.

Jesus is the Fountain of Grace.

Haurietis aquas in gaudio de fontibus Salvatoris.

" You shall draw waters with joy out of the Saviour's fountains."—*Isa.* xii. 3.

Consider the four fountains of grace that we have in Jesus Christ, as contemplated by St. Bernard.

The first is that of mercy, in which we can wash ourselves from all the filthiness of our sins. This fountain was formed for us by our Redeemer with his tears and his blood: *He loved us, and washed us from our sins in his own blood.*[1]

The second fountain is that of peace and consolation in our tribulations: *Call upon me* (saith Jesus Christ) *in the day of trouble, and I will console thee.*[2] *He that thirsteth, let him come to me.*[3] He that thirsteth for true consolations even in this world, let him come to me, for I will satisfy him. He that once tastes the water of my love will forever disdain all the delights of the world: *But he that shall drink of the water that I will give him shall not thirst forever.*[4] And thoroughly contented will he be when he shall enter into the kingdom of the blessed, for the water of my grace shall raise him from earth to heaven. It will *become in him a fountain of water springing up into life*

---

[1] " Dilexit nos, et lavit nos a peccatis nostris in sanguine suo."— *Apoc.* i. 5.

[2] "Invoca me in die tribulationis ; eruam te."—*Ps.* xlix. 15.

[3] "Si quis sitit, veniat ad me, et bibat."—*John*, vii. 37.

[4] "Qui autem biberit ex aqua quam ego dabo ei, non sitiet in æternum."—*John*, iv. 13.

*everlasting.*¹ The peace which God gives to the souls that love him is not the peace that the world promises from sensual pleasures, which leave in the soul more bitterness than peace; the peace which God bestows exceeds all the pleasures of the senses: *Peace which surpasseth all understanding.*² Blessed are those who long for this divine fountain. *Blessed are they that hunger and thirst after justice.*³

The third fountain is that of devotion. Oh, how devout and ready to execute the divine will, and increasing every day in virtue, is he who constantly meditates on all that Jesus Christ has done for our sake! He will be like the tree planted by a stream of water: *He shall be like a tree that is planted near the running waters.*⁴

The fourth fountain is that of love: *In my meditation a fire shall flame out.*⁵ It is impossible to meditate on the sufferings and ignominy borne by Jesus Christ for the love of us, and not to feel inflamed by that blessed fire which he came upon earth to enkindle. How true it is, then, that he who avails himself of these blessed fountains of Jesus Christ will always draw from them waters of joy and of salvation! *You shall draw waters with joy out of the Saviour's fountains.*⁶

Affections and Prayers.

O my sweet and dearest Saviour, how much do I not owe Thee! What an obligation hast Thou put upon me of loving Thee, since Thou hast done for me what no son would have done for his father, and no servant for his master! If Thou, therefore, hast loved me above every one else, it is only just

---

¹ "Fiet in eo fons aquæ salientis in vitam æternam."
² "Pax Dei, quæ exsuperat omnem sensum."—*Phil.* iv. 7.
³ "Beati, qui esuriunt et sitiunt justitiam !"—*Matt.* v. 6.
⁴ "Erit tamquam lignum quod plantatum est secus decursus aquarum."—*Ps.* i. 3.
⁵ "In meditatione mea exardescet ignis."—*Ps.* xxxviii. 4.
⁶ "Haurietis aquas in gaudio de fontibus Salvatoris."

that I should love Thee above all others. I could wish to die with sorrow at the thought that Thou hast suffered so much for me, and that Thou didst accept for my sake the most painful and ignominious death that it is possible for a man to endure; and yet I have so often despised Thy friendship. How many times hast Thou forgiven me, and I have despised Thee afresh? But Thy merits are my hope. I now esteem Thy grace above all the kingdoms of the world. I love Thee, and for Thy love I accept every sorrow, every kind of death. And if I am not worthy to die for Thy glory by the hand of executioners, I accept at least willingly that death which Thou hast allotted to me; and I accept it in the manner and at the time that Thou shalt choose. My dear Mother Mary, obtain for me the grace always to live and to die loving Jesus.

MEDITATION XVII.

THIRD TUESDAY.

Jesus the Charitable Physician of our Souls.

Orietur vobis . . . Sol justitiæ, et sanitas in pennis ejus.

" But unto you the sun of justice shall arise, and health in his wings."—*Mal.* iv. 2.

Your physician will come, says the prophet, to cure the infirm; and he will come swiftly like the bird that flies, and like the sun, which on rising from the horizon, instantly sends its light to the other pole. But behold him, he is already come. Let us console ourselves, and return thanks to him.

St. Augustine says, "He descends to the bed of the sick;"[1] that is to say, even to taking upon him our flesh, for our bodies are the beds of our infirm souls.

Other physicians, if they love their patients, do indeed use all their efforts to cure them; but what physician, in order to cure the sick man, ever took upon himself his disease? Jesus Christ has been that physician, who charged himself with our infirmities in order to cure them. Neither would he content himself with sending

[1] "Descendit usque ad lectum ægrotantis."—*Serm.* 87, *E. B.*

another in his place, but he chose to come himself to fulfil this charitable office, in order to gain to himself all our love: *He hath borne our infirmities and carried our sorrows*.[1] He chose to heal our wounds with his own blood, and by his death to deliver us from eternal death, which we had deserved; in short, he chose to swallow the bitter draught of a life of continual sufferings and a painful death, to obtain for us life, and deliver us from our many evils.

The chalice which My Father hath given Me, shall I not drink it?[2] said he to St. Peter. It was necessary, then, that Jesus Christ should suffer so many ignominies to heal our pride; that he should embrace such a life of poverty to cure our covetousness; that he should be overwhelmed in a sea of troubles, and even die of pure sorrow, to cure our eagerness after sensual pleasures.

Affections and Prayers.

May Thy charity, O my Redeemer! be forever praised and blessed. And what would become of my soul, thus infirm and afflicted with the many sores of my sins, if I had not Thee, my Jesus, who both art able and willing to heal me? O blood of my Saviour, I trust in thee; wash me and cure me. I repent, O my love, of having offended Thee. Thou hast led a life of such tribulations, and hast died so bitter a death to prove to me the love Thou dost bear me. I would fain show Thee how much I love Thee; but what can I do who am so miserable and weak? O God of my soul! Thou art omnipotent; Thou canst heal me, and make me holy. Oh, kindle in me a great desire of pleasing Thee. I renounce all my pleasures to please Thee, my Redeemer, who dost deserve to be pleased at all costs. O sovereign Good! I esteem Thee and love Thee above every good; make me love Thee with all my heart, and always implore Thy love. I have hitherto offended Thee, and have not loved Thee, be-

[1] "Vere languores nostros ipse tulit, et dolores nostros ipse portavit."—*Isa.* liii. 4.
[2] "Calicem quem dedit mihi Pater, non bibam illum?"—*John*, xviii. 11.

cause I have not sought Thy love. I now beg of Thee this love, and the grace always to seek it. Oh, grant my prayer by the merits of Thy Passion. O Mary my Mother! thou art always prepared to hear the prayer of him that calls upon thee. Thou lovest him that loves thee. I love thee, my Queen; obtain for me the grace to love God, and I ask nothing more of thee.

MEDITATION XVIII.

THIRD WEDNESDAY.

We should hope all Things from the Merits of Jesus Christ.

Proprio Filio suo non pepercit; sed pro nobis omnibus tradidit illum.

"He that spared not even His own Son, but delivered Him up for us all."— *Rom.* viii. 32.

Consider that, since the Eternal Father has given us his own Son to be our mediator and advocate with him, and the victim in satisfaction for our sins, we cannot despair of obtaining from God whatever favor we ask of him, if we avail ourselves of the help of such a Redeemer. *How hath he not also, with Him, given us all things?*[1] adds the Apostle. What can God deny us when he has not denied us his Son?

None of our prayers deserve to be heard or granted by the Lord, for we do not deserve graces but punishment for our sins; but Jesus Christ who intercedes for us, and offers for us all the sufferings of his life, his blood, and his death, does indeed deserve to be heard. The Father cannot refuse anything to so dear a Son, who offers him a price of infinite value. He is innocent; all that he pays to divine justice is to satisfy our debts; and the satisfaction he offers is infinitely greater than all the sins of men. It would not be just that a sinner should perish who repents of his sins, and offers to God the merits of Jesus Christ, who has already superabundantly atoned for him.

[1] "Quomodo non etiam cum illo omnia nobis donavit?"

Third Wednesday of Advent.

Let us therefore thank God, and hope all things from the merits of Jesus Christ.

Affections and Prayers.

No, my God and my Father, I can no longer distrust Thy mercy; I cannot fear that Thou wilt refuse me the pardon of all the sins I have committed against Thee, and that Thou wilt withhold from me the graces necessary for my salvation, since Thou hast given me Thy Son, in order that I should offer him to Thee. Thou hast given me Jesus Christ on purpose to pardon me, and to render me capable of receiving Thy grace, and Thou hast commanded me to offer him to Thee, and to hope for salvation from Thee for his merits. Yes, my God, I will obey Thee, and I thank Thee. I offer Thee the merits of this Thy Son, and through them I hope for grace to remedy my weakness, and all the injuries that I have done myself by my sins. I repent, O infinite Goodness! of having offended Thee, and I love Thee above everything; and from this day forth I promise Thee to love none but Thee. But my promise will be of no avail if Thou dost not help me. For the love of Jesus Christ, give me light and strength to accomplish all Thy holy will. Trusting, therefore, in the merits of Jesus Christ, I hope that Thou wilt grant my prayer. Mary, my mother and my hope, I beseech thee also, for the love of Jesus Christ, to obtain for me this grace. O my Mother, listen to my prayer.

Meditations for the Novena for Christmas.*

MEDITATION I.

DECEMBER 16.

God has given Us his only Son to save Us.

Dedi te in lucem gentium, ut sis salus mea usque ad extremum terræ.

"I have given Thee to be the light of the Gentiles, that Thou mayest be My salvation even to the farthest part of the earth."—*Isa.* xlix. 6.

Consider that the Eternal Father addressed these words to the Infant Jesus at the instant of his conception: *I have given Thee to be the light of the Gentiles, that Thou mayest be My salvation.*[1] My Son, I have given Thee to the world for the light and life of all people, in order that Thou mightest procure for them their salvation, which I have as much at heart as if it were my own. Thou must therefore employ Thyself entirely for the well-being of men: "Wholly given to man, Thou must be wholly spent in his service."[2] Thou must therefore, at Thy birth, suffer extreme poverty, in order that men may become rich, "that Thou mayest enrich them by Thy poverty."[3] Thou must be sold as a slave to acquire liberty for man; and Thou must be scourged and crucified as a slave to satisfy my justice for the punishment due to man. Thou must give Thy blood and Thy life to deliver man from eternal death; in short, Thou art no

[1] "Dedi te in lucem gentium, ut sis salus mea usque ad extremum terræ."
[2] "Totus illi datus, totus in suos usus impenderis."—*S. Bern.*
[3] "Ut tua inopia dites."

---

* Further on, page 300, we shall find another Novena of meditations with the chaplet to be recited before every meditation.

longer Thine own, but Thou belongest to man: *A child is born to us, a son is given to us.*[1] Thus, my beloved Son, man will be constrained to love me, and to be mine, when he sees that I give Thee, my only-begotten one, entirely to him, and that there is nothing left for me to give him.

God so loved the world—(O infinite love! only worthy of an infinite God!)—*God so loved the world as to give His only-begotten Son.*[2] The Infant Jesus, far from being sorrowful at this proposal, is pleased at it, accepts it with love, and exults in it: *He hath rejoiced as a giant to run the way;*[3] and from the first moment of his incarnation he gives himself entirely to man, and embraces with pleasure all the sorrows and ignominy that he must suffer on earth for the love of man. These were (says St. Bernard) the mountains and hills that Jesus Christ had to pass with so many labors in order to save man: *Behold, He cometh leaping upon the mountains, skipping over the hills.*[4]

Here consider that the divine Father, in sending his Son to be our Redeemer and mediator between himself and man, has in a certain sense bound himself to forgive us and love us, on account of the covenant he made to receive us into his favor, providing his Son satisfied for us his divine justice. On the other hand, the divine Word, having accepted the decree of his Father (who, by sending him to redeem us, has given him to us), has also bound himself to love us; not, indeed, for our own merits, but in order to fulfil the merciful will of his Father.

[1] " Parvulus natus est nobis, et Filius datus est nobis."—*Isa.* ix. 6.
[2] " Sic Deus dilexit mundum, ut Filium suum unigenitum daret!"—*John*, iii. 16.
[3] " Exsultavit ut gigas ad currendam viam."—*Ps.* lviii. 6.
[4] " Ecce iste venit saliens in montibus, transiliens colles."—*Cant.* ii. 8.

Affections and Prayers.

My dearest Jesus, if it is true (as the law says) that dominion is acquired by gift, since Thy Father hath given Thee to me, Thou art mine; for me Thou wert born, to me hast Thou been given: *A child is born to us, a Son is given to us.*[1] Therefore I may well say, " My Jesus and my all."[2] Since Thou art mine, everything that belongs to Thee is also mine. Of this I am assured by Thy Apostle: *How hath He not also with Him given us all things.*[3] Thy blood is mine, Thy merits are mine, Thy grace is mine, Thy paradise is mine; and if Thou art mine, who shall be able to take Thee from me? " No man can take God away from me,"[4] said with joy the abbot St. Anthony. So, from this day forth, will I also continually say. It is only through my own fault that I can lose Thee and separate myself from Thee; but if in past times I have abandoned Thee and lost Thee, O my Jesus, I now repent of it with all my soul, and I am resolved to lose my life and everything sooner than lose Thee, O infinite Good, and only love of my soul! I thank Thee, Eternal Father, for having given me Thy Son; and since Thou hast given him entirely to me, I, miserable sinner, give myself entirely to Thee. For the sake of this same Son, accept me, and bind me with the chains of love to this my Redeemer; but bind me so strongly that I also may be able to say, *Who shall separate me from the love of Christ?*[5] What good shall there ever be in the world that shall separate me from my Jesus? And Thou, my Saviour, if Thou art all mine, know that I am all Thine. Dispose of me, and of all that belongs to me, as shall best please Thee. And how can I refuse anything to a God who has not refused me his blood and his life? Mary, my Mother, do thou guard me with thy protection. I will no longer be my own. I will be all my Saviour's. Do thou help me to be faithful; I trust in thee.

---

[1] " Parvulus natus est nobis, et Filius datus est nobis."—*Isa.* ix. 6.
[2] " Jesus meus, et omnia."
[3] " Quomodo non etiam cum illo omnia nobis donavit?"—*Rom.* viii. 32.
[4] " Deum a me tollere nemo potest."
[5] " Quis nos separabit a charitate Christi?"—*Rom.* viii. 35.

MEDITATION II.

DECEMBER 17.

Bitterness of the Heart of Jesus in the Womb of his Mother.

Hostiam et oblationem noluisti; corpus autem aptasti mihi.

" Sacrifice and oblation Thou wouldest not ; but a body Thou hast fitted to Me."—*Heb.* x. 5.

Consider the great bitterness with which the heart of the Infant Jesus must have felt itself afflicted and oppressed in the womb of Mary at the first moment when his Father proposed to his consideration all the series of contempt, sorrow, and agonies which he was to suffer during his life, to deliver men from their miseries: *In the morning He wakeneth my ear,*[1] *and I do not resist; I have given my body to the strikers.*[2]

Thus did Jesus speak by the mouth of the prophet: *In the morning He wakeneth my ear;* that is to say, from the first moment of my conception my Father made me feel that it was his will that I should lead a life of sorrows, and in the end should be sacrified on the cross: *And I do not resist; I have given my body to the strikers.* And all this I accepted for your salvation, O ye souls of men, and from that time forth I gave up my body to the scourges, to the nails, and to the death of the cross.

Consider that whatever Jesus Christ suffered in his life and in his Passion, was all placed before him whilst he was yet in the womb of Mary, and he accepted everything that was proposed to him with delight; but in accepting all this, and in overcoming the natural repugnance of sense, O my God, what anguish and oppression did not the innocent heart of Jesus suffer ! Well did he

---

[1] " Mane erigit mihi aurem. . . ."—*Isa.* l. 4.

[2] " Ego autem non contradico . . . ; corpus meum dedi percutientibus."—*Ibid.* 6.

understand what he was first of all to endure, shut up for nine months in the dark prison of the womb of Mary; in suffering the shame and the sorrows of his birth, being born in a cold grotto that was a stable for beasts; in having afterwards to lead for thirty years an humble life in the shop of an artisan; in considering that he was to be treated by men as ignorant, as a slave, as a seducer, and as one guilty of death, and of the most infamous and painful death that ever was allotted to the most worthless of criminals.

All this did our dearest Redeemer accept every moment; but each moment that he accepted it he suffered at once all the the pains and humiliations that he would afterwards have to endure even unto death. The very knowledge of his divine dignity made him feel still more the injuries that he would have to receive from men: *All the day long my shame is before me.*[1] He had continually before his eyes his shame, especially that confusion which he should one day feel at seeing himself stripped naked, scourged, and suspended by three iron nails; and so to end his life in the midst of the insults and curses of those very men for whom he was to die: *Becoming obedient unto death, even to the death of the cross.*[2] And for what? To save us miserable and ungrateful sinners.

Affections and Prayers.

My beloved Redeemer, oh, how much did it cost Thee, even from Thy first entrance into the world, to raise me from the ruin which I have brought on myself by my sins! Thou hast consented to be treated as the lowest of slaves, in order to deliver me from the slavery of the devil, to whom I had willingly sold myself by sin; and yet, knowing all this, I have had the boldness to afflict continually Thy most amiable heart, which

---

[1] "Tota die verecundia mea contra me est."—*Ps.* xliii. 16

[2] "Factus obediens usque ad mortem, mortem autem crucis."—*Phil.* ii 8.

has loved me so much! But since Thou, who art so innocent, and art my God, hast accepted such a painful life and death, I accept for Thy love, O my Jesus, every trouble that shall come to me from Thy hands. I accept it and embrace it, because it comes from those hands which were once pierced through, in order to deliver me from the hell which I have so often deserved. Thy love, O my Redeemer! in offering Thyself to suffer so much for me, does more than oblige me to accept for Thy sake every sorrow, every humiliation. O my Lord! for Thy own merit's sake, give me Thy holy love; Thy love will render all sufferings and ignominy sweet and pleasant to me. I love Thee above everything: I love Thee with my whole heart; I love Thee more than myself. But during Thy whole life how many and what great proofs of Thy love didst Thou not give me; and yet, ungrateful that I am, how many years have I not lived in the world without giving Thee any proofs of my love! I dread appearing before Thee when Thou shalt come to judge me, poor as I now am, without having done anything for the love of Thee. But what can I do without Thy grace? I can do nothing but pray that Thou wilt succor me; but even this prayer comes simply from Thy grace. O my Jesus! help me through the merits of Thy sufferings, and of the blood Thou hast shed for me. Most holy Mary, recommend me to thy Son, for the love that thou bearest him. Behold, I am one of those sheep for which thy Son has died.

MEDITATION III.

DECEMBER 18.

Jesus made Himself a Child to gain our Confidence and our Love.

Parvulus natus est nobis, et Filius datus est nobis.

"A child is born to us, and a son is given to us."—*Isa.* ix. 6.

Consider that after so many centuries, after so many prayers and sighs, the Messias, whom the holy patriarchs and prophets were not worthy to see, whom the nations sighed for, "the Desire of the eternal hills," our Saviour, is come; he is already born, and has given himself entirely to us: *A child is born to us, and a son is given to us.*[1]

The Son of God has made himself little, in order to make us great; he has given himself to us, in order that we may give ourselves to him; he is come to show us his love, in order that we may respond to it by giving him ours. Let us, therefore, receive him with affection; let us love him, and have recourse to him in all our necessities.

"A child gives easily,"[2] says St. Bernard; children readily give anything that is asked of them. Jesus came into the world a child, in order to show himself ready and willing to give us all good gifts: *In whom are hid all treasures.*[3] *The Father hath given all things into His hands.*[4] If we wish for light, he is come on purpose to enlighten us. If we wish for strength to resist our enemies, he is come to give us comfort. If we wish for pardon and salvation, he is come to pardon and save us. If, in short, we desire the sovereign gift of divine love, he is come to inflame our hearts with it; and, above all, for this very purpose, he has become a child, and has chosen to show himself to us worthy of our love, in proportion as he was poor and humble, in order to take away from us all fear, and to gain our affections. "So," says St. Peter Chrysologus, "should he come who willed to drive away fear, and seek for love."[5]

Jesus has, besides, chosen to come as a little child to make us love him, not only with an appreciative but even with a tender love. All infants attract the tender affection of those who behold them; but who will not

---

[1] " Parvulus natus est nobis, et Filius datus est nobis."
[2] "Puer facile donat."—*In Epiph.* s. 1.
[3] " In quo sunt omnes thesauri."—*Col.* ii. 3.
[4] " Omnia dedit in manu ejus."—*John*, iii. 35.
[5] " Taliter venire debuit, qui voluit timorem pellere, quærere charitatem."—*Serm.* 158.

love, with all the tenderness of which they are capable, a God whom they behold as a little child, in want of milk to nourish him, trembling with cold, poor, abased, and forsaken, weeping and crying in a manger, and lying on straw? It was this that made the loving St. Francis exclaim: "Let us love the child of Bethlehem, let us love the child of Bethlehem." Come ye souls, and love a God who is become a child, and poor; who is so amiable, and who has come down from heaven to give himself entirely to you."

Affections and Prayers.

O my amiable Jesus! whom I have treated with so much contempt, Thou hast descended from heaven to save us from hell, and to give Thyself entirely to us; how can we, then, have so often despised Thee, and turned our backs upon Thee? O my God! how different is the gratitude of men towards their fellow-creatures! If any one makes them a gift, if any one comes from afar to pay them a visit, if any one shows them a particular mark of affection, they cannot forget it, and feel themselves obliged to repay their benefactors. And yet they are so ungrateful towards Thee, who art their God, and so worthy of their love, and who, for their sake, didst not refuse to give Thy blood and Thy love. But, alas! I have been worse than others in my conduct towards Thee, because I have been more loved by Thee, and more ungrateful towards Thee. Ah, if Thou hadst bestowed those graces with which I have been favored on a heretic, or an idolater, he would have become a saint; and yet I have done nothing but offend Thee. O my Saviour I pray Thee, forget the injuries I have committed against Thee. But Thou hast indeed said that when a sinner repents, Thou rememberest no longer the injuries Thou hast received from him: *All his iniquities I will not remember.*[1] If in times past I have not loved Thee, in future I will do nothing else but love Thee. Thou hast given Thyself entirely to me, and I give Thee my whole will; O Lord, I love Thee, I love

[1] "Omnium iniquitatum ejus ... non recordabor."—*Ezech.* xviii. 22.

Thee, I love Thee; and I will continually repeat to Thee, I love Thee, I love Thee! While I live, I will constantly say this; and when I die, I will yield my last breath with these sweet words on my lips, "My God, I love Thee;" and from the moment of my entrance into eternity, I will begin to love Thee with a love that shall last forever, without ever again ceasing to love Thee. And in the mean time, O my Lord! my only good and my only love, I intend to prefer Thy will to every pleasure of my own. Let the whole world offer itself to me; I will refuse it; for I will never cease to love him that hath loved me so much; I will never again offend him who deserves from me an infinite love. Do Thou, O my Jesus! aid my desire with Thy grace. O Mary, my Queen! I acknowledge all the graces I have received from God through thy intercession; cease not, then, to intercede for me. Do thou obtain for me perseverance, thou who art the Mother of perseverance.

MEDITATION IV.

DECEMBER 19.

The Passion of Jesus lasted during His Whole Life.

Dolor meus in conspectu meo semper.

"My sorrow is continually before me."—*Ps.* xxvii. 18.

Consider that in the first moment that the soul of Jesus Christ was created and united to his little body in the womb of Mary, the Eternal Father intimated to his Son his will that he should die for the redemption of the world; and in this same moment he presented to his view the entire dreadful scene of the sufferings he would have to endure, even unto death, in order to redeem mankind. He brought before him in that moment all the labors, contempt, and poverty that he would have to suffer during his whole life, as well in Bethlehem as in Egypt and in Nazareth; and then all the sufferings and ignominy of his Passion, the scourges, the thorns, the nails, and the cross; all the weariness, the sadness, the agonies, and the abandonment in which he was to end his life upon Calvary.

When Abraham was leading his son to death, he would not afflict him by giving him notice of it beforehand, even during the short time that was necessary for them to arrive at the mount. But the Eternal Father chose that his Incarnate Son, whom he had destined to be the victim of his justice in atonement of our sins, should suffer then all the pains to which he was to be subject during his life and at his death. Wherefore, from the first moment that he was in his mother's womb, Jesus suffered continually that sorrow which he endured in the garden, and which was sufficient to have taken away his life (as he said, *My soul is sorrowful unto death*[1]). So that from that time forth he felt most vividly, and endured the united weight of all the sorrows and contumely that awaited him.

The whole life, then, of our blessed Redeemer, and all the years that he spent, were a life and years of pains and tears: *My life is wasted with grief, and My years in sighs.*[2] His divine heart never passed one moment free from suffering. Whether he watched or slept, whether he labored or rested, whether he prayed or spoke, he had continually before his eyes that bitter representation which tormented his holy soul more than all their sufferings tormented the holy martyrs. The martyrs have suffered; but, assisted by grace, they suffered with joy and fervor. Jesus Christ suffered; but he suffered with a heart full of weariness and sorrow; and he accepted all for the love of us.

[1] " Tristis est anima mea usque ad mortem."—*Matt.* xxvi. 38.
[2] " Defecit in dolore vita mea, et anni mei in gemitibus."—*Ps.* xxx. 11.

Affections and Prayers.

O sweet, O amiable, O loving Heart of Jesus! even from Thy infancy Thou wert full of bitterness, and Thou didst suffer agonies in the womb of Mary without consolation, and without having any one to look upon Thee and to console Thee by their sympathy. All this Thou didst suffer, O my Jesus! in order to satisfy for the eternal sorrow and agony which I deserved to endure in hell for my sins. Thou didst then suffer, deprived of all relief, to save me, who have had the boldness to forsake God, and to turn my back upon him, in order to satisfy my miserable inclinations. I thank Thee, O afflicted and loving Heart of my Lord! I thank Thee, and I sympathize with Thee, especially when I see that whilst Thou dost suffer so much for the love of man, these very men do not even pity Thee. O love of God, O ingratitude of man! O men, O men, behold this little innocent lamb who is in agony for you, to satisfy the divine justice for the injuries you have committed against him. See how he prays and intercedes for you with his eternal Father; behold him and love him. O my Redeemer! how few are those who think of your sorrows and your love! O God, how few are those that love Thee! But unhappy me, for I also have lived so many years in forgetfulness of Thee! Thou hast suffered so much in order to be loved by me, and I have not loved Thee. Forgive me, my Jesus, forgive me, for I will amend my life and love Thee. Ah, wretched me, O Lord, if I still resist Thy grace, and in resisting it damn myself! All the mercies that Thou hast shown me, and, above all, Thy sweet voice, which now calls me to love Thee, would be my greatest punishment in hell. My beloved Jesus, have pity on me, let me not live any longer ungrateful to Thy love; give me light, give me strength to conquer everything, in order to accomplish Thy will. Grant my prayer, I beseech Thee, for the merits of Thy Passion. In this is all my confidence, and in thy intercession, O Mary! My dearest Mother, help me; it is thou who hast obtained for me all the favors I have received from God: I bless thee for them; but if thou dost not persevere in helping me, I shall persevere in being faithless, as I have been in times past.

MEDITATION V.

DECEMBER 20.

Jesus Offered Himself for our Salvation from the Beginning.

Oblatus est, quia ipse voluit.
"He was offered because it was His own will."—*Isa.* liii. 7.

The divine Word, from the first instant that he was made man and an infant in Mary's womb, offered himself of his own accord to suffer and to die for the ransom of the world : *He was offered because it was His own will.*[1] He knew that all the sacrifices of goats and bulls offered to God in times past had not been able to satisfy for the sins of men, but that it required a divine Person to pay the price of their redemption ; wherefore he said, as the Apostle tells us, *When He cometh into the world He saith : Sacrifice and oblation Thou wouldst not, but a body Thou hast fitted to me. . . . Then said I, Behold, I come.*[2] "My Father," said Jesus, "all the victims hitherto offered to Thee have not sufficed, nor could they suffice, to satisfy Thy justice ; Thou hast given me this passible body, in order that by shedding my blood I might appease Thee and save men : 'Behold, I come ;' here I am ready, I accept everything, and I submit myself in everything to Thy will."

The inferior part felt repugnance, for it naturally was averse to this life and death, so full of sufferings and shame ; but the rational part, which was entirely subordinate to the will of his Father, conquered and accepted everything ; and Jesus began from that moment to suffer all the anguish and sorrows that he would have to suffer during all the years of his life. Thus did our

---

[1] "Oblatus est quia ipse voluit."
[2] "Ideo ingrediens mundum dicit : Hostiam et oblationem noluisti ; corpus autem aptasti mihi. . . . Tunc dixi : Ecce venio."—*Heb.* x. 5.

226 Meditations for the Novena for Christmas.

Redeemer act from the very first moment of his entrance into the world.

But, O God! how have we conducted ourselves towards Jesus since we began, as adults, to know by the light of faith the sacred Mysteries of Redemption? What thoughts, what designs, what goods have we loved! Pleasures, amusements, vengeance, sensuality; these are the goods that have engrossed the affections of our hearts. But if we have faith, we must at last change our life and our affections. Let us love a God who has suffered so much for us. Let us represent to ourselves the sufferings which the heart of Jesus endured for us, even from his infancy; for then we shall not be able to love anything else but that heart which hath loved us so much.

Affections and Prayers.

My Lord, wilt Thou know how I have behaved towards Thee during all my life? Ever since I began to have the use of reason, I began to despise Thy grace and Thy love. But Thou knowest it much better than I do; nevertheless, Thou hast borne with me, because Thou still carest for my welfare. I fled from Thee, and Thou didst follow after and call me. The very same love that made Thee come down from heaven to seek the lost sheep has made Thee bear with me and not forsake me. My Jesus, Thou now seekest me, and I seek Thee. I feel that Thy grace is assisting me: it assists me with the sorrow I feel for my sins, which I abhor above every other evil; it assists me by making me feel a great desire to love Thee and to please Thee. Yea, Lord, I will love Thee and please Thee as much as I can. On one side I feel afraid, it is true, at the thought of my frailty and the weakness which I have contracted by my sins; but Thy grace gives me a greater confidence, and causes me to hope in Thy merits; so that I can say, from the bottom of my heart: *I can do all things in Him who strengtheneth me.*[1] If I am weak, Thou wilt give me strength against my enemies; if I am infirm, I hope that Thy

[1] "Omnia possum in eo qui me confortat."—*Phil.* iv. 13.

blood will be my medicine; if I am a sinner, I hope Thou wilt make me a saint. I acknowledge that I have hitherto cooperated to my own ruin, because I have neglected, on dangerous occasions, to have recourse to Thee. But from this day forth, my Jesus and my hope, I will always have recourse to Thee; and from Thee I hope for every assistance and every good. I love Thee above all things, and I will always love Thee alone. Have pity on me, and help me through the merits of all those sufferings which from Thy infancy Thou hast endured for me. Eternal Father, for the sake of Jesus Christ accept of my love. If I have offended Thee, let the tears of the Infant Jesus, who is praying for me, appease Thy wrath: " Look on the face of Thy Christ."[1] I do not deserve favors, but this Thy guiltless Son deserves them, who offers Thee a life of sufferings, in order that Thou mayest be merciful to me. And thou, O Mary, Mother of mercy, cease not to intercede for me. Thou knowest how much I confide in thee; and I know well that thou dost not forsake him that has recourse to th

MEDITATION VI.

DECEMBER 21.

Jesus a Prisoner in the Womb of Mary.

Factus sum sicut homo sine adjutorio, inter mortuos liber.
" I am become as a man without help, free among the dead."—*Ps.* lxxxvii. 5, 6.

Consider the painful life that Jesus Christ led in the womb of his Mother, and the long-confined and dark imprisonment that he suffered there for nine months. Other infants are indeed in the same state; but they do not feel the miseries of it, because they do not know them. But Jesus knew them well, because from the first moment of his life he had the perfect use of reason. He had his senses, but he could not use them; eyes, but he could not see; a tongue, but he could not speak; hands, but he could not stretch them out; feet, but he could not walk;—so that for nine months he had to re-

[1] " Respice in faciem Christi tui."—*Ps.* lxxxiii. 10.

main in the womb of Mary like a dead man shut up in the tomb : *I am become as a man without help, free among the dead.*[1] He was free, because he had of his own freewill made himself a prisoner of love in this prison ; but love deprived him of liberty, and bound him there so fast in chains that he could not move : "Free among the dead ! oh, great patience of our Saviour !"[2] says St. Ambrose, while he considered the sufferings of Jesus in the womb of Mary.

The womb of Mary was, therefore, to our Redeemer a voluntary prison, because it was a prison of love. But it was also not an unjust prison : he was indeed innocent himself, but he had offered himself to pay our debts and to satisfy for our crimes. It was therefore only reasonable for the divine justice to keep him thus imprisoned, and so begin to exact from him the due satisfaction.

Behold the state to which the Son of God reduces himself for the love of men ! he deprives himself of his liberty and puts himself in chains, to deliver us from the chains of hell. What gratitude and love should we not show in return for the love and goodness of our deliverer and our surety, who, not by compulsion but only out of love, offered himself to pay, and has paid for us, our debts and our penalties by giving up his divine life ! *Forget not the kindness of thy surety; for He hath given His life for thee.*[3]

Affections and Prayers.

Forget not the kindness of thy surety.[4] Yes, my Jesus, the prophet has reason to warn me not to forget the immense favor which Thou hast shown me. I was the debtor, I the criminal, and

[1] "Sicut homo sine adjutorio, inter mortuos liber."
[2] "O grandis patientia Salvatoris !"
[3] "Gratiam fidejussoris ne obliviscaris ; dedit enim pro te animam suam."—*Ecclus.* xxix. 19.
[4] "Gratiam fidejussoris ne obliviscaris."

Thou the innocent one; Thou, O my God! hast chosen to satisfy for my sins by Thy sufferings and Thy death. But after all this kindness I have forgotten Thy favors and Thy love, and I have had the boldness to turn my back upon Thee, as if Thou hadst not been my Lord, and that Lord who has loved me so much. But if in times past I have forgotten Thy mercies, O my dear Redeemer! I will in future never forget them again. Thy sufferings and Thy death shall be the constant subjects of my thoughts, because they will always recall to my mind the love that Thou hast borne me. Cursed be the days in which, forgetting what Thou hast suffered for me, I have made so bad a use of my liberty. Thou hast given it to me to love Thee, and I have used it to despise Thee. But I now consecrate entirely to Thee this liberty which Thou hast given me. I beseech Thee, my Saviour, deliver me from the misery of seeing myself again separated from Thee, and again made the slave of Lucifer. I implore Thee to bind my poor soul to Thy feet by Thy holy love, so that it may never again be separated from Thee. Eternal Father, by the imprisonment of the infant Jesus in the womb of Mary, deliver me from the chains of sin and of hell. And thou, O Mother of God, help me! Thou hast in thy womb the Son of God imprisoned and confined; as, therefore, Jesus is thy prisoner, he will do everything that thou tellest him. Tell him to pardon me; tell him to make me holy. Help me, my Mother, for the sake of the favor and honor that Jesus Christ conferred upon thee by dwelling within thee for nine months.

MEDITATION VII.

DECEMBER 22.

The Sorrow that the Ingratitude of Men has caused Jesus.

In propria venit, et sui eum non receperunt.

"He came unto His own, and His own received Him not."—*St. John*, i. 11.

In these days of the holy Nativity St. Francis of Assisi went about the highways and woods with sighs and tears and inconsolable lamentations. When asked the reason, he answered: How should I not weep when I see that love is not loved! I see a God become, as it were foolish, for the love of man, and man so ungrateful to this God! Now, if this ingratitude of man caused so great a sorrow to the heart of St. Francis, let us consider how much more it must have afflicted the heart of Jesus Christ.

He was hardly conceived in the womb of Mary when he saw the cruel return he was to receive from man. He had descended from heaven to enkindle the fire of divine love, and this desire alone had brought him down to this earth, to suffer there an abyss of sorrows and ignominies: *I am come to cast fire on the earth; and what will I but that it be kindled?*[1] And then he beheld an abyss of sins which men would commit after having seen so many proofs of his love. It was this, says St. Bernardine of Sienna, which made him feel an infinite sorrow: "And therefore he sorrowed infinitely."[2]

Even among us it is an insufferable sorrow for one man to see himself treated with ingratitude by another; for the blessed Simon of Cassia observes that ingratitude often afflicts the soul more than any pain afflicts the body: "Ingratitude often causes more bitter sorrow in the soul than pain causes in the body."[3] What sorrow, then, must our ingratitude have caused to Jesus, who was our God, when he saw that his benefits and his love would be repaid him by offences and injuries! *And they repaid Me evil for good, and hatred for My love.*[4] But even at the present day it seems as if Jesus Christ was going about complaining: *I am become a stranger to My brethren.*[5] For he sees that many neither love nor know him, as if

---

[1] "Ignem veni mittere in terram, et quid volo, nisi ut accendatur?" *Luke*, xii. 49.

[2] "Et ideo infinite dolebat."

[3] "Tristitiam acriorem sæpe in anima fecit ingratitudo, quam dolor inflictus in corpore."

[4] "Et posuerunt adversum me mala pro bonis, et odium pro dilectione mea!"—*Ps.* cviii. 5.

[5] "Extraneus factus sum fratribus meis."—*Ps.* lxviii. 9.

he had not done them any good, nor had suffered anything for love of them. O God, what value do the majority of Christians even now set upon the love of Jesus Christ? Our blessed Redeemer once appeared to the blessed Henry Suso in the form of a pilgrim who went begging from door to door for a lodging, but every one drove him away with insults and injuries. How many, alas! are like those of whom Job speaks: *Who said to God, Depart from us. Whereas he had filled their houses with good things.*[1]

We have hitherto united ourselves to these ungrateful wretches; but shall we always be like them? No; for that loving Infant does not deserve it, who came from heaven to suffer and die for us, in order that we might love him.

Affections and Prayers.

Is it, then, true, O my Jesus, that Thou didst descend from heaven to make me love Thee; didst come down to embrace a life of suffering and the death of the cross for my sake, in order that I might welcome Thee into my heart, and yet I have so often driven Thee from me, and said, " Depart from me, Lord ;[2] go away from me, Lord ; for I do not want Thee?" O God, if Thou wert not infinite goodness, and hadst not given Thy life to obtain my pardon, I should not have courage to ask it of Thee; but I feel that Thou Thyself dost offer me peace: *Turn ye to me, saith the Lord, and I will turn to you.*[3] Thou Thyself, whom I have offended, O my Jesus, hast made Thyself my intercessor: *He is the propitiation for our sins.*[4] I will therefore not do Thee this fresh injury of distrusting Thy mercy. I repent with all my soul of having despised Thee, O sovereign Good! receive me into Thy favor for the sake of the blood which Thou hast shed for me: *Father, I am not worthy to be*

---
[1] " Qui dicebant Deo: Recede a nobis; . . . cum ille implesset domos eorum bonis!"—*Job*, xxii. 17.
[2] " Recede a me, Domine."
[3] " Convertimini ad me, . . . et convertar ad vos."—*Zach.* i. 3.
[4] " Ipse est propititatio pro peccatis nostris."—1 *John*, ii. 2.

called Thy Son.[1] No, my Redeemer and my Father, I am no longer worthy to be Thy son, having so often renounced Thy love; but Thou dost make me worthy of Thy merits. I thank Thee, O my Father! I thank Thee and I love Thee. Ah, the thought alone of the patience with which Thou hast borne with me for so many years, and of the favors Thou hast conferred upon me after so many injuries that I have done Thee, ought to make me live constantly on fire with Thy love. Come, then, my Jesus, for I will not drive Thee away any more, come and dwell in my poor heart. I love Thee, and will always love Thee; but do Thou inflame my heart every day more and more by the remembrance of the love Thou hast borne me. O Mary, my Queen and Mother, help me, pray to Jesus for me; make me during the days that are left me in this world live grateful to that God who has loved me so much, even after I have so greatly offended him.

MEDITATION VIII.

DECEMBER 23.

The Love of God manifested to Men by the Birth of Jesus.

Apparuit gratia Dei Salvatoris nostri omnibus hominibus, erudiens nos, ut . . . pie vivamus in hoc sæculo, expectantes beatam spem et adventum gloriæ magni Dei et Salvatoris nostri Jesu Christi.

" The grace of God our Saviour hath appeared to all men, instructing us that . . . we should live . . . godly in this world, looking for the blessed hope and coming of the glory of the great God and our Saviour Jesus Christ."— *Titus*, ii. 11.

Consider that by the grace that is said here to have appeared is meant the tender love of Jesus Christ towards men,—a love that we have not merited, which therefore is called "grace."

This love was, however, always the same in God, but did not always appear. It was at first promised in many prophecies, and foreshadowed by many figures; but at the birth of the Redeemer this divine love indeed appeared, and manifested itself by the Eternal Word showing him-

[1] " Pater, . . . jam non sum dignus vocari filius tuus."—*Luke*, xv. 21.

self to man as an infant, lying on straw, crying and shivering with cold; beginning thus to make satisfaction for us for the penalties we have deserved, and so making known to us the affection which he bore us, by giving up his life for us: *In this we have known the charity of God, because he hath laid down his life for us.*[1] Therefore the love of our God appeared to all men.[2]

But why is it, then, that all men have not known it, and that even at this day so many are ignorant of it? This is the reason: *The light is come into the world, and men loved darkness rather than the light.*[3] They have not known him, and they do not know him, because they do not wish to know him, loving rather the darkness of sin than the light of grace.

But let us endeavor not to be of the number of these unhappy souls. If in past times we have shut our eyes to the light, thinking little of the love of Jesus Christ, let us try, during the days that may remain to us in this life, to have ever before our eyes the sufferings and death of our Redeemer, in order to love him who hath loved us so much: *Looking for the blessed hope and coming of the glory of the great God and our Saviour Jesus Christ.*[4] Thus may we justly expect, according to the divine promises, that paradise which Jesus Christ has acquired for us by his blood. At his first coming Jesus appeared as an infant, poor and humble, and showed himself on earth born in a stable, covered with miserable rags, and lying on straw; but at his second coming he will come on a throne of majesty: *We shall see the Son of Man coming in*

---

[1] "In hoc cognovimus charitatem Dei, quoniam ille animam suam pro nobis posuit."—1 *John*, iii. 16.

[2] "Omnibus hominibus."

[3] "Lux venit in mundum, et dilexerunt homines magis tenebras quam lucem."—*John*, iii. 19.

[4] "Expectantes beatam spem et adventum gloriæ magni Dei et Salvatoris nostri Jesu Christi."

the clouds with great power and majesty.[1] Blessed then will he be who shall have loved him, and miserable those who have not loved him.

Affections and Prayers.

O my holy Infant! now I see Thee lying on straw, poor, afflicted, and forsaken ; but I know that one day Thou wilt come to judge me, seated on a throne of splendor, and attended by the angels. Forgive me, I implore Thee, before Thou dost judge me. Then Thou wilt have to conduct Thyself as a just judge; but now Thou art my Redeemer, and the Father of mercy. I have been one of those ungrateful ones who have not known Thee, because I did not choose to know Thee, and therefore, instead of being inclined to love Thee by the consideration of the love Thou hast borne me, I have only thought of satisfying my own desires, despising Thy grace and Thy love. But into Thy sacred hands I commend my soul, which I have lost; do Thou save it: *Into Thy hands I commend my spirit; Thou hast redeemed me, O Lord, the God of truth.*[2] In Thee do I place all my hopes, knowing that, to ransom me from hell, Thou hast given Thy blood and Thy life : *Thou hast redeemed me, O Lord, the God of truth.*[3] Thou didst not condemn me to death when I was living in sin, but hast waited for me with infinite patience, in order that, having come to myself, I might repent of having offended Thee, and might begin to love Thee, and that thus Thou mightest be able to forgive and save me. Yes, my Jesus, I will please Thee. I repent, above every other evil, of all the offences I have committed against Thee; I repent, and love Thee above all things. Do Thou save me in Thy mercy, and let it be my salvation to love Thee always in this life and in eternity. My dearest Mother Mary, recommend me to thy Son. Do thou represent to him that I am thy servant, and that I have placed all my hope in thee. He hears thee, and refuses thee nothing.

[1] " Videbunt Filium hominis venientem in nubibus cœli, cum virtute magna et majestate."—*Matt.* xxiv. 30.

[2] " In manus tuas commendo spiritum meum ; redemisti me, Domine, Deus veritatis."—*Ps.* xxx. 6.

[3] " Redemisti me, Domine."

MEDITATION IX.

DECEMBER 24.

Saint Joseph goes to Bethlehem with His Holy Spouse.

Ascendit autem et Joseph . . ., ut profiteretur cum Maria desponsata sibi uxore prægnante.

" And Joseph also went up . . . to be enrolled with Mary his espoused wife, who was with child."—*St. Luke*, ii. 4.

God had decreed that his Son should be born not in the house of Joseph, but in a cavern and stable of beasts, in the poorest and most painful way that a child can be born; and therefore he caused Cæsar to publish an edict, by which people were commanded to go and enroll themselves, every one in his own city whence he drew his origin.

When Joseph heard this order, he was much agitated as to whether he should take with him or leave behind the Virgin Mother, as she was now so near childbirth. My spouse and my lady, said he to her, on the one hand, I do not wish to leave you alone; on the other, if I take you with me, I am much afflicted at the thought of all that you will have to suffer during this long journey, and in such severe weather. My poverty will not permit me to conduct you with that comfort which you require. But Mary answers him, and tries to give him courage with these words: My Joseph, do not fear. I will go with you; the Lord will assist us. She knew, both by divine inspiration, and also because she was well versed in the prophecy of Micheas, that the divine Infant was to be born in Bethlehem. She therefore takes the swaddling-clothes, and the other miserable garments already prepared, and departs with Joseph. *And Joseph also went up . . . to be enrolled with Mary.*[1]

Let us now consider all the devout ond holy discourses

---

[1] " Ascendit autem et Joseph . . ., ut profiteretur cum Maria."

which these two holy spouses must have held together during this journey concerning the mercy, goodness, and love of the divine Word, who was shortly to be born, and to appear on the earth for the salvation of men. Let us also consider the praises, the benedictions, the thanksgivings, the acts of humility and love, which these two illustrious pilgrims uttered on the way. This holy Virgin, so soon to become a mother, certainly suffered much in so long a journey, made in the middle of winter, and over rough roads; but she suffered with peace and with love. She offered to God all these her trials, uniting them to those of Jesus, whom she carried in her womb.

Oh, let us unite ourselves also, and let us accompany Mary and Joseph in the journey of our life; and, with them, let us accompany the King of Heaven, who is born in a cave, and makes his first appearance in the world as an infant, but as the poorest and most forsaken infant that ever was born amongst men. And let us beseech Jesus, Mary, and Joseph that, through the merits of the pains which they suffered in this journey, they would accompany us in the journey that we are making to eternity. Oh, blessed shall we be if, in life and in death, we keep company with these three great personages, and are always accompanied by them!

Affections and Prayers.

My beloved Redeemer, I know that in this journey Thou wast accompanied by hosts of angels from heaven; but on this earth who was there that bore Thee company? Thou hadst but Joseph and Mary who carried Thee with her. Refuse not, O my Jesus! that I also accompany Thee. Miserable ungrateful sinner that I have been, I now see the injuries I have done Thee; Thou didst come down from heaven to make Thyself my companion on earth, and I by my frequent offences have ungratefully abandoned Thee! When I remember, O my Saviour! that for the sake of my own cursed inclinations I have often separated myself from Thee and renounced Thy friendship, I could wish to die of sorrow. But Thou didst come into the world to forgive me; therefore forgive me now, I beseech Thee, for I repent with all my soul of having so often turned my back upon Thee and forsaken Thee. I purpose and hope, through Thy grace, nevermore to leave or separate myself from Thee, O my only love! My soul has become enamoured of Thee, O my amiable Infant God! I love Thee, my sweet Saviour; and since Thou hast come upon earth to save me and to dispense to me Thy graces, I ask this one only grace of Thee, permit me not to be ever again separated from Thee. Unite me, bind me to Thyself, enchain me with the sweet cords of Thy holy love. O my Redeemer and my God, who will then have the heart to leave Thee, and to live without Thee, deprived of Thy grace? Most holy Mary, I come to accompany thee in this journey; and thou, O my Mother, cease not to accompany me in the journey that I am making to eternity. Do thou assist me always, but especially when I shall find myself at the end of my life, and near that moment on which will depend either my remaining always with thee to love Jesus in paradise, or my being forever separated from thee and hating Jesus in hell. My Queen, save me by thy intercession; and may my salvation be to love thee and Jesus forever, in time and in eternity. Thou art my hope; I hope everything from thee.

Meditations for the Octave of Christmas, and for the following Days until the Epiphany.

MEDITATION I.

DECEMBER 25.

The Birth of Jesus.

The birth of Jesus Christ caused a universal joy to the whole world. He was the Redeemer who had been desired and sighed after for so many years; and therefore he was called the desired of the nations, and the desire of the eternal hills. Behold him already come, and born in a little cave. Let us consider that this day the angel announces to us also the same great joy that he announced to the shepherds: *Behold, I bring you good tidings of great joy, that shall be to all the people; for this day is born to you a Saviour.*[1]

What rejoicing is there in a country when the first-born son is born to a king! But surely we ought to keep still greater festival when we see the Son of God born and come down from heaven to visit us, urged to this by the bowels of his mercy: *Through the bowels of the mercy of our God, in which the Orient from on high hath visited us.*[2] We were lost; and behold him who came to save us: *He came down from heaven for our salvation.*[3] Behold the shepherd who came to save his sheep from death by giving his life for their sake: *I am the good shepherd; the good shepherd giveth his life for his sheep.*[4] Behold the Lamb of

[1] "Ecce enim evangelizo vobis gaudium magnum, quod erit omni populo, quia natus est vobis hodie Salvator."—*Luke*, ii. 10.

[2] "Per viscera misericordiæ Dei nostri, in quibus visitavit nos Oriens ex alto."—*Luke*, i. 78.

[3] "Propter nostram salutem, descendit de cœlis."—*Symb. Nic.*

[4] "Ego sum Pastor bonus. Bonus Pastor animam suam dat pro ovibus suis."—*John*, x. 11.

God, who came to sacrifice himself, to obtain for us the divine favor, and to become our deliverer, our life, our light, and even our food in the most Holy Sacrament!

St. Maximus says that for this reason, amongst others, Christ chose to be laid in the manger where the animals were fed, to make us understand that he has become man also to make himself our food: "In the manger, where the food of animals is placed, he allowed his limbs to be laid, thereby showing that his own body would be the eternal food of men."[1] Besides this, he is born every day in the Sacrament by means of the priests and the words of consecration; the altar is the crib, and there we go to feed ourselves on his flesh. Some one might desire to have the Holy Infant in his arms, as the aged Simeon had; but faith teaches us that, when we receive Communion, the same Jesus who was in the manger of Bethlehem is not only in our arms, but in our breasts. He was born for this purpose, to give himself entirely to us: *A child is born to us, a son is given to us.*[2]

Affections and Prayers.

I have gone astray like a sheep that is lost; seek Thy servant.[3] O Lord, I am that sheep which, by following after my own pleasures and caprices, have miserably lost myself; but Thou, who art at once the shepherd and divine Lamb, art he who camest down from heaven to save me by sacrificing Thyself as a victim on the cross in satisfaction for my sins. *Behold, the Lamb of God; behold Him who taketh away the sins of the world.* If, therefore, I desire to amend my life, what need I fear? why should I not confide entirely in Thee, O my Saviour, who wert born on purpose to save me? *Behold, God is my Saviour; I will*

[1] "In præsepio, ubi pastus est animalium, sua collocari membra permittit; in æternam refectionem vescendum a mortalibus suum corpus ostendit."—*In Nat. D.* s. 5.

[2] "Parvulus natus est nobis, et Filius datus est nobis."—*Isa.* ix. 6.

[3] "Erravi sicut ovis quæ periit; quære servum tuum."—*Ps.* cxviii. 176.

[4] "Ecce Agnus Dei, ecce qui tollit peccatum."—*John*, i. 29.

put my trust in him, and will not fear.[1] What greater proof couldst Thou give me of Thy mercy, O my dearest Redeemer, to inspire me with confidence, than to give me Thyself? O my dear Infant, how grieved am I that I have offended Thee! I have made Thee weep in the stable of Bethlehem. But since Thou art come to seek me, I throw myself at Thy feet; and although I behold Thee afflicted and humbled, lying upon straw in the manger, I acknowledge Thee for my supreme king and sovereign. I feel that Thy tender infant-cries invite me to love Thee, and demand my heart. Behold it, my Jesus; I present it to-day at Thy feet; change it and inflame it, O Thou who didst come into the world to inflame the hearts of men with Thy holy love. I feel as if I heard Thee say to me in Thy manger, *Love the Lord thy God with thy whole heart.*[2] And I will answer, Ah, my Jesus, if I do not love Thee, who art my Lord and my God, whom shall I love? Thou callest Thyself mine, because Thou wert born in order to give Thyself entirely to me; and shall I refuse to be Thine? No, my beloved Lord, I give myself entirely to Thee; and I love Thee with my whole heart. I love Thee, I love Thee, I love Thee, O sovereign Good, the one only love of my soul. I beseech Thee accept me this day, and permit me not evermore to cease to love Thee. O Mary, my Queen, I pray thee, through that consolation which thou didst enjoy the first time thou didst behold thy new-born Son and didst give him thy first kiss, beseech him to accept me for his servant, and to enchain me forever to himself by the gift of his holy love.

MEDITATION II.

December 26.

Jesus is born an Infant

Consider that the first sign which the angel gave to the shepherds whereby they might discover the new-born Messias was that they would find him under the form of

---

[1] "Ecce Deus Salvator meus; fiducialiter agam, et non timebo."—*Isa.* xii. 2.

[2] "Diliges Dominum Deum tuum ex toto corde tuo."—*Matt.* xxii. 37.

The Festival of Christmas.

an infant: *You shall find the infant wrapped in swaddling-clothes, and laid in a manger.*[1] The littleness of infants is a great attraction for love; but a still greater attraction must the littleness of the Infant Jesus be to us, who, being the incomprehensible God, has made himself small for the love of us: "For our sake he became a little child."[2]

Adam came into the world at a full age; but the eternal Word chose to appear as an infant—*a child is born to us*[3]—that he might thus attract our hearts to himself with greater force: "so would he be born, who willed to be loved."[4] He came not into the world to inspire terror, but to be loved; and for this reason he preferred to show himself, at his first appearance, as a tender, weak infant. "Our Lord is great, and greatly to be praised,"[5] says St. Peter Chrysologus. My Lord is great, and therefore he deserves highly to be praised for his divine majesty. But when the saint considered him as a little child in the stable of Bethlehem, he exclaimed with tenderness, "My Lord is a little child, and greatly to be loved."[6] My great and supreme God has made himself little for my sake.

Ah, how is it possible that any one can reflect with faith on a God become a little child, crying and wailing on the straw in a cave, and yet not love him, and invite all men to love him, as did St. Francis of Assisi, who said, "Let us love the child of Bethlehem, let us love the child of Bethlehem."[7] He is an infant; he does not

---

[1] "Invenietis infantem pannis involutum, et positum in præsepio."—*Luke*, ii. 12.
[2] "Propter nos factus est parvulus."—*In Ps.* lviii. s. 1.
[3] "Parvulus natus est nobis."
[4] "Sic nasci voluit, qui voluit amari."
[5] "Magnus Dominus et laudabilis nimis."—*Ps.* cxliv. 3.
[6] "Parvus Dominus et amabilis nimis."—*In Cant.* s. 48.
[7] "Amemus Puerum de Bethlehem! Amemus Puerum de Bethlehem!"

speak, he only cries; but, O my God ! are not these cries all voices of love, with which he invites us to love him, and demands our hearts !

Let us consider, besides, that infants also gain our affections because we consider them innocent: but all other infants are born with the infection of original sin; Jesus was born an infant, but he was born holy; " holy, innocent, unpolluted."[1] My beloved, says the holy spouse, is all ruddy with love, and all white with innocence, without a spot of any sin: *My beloved is white and ruddy, chosen out of thousands*.[2] In this Infant did the eternal Father find his delight, because, as St. Gregory says, " in him alone he found no fault."[3]

Let us miserable sinners comfort ourselves, because this divine Infant has come down from heaven to communicate his innocence to us by means of his Passion. His merits, if we only know how to apply them to ourselves, can change us from sinners into innocents and saints: in these merits let us place all our confidence; through them let us continually ask for graces from the eternal Father, and we shall obtain everything.

Affections and Prayers.

Eternal Father, I, a miserable sinner, worthy of hell, have nothing of my own to offer Thee in satisfaction for my sins; I offer Thee the tears, the sufferings, the blood, the death of this Infant, who is Thy Son ; and through them I implore pity from Thee. If I had not this Son to offer Thee, I should be lost; there would be no longer any hope for me ; but Thou hast given him to me for this purpose, in order that, in offering Thee his merits, I might have a good hope of my salvation. My ingratitude, O Lord, is great ; but Thy mercy is still greater. And what greater mercy could I hope for from Thee, than that Thou

---

[1] "Sanctus, innocens, impollutus."—*Heb.* vii. 26.

[2] " Dilectus meus candidus et rubicundus, electus ex millibus."— *Cant.* v. 10.

[3] " In hoc solo non invenit culpam."—*In Ezech. hom.* 8.

shouldst give me Thy own Son for my Redeemer, and for the victim of my sins? For the love, therefore, of Jesus Christ, forgive me all the offences that I have committed against Thee, of which I repent with my whole heart, because by them I have offended Thee, O infinite Goodness. And for the sake of Jesus Christ, I ask of Thee holy perseverance. O my God, if I should again offend Thee, after Thou hast waited for me with so much patience; after Thou hast assisted me with so much light, and forgiven me with so much love,—I should indeed deserve a special hell for myself. O my Father, do not forsake me, I pray Thee. I tremble when I think of the number of times that I have betrayed Thee; how many times have I promised to love Thee, and then have again turned my back upon Thee? O my Creator, let me not have to lament the misfortune of seeing myself again deprived of Thy favor: " Permit me not to be separated from Thee; permit me not to be separated from Thee."[1] I repeat it, and will repeat it to my very last breath; and do Thou always give me the grace to repeat to Thee this prayer: " Permit me not to be separated from Thee."[2] My Jesus, my dearest Infant, enchain me with Thy love. I love Thee, and will always love Thee. Permit me not to be ever again separated from Thy love. I love thee too, my Mother; oh, do thou also love me. And if thou lovest me, this is the favor I beg thee to obtain for me, that I may never cease to love my God.

MEDITATION III.

DECEMBER 27.

Jesus in Swaddling-clothes.

Imagine that you see Mary, having now brought forth her Son, taking him with reverence in her arms, adoring him as her God, and then wrapping him up in swaddling-clothes: *She wrapped Him up in swaddling-clothes.*[3] The Holy Church says the same:

[1] " Ne permittas me separari a te ! ne permittas me separari a te !"
[2] " Ne permittas me separari a te."
[3] " Pannis eum involvit."—*Luke*, ii. 7.

"His limbs, wrapped in swaddling-clothes,
The Virgin Mother binds."[1]

Behold the Infant Jesus, who obediently offers his little hands and feet, and allows himself to be swaddled. Consider that every time the Holy Infant allowed himself to be swathed he thought of the cords with which he should one day be bound and led captive in the garden, and of those also with which he should be tied to the column, and of the nails which should fasten him to the cross; and thinking of these things, he willingly allowed himself to be bound, in order to deliver our souls from the chains of hell.

Bound, then, in these swaddling-clothes, and turning towards us, Jesus invites us to unite ourselves to him with the holy bonds of love. And turning to his eternal Father, he says: My Father, men have abused their liberty, and by rebelling against Thee have made themselves the slaves of sin; but I will make satisfaction for their disobedience, and will be bound and confined in these swaddling-clothes. Bound with these, I offer Thee my liberty, in order that man may be delivered from the slavery of the devil. I accept these swaddling-clothes; they are dear to me, because they are the symbols of the cords with which, from this moment forth, I offer myself to be one day bound and led to death for the salvation of men.

His bands are a healthful binding.[2] The bands of Jesus were the healthful binding, to heal the wounds of our souls. Therefore, O my Jesus, Thou wouldst be bound in swaddling-clothes for the love of me. "O Love, how great is thy bond, which could bind a God."[3] O divine Love, Thou alone couldst make my God Thy prisoner.

[1] "Membra pannis involuta Virgo Mater alligat."—*Off. de Pass.*
[2] "Vincula illius, alligatura salutaris."—*Ecclus.* vi. 31.
[3] "O Charitas! quam magnum est vinculum tuum, quo Deus ligari potuit!"—*Lign. V. de Char.* c. 6.

And shall I then, O Lord, refuse to allow myself to be bound by Thy holy love? Shall I for the future have the courage to detach myself from Thy sweet and amiable chains? And for what? To make myself a slave of hell? O my Lord, Thou remainest bound up in this manger for the love of me; I desire always to remain bound to Thee.

St. Mary Magdalene of Pazzi said that the bands that we ought to take should be a firm resolution of uniting ourselves to God by means of love; detaching ourselves at the same time from all affection for anything that is not God. For this reason, also, it seems that our loving Jesus has allowed himself to be, as it were, bound and made a prisoner in the Most Holy Sacrament of the Altar, under the sacramental species, in order that he might behold his beloved souls made also prisoners of his love.

Affections and Prayers.

And what fear can I have of Thy chastisement, O my beloved Infant, now that I see Thee bound in the swaddling-clothes, depriving Thyself, as it were, of the power of raising Thy hands to punish me? Thou dost give me to understand by these bands that Thou wilt not chastise me, if I will detach myself from the chains of my vices and bind myself to Thee. Yes, my Jesus, I will bind myself. I repent with all my heart of having separated myself from Thee, by abusing that liberty which Thou hast given me. Thou dost offer me a more desirable liberty; a liberty which delivers me from the chains of the devil, and places me among the children of God. Thou hast given Thyself up to be imprisoned in these swaddling-clothes for the love of me; I will be in future a prisoner of Thy infinite love. O blessed chains, O beautiful emblems of salvation, which bind souls to God, bind also my poor heart; but bind it so fast that it may never in future be able to disengage itself from the love of this sovereign Good. My Jesus, I love Thee; I bind myself to Thee; I give Thee my whole heart, my whole will. No, I will never leave Thee again, my beloved Lord. O my Saviour, who, to pay my debts, wouldst not only be wrapped by Mary in swaddling-clothes, but even be bound as a criminal by the executioners, and thus bound wouldst go along the streets of Jerusalem, led to death as an innocent lamb to the slaughter-house; O Thou who wouldst be nailed to the cross, and didst not leave it until Thou hadst given up Thy life upon it,—I beseech Thee permit me not to be ever separated again from Thee, so that I should again find myself deprived of Thy favor and of Thy love. O Mary, who didst one day bind in swaddling-clothes this thy innocent Son, I pray thee, do thou bind me also, a miserable sinner; bind me to Jesus, so that I may never again separate myself from his feet, that I may always live and die bound to him, so that one day I may have the happiness to enter into that blessed country where I shall never be able and shall never be afraid of detaching myself from his holy love.

MEDITATION IV.

DECEMBER 28.

Jesus taking Milk.

As soon as Jesus was swathed, he looked for and took milk from the breast of Mary. The spouse in the Canticles desired to see her little brother taking milk from his mother: *Who shall give thee to me for my brother, sucking the breast of my mother.*[1] The spouse desired it, but did not see him; but we have had the happiness to see the Son of God made Man and become our brother, taking milk from the breasts of Mary. Oh, what a spectacle must it not have been to Paradise to see the divine Word become an infant sucking milk from a virgin who was his own creature!

He, then, who feeds all men and all animals upon the earth, is become so weak and so poor that he requires a little milk to sustain life! Sister Paula, the Camaldolese,

[1] "Quis mihi det te fratrem meum sugentem ubera matris meæ?"— *Cant.* viii. 1.

in contemplating a little image of Jesus taking milk, felt herself immediately all inflamed with a tender love to God. Jesus took but little of this milk, and took it but seldom in the day. It was revealed to Sister Mary Anne, a Franciscan, that Mary only gave him milk three times in the day. O milk most precious to us, to be changed into blood in the veins of Jesus Christ, and so to be made by him a bath of salvation to cleanse our souls!

Let us consider also that Jesus took this milk in order to nourish the body which he wished to leave us as food in the Holy Communion. Therefore, my Blessed Redeemer, whilst Thou dost suck the breast of Mary, Thou art thinking of me; Thou art thinking of changing this milk into blood, to be shed afterwards at Thy death, as the price wherewith to ransom my soul, and as its food in the most Holy Sacrament, which is the salutary milk with which our Lord preserves our souls in the life of grace: "Christ is your milk,"[1] says St. Augustine.

O beloved Infant, O my Jesus, let me also exclaim with the woman in the Gospel, *Blessed is the womb that bare Thee, and the paps that gave Thee suck.*[2] Blessed art thou, O Mother of God, who hadst the happiness to give milk to the Incarnate Word! Oh, admit me, in company with this great Son, to take from thee the milk of a tender and loving devotion to the Infancy of Jesus, and to thyself, my dearest mother.

And I thank Thee, O divine Infant, who didst deign to stand in need of milk for Thy support in order to show me the love that Thou bearest me. This is what our Lord once gave St. Mary Magdalene of Pazzi to understand that he had reduced himself to the necessity of taking milk in order to make us comprehend the love that he has for redeemed souls.

[1] "Lac vestrum Christus est!"—*In 1 Jo. tr.* 3.
[2] "Beatus venter qui te portavit, et ubera quæ suxisti."—*Luke*, xi. 27.

Affections and Prayers.

O my sweet and most amiable Infant, Thou art the bread of heaven, and dost sustain the angels: Thou dost provide all creatures with food ; and yet how art Thou reduced to the necessity of begging a little milk from a Virgin in order to preserve Thy life ! O divine love, how couldst Thou reduce a God to such a state of poverty that he was in want of a little food ? But I understand Thee, O my Jesus! Thou didst take milk from Mary in this stable to offer it to God changed into blood on the cross as a sacrifice, and in satisfaction for our sins. Give, O Mary ! give all the milk thou canst to this Son, because every drop of this milk will serve to wash out the sins of my soul, and to nourish it afterwards in the Holy Communion. O my Redeemer ! how can one not love Thee who believes what Thou hast done and suffered to save us? And I, how could I know this, and yet be so ungrateful to Thee ? But Thy goodness is my hope ; and this makes me sure that if I wish for Thy grace it is mine. I repent, O sovereign Good ! of having offended Thee, and I love Thee above all things. Or, rather, I love nothing, I love and I will love only Thee ; Thou art and shalt always be my only good, my only love. My beloved Redeemer, give me, I pray Thee, a tender devotion to Thy holy Infancy, such as Thou hast given to so many souls, who, meditating on Thee, as an Infant, forgetting all else, seem unable to think of anything but loving Thee. It is true that they are innocent, and I am a sinner ; but Thou didst become a child to make Thyself loved even by sinners. I have been such ; but now I love Thee with my whole heart, and I desire nothing but Thy love. O Mary, give me a little of that tenderness with which thou didst give suck to the Infant Jesus.

MEDITATION V.

DECEMBER 29.

Jesus lying on the Straw.

Jesus is born in the stable at Bethlehem. His poor Mother has neither wool nor down to make a bed for the tender Infant. What does she do, then ? She gathers together a small handful of straw into the manger, and puts it there for him to lie on : *And she laid Him in the manger.*[1] But, O my God, how hard and painful is this bed for an infant just born ; the limbs of a babe are so delicate, and especially the limbs of Jesus, which were formed by the Holy Spirit with a special delicacy, in order that they might be the more sensible to suffering: *A body Thou hast fitted to Me.*[2]

Wherefore the hardness of such a bed must have caused him excessive pain,—pain and shame; for what child, even of the lowest of the people, is ever laid on straw as soon as he is born ? Straw is only a fit bed for beasts; and yet the Son of God had none other on earth than a bed of miserable straw ! St. Francis of Assisi heard one day as he sat at table these words of the Gospel : *And laid Him in the manger;*[3] and exclaimed, " What? my Lord was laid on the straw, and shall I continue to sit?" And thus he arose from his seat, threw himself on the ground, and there finished his scanty meal, mingling it with tears of tenderness as he contemplated the sufferings that the Infant Jesus endured whilst he lay on the straw.

But why did Mary, who had so earnestly desired the birth of this Son—why did she, who loved him so much, allow him to lie and suffer on this hard bed, instead of keeping him in her arms? This is a mystery, says St. Thomas of Villanova : " Nor would she have laid him in such a place, unless there had been some great mystery in it."[4] This great mystery has been explained by many in different ways, but the most pleasing explanation to me is that of St. Peter Damian : Jesus wished as soon as

[1] " Et reclinavit eum in præsepio."—*Luke*, ii. 7.
[2] " Corpus autem aptasti mihi."—*Heb.* x. 5.
[3] " Et reclinavit eum in præsepio."
[4] " Neque illum tali loco posuisset, nisi magnum aliquod **mysterium** ageretur."—*In Natal. D. conc.* 1.

he was born to be placed on the straw, in order to teach us the mortification of our senses: "He laid down the law of martyrdom."[1] The world had been lost by sensual pleasures; through them had Adam and multitudes of his descendants till then been lost. The Eternal Word came from heaven to teach us the love of suffering; and he began as a child to teach it to us by choosing for himself the most acute sufferings that an infant can endure. It was, therefore, he himself who inspired his Mother to cease from holding him in her tender arms, and to replace him on the hard bed, that he might feel the more cold of the cave and the pricking of this rough straw.

Affections and Prayers.

O Lover of souls, O my loving Redeemer! is not, then, the sorrowful Passion that awaits Thee, and the bitter death that is prepared for Thee on the cross, sufficient, but Thou must, even from the commencement of Thy life, even from Thy infancy, begin to suffer? Yes, because even as an infant Thou wouldst begin to be my Redeemer, and to satisfy the divine justice for my sins. Thou didst choose a bed of straw to deliver me from the fire of hell, into which I have so many times deserved to be cast. Thou didst cry and mourn on this bed of straw to obtain for me pardon from Thy Father. Oh, how these Thy tears afflict and yet console me! They afflict me from compassion at seeing Thee, an innocent babe, suffering so much for sins not Thy own; but they console me, because Thy sufferings assure me of my salvation, and of Thy immense love for me. But, my Jesus, I will not leave Thee alone to cry and to suffer. I myself will also weep; for I alone deserve to shed tears on account of the offences I have committed against Thee. I, who have deserved hell, will not refuse any suffering whatever, so that I may regain Thy favor, O my Saviour. Forgive me, I beseech Thee; receive me once more into Thy friendship, make me love Thee, and then chastise me as Thou wilt. Deliver me from eternal punishment, and then treat me as it shall please Thee. I do not

---

[1] "Legem martyrii præfigebat."

seek for pleasures in this life; he does not deserve pleasure who has had the temerity to offend Thee, O infinite Goodness. I am content to suffer all the crosses Thou shalt send me; but, my Jesus, I will love Thee still. O Mary, who didst sympathize by thy sufferings with the sufferings of Jesus, obtain for me the grace to suffer all my trials with patience. Woe to me if, after so many sins, I do not suffer something in this life! And blessed shall I be if I have the happiness to accompany thee in thy sufferings, O my sorrowful Mother, and Thee, O my Jesus, always afflicted and crucified for love of me.

MEDITATION VI.

DECEMBER 30.

Jesus sleeping.

Very short and painful were the slumbers of the Infant Jesus. A manger was his cradle, straw was his bed, and straw his pillow; so that Jesus was constantly interrupted in his sleep by the hardness of this rough and painful little bed, and by the severe cold of the cave. Notwithstanding all this, nature succumbing to its wants, the sweet babe from time to time slept amidst his sufferings.

But the sleep of Jesus differed very much from that of other children. The slumbers of other children are useful for the preservation of life, but not for the operations of the soul, because the soul, being buried in sleep with the senses, cannot then work; but such was not the sleep of Jesus Christ: *I sleep, and My heart watcheth.*[1] His body was asleep, but his soul was watching; because in Jesus there was united the person of the Word, who could not sleep, nor be influenced by the slumber of the senses. The Holy Infant slept therefore; but while he slept he thought of all the sufferings he was to endure for our sake during all his life and at his death. He thought of the labors he was to undergo in Egypt and in Nazareth

[1] "Ego dormio, et cor meum vigilat."—*Cant.* v. 2.

during his miserable and despised life; he thought more particularly on the scourges, the thorns, the ignominies, the agonies, and on that miserable death that he should at last suffer upon the cross; and whilst he was sleeping he offered all this to his Eternal Father to obtain for us pardon and salvation; so that whilst our Saviour was sleeping he was meriting for us and appeasing his Father, and obtaining graces for us.

Let us now beseech him, by the merit of his blessed slumbers, to deliver us from the deadly slumber of sinners who unhappily sleep in the death of sin, forgetful of God and of his love; and to give us instead the blessed sleep of the holy spouse, of which he said, *Stir not up, nor make the beloved to wake till she please*.[1] This is the sleep that God gives to his beloved souls, which is none other, as St. Basil says, "but the most profound oblivion of all things;"[2] and this is when the soul forgets all earthly things, to attend only to God and to the things that concern his glory.

Affections and Prayers.

My beloved and holy Infant, Thou sleepest, and oh, how do Thy slumbers enamour me! With others sleep is the emblem of death; but in Thee it is the sign of eternal life, because whilst Thou art sleeping Thou art meriting for me eternal salvation. Thou sleepest; but Thy heart sleeps not, it is thinking of suffering and dying for me. Whilst Thou art slumbering, Thou art praying for me, and obtaining for me from God the eternal rest of Paradise. But before Thou dost carry me (as I hope) to repose with Thee in heaven, I desire that Thou shouldst repose forever in my soul. There was a time, O my God! when I drove Thee away from me; but I trust that, by means of knocking so often at the door of my heart,—now by

---

[1] "Ne suscitetis neque evigilare faciatis dilectam, quoadusque ipsa velit."—*Cant.* ii. 7.

[2] "Summa rerum omnium oblivio."—*Reg. fus. disp. int.* 6.

making it afraid, now by enlightening it, now by the voice of love,—Thou hast already obtained an entrance there. This, I say, is my hope, because I feel a great confidence that I have been forgiven by Thee; I feel a great hatred and penitence for the offences I have committed against Thee,—penitence that causes me great sorrow; but a sorrow of peace, a sorrow that comforts me and makes me hope most assuredly for pardon from Thy goodness. I thank Thee, my Jesus, and I pray Thee never again to separate Thyself from my soul. I know indeed that Thou wilt not leave me, if I do not drive Thee away; but this is the favor I ask of Thee (and I pray Thee to give me Thy assistance that I may always seek it of Thee), that Thou wouldst not permit me ever to drive Thee from me. Make me forget everything, in order to think of Thee who hast always thought of me and of my welfare. Make me always love Thee in this life, so that I may breathe forth my soul in Thy arms, united to Thee, and may repose eternally in Thee without fear of losing Thee again. O Mary, assist me in life and in death, so that Jesus may always repose in me, and that I may always repose in Jesus.

MEDITATION VII.

DECEMBER 31.

Jesus weeping.

The tears of the Infant Jesus were very different from those of other new-born babes: these weep through pain; Jesus did not weep from pain, but through compassion for us and through love: "They weep because of suffering, Christ because of compassion,"[1] says St. Bernard. Tears are a great sign of love. Therefore did the Jews say when they saw the Saviour weeping for the death of Lazarus: *Behold how He loved him.*[2] Thus also might the angels have said on beholding the tears of the Infant

---

[1] "Illi ex passione lugent, Christus ex compassione."—*In Nat. D.* s. 3.
[2] "Ecce quomodo amat eum!"—*John*, xi. 36.

Jesus: "Behold how he loves them."[1] Behold how our God loves men; since for the love of them we see him made man, become an Infant, and shedding tears.

Jesus wept and offered to his Father his tears to obtain for us the pardon of our sins. "These tears," says St. Ambrose, "washed away my sins;"[2] by his cries and tears he implored mercy for us who were condemned to eternal death, and thus he appeased the indignation of his Father. Oh, how eloquently did the tears of this divine little one plead in our behalf! Oh, how precious were they to God! It was then that the Father caused the angels to proclaim that he made peace with men, and received them into his favor: *And on earth peace to men of good will.*[3]

Jesus wept through love, but he also wept through sorrow at the thought that so many sinners, even after all his tears and the blood he should shed for their salvation, would yet continue to despise his grace. But who would be so hard-hearted, on seeing an Infant God weeping for our sins, as not to weep also, and to detest those sins that have made this loving Saviour shed so many tears? Oh, let us not increase the sorrows of this innocent babe; but let us console him by uniting our tears to his! Let us offer to God the tears of his Son, and let us beseech him for their sake to forgive us!

Affections and Prayers.

My beloved Infant, whilst Thou wert weeping in the stable of Bethlehem, Thou wert thinking of me; beholding even then my sins, which were the cause of Thy tears. And have I, then, O my Jesus! instead of consoling Thee by my love and gratitude at the thought of what Thou hast suffered to save me, have I increased Thy sorrow and the cause of Thy tears? If I

---

[1] "Ecce quomodo amat eos!"
[2] "Mea lacrymæ illæ delicta lavarunt."—*In Luc.* ii.
[3] "Et in terra pax hominibus bonæ voluntatis."—*Luke*, ii. 14.

had sinned less, Thou wouldst have wept less. Weep, oh, weep, for Thou hast cause to weep in seeing such great ingratitude of men to Thy great love. But since Thou weepest, weep also for me; Thy tears are my hope. I also will weep for the offences I have committed against Thee, O my Redeemer! I hate them, I detest them, I repent of them with my whole heart. I weep for all those days and those wretched nights of mine in which I lived as Thy enemy and deprived of Thy beautiful face; but what would my tears avail, O my Jesus, without Thine!

Eternal Father, I offer Thee the tears of the Infant Jesus; for their sake forgive me. And Thou, my dearest Saviour, offer to him all the tears that Thou didst shed for me during Thy life, and with them appease his anger against me. I be-. seech Thee also, O my Love, to soften my heart by these tears, and to inflame it with Thy holy love. Oh that I could from this day forth console Thee by my love for all the pain I have caused Thee by offending Thee! Grant, therefore, O Lord! that the days that remain to me in this life may not any more be spent in offending Thee, but only in weeping for the offences I have committed against Thee, and in loving Thee with all the affections of my soul. O Mary! I beseech thee, by that tender compassion which thou didst so often feel at the sight of the Infant Jesus in tears, obtain for me a constant sorrow for the offences which I have so ungratefully been guilty of against him.

MEDITATION VIII.

JANUARY 1.

The Name of Jesus.*

The name of Jesus is a divine name, announced to Mary on the part of God by St. Gabriel: *and thou shalt call His name Jesus.*[1] For that reason it was called *a name above all names.*[2] And it was also called a name in

[1] " Et vocabis nomen ejus Jesum."—*Luke*, i. 31.
[2] " Nomen quod est super omne nomen."—*Phil.* ii. 9.

---

* To-day is the feast of the circumcision of our Lord. Further on, on page 316, there is a meditation on this mystery.

which alone salvation is found: *whereby we must be saved.*[1]

This great name is likened by the Holy Spirit unto oil: *Thy name is as oil poured out.*[2] For this reason, says St. Bernard, that as oil is light, food, and medicine; so the name of Jesus is light to the mind, food to the heart, and medicine to the soul.

It is light to the mind. By this name the world was converted from the darkness of idolatry to the light of faith. We who have been born in these regions, where before the coming of Christ all our ancestors were Gentiles, should all have been in the same condition had not the Messias come to enlighten us. How thankful ought we not, then, to be to Jesus Christ for the gift of faith! And what would have become of us if we had been born in Asia, in Africa, in America, or in the midst of heretics and schismatics? He who believes not is lost: *He that believeth not shall be condemned.*[3] And thus probably we also should have been lost.

The name of Jesus is also food that nourishes our hearts; yes, because this name reminds us of what Jesus has done to save us. Hence this name consoles us in tribulation, gives us strength to walk along the way of salvation, supplies us with courage in difficulties, and inflames us to love our Redeemer, when we remember what he has suffered for our salvation.

Lastly, this name is medicine to the soul, because it renders it strong against the temptations of our enemies. The devils tremble and fly at the invocation of this holy name, according to the words of the Apostle: *That at the name of Jesus every knee should bow, of those that are in heaven, on earth, and under the earth.*[4] He who

---

[1] "In quo oporteat nos salvos fieri."—*Acts*, iv. 12.

[2] "Oleum effusum, nomen tuum."—*Cant.* i. 2.

[3] "Qui non crediderit, condemnabitur."—*Mark*, xvi. 16.

[4] "In nomine Jesu, omne genu flectatur cœlestium, terrestrium, et infernorum."—*Phil.* ii. 10.

in temptation calls upon Jesus shall not fall; and he who constantly invokes him shall not fall, and shall be saved: *Praising, I will call upon the Lord ; and I shall be saved from my enemies.*[1] And who was ever lost, who when he was tempted invoked Jesus? He alone is lost who does not invoke his aid, or who, whilst the temptation continues, ceases to invoke him.

Affections and Prayers.

Oh, that I had always called upon Thee, my Jesus; for then I should never have been conquered by the devil! I have miserably lost Thy grace, because in temptation I have neglected to call Thee to my assistance. But now I hope for all things through Thy holy name: *I can do all things in Him who comforts me.*[2] Write, therefore, O my Saviour, write upon my poor heart Thy most powerful name of Jesus, so that, by having it always in my heart by loving Thee, I may have it always on my lips by invoking Thee, in all the temptations that hell prepares for me, in order to induce me to become again its slave, and to separate myself from Thee. In Thy name I shall find every good. If I am afflicted, it will console me when I think how much more afflicted Thou hast been than I am, and all for the love of me; if I am disheartened on account of my sins, it will give me courage when I remember that Thou camest into the world to save sinners; if I am tempted, Thy holy name will give me strength, when I consider that Thou canst help me more than hell can cast me down; finally, if I feel cold in Thy love, it will give me fervor, by reminding me of the love that Thou bearest me. I love Thee, my Jesus! Thou art, and I trust Thou wilt always be, my only Love. To Thee do I give all my heart, O my Jesus! Thee alone will I love! Thee will I invoke as often as I possibly can. I will die with Thy name upon my lips; a name of hope, a name of salvation, a name of love. O Mary, if thou lovest me, this is the grace I beg of thee to obtain for me,—the grace constantly to

---

[1] "Laudans invocabo Dominum, et ab inimicis meis salvus ero."—*Ps.* xvii. 4.

[2] "Omnia possum in eo qui me confortat."—*Phil.* iv. 13.

invoke thy name and that of thy Son ; obtain for me that these most sweet names may be the breath of my soul, and that I may always repeat them during my life, in order to repeat them at my death with my last breath. Jesus and Mary, help me ; Jesus and Mary, I love you ; Jesus and Mary, 1 recommend my soul to you.

MEDITATION IX.

JANUARY 2.

The Solitude of Jesus in the Stable.

Jesus chose at his birth the stable of Bethlehem for his hermitage and oratory; and for this purpose he so disposed events as to be born out of the city in a solitary cave, in order to recommend to us the love of solitude and of silence. Jesus remains in silence in the manger; Mary and Joseph adore and contemplate him in silence. It was revealed to Sister Margaret of the Blessed Sacrament, a discalced Carmelite, who was called the Spouse of the Infant Jesus, that all that passed in the cave of Bethlehem, even the visit of the shepherds and the adoration of the holy Magi, took place in silence, and without a word.

Silence in other infants is impotence; but in Jesus Christ it was virtue. The Infant Jesus does not speak; but oh ! how much his silence says ! Oh, blessed is he that converses with Jesus, Mary, and Joseph, in this holy solitude of the manger. The shepherds, though admitted there but for a very short time, came out from the stable all inflamed with love to God; for they did nothing but praise and bless him: *They returned, glorifying and praising God.*[1] Oh, happy the soul that shuts itself up in the solitude of Bethlehem to contemplate the divine mercy, and the love that God has borne, and still

[1] " Reversi sunt pastores glorificantes et laudantes Deum."—*Luke*, ii. 20.

bears, to men! *I will lead her into the wilderness, and I will speak to her heart.*[1] There the divine Infant will speak, not to the ear, but to the heart, inviting the soul to love a God who hath loved her so much. When we see there the poverty of this wandering little hermit, who remains in that cold cave, without fire, with a manger for a crib, and a little straw for a bed; when we hear the cries, and behold the tears of this innocent Child, and consider that he is our God,—how is it possible to think of anything but of loving him! Oh, what a sweet hermitage for a soul that has faith in the stable of Bethlehem!

Let us also imitate Mary and Joseph, who, burning with love, remain contemplating the great Son of God clothed in flesh, and made subject to earthly miseries,— Wisdom become an infant that cannot speak,—the Great One become little,—the Supreme One become so abased, —the Rich One become so poor,—the Omnipotent so weak. In short, let us meditate on the divine majesty shrouded beneath the form of a little Infant, despised and forsaken by the world, and who does and suffers everything in order to make himself loved by men, and let us beseech him to admit us into this sacred retreat;— there stop, there remain, and never leave it again. "O solitude," says St. Jerome, "in which God speaks and converses familiarly with his servants;"[2] O beautiful solitude, in which God speaks and converses with his chosen souls, not as a sovereign, but as a friend, as a brother, as a spouse! Oh, what a paradise it is to converse alone with the Infant Jesus in the little grotto of Bethlehem!

[1] "Ducam eam in solitudinem, et loquar ad cor ejus."—*Os.* ii. 14.
[2] "O solitudo, in qua Deus cum suis familiariter loquitur et conversatur!"

Ninth Meditation.

Affections and Prayers.

My dearest Saviour, Thou art the King of Heaven, the King of kings, the Son of God ; and how is it, then, that •I see Thee in this cave, forsaken by all ? I see no one assisting Thee but Joseph and Thy holy Mother. I desire to unite myself also to them in keeping Thee company. Do not reject me. I do not deserve it; but I feel that Thou dost invite me by Thy sweet voice, speaking to my heart. Yes, I come, O my beloved Infant ! I will leave all things to pass my whole life alone with Thee, my dear little hermit, the only love of my soul. Fool that I was, I have hitherto forsaken Thee and left Thee alone, O my Jesus, whilst I was seeking miserable and empoisoned pleasures from creatures; but now, enlightened by Thy grace, I desire nothing but to live in solitude with Thee, who didst will to live Thyself in solitude on this earth : *Who will give me wings like a dove, and I will fly and be at rest?*[1] Ah, who will enable me to fly from this world, where I have so often found my ruin,— to fly, and to come and remain always with Thee, who art the joy of paradise and the true lover of my soul ? Oh, bind me, I pray Thee, to Thy feet, so that I may no longer be separated from Thee, but may find my happiness in continually keeping company with Thee ! Ah, by the merits of Thy solitude in the cave of Bethlehem, give me a constant interior recollection, so that my soul may become a solitary little cell, where I may attend to nothing but to conversing with Thee ; where I may take counsel with Thee in all my thoughts and all my actions ; where I may dedicate to Thee all my affections ; where I may always love Thee, and sigh to leave the prison of this body to come and love Thee face to face in heaven. I love Thee, O infinite Goodness, and I hope always to love Thee, in time and in eternity. O Mary, thou who canst do all things, pray to him to enchain me with his love, and not to permit me ever again to lose his grace.

[1] " Quis dabit mihi pennas sicut columbæ, et volabo, et requiescam ?"—*Ps.* liv. 7.

MEDITATION X.

JANUARY 3.

The Occupations of the Infant Jesus in the Stable of Bethlehem.

There are two principal occupations of a solitary,—to pray, and to do penance. Behold the Infant Jesus in the little grotto of Bethlehem giving us the example. He, in the crib which he chose for his oratory upon earth, never ceases to pray, and to pray continually, to the Eternal Father. There he constantly makes acts of adoration, of love, and of prayer.

Before this time the divine Majesty had been, it is true, adored by men and by angels; but God had not received from all these creatures that honor which the Infant Jesus gave him by adoring him in the stable where he was born. Let us, therefore, constantly unite our adorations to those of Jesus Christ when he was upon this earth.

Oh, how beautiful and perfect were the acts of love which the Incarnate Word made to his Father in his prayer! God had given to man the commandment to love him with all his heart and all his strength; but this precept had never been perfectly fulfilled by any man. The first to accomplish it amongst women was Mary, and amongst men the first was Jesus Christ, who fulfilled it in a degree infinitely superior to Mary. The love of the seraphim may be said to be cold in comparison with the love of this Holy Infant. Let us learn from him to love the Lord our God as he ought to be loved; and let us beseech him to communicate to us a spark of that pure love with which he loved the divine Father in the stable of Bethlehem.

Oh, how beautiful, perfect, and dear to God were the

prayers of the Infant Jesus! At every moment he prayed to his Father, and his prayers were all for us and for each one of us in particular. All the graces that each one of us has received from the Lord, and our being called to the true faith, our having had time given us for repentance, the lights, the sorrow for sins, the pardon of them, the holy desires, the victory over temptations, and all the other good acts that we have made, or shall make, of confidence, of humility, of love, of thanksgiving, of offering, of resignation,—all these Jesus has obtained for us, and all has been the effect of the prayers of Jesus. Oh, how much do we owe him! and how much ought we not to thank him and to love him!

Affections and Prayers.

My dear Redeemer, how much do I owe Thee! If Thou hadst not prayed for me, in what a state of ruin should I find myself! I thank Thee, O my Jesus; Thy prayers have obtained for me the pardon of my sins, and I hope that they will also obtain for me perseverance unto death. Thou hast prayed for me, and I bless Thee with my whole heart for it; but I beseech Thee not to leave off praying. I know that Thou dost continue even in heaven to be our advocate: *We have an advocate, Jesus Christ;*[1] and I know that Thou dost continue to pray for us: *Who also maketh intercession for us.*[2] Continue therefore to pray; but pray, O my Jesus, more particularly for me, who am more in want of Thy prayers. I hope God has already pardoned me through Thy merits; but as I have already so often fallen, I may therefore fall again. Hell does not cease, and will not cease, to tempt me, in order to make me again lose Thy friendship. Ah, my Jesus, Thou art my hope; it is Thou that must give me fortitude to resist; from Thee I seek it, and of Thee I hope for it! But I will not content myself only with the grace not to fall again; I desire also the grace to love Thee exceeding-

[1] "Advocatum habemus apud Patrem, Jesum Christum."—1 *John*, ii. 1.
[2] "Qui etiam interpellat pro nobis."—*Rom.* viii. 34.

ly. My death approaches. If I were to die now, I should indeed hope to be saved; but I should love Thee but little in paradise, because I have hitherto loved Thee so little. I will love Thee much in the days that remain to me, that I may love Thee still more in eternity. O Mary, my Mother! do thou also pray, and beseech Jesus for me; thy prayers are all-powerful with thy Son, who loves thee so much. Thou dost so much desire that he should be loved, beseech him to give me a great love for his goodness, and let this love be constant and eternal.

MEDITATION XI.

JANUARY 4.

The Poverty of the Infant Jesus.

O God! who would not feel compassion if he saw a little prince, the son of a monarch, born in such poverty as to be left to lie in a damp, cold cavern, not having bed, servants, fire, or clothes sufficient to warm him? Ah, my Jesus, Thou art the Son of the Lord of heaven and earth, and yet Thou liest in this cold grotto without other cradle than a manger, with nothing but straw for Thy bed, and miserable rags to cover Thee. The angels stand round Thee and sing Thy praises, but they do not relieve Thy poverty. My dear Redeemer, the poorer Thou art, the more amiable Thou dost render Thyself in our eyes, because Thou hast embraced so great a poverty for this end, to make us love Thee more. If Thou hadst been born in a palace, if Thou hadst had a cradle of gold, if Thou hadst been assisted by the first princes of the earth, Thou wouldst have acquired more respect from men, but less love; but this stable where Thou dost sleep, these miserable rags that cover Thee, this straw that serves as Thy bed, this manger that is Thy only cradle,—oh, how do they attract our souls to love Thee, because Thou hast made Thyself thus poor in order to become more dear to us! " The viler he was for me," says St. Bernard, "the dearer he is to me." Thou hast made Thyself poor to enrich us with Thy riches; that is, with grace and glory: *He became poor, that through His poverty you might be rich.*[2]

The poverty of Jesus Christ was for us great riches, inasmuch as it moves us to acquire the treasures of heaven and to despise those of earth. Ah, my Jesus! this Thy poverty has induced so many saints to leave all— riches, honors, and kingdoms—in order to become poor with Thee! Oh, detach me also, my Saviour, from all affection to earthly goods, so that I may be made worthy to acquire Thy holy love, and thus to possess Thee, who art the infinite Good!

Affections and Prayers.

Oh that I also could say to Thee, O holy Infant, with thy dear St. Francis, "My God and my All!"[3] and with David, *What have I in heaven? and besides Thee, what do I desire upon earth? . . . God of my heart, and the God that is my portion forever;*[4] so that from this day forth I might desire no other riches but those of Thy love, and that my heart might be no more under the dominion of the vanities of the world, but that Thou alone, my love, mightest be its only Lord. But I even now wish to begin to say it: *God of my heart, and the God that is my portion forever.*[5] Miserable that I was, I have hitherto only sought after worldly goods, and have found nothing but thorns and gall. I feel more satisfaction at finding myself at Thy feet, to thank Thee and love Thee, than I have ever experienced from all my sins. One fear alone afflicts me—the fear that Thou hast not yet forgiven me; but Thy promises of forgiveness to the peni-

---

[1] "Quanto pro me vilior, tanto mihi carior!"—*In Epiph.* s. 1.

[2] "Egenus factus est . . . , ut illius inopia vos divites essetis."— 2 *Cor.* viii. 9.

[3] "Deus meus, et omnia!"

[4] "Quid enim mihi est in cœlo? et a te quid volui super terram? . . . Deus cordis mei, et pars mea, Deus, in æternum!"—*Ps.* lxxii. 25.

[5] "Deus cordis mei, et pars mea, Deus, in æternum!"

tent, the thought that Thou didst make Thyself poor for the love of me, that Thou art still calling me to love Thee; the tears, the blood Thou hast shed for me, the sorrows, the ignominy, the bitter death Thou hast endured for me,—all console me, and make me hope certainly for pardon. And supposing Thou hast not forgiven me, what shall I then do? Dost Thou desire that I should repent? I repent with my whole heart of having offended Thee, O my Jesus! Dost Thou desire that I should love Thee? I love Thee more than myself. Dost Thou desire that I should give up everything? Behold, I give up all and give myself to Thee; and I know that Thou dost accept me, otherwise I should not have sorrow, nor love, nor the desire to give myself to Thee. I give myself then to Thee, and Thou hast already accepted me. I love Thee, and Thou dost also love me. Do not permit that this love between Thee and me should evermore be interrupted. O my Mother Mary! do thou obtain for me the grace that I may always love Jesus, and that I may always be loved by him!

MEDITATION XII.

JANUARY 5.

The Abasement of Jesus.*

The eternal Word descends on earth to save man; and whence does he descend? *His going out is from the end of heaven.*[1] He descends from the bosom of his divine Father, where from eternity he was begotten in the brightness of the saints. And where does he descend? He descends into the womb of a virgin, a child of Adam, which in comparison with the bosom of God is an object of horror; wherefore the Church sings, "Thou didst not abhor the Virgin's womb."[2] Yes, because the Word, being in the bosom of the Father, is God like the Father —is immense, omnipotent, most blessed and supreme Lord, and equal in everything to the Father. But in the womb of Mary he is a creature, small, weak, afflicted,

---
[1] "A summo cœlo egressio ejus."—*Ps.* xviii. 7.
[2] "Non horruisti virginis uterum."

* This meditation is the same as Meditation V., for the first Thursday of Advent, p. 182.

a servant inferior to the Father, *Taking the form of a servant.*[1]

It is related as a great prodigy of humility in St. Alexis that, although he was the son of a Roman gentleman, he chose to live as a servant in his father's house. But how is the humility of this saint to be compared with the humility of Jesus Christ? Between the son and the servant of the father of St. Alexis there was, it is true, some difference; but between God and the servant of God there is an infinite difference. Besides, this Son of God having become the servant of his Father in obedience to him, made himself also the servant of his creatures; that is to say, of Mary and Joseph: *And he was subject to them.*[2] Moreover, he made himself even a servant of Pilate, who condemned him to death, and he was obedient to him, and accepted it; he became a servant to the executioners, who scourged him, crowned him with thorns, and crucified him: and he humbly obeyed them all, and yielded himself into their hands.

O God! and shall we, after this, refuse to submit ourselves to the service of so loving a Saviour, who, to save us, has subjected himself to so painful and degrading a slavery? And rather than be the servants of this so great and so loving a Lord, shall we be content to be slaves of the devil, who does not love his servants, but hates them and treats them like a tyrant, making them miserable and wretched in this world and in the next? But if we have been guilty of this great folly, why do we not quickly give up this unhappy servitude? Courage, then, since we have been delivered by Jesus Christ from the slavery of hell; let us now embrace and bind around us with love those sweet chains, which will render us servants and lovers of Jesus Christ, and hereafter obtain for us the crown of the eternal kingdom amongst the blessed in Paradise.

[1] "Formam servi accipens."—*Phil.* ii. 7.
[2] "Et erat subditus illis."—*Luke*, ii. 51.

Affections and Prayers.

My beloved Jesus, Thou art the Sovereign of heaven and earth; but for the love of me Thou hast made Thyself a servant even of the executioners who tore Thy flesh, pierced Thy head, and finally left Thee nailed on the cross to die of sorrow. I adore Thee as my God and Lord, and I am ashamed to appear before Thee when I remember how often, for the sake of some miserable pleasure, I have broken Thy holy bonds, and have told Thee to Thy face that I would not serve Thee. Ah, Thou mayest justly reproach me: *Thou hast burst my bands, and Thou saidst: I will not serve.*[1] But still, O my Saviour, Thy merits and Thy goodness, which cannot despise a heart that repents and humbles itself, give me courage to hope for pardon: *A contrite and humble heart, O God, Thou wilt not despise.*[2] I confess, my Jesus, that I have offended Thee greatly; I confess that I deserve a thousand hells for the sins that I have committed against Thee; chasten me as Thou seest fit, but do not deprive me of Thy grace and love. I repent above every other evil for having despised Thee. I love Thee with my whole heart. I propose from this day forth to desire to serve Thee and love Thee alone. I pray Thee bind me by Thy merits with the chains of Thy holy love, and never suffer that I see myself released from them again. I love Thee above everything, O my Deliverer, and I would prefer being Thy servant to being master of the whole world. And of what avail would all the world be to him who lives deprived of Thy grace? *My sweetest Jesus, permit me not to separate myself from Thee, permit me not to separate myself from Thee.*[3] This grace I ask of Thee, and I intend always to ask it; and I beg of Thee to grant me this day the grace to repeat continually to the end of my life this prayer: My Jesus, grant that I may never again separate myself from Thy love. I ask this favor of thee also, O Mary, my Mother: help me by thy intercession, that I may never separate myself again from my God.

[1] "Rupisti vincula mea, et dixisti: Non serviam."—*Jer.* ii. 20.
[2] "Cor contritum et humiliatum, Deus, non despicies."—*Isa.* l., 19.
[3] "Jesu dulcissime! ne permittas me separari a te; ne permittas me separari a te."

Meditations for the Octave of the Epiphany.

MEDITATION I.

JANUARY 6.

The Adoration of the Magi.

Jesus is born poor in a stable; the angels of heaven indeed acknowledge him, but men abandon and forsake him on earth. Only a few shepherds come and pay him homage. But our Redeemer was desirous of communicating to us the grace of his redemption, and begins therefore to manifest himself to the Gentiles, who knew him least. Therefore he sends a star to enlighten the holy Magi, in order that they may come and acknowledge and adore their Saviour. This was the first and sovereign grace bestowed upon us,—our vocation to the faith; which was succeeded by our vocation to grace, of which men were deprived.

Behold the wise men, who immediately, without delay, set off upon their journey. The star accompanies them as far as the cavern where the holy Infant lies: on their arrival they enter; and what do they find? *They found the child with Mary.*[1] They find a poor maiden and a poor Infant wrapped in poor swaddling-clothes, without any one to attend on him or assist him. But, lo! on entering into the little shed these holy pilgrims feel a joy which they had never felt before; they feel their hearts chained to the dear little Infant which they behold. The straw, the poverty, the cries of their little Saviour,—oh, what darts of love! oh, what blessed flames are they to

[1] "Invenerunt puerum cum Maria."—*Matt.* ii. 11.

First Meditation.

their enlightened hearts! The Infant looks upon them with a joyful countenance, and this is the mark of affection with which he accepts them amongst the first-fruits of his redemption.

The holy kings then look at Mary, who does not speak —she remains silent; but with her blessed countenance that breathes the sweetness of paradise she welcomes them, and thanks them for having been the first to come and acknowledge her son (as indeed he is) for their Sovereign Lord. See also how, out of reverence, they adore him in silence, and acknowledge him for their God, kissing his feet, and offering him their gifts of gold, frankincense, and myrrh. Let us also with the holy Magi adore our little King Jesus, and let us offer him all our hearts.

Affections and Prayers.

O amiable Infant! though I see Thee in this cavern lying on straw poor and despised, yet faith teaches me that Thou art my God, who camest down from heaven for my salvation. I acknowledge Thee, then, for my sovereign Lord and Saviour; but I have nothing, alas! to offer Thee. I have no gold of love, because I have loved creatures; I have loved my own caprices, but I have not loved Thee. O amiable infinite One! I have not the incense of prayer, because I have lived in a miserable state of forgetfulness of Thee. I have no myrrh of mortification, for I have often displeased Thy infinite goodness that I might not be deprived of my miserable pleasures. What then shall I offer Thee? I offer Thee my heart, filthy and poor as it is; do Thou accept it, and change it. Thou camest into the world for this purpose, to wash the hearts of men from their sins by Thy blood, and thus change them from sinners into saints. Give me, therefore, I pray Thee, this gold, this incense, and this myrrh. Give me the gold of Thy holy love; give me the spirit of holy prayer, give me the desire and strength to mortify myself in everything that displeases Thee. I am resolved to obey Thee and to love Thee; but Thou knowest my weakness, oh, give me the grace to be faithful to Thee! Most holy Virgin, thou who didst welcome with such affection and didst console the holy Magi, do thou welcome and console me also, who come to visit thy Son and to offer myself to him. O my Mother, I have great confidence in thy intercession! Do thou recommend me to Jesus. To thee do I intrust my soul and my will; bind it forever to the love of Jesus!

MEDITATION II.

JANUARY 7.

The Presentation of Jesus in the Temple.

The time having now come when, according to the law, Mary had to go to the Temple for her purification, and to present Jesus to the divine Father, behold she sets out in company with Joseph. Joseph carries the two turtle-doves that they are to offer to God, and Mary carries her dear Infant: she takes the Lamb of God to offer him to the Almighty, in token of the great sacrifice that this Son should one day accomplish on the cross.

Consider the holy Virgin entering the Temple; she makes an oblation of her Son on the part of the whole human race, and says: Behold, O Eternal Father, Thy beloved only-begotten One, who is Thy Son and mine also; I offer him to Thee as a victim to Thy divine justice, in order to appease Thy wrath against sinners. Accept him, O God of mercy! have pity on our miseries; for the love of this immaculate Lamb do Thou receive men into Thy grace.

The offering of Mary is joined to that of Jesus. Behold me (says also the holy Infant), behold me, O My Father; to Thee do I consecrate my whole life; Thou hast sent me into the world to save it by my blood; behold my blood and my whole self. I offer myself entirely to Thee for the salvation of the world. *He delivered Himself . . . an oblation and a sacrifice to God.*[1]

[1] "Tradidit semetipsum pro nobis oblationem et hostiam Deo."— *Eph.* v. 2.

No sacrifice was ever so acceptable to God as this which his dear Son then made to him; who had become, even from his infancy, a victim and priest. If all men and angels had offered their lives, their oblation could not have been so dear to God as was this of Jesus Christ, because in this offering alone the Eternal Father received infinite honor and infinite satisfaction.

If Jesus offers his life to his Father for the love of us, it is just that we should offer him our life and our entire being. This is what he desires, as he signified to the blessed Angela da Foligno, saying to her, " I have offered myself for thee, in order that thou shouldest offer thyself to me."

Affections and Prayers.

Eternal Father, I, a miserable sinner, who have deserved a thousand hells, present myself this day before Thee, O God of infinite majesty, and I offer Thee my poor heart. But, O God, what a heart is it that I offer Thee?—a heart that has never known how to love Thee, but has, on the contrary, so often offended Thee and so often betrayed Thee ; but now I offer it to Thee full of penitence, and resolved to love Thee at all costs and to obey Thee in all things. Pardon me, and draw me entirely to Thy love. I do not deserve to be heard ; but Thy infant Son, who offers himself to Thee in the Temple as a sacrifice for my salvation, merits for me this grace. I offer Thee this Thy Son and his sacrifice, and in this I place all my hopes. I thank Thee, O my Father, for having sent him upon the earth to sacrifice himself for me. And I bless Thee, O Incarnate Word, Lamb of God, who didst offer Thyself to die for my soul. I love Thee, my dear Redeemer, and Thee alone will I love ; for I find none but Thee that has offered and sacrificed his life to save me. It makes me shed tears to think how grateful I have been to others and how ungrateful to Thee alone ; but Thou willest not my death, but that I should be converted and live. Yes, my Jesus, I turn to Thee, and repent with my whole heart of having offended Thee, and of having offended my God, who has thus sacrificed himself for me. Do Thou give me life, and that life shall consist in loving Thee, the sovereign Good; make me love Thee, I ask Thee nothing more. Mary, my Mother, thou didst offer at that time thy Son in the Temple even for me; do thou offer him again for me; and beseech the Eternal Father, for the love of Jesus, to accept me for his own. And thou, my Queen, do thou also accept me for thy perpetual servant. If I am thy servant, I shall also be the servant of thy Son.

MEDITATION III.

January 8.

The Flight of Jesus into Egypt.

The angel appeared to St. Joseph in a dream, and informed him that Herod was seeking the Infant Jesus to destroy his life; wherefore he said, *Arise, and take the Child and His Mother, and fly into Egypt.*[1] Behold, then, how Jesus is no sooner born than he is persecuted unto death. Herod is a figure of those miserable sinners who, as soon as they see Jesus Christ born again in their souls by the pardon of sin, persecute him to death by returning to their sins: *They seek the Child to destroy Him.*[2]

Joseph immediately obeys the command of the angel without delay, and gives notice of it to his holy spouse. He then takes the few tools that he can carry, in order to make use of them in his trade, and to be able in Egypt to support his poor family. Mary at the same time puts together a little bundle of clothes for the use of the holy Child; and then she goes into her cell, kneels down first before her Infant Son, kisses his feet, and then with tears of tenderness says to him, O my Son and my God, hardly art Thou born and come into the world to save men, when these men seek Thee to put Thee to death. She then takes him; and the two holy spouses, shedding tears

---

[1] "Surge, et accipe Puerum et Matrem ejus et fuge in Ægyptum." —*Matt.* ii. 13.

[2] "Quærunt Puerum ad perdendum eum."

as they go, shut the door, and the same night set out on their journey.

Let us consider the occupations of these holy pilgrims during their journey. All their conversation is upon their dear Jesus alone, on his patience and his love; and thus they console themselves in the midst of the trials and inconveniences of so long a journey. Oh, how sweet it is to suffer at the sight of Jesus suffering! O my soul, says St. Bonaventure, do thou also keep company with these three poor holy exiles; and have compassion with them in the long, wearisome, and painful journey which they are making. And beseech Mary that she will give thee her divine Son to carry in thy heart.

Consider how much they must have suffered, especially in those nights which they had to pass in the desert of Egypt. The bare earth serves them for a bed in the cold open air. The Infant weeps, Mary and Joseph shed tears of compassion. O holy faith! who would not weep at seeing the Son of God become an infant, poor and forsaken, flying across a desert in order to escape death?

Affections and Prayers.

My dear Jesus, Thou art the King of Heaven, but now I behold Thee as an infant wandering over the earth; tell me whom art Thou in search of? I pity Thee when I see Thee so poor and humbled; but I pity Thee more when I see Thee treated with such ingratitude by those same men whom Thou camest to save. Thou dost weep; but I also weep, because I have been one of those who in times past have despised and persecuted Thee. But now I value Thy grace more than all the kingdoms of the world; forgive me, O my Jesus! all the evil I have committed against Thee, and permit me to carry Thee always in my heart during the journey of my life to eternity, even as Mary carried Thee in her arms during the flight into Egypt. My beloved Redeemer, I have many times driven Thee out of my soul; but now I hope that Thou hast again taken possession of it. I beseech Thee, do Thou bind it to Thyself with the sweet chains of Thy love. I will never again drive Thee from me. But I fear lest I should again abandon Thee, as I have done in past times. O my Lord! let me die rather than treat Thee with fresh and still more horrible ingratitude. I love Thee, O infinite Goodness; and I will always repeat to Thee, I love Thee, I love Thee, I love Thee; and so I hope to die saying, *God of my heart, and the God that art my portion forever.*[1] O my Jesus! Thou art so good, so worthy of being loved, oh do Thou make Thyself loved; make Thyself loved by all the sinners who persecute Thee; give them light, make them know the love Thou hast borne them and the love that Thou deservest since Thou goest wandering about the earth as a poor Infant, weeping and trembling with cold, and seeking souls to love Thee! O Mary, most holy Virgin, O dearest Mother and companion of the sufferings of Jesus, do thou help me always to carry and preserve in my heart thy Son, in life and in death!

MEDITATION IV.

JANUARY 9.

The Dwelling of Jesus in Egypt.

Jesus chose to dwell in Egypt during his infancy, that he might lead a more hard and abject life. According to St. Anselm and other writers, the holy family lived in Heliopolis. Let us with St. Bonaventure contemplate the life that Jesus led during the seven years that he remained in Egypt, as it was revealed to St. Mary Magdalene of Pazzi.

The house they live in is very poor, because St. Joseph has but little wherewith to pay rent; their bed is poor, their food poor; their life, in short, is one of strict poverty, for they barely gain their livelihood day by day by the work of their hands, and they live in a country where

---

[1] "Deus cordis mei, et pars mea, Deus, in æternum."—*Ps.* lxxii. 26.

they are unknown and despised, having there neither relatives nor friends.

This holy family does indeed live in great poverty; but oh, how well-ordered are the occupations of these three sojourners! The holy Infant speaks not with his tongue; but in his heart he speaks indeed and continually to his heavenly Father, applying all his sufferings, and every moment of his life, for our salvation. Neither does Mary speak; but at the sight of that dear Infant she meditates on the divine love, and the favor that God has conferred upon her by choosing her for his Mother. Joseph also works in silence; and at the sight of the divine Child his heart is inflamed, while he thanks him for having chosen him for the companion and guardian of his life.

In this house Mary weans Jesus: at first she fed him from her breast, now she feeds him with her hands; she holds him on her lap, takes from the porringer a little bread soaked in water, and then puts it into the sacred mouth of her Son. In this house Mary made her Infant his first little garment; and when the time was come, she took off his swaddling-clothes, and began to put on this vestment. In this house the Child Jesus began to walk and speak. Let us adore the first steps that the Incarnate Word began to take in this house, and the first words of eternal life that he began to utter. Here he began also to do the work of a little servant-boy, occupying himself in all the little services that a child can render.

Ah, weaning! ah, little garment! ah, first steps! ah, lisping words! ah, little services of the little Jesus, how do you not wound and inflame the hearts of those who love Jesus and meditate on you! Behold a God trembling and falling, a God lisping, a God become so weak that he can occupy himself in nothing but in little household affairs, and unable even to lift a bit of wood, if too heavy for the strength of a child ! O holy faith, enlighten us, and make us love this good Lord, who for the love of us has submitted himself to so many miseries ! It is said that on the entrance of Jesus into Egypt all the idols of the country fell down; oh, let us pray to God that he will make us love Jesus from our hearts, since in that soul where the love of Jesus enters, all the idols of earthly affections are overthrown.

Affections and Prayers.

O Holy Infant, who livest in this country of barbarians poor, unknown, and despised, I acknowledge Thee for my God and Saviour, and I thank Thee for all the humiliations and sufferings Thou didst endure in Egypt for the love of me. By Thy manner of life there Thou dost teach me to live as a pilgrim on this earth, giving me to understand that this is not my country; but that Paradise, which Thou hast purchased for me by Thy death is my home. Ah, my Jesus, I have been ungrateful to Thee because I have thought but little of what Thou hast done and suffered for me. When I think that Thou, the Son of God, didst lead a life of such tribulation upon this earth, so poor and neglected, how is it possible that I should go about seeking the amusements and good things of the earth ? Take me, I pray Thee, my dear Redeemer, for Thy companion ; admit me to live always united with Thee upon this earth, in order that united with Thee in heaven, I may love Thee there, and be Thy companion throughout eternity. Give me light, increase my faith. What goods, what pleasures, what dignities, what honors ! All is vanity and folly. The only real riches, the only real good, is to possess Thee, who art the infinite Good. Blessed he who loves Thee ! I love Thee, O my Jesus, and I seek none other but Thee. I desire Thee, and Thou desirest me. If I had a thousand kingdoms, I would renounce them all to please Thee, "my God and my All."[1] If in times past I have sought after the vanities and pleasures of this world, I now detest them, and am sorry that I have done so. My beloved Saviour, from this

[1] " Deus meus, et omnia."

day forward Thou shalt be my only delight, my only love, my only treasure. Most holy Mary, pray to Jesus for me; beseech him to make me rich in his love alone, and I desire nothing else.

MEDITATION V.

JANUARY 10.

The Return of Jesus from Egypt.

After the death of Herod, and an exile of seven years, according to the common opinion of the Doctors, during which time Jesus lived in Egypt, the angel again appeared to St. Joseph, and commanded him to take the Holy Child and his Mother and return to Palestine. St. Joseph, consoled by this command, communicates it to Mary. Before their departure, these holy spouses courteously informed the friends whom they had made in the country. Joseph then collects the few instruments of his trade, Mary her little bundle of clothes, and taking by the hand the divine Child, they set out on their journey homewards, leading him between them.

St. Bonaventure considers that this journey was more fatiguing to Jesus than was the flight into Egypt, because he was now become too large for Mary and Joseph to carry him much in their arms ; but at the same time the Holy Child, at his age, was not able to make a long journey ; so that Jesus was obliged through fatigue frequently to stop and rest himself on the way. But Joseph and Mary, whether they walk or sit, always keep their eyes and thoughts fixed upon the beloved little Child, who was the object of all their love. Oh, with what recollection does that happy soul travel through this life who keeps before its eyes the love and the examples of Jesus Christ!

The holy pilgrims interrupt now and then the silence of this journey by some holy conversation ; but with whom and of whom do they converse? They speak only with Jesus and of Jesus. He who has Jesus in his heart speaks only with Jesus or only speaks of him.

Consider again the pain that our little Saviour must have endured during the nights of this journey, in which he had no longer the bosom of Mary for his bed, as in his flight, but the bare ground ; and for his food he had no more milk, but a little hard bread, too hard for his tender age. He was probably also afflicted by thirst in this desert, in which the Jews had been in such want of water that a miracle was necessary to supply them with it. Let us contemplate and lovingly adore all these sufferings of the Child Jesus.

Affections and Prayers.

Beloved and adored Child, Thou dost return to Thy country; but where, O God, where dost Thou return ? Thou comest to that place where Thy countrymen prepare for Thee insults during life, and then scourges, thorns, ignominy, and a cross at Thy death. But all was already present to Thy divine eyes, O my Jesus ! and yet Thou comest of Thy own will to meet that Passion which men prepare for Thee. But, my Redeemer, if Thou hadst not come to die for me, I could not go to love Thee in Paradise, but must have always remained far away from Thee. Thy death hath been my salvation. But how is it, Lord, that by despising Thy grace I have again condemned myself to hell, even after Thy death, by which Thou didst deliver me from it. I acknowledge that hell is but a slight punishment for me. But Thou hast waited to pardon me. I thank Thee for it, O my Redeemer, and I repent, and detest all the offences I have committed against Thee. O Lord, I beseech Thee, deliver me from hell. Ah, if I were miserable enough to damn myself, how would my torments in hell be increased by the remorse caused by my having meditated during my life on the love that Thou hast borne me ! It would not be so much the fire of hell as Thy love, O my Jesus, that would be my hell. But Thou didst come into the world to kindle the fire of Thy holy love; I desire to burn with this fire, and not with that which would keep me forever separated from Thee. I repeat, therefore, O my Jesus! deliver me from hell, because in hell I cannot love Thee. O Mary, my Mother! I hear it everywhere said and preached that those who love thee and trust in thee, provided they desire to amend their lives, will not go to hell. I love thee, my Lady, and I trust in thee; I will amend my life: O Mary, do thou remember to deliver me from hell!

MEDITATION VI.

JANUARY 11.

The Dwelling of Jesus at Nazareth.

St. Joseph, on his return to Palestine, heard that Archelaus reigned in Judea instead of his father, Herod, wherefore he was afraid to go and live there; and being warned in a dream, he went to live in Nazareth, a city of Galilee, and there in a poor little cottage he fixed his dwelling. O blessed house of Nazareth, I salute and venerate you! There will come a time when you will be visited by the great ones of the earth: when the pilgrims find themselves inside your poor walls, they will never be satisfied with shedding tears of tenderness at the thought that within them the King of Paradise passed nearly all his life.

In this house, then, the Incarnate Word lived during the remainder of his infancy and youth. And how did he live? Poor and despised by men, performing the offices of a common working-boy, and obeying Joseph and Mary: *and He was subject to them.*[1] O God, how touching it is to think that in this poor house the Son of God lives as a servant! Now he goes to fetch water; then he opens or shuts the shop; now he sweeps the room; now he collects the shavings for the fire; now he labors in assisting Joseph at his trade. O wonder! To see a God sweeping! A God serving as a boy! O

[1] " Et erat subditus illis."—*Luke*, ii. 51.

thought that ought to make us all burn with holy love to our Redeemer, who has reduced himself to such humiliations in order to gain our love!

Let us adore all these servile actions of Jesus, which were all divine. Let us adore, above all, the hidden and neglected life that Jesus Christ led in the house of Nazareth! O proud men, how can you desire to make yourselves seen and honored, when you behold your God, who spends thirty years of his life in poverty, hidden and unknown, to teach us the love of retirement and of an humble and a hidden life!

Affections and Prayers.

O my adorable Infant, I see Thee an humble servant-boy, working even in the sweat of Thy brow in this poor shop. I understand it all; Thou art serving and working for me. But since Thou dost employ Thy whole life for the love of me, so grant, I pray Thee, my dear Saviour, that I may employ all the rest of my life for Thy love. Look not at my past life: it has been a life of sorrow and tears both for me and for Thee,—a life of disorder, a life of sins. Oh, permit me at least to keep Thee company during the remainder of my days, and to labor and suffer with Thee in the shop of Nazareth, and afterwards to die with Thee on Calvary, embracing that death which Thou hast destined for me. My dear Jesus, my love, suffer me not to leave and forsake Thee again, as I have done in times past. Thou, my God, art suffering such poverty in a shop, hidden, unknown, and despised; and I, a vile worm, have gone about seeking honors and pleasures, and for the sake of these have separated myself from Thee, O sovereign Good! No, my Jesus, I love Thee; and because I love Thee, I will not remain any longer separated from Thee. I renounce all things, in order to unite myself to Thee, my hidden and despised Redeemer. Thy grace gives me more happiness than have all the vanities and pleasures of the world, for which I have so miserably forsaken Thee. Eternal Father, for the merits of Jesus Christ, unite me to Thyself by the gift of Thy holy love. Most holy Virgin, how blessed wert thou, who, being the companion of thy Son in his poor and hidden life, didst make thyself so like to thy Jesus! O my Mother, grant that I also, at least during the short remainder of my life, may endeavor to become like to thee and to my Redeemer.

MEDITATION VII.

JANUARY 12.

The Same Subject continued.

St. Luke, speaking of the residence of the Infant Jesus in the house at Nazareth, writes: *And Jesus advanced in wisdom and age, and grace with God and men.*[1] As Jesus grew in age, so did he increase in wisdom: not that he went on every year acquiring a greater knowledge of things, as is the case with us; for, from the first moment of his life, Jesus was full of all divine knowledge and wisdom: *In whom are hid all the treasures of wisdom and knowledge;*[2] but it is said that he advanced, because every day as he advanced in age he manifested more and more his sublime wisdom.

Thus it is also said that he advanced in grace with God and men; with God, because all his divine actions, though they did not render him more holy or increase his merit,—since Jesus was from the first full of sanctity and merit, of whose fulness we have received all graces: *of his fulness we have all received;*[3]—yet, nevertheless, these operations of the Redeemer were all sufficient in themselves to increase his grace and merit.

He advanced also in grace with men, increasing in beauty and amiability. Oh, how Jesus showed himself more and more amiable every day of his youth, showing

---

[1] "Et Jesus proficiebat sapientia, et ætate, et gratia, apud Deum et homines."—*Luke*, ii. 52.

[2] "In quo sunt omnes thesauri sapientiæ, et scientiæ absconditi."—*Col.* ii. 3.

[3] "De plenitudine ejus nos omnes accepimus"—*John*, i. 16.

more and more every day the claims he had upon men's love! With what delight did the holy youth obey Mary and Joseph! With what recollection of mind did he work! With what moderation did he take his food! With what modesty did he speak! With what sweetness and affability did he converse with all! With what devotion did he pray! In a word, every action, every word, every motion of Jesus, inflamed with love the hearts of all those who beheld him, and especially of Mary and of Joseph, who had the good fortune to see him always at their side. Oh, how these holy spouses remained always intent on contemplating and admiring all the operations, the words, and gestures of this Man-God!

Affections and Prayers.

Grow, my beloved Jesus, grow continually for me; grow to teach me Thy virtues by Thy divine examples; grow to consummate the great sacrifice on the cross, on which depends my eternal salvation! Grant also, my Saviour, that I too may grow more in Thy love and grace. Miserable that I have been, I have hitherto only increased in ingratitude towards Thee who hast loved me so much. O my Jesus, grant that in future it may be just the contrary with me; Thou knowest all my weakness, it is from Thee that I must receive light and strength. Make me know the claims which Thou hast to my love. Thou art a God of infinite beauty and of infinite majesty, who didst not refuse to come down upon this earth and become man for us, and for our sakes to lead an abject and painful life, and to end it by a most cruel death. And where can we ever find an object more amiable and more worthy of love than Thee? Fool that I was, in times past I refused to know Thee, and therefore I have lost Thee. I implore Thy pardon; I am heartily sorry, and I am determined to be entirely devoted to Thee in future. But do Thou assist me; remind me constantly of the life of suffering and the bitter death Thou hast endured for the love of me. Give me life and give me strength. When the devil presents to me forbidden fruit, grant me strength to despise it;

and let me not for some vile and momentary good risk losing Thee, O infinite Good. I love Thee, my Jesus, who hast died for me ; I love Thee, infinite Goodness ; I love Thee, O Beloved of my soul. O Mary, thou art my hope ; through thy intercession I hope to obtain grace to love my God from this time forth and forever, and never to love any but God.

MEDITATION VIII.

JANUARY 13.

The Loss of Jesus in the Temple.

St. Luke relates that Mary and Joseph went every year to Jerusalem on the Feast of the Pasch, and took the Infant Jesus with them. It was the custom, says the Venerable Bede, for the Jews to make this journey to the temple, or at least on their return home, the men separated from the women ; and the children went at their pleasure, either with their fathers or their mothers. Our Redeemer, who was then twelve years old, remained during this solemnity for three days in Jerusalem. Mary thought he was with Joseph, and Joseph that he was with Mary: *Thinking that He was in the company.*[1]

The Holy Child employed all these three days in honoring his eternal Father by fasts, vigils, and prayers, and in being present at the sacrifices, which were all figures of his own great sacrifice on the cross. If he took a little food, says St. Bernard, he must have procured it by begging ; and if he took any repose, he could have had no other bed but the bare ground.

When Mary and Joseph arrived in the evening at their home, they did not find Jesus ; wherefore, full of sorrow, they began to seek him amongst their relatives and friends. At last, returning to Jerusalem, the third day they found him in the Temple, disputing with the Doctors, who, full of astonishment, admired the ques-

[1] " Existimantes illum esse in comitatu."—*Luke*, ii. 44.

tions and answers of this wonderful child. On seeing him, Mary said, *Son, why hast Thou done so to us? Behold Thy father and I have sought Thee sorrowing.*[1]

There is not upon earth a sorrow like to that which is felt by a soul that loves Jesus, when she fears that Jesus Christ has withdrawn himself from her through some fault of hers. This was the sorrow of Mary and Joseph, which afflicted them so much during these days; for they perhaps feared, through their humility, as says the devout Lanspergius, that they had rendered themselves unworthy of the care of such a treasure. Wherefore, on seeing him, Mary said to him, in order to express to him this sorrow: *Son, why hast Thou done so to us? Behold Thy father and I have sought Thee sorrowing.*[1] And Jesus answered, *Did you not know that I must be about My Father's business?*[2]

Let us learn from this mystery two lessons; the first, that we must leave all our friends and relatives when the glory of God is in question. The second, that God easily makes himself found by those who seek him: *The Lord is good to the soul that seeketh Him.*[3]

Affections and Prayers.

O Mary, thou weepest because thou hast lost thy Son for a few days; he has withdrawn himself from thy eyes, but not from thy heart. Dost thou not see that that pure love with which thou lovest him keeps him constantly united and bound to thee? Thou knowest well that he who loves God cannot but be loved by God, who says, *I love those that love Me;*[4] and with St. John, *He that abideth in charity abideth in God, and*

---

[1] "Fili, quid fecisti nobis sic? ecce pater tuus et ego dolentes quærebamus te."

[2] "Nesciebatis quia, in his quæ Patris mei sunt, oportet me esse?"

[3] "Bonus est Dominus . . . . animæ quærenti illum."—*Lam.* iii. 25.

[4] "Ego diligentes me diligo."—*Prov.* viii. 17.

God in him.[1] Wherefore, then, dost thou fear? Wherefore dost thou weep? Leave these tears to me, who have so often lost God through my own fault, by driving him away from my soul. O my Jesus! how could I offend Thee thus with my eyes open, when I knew that by sinning I should lose Thee? But Thou willest not that the heart that seeks Thee should despair, but rather that it should rejoice : *Let the heart of them rejoice that seek the Lord.*[2] If hitherto I have forsaken Thee, O my Love, I will now seek, and will seek none but Thee. And provided I possess Thy grace, I renounce all the goods and pleasures of this world ; I renounce even my own life, Thou hast said that Thou lovest him who loves Thee ; I love Thee, do Thou also love me. I esteem Thy love more than the dominion of the whole world. O my Jesus, I desire not to lose Thee any more ; but I cannot trust to myself, I trust in Thee : *In Thee, O Lord, have I put my trust ; I shall not be confounded forever.*[3] I beseech Thee, do Thou bind me to Thee, and permit me not to be again separated from Thee. O Mary! through thee have I found my God, whom I had once lost ; do thou obtain for me also holy perseverance ; wherefore I will also say to thee, with St. Bonaventure, *In thee, O Lady, have I hoped ; let me not be confounded forever.*[4]

[1] "Qui manet in charitate, in Deo manet, et Deus in eo."—1 *John*, iv. 16.

[2] "Lætetur cor quærentium Dominum."—*Ps.* civ. 3.

[3] "In te, Domine, speravi ; non confundar in æternum."—*Ps.* xxx. 6.

[4] "In te, Domina, speravi ; non confundar in æternum."

Other Meditations for the First Eight Days of Advent.*

MEDITATION I.

The Love that God has manifested to us in the Incarnation of the Word.

Et Verbum caro factum est.
"And the Word was made flesh."—*John*, i. 14.

I.

God has created us to love him in this life, and afterwards to enjoy him in the next; but we ungratefully rebelled against God by sinning, and refused to obey him, and therefore we have been deprived of divine grace, and excluded from paradise, and besides condemned to the eternal pains of hell. Behold us, therefore, all lost; but this God, moved by compassion for us, resolved to send on earth a Redeemer, who should repair our great ruin.

II.

But who shall this Redeemer be? Shall it be an angel, or a seraph? No; to show us the immense love that he bears us, God sends us his own Son: "*God sent His Son in the likeness of sinful flesh.*"[1] He sent his only-begotten Son to clothe himself with the same flesh as we sinners, but without the stain of sin; and he willed that by his sufferings and his death he should satisfy the divine justice for our crimes, and should thus deliver us from

[1] "Deus Filium suum mittens in similitudinem carnis peccati."
—*Rom.* viii. 3.

* These eight meditations, with the twelve others that follow them, did not form a part of the *Novena of Christmas*. They appeared some years later, in 1767.—ED.

eternal death, and render us worthy of divine grace and eternal glory.

I thank Thee, O my God, on behalf of all mankind; for, if Thou hadst not thought of saving us, I and all the world would have been lost forever.

III.

Let us dwell here on the infinite love which our God has shown for us in this great work of the Incarnation of the Word, ordaining that his Son should come and sacrifice his life upon the Cross by the hands of executioners, in a sea of sorrows and of shame, to obtain for us pardon and eternal salvation. O infinite goodness! O infinite mercy! O infinite love! A God to become man and die for us poor worms!

I beseech Thee, my Saviour, make me know how much Thou hast loved me, in order that, at the sight of Thy loving-kindness, I may discover my own ingratitude. Thou hast delivered me by Thy death from perdition; and I, ungrateful that I am, have turned my back upon Thee, to ruin myself again! I repent with all my heart of having done Thee this great injury. O my Saviour! forgive me and save me in future from sin; do not suffer me again to lose Thy grace. I love Thee, O my dear Jesus; Thou art my hope and my love! O Mary, Mother of this great Son, recommend to him my soul!

MEDITATION II.

Goodness of God the Father and of God the Son in the Work of the Redemption.

Et incarnatus est de Spiritu Sancto ex Maria Virgine, et homo factus est.

"And became incarnate by the Holy Ghost of the Virgin Mary, and was made man."—*Symb. Const.*

I.

God created Adam, and enriched him with gifts; but man, ungrateful, offended him by sinning, and thus both he and all we, his descendants, remained deprived of divine grace and paradise. Thus, then, all mankind was lost and without a remedy. Man had offended God, and therefore was incapable of giving him an adequate satisfaction; it was necessary then that a divine person should satisfy for man. What does the eternal Father to save lost man? He sent this same Son to become man, and clothe himself with the same flesh as sinful men, in order that by his death he might pay their debts to divine justice, and thus obtain for them a restoration to divine grace.

O my God, if Thy infinite bounty had not discovered this remedy, who of us could ever have asked it, or even imagined it?

II.

O God, what a subject of wonder must not this great love which God showed to rebellious man have been to the angels! What must they have said when they saw the eternal Word become man, and assume the same flesh as sinful man, insomuch that this Word incarnate appeared to the whole world in the form of a sinful man, as were all others. O my Jesus, how much do we not owe Thee, and how much more than others am I not indebted to Thee, who have offended Thee so much more than others! If Thou hadst not come to save me, what would have become of me for all eternity? Who could have saved me from the pains that I deserve? Mayest Thou be ever blessed and praised for so great love!

III.

Thus, then, the Son of God comes from heaven on earth, and becomes man; he comes to live a life of suffering; he comes to die upon the cross for the love of man; and shall men who believe all this love any other object besides this incarnate God?

O Jesus my Saviour, I will love none other but Thee;

Thou alone hast loved me, Thee alone will I love. I renounce all created goods; Thou alone art sufficient for me, O immense and infinite Good! If hitherto I have displeased Thee, I am now heartily sorry for it, and would wish that this sorrow might make me die, to compensate in some measure for the displeasure I have caused Thee. Oh, permit me not in future to be ever again ungrateful for the love Thou hast borne me. No, my Jesus, make me love Thee, and then treat me as Thou pleasest. O infinite Bounty, O infinite Love, I will only live henceforth to love Thee ! O Mary, Mother of mercy, this one favor I ask of thee, obtain for me the grace of always, always loving God.

MEDITATION III.

Motives of Confidence that are given to us by the Incarnation of the Word.

Quomodo non etiam cum illo omnia nobis donavit?
" How hath he not also, with him, given us all things ?"—*Rom.* viii. 32.

I.

Consider, my soul, that the eternal Father, in giving us his beloved Son for our Redeemer, could have given us no stronger motives for confiding in his mercy and loving his infinite bounty; for he could have given us no more certain token of the desire he has for our good, and of the immense love which he bears us, inasmuch as in giving us his Son, he has nothing left to give us. Let all men, therefore, O eternal God, praise Thy infinite charity.

II.

How hath He not also, with Him, given us all things ?[1] Since God has given us his Son, whom he loved as himself, how can we fear that he will deny us any other

[1] " Quomodo non etiam cum illo omnia nobis donavit ?"

good that we ask of him? If, therefore, he has given us his Son, he will not refuse us pardon for the offences which we have committed against him, provided we detest them; he will not refuse us the grace to resist temptations, if we implore it of him; he will not refuse us his holy love, if we desire it; he will not, finally, refuse us Paradise, if we do not render ourselves unworthy of it by falling into sin. Behold how Jesus himself assures us of this: *If you ask the Father anything in My name, He will give it you.*[1]

Encouraged, therefore, O my God, by this promise, I beg of Thee, for the love of Jesus Thy Son, to pardon me all the injuries that I have done Thee; give me holy perseverance in Thy grace until death; give me Thy holy love; may I detach myself from everything to love Thee alone, O infinite Goodness; give me Paradise in order that I may come and love Thee there with all my strength, and forever, without fear of ever ceasing to love Thee.

III.

In a word, the Apostle says that, having obtained Jesus Christ, we have been enriched with every good, so that there is no grace wanting to us: *In all things you are made rich in Him . . ., so that nothing is wanting to you in any grace.*[2]

Yes, my Jesus, Thou art every good; Thou alone sufficest me; for Thee alone do I sigh; if once I drove Thee away from me by my sins, I repent of it now with my whole heart. Forgive me, and return to me, O Lord; and if Thou art already with me, as I hope, leave me not again, or, rather, suffer me not to drive Thee away

---

[1] "Si quid petieritis Patrem in nomine meo, dabit vobis."—*John*, xvi. 23.

[2] "In omnibus divites facti estis in illo . . ., ita ut nihil vobis desit in ulla gratia."—1 *Cor.* i. 5.

from my soul again. My Jesus, my Jesus, my treasure, my love, my All, I love Thee, I love Thee, I love Thee, and will love Thee forever. O Mary, my hope, make me always to love Jesus.

MEDITATION IV.

Happiness of having been born after the Redemption and in the True Church.

Ubi venit plenitudo temporis, misit Deus Filium suum . . . , ut eos qui sub lege erant, redimeret.

"When the fulness of the time was come, God sent His Son . . . that he might redeem them who were under the law."—*Gal.* iv. 4.

I.

How thankful should we not be to Almighty God for having caused us to be born after the great work of man's redemption was accomplished! This is what is meant by *the fulness of time*,[1] a time blessed by the fulness of grace, which Jesus Christ obtained for us by coming into the world. Miserable should we have been if, guilty as we are of manifold sins, we had lived on this earth before the coming of Jesus Christ.

II.

Oh, what a miserable state were all men in before the coming of the Messias; the true God was hardly known even in Judea, and in every other part of the world idolatry reigned, so that our forefathers worshipped stones, and wood, and devils; they worshipped innumerable false gods, but the true God was neither loved nor known by them. Even now, how many countries are there in which there are scarcely any Catholics, and all the rest of the inhabitants are either infidels or heretics! and all these are certainly in the way to be lost. What obligation do we not owe to God for causing us to be born,

---

[1] "Plenitudo temporis."

not only after the coming of Jesus Christ, but also in countries where the true faith reigns!

I thank Thee, O Lord, for this. Woe to me if, after so many transgressions, it had been my lot to live in the midst of infidels or heretics! I know, O my God, that Thou willest that I should be saved; and I, miserable wretch, have willed so many times to damn myself by losing Thy favor. Have pity, my Blessed Redeemer, on my soul, which has cost Thee so much.

III.

God sent His Son that He might redeem them that were under the law.[1] The slave therefore sins, and by sinning gives himself into the power of the devil, and his own Lord comes and ransoms him by his death.

O immense love, O infinite love of God towards man! O my Saviour, if Thou hadst not redeemed me by Thy death, what would have become of me? Of me, who so many times have deserved hell by my sins. Oh, if Thou, my Jesus, hadst not died for me, I should have lost Thee forever, and there would have been no hope for me of recovering Thy grace, or of seeing Thy beautiful face in paradise. My dearest Saviour, I thank Thee; and I hope to come to heaven, there to thank Thee for all eternity. I regret above every evil that of having despised Thee in times past. In future, I purpose to choose every trouble, every kind of death, rather than offend Thee. I beseech Thee, my Jesus, let me never do so;"'never let me be separated from Thee, never let me be separated from Thee."[2] I love Thee, O infinite Goodness! and I will always love Thee in this life, and in all eternity. O my queen and advocate, Mary, keep me always under thy protection, and deliver me from sin.

[1] "Misit Filium suum, ut eos, qui sub lege erant, redimeret."—*Gal.* iv. 4.

[2] " Noli me separari a te; noli me separari a te."

MEDITATION V.

Jesus has done and suffered Everything to save us.

Dilexit me, et tradidit semetipsum pro me.
"He loved me, and delivered Himself for me."—*Gal.* ii. 20.

I.

If, therefore, my Jesus, Thou hast for love of me embraced a laborious life and a bitter death, I may, indeed, say that Thy death is mine, Thy sufferings are mine, Thy merits are mine, Thou Thyself art mine; since for me Thou hast given Thyself up to so great sufferings. Ah, my Jesus, there is no trouble that afflicts me more than the thought that once Thou wert mine, and that I have so often willingly lost Thee. Forgive me, and unite me to Thyself; suffer me not in future ever to offend Thee again. I love Thee with all my heart. Thou willest to be all mine; and I will be entirely Thine.

II.

The Son of God being true God is infinitely happy; and yet, as St. Thomas says, he has done and suffered as much for man as if he could not be happy without him.[1] If Jesus Christ had been obliged to earn for himself upon this earth his eternal beatitude, what could he have done more than to burden himself with all our weaknesses, and assume all our infirmities, and then end his life with a death so severe and ignominious? But no, he was innocent, he was holy, and was in himself blessed; whatever he did and suffered was all to gain for us divine grace and paradise, which we had lost.

Miserable is he that does not love Thee, my Jesus, and that does not pass his life enamoured with so much goodness.

[1] "Quasi sine ipso beatus esse non posset."—*Opusc.* 63, c. 7.

III.

If Jesus Christ had permitted us to ask him for the greatest proofs of his love, who would have dared to propose to him to become a child like one of us, to embrace all our miseries, to make himself of all men the most poor, the most despised, the most ill-used, even to dying in torments the infamous death of the cross, cursed and forsaken by all, even by his own Father? But that which we should not have dared even to think of, he has both thought of and done.

My beloved Redeemer, I beseech Thee to obtain for me that grace which Thou hast merited for me by Thy death. I love Thee, and am sorry for having offended Thee. Oh, take my soul into Thy hands; I will not let the devil have dominion over it any more; I desire that it may be entirely Thine, since Thou hast bought it with Thy blood. Thou alone lovest me, and Thee alone will I love. Deliver me from the misery of living without Thy love, and then chastise me as Thou willest. O Mary, my refuge, the death of Jesus and thy intercession are my hopes.

MEDITATION VI.

The Sight of our Sins afflicted Jesus from the First Moment of his Life.

Dolor meus in conspectu meo semper.
"My sorrow is continually before me."—*Ps.* xxxvii. 18.

I.

All the afflictions and ignominies which Jesus Christ suffered in life and death, all were present to his mind from the first moment of his life.[1] And he offered them all every moment of his life in satisfaction for our sins. Our Lord revealed to one of his servants that every sin

[1] " Dolor meus in conspectu meo semper."

of men gave him during his life so much sorrow that it would have sufficed to cause his death, if his life had not been preserved in order that he might suffer more. Behold, O my Jesus! what gratitude hast Thou received from men, and especially from me. Thou hast spent thirty-three years of life for my salvation, and I have done as much as I could, as far as it depended on me, to make Thee die with sorrow, as often as I have committed sin.

II.

St. Bernardine of Sienna writes that Jesus Christ "had a particular regard to every single sin."[1] Each of our sins was present continually to our Saviour, even from his infancy, and afflicted him grievously. St. Thomas adds[2] that this one sorrow of knowing all the injury which resulted to the Father from every sin, and all the evil which it occasioned to us, surpassed the sorrow of all the contrite sinners that ever were, even of those who died of pure contrition; because no sinner ever arrived at loving God and his own soul as Jesus Christ has loved the Father and our souls.

Therefore, my Jesus, if no man ever loved me more than Thou hast done, it it only just that I should love Thee above all men. Since, then, I can say that Thou alone hast really loved me, so will I love Thee alone.

III.

That agony which Jesus suffered in the garden at the sight of our sins, for which he had taken upon himself to satisfy, he suffered from the time he was conceived in his mother's womb. If, therefore, Jesus Christ passed a life full of tribulations for no other reason than on account of our sins, we ought not, during our life, to afflict

[1] "Ad quamlibet culpam singularem habet aspectum."—*T*. ii. s. 56, a. 1, c. 1.
[2] P. 3, q. 46, a. 6.

ourselves for any other evils than for the sins which we have committed.

My beloved Redeemer, I could wish to die of sorrow at the thought of all the bitterness that I have caused Thee during my life. My Love, if Thou lovest me, give me such a sorrow as may take away my life, and so obtain for me Thy pardon, and the grace to love Thee with all my strength. I give Thee my whole heart; and if I do not know how to give it to Thee entirely, oh, do Thou take it Thyself, and inflame it with Thy holy love. O Mary, advocate of the wretched, I recommend myself to thee.

MEDITATION VII.

Baptismo habeo baptizari; et quomodo coarctor, usquedum perficiatur?

"I have a baptism wherewith I am to be baptized; and how am I straitened until it be accomplished?"—*Luke*, xii. 50.

The Desire that Jesus had to suffer for us.

I.

Jesus could have saved us without suffering; but he chose rather to embrace a life of sorrow and contempt, deprived of every earthly consolation, and a death of bitterness and desolation, only to make us understand the love which he bore us, and the desire which he had that we should love him. He passed his whole life in sighing for the hour of his death, which he desired to offer to God, to obtain for us eternal salvation. And it was this desire which made him exclaim: *I have a baptism wherewith I am to be baptized; and how am I straitened until it be accomplished?*[1] He desired to be baptized in his own blood, to wash out, not, indeed, his own, but our sins. O infinite Love, how miserable is he who does not know Thee, and does not love Thee!

[1] "Desiderio desideravi hoc pascha manducare vobiscum."—*Luke*, xxii. 15.

II.

This same desire caused him to say, on the night before his death, *With desire I have desired to eat this pasch with you*. By which words he shows that his only desire during his whole life had been to see the time arrive for his Passion and death, in order to prove to man the immense love which he bore him. So much, therefore, O my Jesus, didst Thou desire our love, that to obtain it Thou didst not refuse to die. How could I, then, deny anything to a God who, for love of me, has given his blood and his life?

III.

St. Bonaventure says that it is a wonder to see a God suffering for the love of men; but that it is a still greater wonder that men should behold a God suffering so much for them, shivering with cold as an infant in a manger, living as a poor boy in a shop, dying as a criminal on a cross, and yet not burn with love to this most loving God; but even go so far as to despise this love, for the sake of the miserable pleasures of this earth. But how is it possible that God should be so enamoured with men, and that men, who are so grateful to one another, should be so ungrateful to God?

Alas! my Jesus, I find myself also among the number of these ungrateful ones. Tell me, how couldst Thou suffer so much for me, knowing the injuries that I should commit against Thee? But since Thou hast borne with me, and even desirest my salvation, give me, I pray Thee, a great sorrow for my sins, a sorrow equal to my ingratitude. I hate and detest, above all things, my Lord, the displeasure which I have caused Thee. If, during my past life, I have despised Thy grace, now I value it above all the kingdoms of the earth. I love Thee with my whole soul, O God, worthy of infinite love, and I desire only to live in order to love Thee.

Increase the flames of Thy love, and give me more and more love. Keep alive in my remembrance the love that Thou hast borne me, so that my heart may always burn with love for Thee, as Thy heart burns with love for me. O burning heart of Mary, inflame my poor heart with holy love.

MEDITATION VIII.

Haurietis aquas in gaudio de fontibus Salvatoris.

"You shall draw waters with joy out of the Saviour's fountains."—*Isa.* xii. 3.

Three Fountains of Grace that We have in Jesus Christ.

I.

We have three fountains of grace in Jesus Christ. The first is the fountain of *mercy*, in which we may purify ourselves from all the filth of our sins. For this end did our blessed Redeemer form, for our good, this fountain out of his own blood. *He hath loved us, and washed us from our sins in His own blood.*[1]

My dearest Saviour, how much do I owe Thee! Thou hast done for me what no servant would have done for his master, and no son for his father. No, I cannot cease to love Thee; for Thou hast, by Thy love, entailed on me the necessity of loving Thee.

II.

The second fountain is that of *love*. He that meditates on the sufferings and degradations undergone by Jesus Christ, for the love of us, from his birth even until his death, must of necessity feel himself inflamed with that blessed fire which he came on earth to enkindle in the hearts of men. Thus it is that the waters of this fountain wash, and at the same time inflame, our souls. Grant, therefore, O my Jesus! that the blood which

[1] "Dilexit nos, et lavit nos a peccatis nostris in sanguine suo."—*Apoc.* i. 5.

Thou hast shed for me may not only wash away all the sins which I have committed against Thee, but may also inflame me with holy ardor towards Thee. Make me forget everything, so that I may be intent only on loving Thee, my God, who art worthy of infinite love.

III.

The third fountain is that of *peace*. This is what Jesus Christ meant when he said, *If any man thirst, let him come to Me*.[1] He that desireth peace of mind, let him come to me, who am the God of peace. The peace which the Lord gives to the souls that love him is not the peace which the world promises in the pleasures of sense or in temporal goods which do not satisfy the heart of man. The peace which God gives to his servants is true peace, perfect peace, which satisfies the heart, and surpasses all the enjoyments that creatures can afford. *But he that shall drink of the water that I will give him shall not thirst forever*.[2] He that truly loves God leaves everything, despises everything, and seeks nothing but God. "Yes, my God, I desire Thee alone, and nothing else." There was, indeed, a time when I sought for other goods besides Thee; but when I think of the injustice which I have done Thee, in preferring so vile and fleeting goods to Thee, I am ready to die of sorrow. I acknowledge the sin I have committed, and I grieve for it with my whole heart. I acknowledge also that Thou art worthy of all my love; and therefore I repeat, and hope always to repeat in this life and in the next, "My God, my God, I desire Thee alone, and nothing more; I desire Thee alone, and nothing more." O Mary, thou wert the first lover of this God; oh, make me partake in thy love!

---

[1] "Si quis sitit, veniat ad me."—*John*, vii. 37.

[2] "Qui autem biberit ex aqua quam ego dabo ei, non sitiet in æternum."—*John*, iv. 13.

Other Meditations for the Novena of Christmas.

Chaplet to be recited before every Meditation.

1. My most sweet Jesus, who wert born in a cave and wert afterwards laid in a manger upon straw, have mercy upon us. *R.* Have mercy, O Lord, have mercy upon us. *Our Father, Hail Mary, Glory be to the Father*, etc.

2. My most sweet Jesus, who wert presented and offered by Mary in the temple, to be afterwards one day sacrificed for us upon the cross, have mercy upon us. *R.* Have Mercy, O Lord, have mercy upon us. *Our Father, Hail Mary, Glory be to the Father*, etc.

3. My most sweet Jesus, who wert persecuted by Herod and constrained to fly into Egypt, have mercy upon us. *R.* Have mercy, O Lord, have mercy upon us. *Our Father, Hail Mary, Glory be to the Father*, etc.

4. My most sweet Jesus, who didst dwell in Egypt for seven years, poor, unknown, and despised by that barbarous nation, have mercy upon us. *R.* Have mercy, O Lord, have mercy upon us. *Our Father, Hail Mary, Glory be to the Father*, etc.

5. My most sweet Jesus, who didst return to Thy country to be one day crucified there in the midst of two thieves, have mercy upon us. *R.* Have mercy O Lord, have mercy upon us. *Our Father, Hail Mary, Glory be to the Father*, etc.

6. My most sweet Jesus, who at the age of twelve years didst remain in the temple to dispute with the Doctors, and after three days wert found by Mary, have mercy upon us. *R.* Have mercy, O Lord, have mercy upon us. *Our Father, Hail Mary, Glory be to the Father*, etc.

7. My most sweet Jesus, who didst live concealed from the world for so many years in the shop at Nazareth, serving Mary and Joseph, have mercy upon us. *R.* Have mercy, O Lord, have mercy upon us. *Our Father, Hail Mary, Glory be to the Father,* etc.

8. My most sweet Jesus, who for three years before Thy Passion didst go about preaching and teaching the way of salvation, have mercy upon us. *R.* Have mercy, O Lord, have mercy upon us. *Our Father, Hail Mary, Glory be to the Father,* etc.

9. My most sweet Jesus, who for the love of us didst terminate Thy life by dying on the cross, have mercy upon us. *R.* Have mercy, O Lord, have mercy upon us. *Our Father, Hail Mary, Glory be to the Father,* etc.

MEDITATION I.

DECEMBER 16.

The Love that God has shown to us in becoming Man.

Let us consider the immense love which God showed us in becoming man in order to procure us eternal life.

Our first parent, Adam, having sinned and rebelled against God, was driven out of paradise and condemned to everlasting death with all his descendants. But behold the Son of God, who, seeing man thus lost, in order to deliver him from death offers to take upon himself human flesh, and to die condemned as a malefactor upon the cross. But, my Son, we may suppose the Father saying to him: Consider what a life of humiliation and suffering Thou wilt have to lead upon earth. Thou wilt have to be born in a cold cave, and to be laid in a manger for beasts. Thou wilt have to fly as an infant into Egypt to escape from the hands of Herod. On Thy return from Egypt Thou wilt have to live in a shop as an humble servant, poor and despised. And, finally, worn out by sufferings, Thou wilt have to give up Thy life upon a cross, insulted and forsaken by all.—Father, all this matters not, replies the Son ; I am content with enduring all, provided man is saved.

What should we say if a prince were to take compassion upon a dead worm, and were to choose to become a worm himself, and to make, as it were, a bath of his own blood, to die in order to restore the worm to life? But the eternal Word has done even more than this for us ; for, being God, he has chosen to become a worm like us, and to die for us, in order to purchase for us the life of divine grace which we had lost. When he saw that all the gifts he had bestowed upon us could not secure to him our love, what did he do ? He became man, and he gave himself entirely to us : " *The Word was made flesh, and gave Himself for us.*" [1]

Man by despising God, says St. Fulgentius, separated himself from God ; but God, through his love for man, came from heaven to seek him. And why did he come ? He came in order that man might know how much God loved him, and that thus, out of gratitude at least, he might love him in return. Even the beasts, when they approach themselves to us, make us love them ; and why, then, are we so ungrateful towards a God who descends from heaven to earth to make us love him?

One day, when a priest was saying these words in Mass, *Et verbum caro factum est*—" And the Word was made flesh"—a man who was present neglected to make an act of reverence ; upon which the devil gave him a blow, saying, " Ah, ungrateful man ! if God had done as much for me as he has done for thee, I should remain with my face always bent down to the ground returning thanks to him."

---

[1] " Verbum caro factum est "—*John*, i. 14—" et tradidit semetipsum pro nobis."—*Eph.* v. 2.

Affections and Prayers.

O great Son of God! Thou hast become man in order to make Thyself loved by men; but where is the love that men bear to Thee? Thou hast given Thy blood and Thy life to save our souls; and why are we so ungrateful to Thee, that, instead of loving Thee, we despise with such ingratitude? Alas! I myself, Lord, have been one of those who more than others have thus illtreated Thee. But Thy Passion is my hope. Oh, for the sake of that love that induced Thee to assume human flesh, and to die for me upon the cross, forgive me all the offences I have committed against Thee. I love Thee, O Incarnate Word; I love Thee, O my God; I love Thee, O Infinite Goodness; and I repent of all the injuries I have done Thee. Would that I could die of sorrow for Thee! O my Jesus! grant me the gift of Thy love; let me not live any longer ungrateful for the affliction Thou hast borne me. I am determined to love Thee always. Give me holy perseverance. O Mary, Mother of God, and my Mother, obtain for me from thy Son the grace to love him always even unto death.

MEDITATION II.

DECEMBER 17.

The Love of God in being born an Infant.

The Son of God, in becoming man for our sake, might have appeared in the world at the age of a perfect man, as Adam appeared when he was created; but, as children generally attract to themselves greater love from those who take care of them, therefore he chose to appear upon earth as an infant; and as the poorest and most abject infant that ever was born. St. Peter Chrysologus writes: "Thus did our God choose to be born; because thus did he wish to be loved." The prophet Isaias had already predicted that the Son of God was to be born an infant, and thus to give himself entirely to us through the love that he bore us: *A Child is born to us, a Son is given to us.*[1]

O my Jesus, my supreme and true God! what can have attracted Thee from heaven to be born in a cave, if it be not the love that Thou bearest to man? What has drawn Thee from the bosom of Thy Father to lay Thyself down in a manger? What has brought Thee down from Thy throne above the stars, to stretch Thyself on a little straw? What, from the midst of the nine choirs of angels, has placed Thee between two animals? Thou dost inflame the seraphim with holy fire, and lo, Thou art trembling with cold in this stable! Thou dost give motion to the heavens and the sun, and now Thou canst not move without being carried in some one's arms! Thou dost provide with food both man and beast, and dost Thou now require a little milk to sustain Thy life? Thou art the delight of heaven, and now how is it that I hear Thee weep and moan? Tell me who hath reduced Thee to such misery? "Who hath done this? Love hath done it,"[2] says St. Bernard; the love that Thou bearest to man hath done it.

Affections and Prayers.

O dearest Infant! tell me what Thou camest on earth to do? Tell me whom Thou art seeking? Ah, I understand Thee now; Thou art come in order to die for me, to deliver me from hell. Thou art come to seek me, a lost sheep, in order that I may no more fly from Thee, but love Thee. Ah, my Jesus, my treasure, my life, my love, my all; if I do not love Thee, whom then shall I love? Where can I find a father, a friend, a spouse more amiable than Thou, and who has loved me more than Thou hast done? I am sorry to have been so many years in the world, and yet not to have loved Thee; yea, rather to have offended and despised Thee. Forgive me, O my beloved Redeemer; for I repent of having treated Thee thus; I am sorry for it with all

---

[1] " Parvulus natus est nobis, et Filius datus est nobis."—*Isa.* ix. 6.
[2] " Quis hoc fecit? Amor fecit."

my heart. Pardon me, and give me Thy grace, that I may never again separate myself from Thee, and that I may love Thee constantly during the years that remain to me in this life. My love, I give myself entirely to Thee; accept me, and do not reject me, though I deserve it. O Mary, thou art my advocate; thou dost obtain by thy prayers whatever thou wilt from thy Son; beg of him to forgive me, and to give me holy perseverance unto death.

MEDITATION III.

DECEMBER 18.

The Life of Poverty which Jesus led even from His Birth.

It was ordained by God that at the time when his Son was born on this earth the decree of the emperor should be promulgated, obliging every one to go and enroll himself in the place of his birth. And thus it happened that Joseph had to go with his spouse to Bethlehem to enroll himself according to the decree of Cæsar. And now, the time of her delivery having arrived, Mary, having been driven from the other houses, and even from the common asylum for the poor, was obliged to remain that night in a cave, and there brought forth the King of Heaven. It is true that, if Jesus had been born in Nazareth, he would equally have been born in a state of poverty; but then he would at least have had a dry room, a little fire, warm clothes, and a more comfortable cradle. But no, he chose to be born in this cold cavern without a fire to warm him; he chose to have a manger for a cradle, and a little prickly straw for a bed, in order that he might suffer more.

Let us, then, enter into the cave of Bethlehem; but let us enter there with faith. If we go there without faith, we shall see nothing but a poor infant, who moves us to compassion at beholding him so beautiful, shivering and crying with cold, and with the prickling of the straw on which he lies. But if we enter in with faith, and consider that this Child is the Son of God, who for the love of us has come down to this earth and suffered so much to pay the penalty of our sins, how can it be possible not to thank him and love him?

Affections and Prayers.

O my sweet Infant! how is it possible that, knowing how much Thou hast suffered for me, I can have been so ungrateful to Thee, and offended Thee so often? But these tears which Thou sheddest, this poverty which Thou hast chosen for the love of me, make me hope for the pardon of all the offences that I have committed against Thee. I repent, my Jesus, of having so often turned my back upon Thee; and I love Thee above all things, "my God and my All."[1] My God, from this day forth Thou shalt be my only treasure and my only good. I will say to Thee, with St. Ignatius of Loyola, "Give me Thy love, give me Thy grace, and I am sufficiently rich." I wish for, I desire nothing else. Thou alone art sufficient for me, my Jesus, my life, my love.

MEDITATION IV.

DECEMBER 19.

The Life of Humility which Jesus led even from His Infancy.

All the marks that the angel gave to the shepherds to find the Saviour, who was just born, were marks of humility: *And this shall be a sign unto you; you shall find the infant wrapped in swaddling-clothes, and laid in a manger.*[2] This shall be the sign, said the angel, to find the new-born Messias: you will find him an infant, wrapped in poor ragged clothes, in a stable, lying on straw in a manger for animals. Thus would the King of Heaven, the Son of God, be born, because he came to destroy the pride which had been the cause of man's ruin.

[1] "Deus meus, et omnia."
[2] "Et hoc vobis signum: invenietis infantem pannis involutum, et positum in præsepio."—*Luke*, ii. 12.

The prophets had already foretold that our Redeemer should be treated as the vilest man upon earth, and overwhelmed with insults. How much contempt had not Jesus to suffer from men! He was treated as a drunkard, as a magician, as a blasphemer, and a heretic. How many affronts did he endure during his Passion! He was forsaken by his own disciples; even one of them sold him for thirty pieces of silver, and another denied having ever known him. He was led through the streets bound like a criminal, scourged like a slave, treated like a madman, as a mock king; struck, spit upon in the face; and at length he was put to death on a cross, suspended between two thieves, as the greatest malefactor in the world.

Thus, says St. Bernard, the noblest of men is treated like the vilest of all. "But, my Jesus," adds the saint, "the viler Thou art, the dearer art Thou to me."[1] The more Thou appearest to me humbled and despised, the more dear and worthy of love dost Thou become to me.

Affections and Prayers.

O my sweet Saviour! Thou hast embraced so much contempt for the love of me, and I have not been able to bear a word of insult without thinking immediately of revenging myself of it, —I who so often have deserved to be trodden underfoot by the devils in hell! I am ashamed of appearing before Thee, a proud sinner that I am. O Lord! do not drive me from Thy presence, as I deserve. Thou hast said that Thou couldst not despise a heart that repents and humbles itself: I repent of all the offences I have committed against Thee. Forgive me, my Jesus; for I will not offend Thee any more. Thou hast suffered so many injuries for my sake, I will for Thy sake bear with all the injuries that may be offered me. I love Thee, my Jesus, despised for my sake; I love Thee, my Good, above every other good. Give me Thy help, that I may always love Thee, and suffer every insult for the love of Thee. O Mary! recommend me to thy Son; pray to Jesus for me.

[1] "Quanto pro me vilior, tanto mihi carior."

MEDITATION V.
DECEMBER 20.
The Life of Sorrow which Jesus led even from His Birth.

Jesus Christ could have saved man without suffering and without dying; but no, he chose a life full of tribulations, in order to make us know how much he loved us. Therefore the prophet Isaias called him the Man of sorrows,[1] because the life of Jesus Christ was to be a life full of sorrows. His Passion did not commence at the time of his death, but from the commencement of his life.

Behold him, as soon as he is born, laid in a stable, where for Jesus everything is a torment. His sight is tormented by seeing nothing else in this cave but black rough walls. His sense of smelling is tormented by the stench of the dung of the beasts that are lying there. His sense of touch is tormented by the pricking of the straw that serves him for a bed. Soon after his birth he is obliged to fly into Egypt, where he passed several years of his childhood poor and despised; the life which he led afterwards in Nazareth was not much better. Behold him at length terminating his life in Jerusalem, dying on a cross by dint of torments.

Thus, then, the life of Jesus was one continual suffering, and indeed a double suffering; for he had constantly before his eyes all the sorrows that would afflict him until the day of his death. Sister Mary Magdalene Orsini, complaining one day before the crucifix, said to him: "O Lord, Thou didst remain on the cross for three hours, but I have suffered this pain for several years." But Jesus answered her: "Oh, ignorant that thou art, what dost thou say? I suffered even from my Mother's womb all the pains of my life and my death." But all these sufferings did not so much afflict Jesus Christ—

[1] "Virum dolorum."—*Isa*. liii. 3.

Novena of Christmas. VI.

because he chose voluntarily to suffer them—as did the sight of our sins and our ingratitude for his great love. St. Margaret of Cortona was never satisfied with lamenting over the offences committed against God; wherefore her confessor said to her one day: " Margaret, cease crying, because God has already forgiven thee." But she replied: " Ah, Father, how can I cease crying, when I know that my sins kept Jesus Christ in a state of affliction all his life?"

Affections and Prayers.

O my sweet Love, have I then by my sins kept Thee in a state of affliction all Thy life long? Oh, tell me, then, what I can do, in order that Thou mayest forgive me; for I will leave nothing undone. I repent, O sovereign Good, of all the offences I have committed against Thee; I repent, and love Thee more than myself. I feel a great desire to love Thee; it is Thou that givest me this desire; give me, therefore, strength to love Thee ardently. It is only just that I, who have offended Thee so much, should also love Thee much. Oh, remind me constantly of the love Thou hast borne me, in order that my soul may always burn with the love of Thee; that it may think of Thee alone, desire Thee alone, and strive to please Thee alone. O God of love, I, who once was the slave of hell, now give myself entirely to Thee. Accept me in Thy mercy, and bind me with Thy love, my Jesus, from this day forth. I will love Thee in life; and in loving Thee I will die. O Mary, my Mother and my hope, help me to love thy dear Jesus and mine; this favor alone I desire and hope from thee.

MEDITATION VI.

DECEMBER 21.

The Mercy of God in coming down from Heaven to save Us by His Death.

St. Paul says, *The goodness and kindness of God our Saviour appeared.*[1] When, therefore, the Son of God made

[1] " Benignitas et humanitas apparuit Salvatoris nostri Dei."—*Tit.* iii. 4.

Man appeared upon earth, then was seen how great the goodness of God was towards us. St. Bernard writes that the power of God appeared first in the creation of the world, and his wisdom in sustaining it; but his mercy appeared to a still greater degree when he took human flesh to save lost man by his sufferings and death. And what greater mercy could the Son of God show us than to take upon him the pains we have deserved?

Behold him a new-born infant, weak, and wrapped in swaddling-clothes in a manger; not able either to move or feed himself, he requires for his sustenance that Mary should feed him with a little milk. Behold him afterwards in the judgment-hall of Pilate, bound to a column by cords from which he cannot loosen himself, and there scourged from head to foot. Behold him in the journey to Calvary, falling down as he goes along the road through weakness and the weight of the cross that he carries. Behold him finally nailed to that infamous tree, whereon he finishes his life by dint of suffering.

Jesus Christ wished to gain all the affections of our hearts by his love for us, and therefore he would not send an angel to redeem us, but he would come himself to save us by his Passion. If an angel had been our redeemer, man must have divided his heart, loving God as his Creator, and the angel as his redeemer; but God, who desired the whole heart of man, as he was his Creator, chose also to be his Redeemer.

Affections and Prayers.

Ah, my dear Redeemer, where should I be now, if Thou hadst not borne with me with so much patience, but hadst condemned me to death whilst I was yet in sin? Since, then, Thou hast hitherto waited for me, my Jesus, forgive me speedily, before death surprises me whilst I am guilty of so many offences against Thee. I repent, O sovereign Good, of having thus despised Thee; I should like to die of sorrow for my sins. Thou canst not forsake a soul that seeks Thee; if I have hitherto neglected Thee, I will henceforth seek Thee and love Thee. Yes, O my God! I love Thee above all things; I love Thee more than myself. Help me, Lord, to love Thee always during the remainder of my life; I ask nothing more; I ask this, and I hope it of Thee. Mary, my hope, do thou pray for me; if thou prayest for me, I am sure of grace.

MEDITATION VII.

DECEMBER 22.

The Journey of the Infant Jesus to Egypt.

The Son of God came from heaven to save mankind; but as soon as he was born, they began to persecute him even until death. Herod, fearing that this Infant would deprive him of his kingdom, tried to put him to death; wherefore St. Joseph was advised by the angel in a dream to take Jesus with his Mother and to fly into Egypt. Joseph promptly obeyed, and informed Mary of it; so he took the few implements of his trade that he possessed, in order that they might serve him to gain a livelihood in Egypt for himself and his poor family. Mary, on her part, added a small packet of clothes that were to serve for the Holy Infant; and then, drawing near to the crib, she said with tears to her sleeping child, "O my Son and my God, Thou art come down from heaven to save men, and hardly art Thou born when they seek Thee to take away Thy life." She then took him, and, continuing to weep, in the same night she and Joseph set off on their journey.

Let us consider how much these holy pilgrims must have suffered whilst they were making so long a journey, deprived of every comfort. The Infant was not yet able to walk; therefore first Mary and then Joseph were obliged by turns to carry him in their arms. During their journey through the desert of Egypt, their only bed at night was the bare earth in the open air. The Infant weeps with the cold, and Joseph and Mary weep also from compassion. And who would not weep, in seeing the Son of God, poor and persecuted, wandering about on the earth, that he may not be killed by his enemies?

Affections and Prayers.

Ah, dearest Infant, Thou dost weep; and well mayest Thou weep, in seeing Thyself so persecuted by those men whom Thou hast so much loved. Alas, my God, I also have persecuted Thee by my sins; but now I love Thee more than myself; and there is no sorrow that afflicts me more than the remembrance that I have despised Thee, my sovereign Good. Oh, forgive me, my Jesus, and permit me to carry Thee with me in my heart in all the journey of life that I have yet to make, and then to enter together with Thee into eternity. I have so often driven Thee from my soul by offending Thee; but now I love Thee above everything, and I repent above every other evil of having offended Thee. My beloved Lord, I will never leave Thee more; but do Thou give me strength to resist temptations; permit me not to separate myself any more from Thee; let me rather die than ever again lose Thy favor. O Mary, my hope, make me always live and die in the love of God.

MEDITATION VIII.

DECEMBER 23.

The Sojourn of the Infant Jesus in Egypt and in Nazareth.

Our blessed Redeemer passed his first infancy in Egypt, leading there for seven years a life of poverty and contempt. Joseph and Mary were both strangers and unknown there, having there neither relatives nor friends; and they could hardly earn their daily bread by the labor of their hands. Their cottage was poor, their bed was poor, and their food was poor. In this miserable hut Mary weaned Jesus. First she had fed him from her breast; and afterwards with her hands she took from the porringer a little bread soaked in water, and then she put it in the sacred mouth of her Son. In this cottage she made him his first little garment; she took off his swaddling-clothes and began to dress him. In this cottage the Child Jesus began to take his first steps; but he kept falling—many times and trembling, as it happens to other children. Here he began to utter his first words, but in stammering. O wonder! to what has not a God reduced himself for the love of us! A God trembling and falling as he walks! a God stammering whilst he speaks!

Not unlike this was the poor and abject life that Jesus led on his return from Egypt to the house of Nazareth. Until the age of thirty he held no other office than that of a simple shop-boy, being obedient to Joseph and Mary. *And he was subject to them.*[1] Jesus went to fetch the water; Jesus opened and shut up the shop; Jesus swept the house; he collected the fragments of wood for the fire, and worked all day, helping Joseph in his labors. O wonder! A God serving as a boy! a God sweeping the house! a God working and sweating to plane a piece of wood! And who is this? The omnipotent God, who by a nod created the world, and can destroy it when he pleases! Ought not the mere thought of this to move our hearts to love him? How sweet it must have been to observe the devotion with which Jesus said his prayers, the patience with which he labored, the promptitude with which he obeyed, the modesty with which he took his food, and the sweetness and affability with which he spoke and conversed! Oh, every word, every action of Jesus was so holy that it filled every one with love for him; but especially Mary and Joseph, who were constantly observing him!

[1] "Et erat subditus illis."—*Luke*, ii. 51.

MEDITATION IX.

DECEMBER 24.

The Birth of the Infant Jesus in the Cave of Bethlehem.

The edict of the Roman emperor having gone forth, by which every one was to go and enroll himself in his own country, Joseph and his spouse Mary departed, to go and enroll themselves in Bethlehem. O God! how much must the Blessed Virgin have suffered in this journey, which was of four days, over mountainous roads, and in the winter, with cold, wind, and rain!

As soon as they arrived there, the time of her delivery was at hand; wherefore Joseph went about the town looking for a lodging, where Mary could bring forth her child. But, because they are poor, they are driven away by every one; they are even driven from the inn where the other poor had been received. They went away therefore from the town in the night; and having found a cave, Mary entered in there. But Joseph said to her: "My spouse, how can you pass the night in this damp, cold place? Do you not see that this is a stable for animals?" But Mary answered: "O my Joseph! it is nevertheless true that this shed is the royal palace in which the Son of God chooses to be born."

And behold, the hour of the birth being come, whilst the Holy Virgin was kneeling in prayer, she saw all at once the cave illuminated by a brilliant light; she cast her eyes upon the ground, and beheld the Son of God already born, a tender infant, crying and trembling with cold: whereupon she first adores him as her God; she then places him in her bosom, and wraps him in the poor swaddling-clothes which she had with her; and, finally, she lays him on a little straw in the manger. Behold, how the Son of the eternal Father chose to be born for the love of us.

Novena of Christmas. IX.

St. Mary Magdalene of Pazzi says that the souls enamoured of Jesus Christ ought to kneel in spirit at the feet of the Holy Child, and perform for him the same office that the beasts of the stable of Bethlehem did, which warmed Jesus with their breath; they should, therefore, warm him also with the sighs of love.

Affections and Prayers.

O my adorable Infant! I should not have the boldness to prostrate myself at Thy feet, if I did not know that Thou Thyself invitest me to approach Thee. I am he who by my sins have caused Thee to shed so many tears in the stable of Bethlehem. But since Thou camest upon earth to forgive repentant sinners, forgive me also; for I repent with all my heart of having despised Thee, my Saviour, my God, who art so good, and hast loved me so much. Thou dost dispense great graces to so many souls during this sacred night; do Thou, therefore, console my soul also. The grace I desire is the grace to love Thee from this day forth with my whole heart. Oh, inflame me wholly with Thy holy love! I love Thee, my God, become a child for me. Oh, permit me not ever to cease from loving Thee. O Mary, my Mother, thou canst do all things by thy prayers; I ask thee only this, to pray to Jesus for me.

Another Meditation for the Feast of the Circumcision.

I.

Behold the eternal Father, having sent his Son to suffer and die for us, commands that on this day he should be circumcised, and should begin to shed his divine blood, which he was to shed for the last time on the day of his death upon the cross in a sea of contumely and sorrow. And wherefore? In order that this innocent Son should thus pay the penalties which we have deserved. "O admirable," sings the Holy Church, "admirable condescension of divine pity towards us! O inestimable love of charity! to redeem Thy servant Thou hast given Thy Son to death!"

O eternal God, who could ever have bestowed upon us this infinite gift, but Thou who art infinite goodness and infinite love? O my Lord, if in giving me Thy Son Thou hast given me the dearest treasure Thou hast, it is but right that I should give myself entirely to Thee. Yes, my God, I give Thee my whole self; accept of me, I pray Thee, and let me never depart from Thee again.

II.

Behold, on the other hand, the divine Son, who, full of humility and love towards us, embraces the bitter death destined for him in order to save us sinners from eternal death, and willingly begins on this day to make satisfaction for us to the divine justice with the price of his blood. *He humbled Himself*, says the Apostle, *becoming obedient unto death, even to the death of the cross.*[1]

[1] " Humiliavit semetipsum, factus obediens usque ad mortem, mortem autem crucis."—*Phil.* ii. 8.

Thou, therefore, O my Jesus, hast accepted death for my sake; what, then, shall I do? shall I continue to offend Thee by my sins? No, my Redeemer, I will no longer be ungrateful to Thee. I am sorry from my heart that I have caused Thee so much bitterness in times past. I love Thee, O infinite Goodness, and for the future I will never cease to love Thee.

III.

Our Redeemer said, *Greater love can no man have than to lay down his life for his friends*.[1] But Thou, O my Jesus, says St. Paul, hast shown greater love than this towards us, by giving Thy life for us who were Thy enemies.

Behold one of them, O Lord, at Thy feet. How many times have I, a miserable sinner, renounced Thy friendship because I would not obey Thee! I now see the evil I have done; forgive me, O my Jesus. Would that I could die of sorrow for my sins! I now love Thee with my whole soul, and I desire nothing else but to love Thee and to please Thee. O Mary, Mother of God and my Mother, pray to Jesus for me.

[1] " Majorem hac dilectionem nemo habet, ut animam suam ponat quis pro amicis suis."—*John*, xv. 13.

Another Meditation for the Feast of the Epiphany.

I.

The Son of God is born humble and poor in a stable. There indeed the angels of heaven acknowledge him, singing, *Glory to God in the highest;*[1] but the inhabitants of the earth, for whose salvation Jesus was born, leave him neglected: only a few shepherds come and acknowledge him, and confess him to be their Saviour. But our loving Redeemer desired from the very beginning to communicate to us the grace of redemption, and therefore he begins to make himself known even to the Gentiles, who neither knew him nor expected him. For this purpose he sends the star to give notice to the holy Magi, enlightening them at the same time with internal light, in order that they might come and acknowledge and adore him as their Redeemer. This was the first and sovereign grace bestowed upon us; our calling to the true faith.

O Saviour of the world, what would have become of us if Thou hadst not come to enlighten us? we should be like our forefathers, who worshipped as gods animals, stones, and wood, and consequently we should have been all damned. I give Thee thanks to-day on the part of all men

II.

Behold, the Magi without delay set out on their journey; and by means of the star they arrive at the place where the Holy Infant is lying: *They found the child with*

---

[1] "Gloria in altissimis Deo."—*Luke*, ii. 14.

Mary.¹ They find there only a poor maiden, and a poor infant wrapped in poor swaddling-clothes; on entering into that abode, which was a stable for beasts, they feel an interior joy, and their hearts are drawn towards this sweet infant. That straw, that poverty, those cries of their Infant Saviour, are all darts of love and fire to their enlightened hearts.

Yes, my Infant Jesus, the more humbled and poor I behold Thee, the more dost Thou inflame me with Thy love.

III.

The Infant looks upon these holy pilgrims with a joyful countenance, and thus shows that he accepts these first-fruits of his redemption. The divine Mother is also silent, but by her smiling looks welcomes them, and thanks them for the homage done to her Son. They adore him also in silence, and acknowledge him for their Saviour and their God, offering him gifts of gold, frankincense, and myrrh.

O Jesus, my Infant King! I also adore Thee, and offer Thee my miserable heart. Accept of it and change it. Make it wholly Thine own, so that it may love nothing but Thee. My sweet Saviour, save me, and let my salvation be to love Thee always and without reserve. O Mary, most holy Virgin! I hope for this grace from thee.

¹ "Invenerunt Puerum cum Maria."—*Matt.* ii. 11.

Another Meditation for the Feast of the Holy Name of Jesus.*

I.

The name of Jesus was given to the Incarnate Word not by men, but by God himself: *And his name shall be called Jesus,*[1] that is, Saviour. A name of gladness, a name of hope, a name of love.

A name of *gladness*, because if the remembrance of past transgressions afflicts us, this name comforts us, reminding us that the Son of God became man for this purpose, to make himself our Saviour.

My beloved Saviour, Thou camest down from heaven to seek me, and I, a miserable sinner, have turned my back upon Thee and despised Thy grace and Thy love! But, notwithstanding this, Thou willest my salvation, O my Jesus! and I thank Thee for it and love Thee.

II.

A name of *hope*, because he that prays to the Eternal Father in the name of Jesus may hope for every grace he asks for: *If you ask the Father anything in My name, He will give it you.*[2]

O my God! trusting to this promise, in the name of Jesus I ask of Thee the pardon of my sins, holy perseverance, and the gift of Thy love. Grant, above all, that the remainder of my life may not be spent in displeasing Thee, but only in loving Thee and doing Thy will, as Thou deservest that I should do.

[1] "Et vocabis nomen ejus Jesum."—*Luke*, i. 31.
[2] "Si quid petieritis Patrem in nomine meo, dabit vobis."—*John*, xvi. 23.

---

* On page 151 there is a discourse, and on page 255 a meditation, and at the end of the volume, page 451, a novena on the same subject.—ED,

III.

A name of *love*. St. Bernardine of Sienna says that the name of Jesus is a sign that represents to us how much God has done for the love of us. For the name of Jesus brings to our remembrance all the sufferings which Jesus has endured for us in his life and at his death. Wherefore a devout writer says to him, "O Jesus! how much hath it cost Thee to be Jesus,—that is to say, my Saviour!"[1]

O my Jesus! I beseech Thee, do Thou write Thy name on my poor heart and on my tongue, in order that when I am tempted to sin, I may resist by invoking Thee; so that if I am tempted to despair, I may trust in Thy merits; and that if I feel myself tepid in loving Thee, Thy name may inflame my heart at the recollection of how much Thou hast loved me. Thy name, then, will always be my defence, my comfort, and the fire that shall keep me always inflamed with Thy love. Make me, therefore, always to call Thee my Jesus, and to live and die with Thy holy name on my lips, saying even with my last breath, "I love Thee, my Jesus; my Jesus, I love Thee." O Mary, my Queen! make me when I am dying invoke thee continually, together with thy Son Jesus.

[1] "O Jesu! quanti tibi constitit esse Jesum, Salvatorem meum!"

Hymns.

HYMNS

I.

Ode on the Birth of Our Saviour Jesus Christ.

WHEN Jesus first appeared on earth
    A babe in Bethlehem,
The winter midnight of his birth
    Did fair as noontide seem ;
      Ne'er shone the stars so bright
      As on that wondrous night :
Swift to the East the brightest of them all
Darts through the sky, the Magi kings to call.

Awakened by th' unwonted light,
    The startled songster birds
Broke the lone stillness of the night
    With songs like angels' words ;
      While chirping in the field,
      The grasshoppers revealed
The joy of earth : "Jesus is born !" they cried ;
"Our God is born !" the warbling birds replied.

Fresh, as when washed by summer showers,
    Now bud the roses sweet ;
And thousand, thousand fragrant flowers
    The Infant Saviour greet ;
      While e'en the arid hay
      That in the manger lay
Decked out with leaf and bloom the poor abode,
And kissed the infant members of its God.

    In fair Engaddi's flowery clime
      Now blooms the fragrant vine,

Hymns.

And ripening grapes, ere nature's time,
    In purple clusters twine.
    Sweet Babe! divinely fair!
    Thou art Love's cluster rare!
Coolness to burning lips Thou dost impart,
And warmth of love divine to frozen heart.

Now gentle peace reigned far and wide,
    In joy and liberty;
The sheep and lion side by side
    Were pastured happily;
        The kid, with frolic gay,
        Near tiger fierce can play,
And ox with savage bear secure from harm,
And lambkin near the wolf without alarm.

Joy, too, awoke at Jesus' birth,
    And roamed creation free,
In heaven, in every tribe of earth,
    O'er every land and sea;
        And many a sleeper smiled
        As when a little child,
And felt his heart rebounding in his breast,
While dreams of gladness mingled with his rest.

The watchful shepherds kept by night
    The flocks of Bethlehem,
When lo! an angel clothed in light
    Appeared, and said to them,
        " Good shepherds! do not fear,
        Our gladsome tidings hear;
For peace and joy upon the world arise,
And sinful earth becomes a paradise!

" To you this day in Bethlehem
    A Saviour king is born;
The long-expected,—to redeem
    And save a world forlorn,

Then haste, and you will find
The Saviour of mankind,
An infant, swathed, and lying in a stall,
Amongst the poor, the poorest one of all."

The angel choirs in glittering throng
   From heaven to earth descend,
And in one sweet melodious song
   Their countless voices blend.
     " Glory to God above!
     Born is the King of Love!
Peace be, on earth, to men who have good will;
Let grateful concerts earth and heaven fill!"

Each shepherd's heart within his breast
   Bounded with love inflamed,
And eagerly unto the rest
   His ardor thus proclaimed:
     " Why longer thus delay?
     Come, haste, away, away!
For ah! I languish with desire untold
My Infant God and Saviour to behold!"

The shepherds o'er the hill-top hie,
   Like herd of startled deer;
With joy they soon the cave descry,
   And to the crib draw near;
     They see that Infant sweet,
     With Mary at his feet,
And looks of love all beaming from his eyes
Appear like rays of bliss from paradise.

Astonished, raptured, and enchained
   At this great sight they saw,
Long time the shepherds thus remained
   In solemn silent awe;
     Then sweet and loving sighs
     Deep from their hearts arise,
While mingled tears and words their love confess,
And in a thousand fervent acts express.

Then entering the poor abode,
    With knees devoutly bent,
They humbly to the Infant God
    Their simple gifts present;
        And Jesus does not scorn
        The poor and lowly-born,
But raising up to them his tiny hand,
He smiles a blessing on this humble band.

Then do the flames of heavenly fire,
    Which in their bosoms glow,
Such tender confidence inspire
    As love alone can know.
        They venture to embrace
        That Child of heavenly grace,
And on his hands and feet—O happiness!—
A thousand times their fervent lips they press.

Then in their pipes these joyful swains
    Such heavenly music breathed,
And rivalling angelic strains,
    With tuneful Mary wreathed
        In sweetest harmony
        Such soothing lullaby,
That slumber o'er the infant eyelids crept,
And Jesus closed his lovely eyes, and slept.

The lullaby these shepherds blest
    To Jesus sung was this;
Which gently, softly, lulled to rest
    The Infant God of bliss.
        But while I now repeat
        This cradle-song so sweet,
Think that with them beside the crib you kneel,
And pray the ardors of their love to feel.

"Gentle slumber, from above,
    Hush to sleep your heavenly king,
Born an Infant for our love!
    Hasten, sleep, soft slumbers bring!

"Lovely Jewel of my heart!
   Would that I could be the sleep,
Softly, swiftly, to impart
   Closing eyes and slumbers deep.

"But, if love of men to gain,
   Thus a babe Thou deign'st to be,
Love alone can sing the strain,
   Which can slumbers bring to Thee!

"Since, then, love has power on Thee,
   Lo! my heart and soul are Thine!
Yes! I love Thee, love—but see!—
   Sleep has closed those eyes divine.

"Thee, my God, alone I love!
   Treasure! Beauty! Love, I . . ."
  *   *   *   *   *
  *   *   *   *   *

Then breaking off their loving strain,
   All happy and content,
They hastened to their flocks again,
   Rejoicing as they went;
      But such a heavenly fire,
      So ardent a desire
Of this dear Infant in their bosoms burns
That to their thoughts he evermore returns.

In hell alone, where mortal hate,
   Despair, and terror dwell,
And in the hearts as obstinate
   As demons loosed from hell,
      The splendors of that night
      Awakened strange affright;
Hardened in guilt, they trembled with dismay;
They hate the light which shows to heaven the way.

Hymns.

Jesus! Thou art a Sun of Love,
  Whence beams of mercy dart;
Thy rays enlighten from above,
  And warm the sinner's heart.
    Though black and hard his soul,
    As changed to earthy coal,
Yet if repentant once he turns to Thee,
Thou show'st still more Thy loving clemency.

But, sweetest child, ah! Jesus, say,
  Why flow those infant tears?
Yes, 'tis that I may wash away,
  My sins of bygone years!
    Alas! what have I done?
    Unkind, ungrateful one!
I sinned, I sinned, yet still Thou lovedst me:
Would I had died ere I offended Thee!

Oh for a fountain flowing o'er
  With tears both night and day,
My sins unnumbered to deplore,
  And weep them all away
    To bathe my Infant's feet,
    And by my sobs entreat
His mercy! Then, oh, grant me once to hear
The word *Thou art forgiven; do not fear!*

Thrice blest, thrice happy should I be
  With this too favored lot!
All else on earth would seem to me
  Not worth one care, one thought.
    Thou Hope of the distressed,
    Hear, Mary, my request!
Cease not to pray for this poor sinful one,
Who asks to love once more thy Blessed Son!

II.

The Madonna's Lullaby.

Mary sings, the ravished heavens
   Hush the music of their spheres;
Soft her voice, her beauty fairer
   Than the glancing stars appears:
While to Jesus, slumbering nigh,
Thus she sings her lullaby:

"Sleep, my Babe, my God, my Treasure,
   Gently sleep; but ah! the sight
With its beauty so transports me,
   I am dying with delight;
Thou canst not Thy mother see,
Yet Thou breathest flames to me.

"If within your lids unfolded,
   Slumbering eyes, you seem so fair;
When upon my gaze you open,
   How shall I your beauty bear?
Ah! I tremble when you wake,
Lest my heart with love should break.

Cheeks than sweetest roses sweeter,
   Mouth where lurks a smile divine,
Though the kiss my Babe should waken,
   I must press those lips to mine.
Pardon, Dearest, if I say
Mother's love will take no nay."

As she ceased, the gentle Virgin
   Clasped the Infant to her breast,
And, upon his radiant forehead
   Many a loving kiss impressed,
Jesus woke and on her face
Fixed a look of heavenly grace.

Ah! that look, those eyes, that beauty,
  How they pierce the Mother's heart!
Shafts of love from every feature
  Through her gentle bosom dart.
Heart of stone! can I behold
Mary's love, and still be cold?

Where, my soul, thy sense, thy reason?
  When will these delays be o'er?
All things else, how fair so ever,
  Are but smoke: resist no more!
Yes! 'tis done! I yield my arms
Captive to those double charms.

If, alas, O heavenly beauty!
  Now so late those charms I learn,
Now at least, and ever, ever
  With thy love my heart will burn,
For the Mother and the Child,
Rose and Lily undefiled.

Plant and fruit, and fruit and blossom,
  I am theirs, and they are mine;
For no other prize I labor,
  For no other bliss I pine.
Love can every pain requite,
Love alone is full delight.

III.

St. Joseph addressing the Divine Child Jesus.

Since Thou the name of Father hast bestowed
   On me, my Jesus, let me call Thee Son.
My Son! I love—I love Thee; yes, my God!
   Forever wi'' I love Thee, dearest One!

Thou art my God! I humbly Thee adore;
   But, as my Son, ah! bid me kiss Thy face,
And make my heart remain for evermore
   Close bound with sweetest chains in Thy embrace!

Since Thou hast deigned to choose me here below
   The nurse and guardian of Thy life to be,
My sweetest Love! my Good! ah! let me know
   What willest Thou?—what dost Thou ask of me?

All, all I am, to Thee I now resign;
   My love I consecrate to Thee alone;
And know, my heart is mine no more—'Tis Thine;
   My very life I do not call my own.

Since Thou art pleased to share my humble home,
   And be on earth companion of my love,
Well may I hope, dear Jesus, to become
   Thy loved companion in Thy home above.

IV.

To the Infant Jesus in the Crib

Oh, how I love Thee, Lord of Heaven above!
Too well hast Thou deserved to gain my love;
Sweet Jesus, I would die for love of Thee,
For Thou didst not disdain to die for me.

I leave Thee, faithless world,—farewell! depart!
This lovely Babe has loved and won my heart.
I love Thee, loving God, who from above
Didst come on earth, a Babe, to gain my love.

Thou tremblest, darling Child, and yet I see
Thy heart is all on fire with love for me:
Love makes Thee thus a child, my Saviour dear;
Love only brought Thee down to suffer here;

Love conquered Thee, Great God, love tied Thy hands,
A captive here for me, in swathing-bands;
And love, strong love, awaits Thy latest breath,
To make Thee die for me a cruel death.

Hymns.

V.
To the Infant Jesus.

O King of Heaven! from starry throne descending,
  Thou takest refuge in that wretched cave;
O God of bliss! I see Thee cold and trembling,
  What pain it cost Thee fallen man to save!

Thou, of a thousand worlds the great Creator,
  Dost now the pain of cold and want endure;
Thy poverty but makes Thee more endearing,
  For well I know 'tis love has made Thee poor.

I see Thee leave Thy Heavenly Father's bosom,
  But whither has Thy love transported Thee?
Upon a little straw I see Thee lying;
  Why suffer thus? 'Tis all for love of me.

But if it is Thy will for me to suffer,
  And by these sufferings my heart to move,
Wherefore, my Jesus, do I see Thee weeping?
  'Tis not for pain Thou weepest, but for love.

Thou weepest thus to see me so ungrateful;
  My sins have pierced Thee to the very core;
I once despised Thy love, but now I love Thee,
  I love but Thee; then, Jesus, weep no more.

Thou sleepest, Lord, but Thy heart ever watches,
  No slumber can a heart so loving take;
But tell me, darling Babe, of what Thou thinkest,
  "I think," he says, "of dying for Thy sake."

Is it for me that Thou dost think of dying!
  What, then, O Jesus! can I but love Thee?
Mary, my hope! If I love him too little,—
  Be not indignant,—love him thou for me.

It is not certain that this devotion is by St. Alphonsus; but the tradition in the Congregation of the Most Holy Redeemer has always ascribed it to him. It is found in the Italian Directory of the Novices, which was certainly written by the saint, and which has always been used in the novitiate of the Congregation.—ED.

Stations of the Infant Jesus.

V. Incline unto my aid, O God.
R. O Lord, make haste to help me.
Glory be to the Father, etc.

STATION I.
The Son of God becomes an Infant.

O Jesus, born of Virgin bright,
Immortal glory be to Thee;
Praise to the Father infinite,
And Holy Ghost eternally.

Consideration.

Consider that the Son of God, the Infinite Majesty, the Creator of the world, and who has need of no one, became incarnate to save lost man by his sufferings, and was for nine months enclosed as a little Infant in the most chaste womb of Mary.

Affections.

O most amiable Infant Jesus, God and Man, it was Thy burning love for me which urged Thee do do all this. I give Thee thanks; and I beseech Thee, by Thy Incarnation, to give me the grace to correspond to such great goodness.

O my sweetest Love, I am sorry that I have offended Thee. I desire to be always faithful in Thy service: enkindle in me Thy love; make me chaste and holy

The Way of Bethlehem. 335

O Mary, grant that I may belong entirely to thee and to thy Son Jesus.

Hail Mary, etc. Glory be to the Father, etc.

V. Blessed is the womb of the Virgin Mary, which bore the Son of the Eternal Father.

R. And blessed are the breasts which gave suck to Christ our Lord.

<blockquote>
O Jesus, ever sweetest Lord,
And ever loving still;
From this dear crib sweet drops of love
Into my heart distil.
</blockquote>

STATION II.

Jesus is born an Infant.

<blockquote>
O Jesus, born of Virgin bright,
Immortal glory be to Thee;
Praise to the Father infinite,
And Holy Ghost eternally.
</blockquote>

Consideration.

Consider that Jesus at his birth has not even a wretched cabin, such as the poorest have; but is born in a cold cavern, and is laid in a manger upon straw.

Affections.

O most holy Infant Jesus, I thank Thee for this; and I beseech Thee, by Thy most poor and bitter birth, grant that I may reap the fruits of Thy coming on this earth.

O my sweetest Love, I am sorry that I have offended Thee. I desire to be always faithful in Thy service: enkindle in me Thy love; make me chaste and holy.

O Mary, grant that I may belong entirely to thee and to thy Son Jesus.

Hail Mary, etc. Glory be to the Father, etc.

V. Blessed is the womb of the Virgin Mary, which bore the Son of the Eternal Father.

R. And blessed are the breasts which gave suck to Christ our Lord.

> O Jesus, ever sweetest Lord,
> And ever loving still;
> From this dear crib sweet drops of love
> Into my heart distil.

STATION III.

Jesus is suckled.

> O Jesus, born of Virgin bright,
> Immortal glory be to Thee;
> Praise to the Father infinite,
> And Holy Ghost eternally.

Consideration.

Consider that God, Majesty itself, who gives food to men and beasts, is born an Infant, and has recourse to Mary for his food; and he, through whom not a sparrow hungers, is fed with a little milk.

Affections.

O most lovely Infant, Thou takest milk, to be changed into that flesh which one day is to be bruised and torn for me. I thank Thee for this goodness; and I beseech Thee by this purest milk, grant me grace to act always with a pure intention of pleasing Thee, even as Thou didst ever act with the sole aim of obtaining my eternal happiness.

O my sweetest Love, I am sorry that I have offended Thee. I desire to be always faithful in Thy service: enkindle in me Thy love; make me chaste and holy.

O Mary, grant that I may belong entirely to thee and to thy Son Jesus.

The Way of Bethlehem.

Hail Mary, etc. Glory be to the Father, etc.

V. Blessed is the womb of the Virgin Mary, which bore the Son of the Eternal Father.

R. And blessed are the breasts which gave suck to Christ our Lord.

> O Jesus, ever sweetest Lord,
> And ever loving still;
> From this dear crib sweet drops of love
> Into my heart distil.

STATION IV.

Jesus is wrapped in Swaddling-clothes.

> O Jesus, born of Virgin bright,
> Immortal glory be to Thee;
> Praise to the Father infinite,
> And Holy Ghost eternally.

Consideration.

Consider that the Infinite God, whom the heavens cannot contain, made an Infant for us, vouchsafed to be wrapped by Mary in swaddling-clothes, and covered with poor rags. And thus the hands and feet of God by swathing-bands are tied.

Affections.

O gentlest Infant, Thou art tied in swathing-bands to deliver my soul from the chains of sin and hell. I thank Thee; grant, by Thy holy humility, that, casting away every other bond, I may ever live bound and united to Thee.

O my sweetest Love, I am sorry that I have offended Thee. I desire always to be faithful in Thy service: enkindle in me Thy love; make me chaste and holy.

O Mary, grant that I may belong entirely to thee and to thy Son Jesus.

Hail Mary, etc. Glory be to the Father, etc.

V. Blessed is the womb of the Virgin Mary, which bore the Son of the eternal Father.

R. And blessed are the breasts which gave suck to Christ our Lord.

> O Jesus, ever sweetest Lord,
> And ever loving still;
> From this dear crib sweet drops of love
> Into my heart distil.

STATION V.

Jesus is circumcised.

> O Jesus, born of Virgin bright,
> Immortal glory be to Thee;
> Praise to the Father infinite,
> And Holy Ghost eternally.

Consideration.

Consider that the Infant Jesus, eight days after his birth, showed himself to be even then our Saviour, by shedding for us his divine blood in the Circumcision.

Affections.

O most merciful Infant God, I give Thee thanks; and I beseech Thee, by the pain which Thou didst feel, and by the blood which Thou didst shed in Thy Circumcision, grant me grace and power to pluck out of my heart, and to cast from it, all earthly affections.

O my sweetest love, I am sorry that I have offended Thee. I desire to be always faithful in Thy service: enkindle in me Thy love; make me chaste and holy.

O Mary, grant that I may belong entirely to thee and to thy Son Jesus.

Hail Mary, etc. Glory be to the Father, etc.

℣. Blessed is the womb of the Virgin Mary, which bore the Son of the eternal Father.
℟. And blessed are the breasts which gave suck to Christ our Lord.

> O Jesus, ever sweetest Lord,
> And ever loving still;
> From this dear crib sweet drops of love
> Into my heart distil.

STATION VI.

Jesus is adored by the Magi.

> O Jesus, born of Virgin bright,
> Immortal glory be to Thee;
> Praise to the Father infinite,
> And Holy Ghost eternally.

Consideration.

Consider that the Infant God is visited and adored by the Magi, who, though Gentiles, were enlightened by faith to acknowledge this Man-God for their Saviour, and offered him gold, frankincense, and myrrh.

Affections.

Most adorable Redeemer, I too have received from Thee this great gift of faith. I thank Thee for it; and I beseech Thee, by the glory of this Thy manifestation, grant that, like the Magi, I may correspond and be faithful to Thy grace.

O my sweetest Love, I am sorry that I have offended Thee. I desire to be always faithful in Thy service: enkindle in me Thy love; make me chaste and holy.

O Mary, grant that I may belong entirely to thee and to thy Son Jesus.

Hail Mary, etc. Glory be to the Father, etc.

V. Blessed is the womb of the Virgin Mary, which bore the Son of the eternal Father.

R. And blessed are the breasts which gave suck to Christ our Lord.

> O Jesus, ever sweetest Lord,
> And ever loving still ;
> From this dear crib sweet drops of love
> Into my heart distil.

STATION VII.

Jesus is presented in the Temple.

> O Jesus, born of Virgin bright,
> Immortal glory be to Thee;
> Praise to the Father infinite,
> And holy Ghost eternally.

Consideration.

Consider that the Virgin Mary, forty days after the birth of the Infant Jesus, carries him in her arms to the Temple, and, offering him to God for us, consents that by his Passion and Death he should become our Redeemer.

Affections.

O most loving Infant, for this one end didst Thou deliver Thyself up to death, to bestow on me eternal life. I give Thee thanks, and pray Thee, by this offering of Thyself, to make me constantly ready to mortify and die to myself for the love of Thee.

O my sweetest Love, I am sorry that I have offended Thee. I desire to be always faithful in Thy service : enkindle in me Thy love ; make me chaste and holy.

O Mary, grant that I may belong entirely to thee and to thy Son Jesus.

Hail Mary, etc. Glory be to the Father, etc.

The Way of Bethlehem. 341

V. Blessed is the womb of the Virgin Mary, which bore the Son of the eternal Father.

R. And blessed are the breasts which gave suck to Christ our Lord.

> O Jesus, ever sweetest Lord,
> And ever loving still;
> From this dear crib sweet drops of love
> Into my heart distil.

STATION VIII.

Jesus flees into Egypt.

> O Jesus, born of Virgin bright,
> Immortal glory be to Thee;
> Praise to the Father infinite,
> And Holy Ghost eternally.

Consideration.

Consider that Herod, fearing that Jesus would deprive him of his kingdom, plans his death; and therefore orders all the children of Bethlehem to be murdered. The most blessed Virgin, warned by an angel, takes the Infant Jesus into Egypt.

Affections.

O dearest Infant, what sufferings didst Thou not endure during this journey of a whole month and even longer, and that too in the depth of winter! How often wert Thou drenched with rain and stiffened with the cold! How many nights didst Thou pass in the open air!

I thank Thee; and beseech Thee by Thy flight to give me strength to avoid all the dangers of eternal death.

O my sweetest Love, I am sorry that I have offended Thee. I desire to be always faithful in Thy service: enkindle in me Thy love; make me chaste and holy.

O Mary, grant that I may belong entirely to Thee and to thy Son Jesus.

Hail Mary, etc. Glory be to the Father, etc.

V. Blessed is the womb of the Virgin Mary, which bore the Son of the Eternal Father.

R. And blessed are the breasts which gave suck to Christ our Lord.

> O Jesus, ever sweetest Lord,
> And ever loving still :
> From this dear crib sweet drops of love
> Into my heart distil.

STATION IX.

Jesus with His Hands freed from the Swaddling-clothes.

> O Jesus, born of Virgin bright,
> Immortal glory be to Thee ;
> Praise to the Father infinite,
> And Holy Ghost eternally.

Consideration.

Consider that the Infant Jesus, some months after his birth, is still swathed by the blessed Virgin, though his hands are freed from the swaddling-clothes.

Affections.

Most tender Infant, I imagine to myself that first moment when Thou didst join Thy little hands, and, lifting up Thy divine eyes to heaven, didst intercede with the Eternal Father in my behalf. I give Thee thanks; and beseech Thee to grant by the merits of Thy prayer that my prayers may be always pleasing and acceptable in Thy sight.

O my sweetest Love, I am sorry that I have offended Thee. I desire to be always faithful in Thy service : enkindle in me Thy love; make me chaste and holy.

O Mary, grant that I may belong entirely to thee and to thy Son Jesus.

Hail Mary, etc. Glory be to the Father, etc.

V. Blessed is the womb of the Virgin Mary, which bore the Son of the Eternal Father.

R. And blessed are the breasts which gave suck to Christ our Lord.

> O Jesus, ever sweetest Lord,
> And ever loving still;
> From this dear crib sweet drops of love
> Into my heart distil.

STATION X.

Jesus begins to walk.

> O Jesus, born of Virgin bright,
> Immortal glory be to Thee;
> Praise to the Father infinite,
> And Holy Ghost eternally.

Consideration.

Consider that the Infant Jesus, now a little older, begins to walk, and plans out in his mind the journeys he would make in the surrounding country of Judæa to preach by his most holy words the way of salvation; and at the same time figures to himself the road to Calvary, which he would tread in going to die for us.

Affections.

O most loving Infant, I thank Thee; and beseech Thee by Thy first steps, grant me grace always to walk in the way which Thou hast pointed out to me.

O my sweetest Love, I am sorry that I have offended Thee. I desire to be always faithful in Thy service: enkindle in me Thy love; make me chaste and holy.

O Mary, grant that I may belong entirely to thee and to thy Son Jesus.

Hail Mary, etc. Glory be to the Father, etc.

V. Blessed is the womb of the Virgin Mary, which bore the Son of the Eternal Father.

R. And blessed are the breasts which gave suck to Christ our Lord.

> O Jesus, ever sweetest Lord,
> And ever loving still ;
> From this dear crib sweet drops of love
> Into my heart distil.

STATION XI.

Jesus sleeps.

> O Jesus, born of Virgin bright,
> Immortal glory be to Thee ;
> Praise to the Father infinite,
> And Holy Ghost eternally.

Consideration.

Consider that the Infant Jesus lies in a poor cradle in the little house of his Mother Mary, and takes his rest; and oftentimes the bare ground serves him as a bed.

Affections.

O most amiable Infant, even while sleeping Thy heart watches, and Thou wert loving me, and thinking upon me; and Thy heart was consoled with the good which Thou hadst bestowed, and would bestow, upon me. I thank Thee ; and pray Thee, by Thy loving slumbers, to give me grace to live forever in loving Thee, who art the most loving Good.

O my sweetest Love, I am sorry that I have offended Thee. I desire to be always faithful in Thy service: enkindle in me Thy love ; make me chaste and holy.

O Mary, grant that I may belong entirely to thee and to thy Son Jesus.

Hail Mary, etc. Glory be to the Father, etc.

V. Blessed is the womb of the Virgin Mary, which bore the Son of the Eternal Father.

R. And blessed are the breasts which gave suck to Christ our Lord.

> O Jesus, ever sweetest Lord,
> And ever loving still;
> From this dear crib sweet drops of love
> Into my heart distil.

STATION XII.

Jesus in the Form of a Fisher.

> O Jesus, born of Virgin bright,
> Immortal glory be to Thee;
> Praise to the Father infinite,
> And Holy Ghost eternally.

Consideration.

Consider to yourself the Infant Jesus represented in the form of a fisher, holding in his hands a rod, to which is attached the hook wherewith he will catch the hearts of men. When we think on his beauty, and on the love with which he seeks us, and on all that he has done to allure us to his love, we must needs consecrate our hearts to his service.

Affections.

O Divine Infant, I give Thee thanks; and pray Thee by the zeal which Thou hast shown in endeavoring to draw my heart to Thee, give me the grace never to leave Thee more, and grant that, having continual recourse to Thee, I may become one with Thee, and never separate myself from Thee again.

O my sweetest Love, I am sorry that I have offended Thee. I desire to be faithful in Thy service: enkindle in me Thy love; make me chaste and holy.

O Mary, grant that I may belong entirely to thee and to thy Son Jesus.

Hail Mary, etc. Glory be to the Father, etc.

V. Blessed is the womb of the Virgin Mary, which bore the Son of the Eternal Father.

R. And blessed are the breasts which gave suck to Christ our Lord.

> O Jesus, ever sweetest Lord,
> And ever loving still;
> From this dear crib sweet drops of love
> Into my heart distil.

Prayer.

I offer and present unto Thee, O most sweet Infant Jesus, the steps which I have made to venerate the mysteries of Thy Infancy, and the homage which I have paid Thee.

I pray Thee graciously to accept it, and to reward me with the virtues of childhood,—chastity, humility, and simplicity.

It is a joy and consolation to me when I behold Thee on the altar, surrounded with so many and so lovely flowers. I ardently desire and wish to see my heart in like manner adorned with the flowers of all holy virtues, that Thou mayest find Thy pleasure, and dwell in it; and may it be my lot to live in this world ever united to Thee, that, one with Thee, I may dwell in Thy presence in heaven for all eternity. Amen.

Indulgences Attached to the Exercises of Piety in Honor of the Infant Jesus.

I.

EVERY YEAR.

Novena Preparatory to Christmas-day.

AN INDULGENCE OF THREE HUNDRED DAYS, every day, to all those who, with at least contrite heart and devotion, prepare themselves for this solemnity by a novena (from the 16th to the 25th of December) with pious exercises, prayers, acts of virtue, etc. (As the good works have not been determined, it seems to be sufficient for gaining this indulgence that we make every day a spiritual reading or a meditation, or say some prayer, such as the Chaplet, page .

A PLENARY INDULGENCE on Christmas-day, or on any day in its octave, to those who have made this novena, provided that, being truly penitent after confession and Communion, they pray devoutly (for instance, by saying five *Our Fathers* and five *Hail Marys*) for the welfare of the Church, and for the intention of the Holy Father.

These indulgences may be gained once more within the year by making the novena in honor of the Child Jesus, as directed above.

---

* We think that it will be pleasing to St. Alphonsus, as well as to his pious readers, to add here, as an appendix, the list of indulgences with which the Sovereign Pontiffs have enriched the devotion to the Infant Jesus, and which we copy from the *Raccolta*. All these indulgences are applicable to the souls in purgatory.—ED.

Christmas-day.

INDULGENCE OF A HUNDRED YEARS for each of the following offices which the faithful recite or at which they are present in any church, being truly contrite, after confession and Communion, namely: The First Vespers, Matins and Lauds, the Mass (without doubt each of the three Masses), and the Second Vespers.

AN INDULGENCE OF FORTY YEARS, on the same conditions, for each of the following Hours: Prime, Tierce, Sext, None, and Complins.

II.

EVERY MONTH.

Novena from the 16th to the 24th.

AN INDULGENCE OF ONE YEAR for every day of the novena on which, with a contrite heart, we make, either in public or private, the following offering:

In the name of the Father, and of the Son, and of the Holy Ghost. Amen.

I. *Offering.*—Eternal Father, I offer to Thy honor and glory, and for my own salvation, and for the salvation of the whole world, the mystery of the birth of our divine Saviour.

Glory be to the Father, etc.

II. *Offering.*—Eternal Father, I offer to Thy honor and glory, and for my eternal salvation, the sufferings of the most holy Virgin and of St. Joseph in that long and weary journey from Nazareth to Bethlehem. I offer Thee the sorrows of their hearts when they found no place wherein to shelter themselves, when the Saviour of the world was to be born.

Glory be to the Father, etc.

III. *Offering.*—Eternal Father, I offer to Thy honor and glory, and for my eternal salvation, the sufferings of

Jesus in the stable where he was born, and the cold he suffered, the swaddling-clothes which bound him, the tears that he shed, and his tender infant cries.

Glory be to the Father, etc.

IV. *Offering.*—Eternal Father, I offer to Thy honor and glory, and for my eternal salvation, the pain which the holy child Jesus felt in his tender body when he submitted to circumcision. I offer Thee that precious blood which then, for the first time, he shed for the salvation of the whole human race.

Glory be to the Father, etc.

V. *Offering.*—Eternal Father, I offer to Thy honor and glory, and for my eternal salvation, the humility, mortification, patience, charity, all the virtues of the child Jesus; and I thank Thee, and I love Thee, and I bless Thee without end, for the ineffable mystery of the Incarnation of the divine Word.

Glory be to the Father, etc.

Verbum caro factum est.	The Word was made flesh.
Et habitavit in nobis.	And dwelt amongst us.
Oremus.	*Let us pray.*
Deus, cujus Unigenitus in substantia nostræ carnis apparuit: præsta, quæsumus, ut per eum, quem similem nobis foris agnovimus, intus reformari mereamur. Qui tecum vivit et regnat in sæcula sæculorum. Amen.	O God, whose only-begotten Son was made manifest to us in the substance of our flesh! grant, we beseech Thee, that through him, whom we acknowledge to be like unto ourselves, our souls may be inwardly renewed. Who liveth and reigneth with Thee for ever and ever. Amen.

The 25th of the Month.

A PLENARY INDULGENCE for those who, being truly contrite, after confession and Communion, are present in some church or public oratory at the pious exercise that is performed in honor of the Infant Jesus, recite the following prayer, to venerate the twelve mysteries of the holy infancy, and pray to the intention of his Holiness.

V. Deus, in adjutorium meum intende.
R. Domine, ad adjuvandum me festina.
V. Gloria Patri et Filio et Spiritui Sancto.
R. Sicut erat in principio, et nunc, et semper, et in sæcula sæculorum. Amen.

Pater noster.

V. Incline unto my aid, O God.
R. O Lord, make haste to help me.
V. Glory be to the Father, and to the Son, and to the Holy Ghost.
R. As it was in the beginning, is now, and ever shall be, world without end. Amen.

Our Father.

1ST MYSTERY. THE INCARNATION.

Jesu Infans dulcissime! e sinu Patris propter nostram salutem descendens, de Spiritu Sancto conceptus, Virginis uterum non horrens, et, Verbum caro factum, formam servi accipiens, miserere nostri.

R. Miserere nostri, Jesu Infans! miserere nostri.

Ave Maria.

Jesus, sweetest child, who' coming down from the bosom of the Father for our salvation, didst not disdain the womb of the Virgin, where, conceived by the Holy Ghost, Thou, the Word incarnate, didst take upon Thee the form of a servant: have mercy on us.

R. Have mercy on us, child Jesus, have mercy on us.

Hail Mary.

2. VISITATION.

Jesu Infans dulcissime! per Virginem Matrem tuam visitans Elisabeth, Joannem Baptistam præcursorem tuum Spiritu Sancto replens, et adhuc in utero

Jesus, sweetest child, who in Thy virgin mother's womb, didst visit St. Elizabeth, and fill Thy precursor, John the Baptist, with the Holy Ghost,

Indulgences. 351

matris suæ sanctificans, miserere nostri.
R. *Miserere nostri, Jesu Infans! miserere nostri.*
Ave Maria.

sanctifying him from his mother's womb: have mercy on us.
R. Have mercy on us, child Jesus, have mercy on us.
Hail Mary.

3. THE EXPECTATION.

Jesu Infans dulcissime! novem mensibus in utero clausus, summis votis a Maria Virgine et a Sancto Joseph expectatus, et Deo Patri pro salute mundi oblatus, miserere nostri.

Jesus, sweetest child, who, for nine months hidden in Thy mother's womb, and awaited with eager expectation by the Virgin Mother Mary and by St. Joseph, wast by them offered to God the Father for the salvation of the world: have mercy on us.

R. *Miserere nostri, Jesu Infans! miserere nostri.*
Ave Maria.

R. Have mercy on us, child Jesus, have mercy on us.
Hail Mary.

4. THE BIRTH.

Jesu Infans dulcissime! in Bethlehem ex Virgine Maria natus, pannis involutus, in præsepio reclinatus, ab Angelis annuntiatus, et a pastoribus visitatus, miserere nostri.

Jesus, sweetest child, born in Bethlehem of the Virgin Mary, wrapped in swaddling-clothes, laid in the manger, heralded by angels, visited by shepherds: have mercy on us.

R. *Miserere nostri, Jesu Infans! miserere nostri.*
Ave Maria.

R. Have mercy on us, child Jesus, have mercy on us.
Hail Mary.

Jesu, tibi sit gloria,
Qui natus es de Virgine,
Cum Patre et almo Spiritu,
In sempiterna sæcula!
Amen.

O Jesus, born of Virgin bright,
Infinite glory be to Thee;
Praise to the Father infinite,
And Holy Ghost eternally.
Amen.

Christus prope est nobis.
Venite, adoremus.

V. Christ is at hand.
R. Come, let us adore him.

Pater noster.

Our Father.

5. THE CIRCUMCISION.

Jesu Infans dulcissime! in circumcisione post dies octo vulneratus, glorioso Jesu nomine vocatus, et in nomine simul et sanguine Salvatoris officio præsignatus, miserere nostri.

R. Miserere nostri, Jesu Infans! miserere nostri.

Ave Maria.

Jesus, sweetest child, wounded in the circumcision on the eighth day, called by the glorious name of Jesus, and, by Thy name and by Thy blood, foreshown as the Saviour of the world: have mercy on us.

R. Have mercy on us, child Jesus, have mercy on us.

Hail Mary.

6. THE ADORATION OF THE MAGI.

Jesu Infans dulcissime! stella duce tribus Magis demonstratus, in sinu Matris adoratus, et mysticis muneribus, auro, thure, et myrrha, donatus, miserere nostri.

R. Miserere nostri, Jesu Infans! miserere nostri.

Ave Maria.

Jesus, sweetest child, made known to three Magi by a star, adored on Mary's bosom, honored with the mystical gifts of gold, frankincense, and myrrh: have mercy on us.

R. Have mercy on us, child Jesus, have mercy on us.

Hail Mary.

7. THE PRESENTATION.

Jesu Infans dulcissime! in Templo a Matre Virgine præsentatus, inter brachia a Simeone amplexatus, et ab Anna prophetissa Israeli revelatus, miserere nostri.

R. Miserere nostri, Jesu Infans! miserere nostri.

Ave Maria.

Jesus, sweetest child, presented in the temple by Thy Virgin Mother; Jesus, whom Simeon took into his arms and embraced, and Anna the prophetess made known to Israel: have mercy on us.

R. Have mercy on us, child Jesus, have mercy on us.

Hail Mary.

Indulgences. 353

8. The Flight into Egypt.

Jesu Infans dulcissime! ab iniquo Herode ad mortem quæsitus, a Sancto Joseph in Ægyptum cum matre deportatus, a crudeli cæde sublatus, et a præconiis martyrum Innocentium glorificatus, miserere nostri.

Jesus, sweetest child, whom Herod sought to slay, whom St. Joseph carried with Mary into Egypt, who was saved by flight from a cruel death, and glorified by the praises of the holy Innocents: have mercy on us.

R. Miserere nostri, Jesu Infans! miserere nostri.

R. Have mercy on us, child Jesus, have mercy on us.

Ave Maria.

Hail Mary.

*Jesu, tibi sit gloria,
Qui natus es de Virgine,
Cum Patre et almo Spiritu,
In sempiterna sæcula!
Amen.*

O Jesus, born of Virgin bright,
Infinite glory be to Thee;
Praise to the Father infinite,
And Holy Ghost eternally.
Amen.

Christus prope est nobis.
Venite, adoremus.

V. Christ is at hand.
R. Come, let us adore him.

Pater noster.

Our Father.

9. The Sojourn in Egypt.

Jesu Infans dulcissime! in Ægypto cum Maria sanctissima et patriarcha Sancto Joseph usque ad obitum Herodis commoratus, miserere nostri.

Jesus, sweetest child, who, with Mary most holy and the patriarch St. Joseph, didst dwell in Egypt until the death of Herod: have mercy on us.

R. Miserere nostri, Jesu Infans! miserere nostri.

R. Have mercy on us, child Jesus, have mercy on us.

Ave Maria.

Hail Mary.

10. The Return from Egypt.

Jesu Infans dulcissime! ex Ægypto cum parentibus in terram Israel reversus, multos labores in itinere perpessus, et in

Jesus, sweetest child, who didst return with Thy parents from Egypt into the land of Israel, who didst suffer many

civitatem Nazareth ingressus, miserere nostri.

R. *Miserere nostri, Jesu Infans! miserere nostri.*

Ave Maria.

toils by the way, and enter the city of Nazareth: have mercy on us.

R. Have mercy on us, child Jesus, have mercy on us.

Hail Mary.

11. THE LIFE OF JESUS AT NAZARETH.

Jesu Infans dulcissime! in sancta Nazarena domo subditus parentibus sanctissime commoratus, paupertate et laboribus fatigatus, in sapientia, ætatis, et gratiæ, profectu confortatus, miserere nostri.

R. *Miserere nostri, Jesu Infans! miserere nostri.*

Ave Maria.

Jesus, sweetest child, who didst live most holily in the blessed house of Nazareth, subject to Thy parents, spending Thy life in poverty and toil, and growing in wisdom, in age, and in grace: have mercy on us.

R. Have mercy on us, child Jesus, have mercy on us.

Hail Mary.

12. JESUS IN THE MIDST OF THE DOCTORS.

Jesu Infans dulcissime! in Jerusalem duodennis ductus, a parentibus cum dolore quæsitus, et post triduum cum gaudio inter Doctores inventus, miserere nostri.

R. *Miserere nostri, Jesu Infans! miserere nostri.*

Ave Maria.

Jesu, tibi sit gloria,
Qui natus es de Virgine,
Cum Patre et almo Spiritu,
In sempiterna sæcula.
Amen.
Christus prope est nobis.
Venite, adoremus.
Pater noster.

Jesus, sweetest child, brought to Jerusalem when twelve years old, sought by Thy parents with much sorrow, and, after three days, found, to their great joy, among the doctors: have mercy on us.

R. Have mercy on us, child Jesus, have mercy on us.

Hail Mary.

O Jesus, born of Virgin bright,
Infinite glory be to Thee;
Praise to the Father infinite,
And Holy Ghost eternally.
Amen.
V. Christ is at hand.
R. Come, let us adore him.
Our Father.

Indulgences.

Versicle for the Feast and Octave of Christmas.

V. *Verbum caro factum est. Alleluia.*
R. *Et habitavit in nobis. Alleluia.*

V. The Word was made flesh. Alleluia.
R. And dwelt amongst us. Alleluia.

This versicle is also recited throughout the year, but the Alleluia is omitted.

For the Feast of Epiphany and its Octave we say:

V. *Christus manifestavit se nobis. Alleluia.*
R. *Venite, adoremus. Alleluia.*

V. Christ manifested himself to us. Alleluia.
R. Come, let us adore him. Alleluia.

Oremus.

Omnipotens sempiterne Deus, Domine cœli et terræ, qui te revelas parvulis! concede, quæsumus, ut nos sacrosancta Filii tui Infantis Jesu mysteria digno honore recolentes, ac digna imitatione sectantes, ad Regnum cœlorum promissum parvulis pervenire valeamus. Per eumdem Christum Dominum nostrum. Amen.

Let us pray.

Almighty and everlasting God, Lord of heaven and earth, who dost reveal Thyself to little ones; grant us, we beseech Thee, to honor meekly the holy mysteries of Thy Son, the child Jesus, and to follow him humbly in our lives, so that we may come to the eternal kingdom promised by Thee to little ones. Through the same Jesus Christ Amen.

III.

Every Day.

INDULGENCE OF THREE HUNDRED DAYS, once a day, if privately, with a contrite heart, we recite the aforesaid exercise in honor of the twelve mysteries of the Holy Infancy of Jesus.

A PLENARY INDULGENCE once a month to all the faithful who every day, at the sound of the bell in the morning, or at noon, or in the evening at sunset, shall devoutly say the *Angelus Domini* with the *Hail Mary* three times, on any day when, being truly penitent, after confession and Communion, they shall pray to the intention of the Church. This prayer is said kneeling during the week and standing on Saturday evenings and Sundays. During the Paschal time this prayer is replaced by the *Regina Cœli* with the proper versicle and prayer, and is recited every day standing; but if the faithful do not know it by heart they may say the *Angelus* standing.

AN INDULGENCE OF A HUNDRED DAYS each time that the faithful, being truly contrite, recite the above-mentioned prayer in the manner indicated.

In regard to the recitation of the *Angelus*, we here subjoin the translation of a late decree published by Pope Leo XIII.:

To gain the indulgences which Benedict XIII. granted the faithful who recite the *Angelus Domini*, with the three *Hail Marys*, and which were extended by Benedict XIV. to all who, during the Paschal season, say the *Regina Cœli*, with the versicles and proper prayer, it was necessary to recite the *Hail Marys*, versicles, and prayer at the sound of the bell. It was further necessary to recite the *Angelus* and the *Hail Marys* on bended knees, except on Saturday evenings and Sundays, when they were said standing, and the Paschal season, when the *Regina Cœli*, with its versicle and prayer, was likewise said standing. Recently, many pious men implored the Sacred Congregation of Indulgences to mitigate to some extent these two conditions. For the Angelus bell is not rung in all places, nor rung three times a day, nor at the same hours; and if rung it is not always heard; and even if heard, the faithful may be prevented by reasonable cause from kneeling down just at that moment to say the prayer. Besides, there are any number of the faithful who know neither the *Angelus* nor the *Regina Cœli* by heart, and cannot even read it in print.

Wherefore, his Holiness Pope Leo XIII., in order not to have so many of the faithful deprived of these spiritual favors, owing to the non-fulfilment of the conditions, and in order to stir up in all an abiding and grateful remembrance of the mysteries of our Lord's incarnation and resurrection, in an audience granted the undersigned secretary of the Sacred Congregation of Indulgences on the 15th of March last, graciously granted that all the faithful (*a*) who say the *Angelus*, with the three *Hail Marys*, the *Pray for us, O Holy Mother of God*, and the prayer *Pour forth, we beseech Thee*, though for reasonable cause they do not say them on bended knees, nor at the sound of the bell; or (*b*) who recite during Paschal time the *Regina Cæli*, with its versicle and prayer; or who say in the morning, about midday, and evening, five *Hail Marys* in a becoming manner with attention and devotion (in case they do not know the *Angelus* or the *Regina Cæli* and cannot read it), may gain the indulgences mentioned above.

Given at the Secretariate of the same Congregation, Rome, April 3, 1884.

A. Cardinal OREGLIA, a S. STEPHANO, *Prefect.*

F. DELLA VOLPE, *Secretary.*

IV.
At all Times.

AN INDULGENCE OF FIFTY DAYS each time for saying to one another when meeting:

Laudetur Jesus Christus.   Praise be to Jesus Christ.
In sæcula. Amen.   Forever. Amen.

AN INDULGENCE OF TWENTY-FIVE DAYS granted every time to all those who devoutly invoke the most holy names of Jesus and Mary.

A PLENARY INDULGENCE, at the hour of death granted to all those who during life have had the pious practice of saluting one another and answering as above directed, or of frequently invoking the above-mentioned most holy names, provided they invoke them then, at least with the heart, if they are unable to do so with their lips.

The same indulgences are granted to preachers, and to all those who exhort the faithful to salute one another in the manner prescribed, and to invoke frequently the most holy names of Jesus and Mary.

AN INDULGENCE OF ONE HUNDRED DAYS every time the faithful say this pious ejaculation:

My Jesus, mercy !

AN INDULGENCE OF A HUNDRED DAYS granted every time to all who with at least contrite heart and devotion recite these three ejaculations:

Jesus, Mary, and Joseph, I give you my heart and my soul.

Jesus, Mary, and Joseph, assist me in my last agony.

Jesus, Mary, and Joseph, may I breathe forth my sou in peace with you.

AN INDULGENCE OF FIFTY DAYS granted every time to those who recite the following ejaculation:

Dulcissime Jesu, ne sis mihi My sweetest Jesus, be not my
Judex, sed Salvator. judge, but my Saviour.

A PLENARY INDULGENCE is granted once a year, on the feast of St. Jerome Emiliani (July 20), beginning from the first vespers and during the whole octave, on the day when, being truly penitent, after confession and Communion, they visit any church or public oratory and pray there for some time, to the intention of his Holiness.

Darts of Fire;

OR PROOFS THAT JESUS CHRIST HAS GIVEN US OF HIS LOVE IN THE WORK OF REDEMPTION.*

To any one who considers the immense love which Jesus Christ has shown us in his life, and especially in his death, it is impossible not to be stirred up and excited to love a God who is so enamoured of our souls. St. Bonaventure calls the wounds of our Redeemer wounds which pierce the hardest hearts, and inflame divine love in the coldest souls.[1]

Therefore, in this short examination of the love of Jesus Christ, let us consider, according to the testimony of the divine Scriptures, how much our loving Redeemer has done to make us understand the love that he bears us, and to oblige us to love him.

[1] "Vulnera corda saxea vulnerantia et mentes congelatas inflammantia."—*Stim. div. am.* p. I, c. I.

---

* Saint Alphonsus set a high value on this little treatise. He recommends it in several places of his works, and we read in one of his spiritual letters (December 18, 1767) that he himself used it nearly every day. In it is to be found the expression of those sentiments with which the saintly author mostly loved to nourish himself, and by which he sanctified his soul. In this treatise are chiefly repeated, under every form, the most fervent acts of contrition and of love. "They are irresistible darts that pierce the hardest hearts, and inflame divine love in the coldest souls." These pious reflections may be especially used when we are in the presence of the Blessed Sacrament, in our Visits, before and after Holy Communion, during Holy Mass and other divine services, or when we meditate on the Passion of our Lord. This treatise, entitled *Darts of Fire*, was published by the holy author in 1767.—Ed.

I.

Dilexit nos, et tradidit semetipsum pro nobis.
"He hath loved us, and hath delivered Himself for us."—*Ephes.* v. 2.

God had conferred so many blessings on men, thereby to draw them to love him; but these ungrateful men not only did not love him, but they would not even acknowledge him as their Lord. Scarcely in one corner of the earth, in Judea, was he recognized as God by his chosen people; and by them he was more feared than loved. He, however, who wished to be more loved than feared by us, became man like us, chose a poor, suffering, and obscure life, and a painful and ignominious death; and why? to draw our hearts to himself. If Jesus Christ had not redeemed us, he would not have been less great or less happy than he has always been; but he determined to procure our salvation at the cost of many labors and sufferings, as if his happiness depended on ours. He might have redeemed us without suffering; but no,—he willed to free us from eternal death by his own death; and though he was able to save us in a thousand ways, he chose the most humiliating and painful way of dying on the cross of pure suffering, to purchase the love of us, ungrateful worms of the earth. And what indeed was the cause of his miserable birth and his most sorrowful death, if not the love he had for us?

Ah, my Jesus, may that love which made Thee die for me on Calvary destroy in me all earthly affections, and consume me in the fire which Thou art come to kindle on the earth. I curse a thousand times those shameful passions which cost Thee so much pain. I repent, my dear Redeemer, with all my heart for all the offences I have committed against Thee. For the future I will rather die than offend Thee; and I wish to do all that I can to please Thee. Thou hast spared nothing for my love; neither will I spare anything for Thy love. Thou hast loved me without reserve; I also without reserve will love Thee. I love Thee, my only good, my love, my all.

II.

Sic Deus dilexit mundum, ut Filium suum unigenitum daret.
" God so loved the world, as to give His only-begotten Son."—*John*, iii. 16.

Oh, how much does that little word *so* mean! It means that we shall never be able to comprehend the extent of such a love as this which made a God send his Son to die, that lost man might be saved. And who would ever have been able to bestow on us this gift of infinite value but a God of infinite love?

I thank thee, O Eternal Father! for having given me Thy Son to be my Redeemer; and I thank Thee, O great Son of God, for having redeemed me with so much suffering and love. What would have become of me, after the many sins that I have committed against Thee, if Thou hadst not died for me? Ah, that I had died before I had offended Thee, my Saviour! Make me feel some of that detestation for my sins which Thou hadst while on earth and pardon me. But pardon is not sufficient for me, Thou dost merit my love; Thou hast loved me even to death, unto death will I also love Thee. I love Thee, O infinite goodness, with all my soul; I love Thee more than myself; in Thee alone will I place all my affections. Do thou help me; let me no longer live ungrateful to Thee, as I have done hitherto. Tell me what Thou wouldst have of me, for, by Thy grace, all, all will I do. Yes, my Jesus, I love Thee, my treasure, my life, my love, my all.

III.

Neque per sanguinem hircorum aut vitulorum, sed per proprium sanguinem introivit semel in sancta, æterna redemptione inventa.
"Neither by the blood of goats or of calves, but by His own blood, entered once into the Holies, having obtained eternal redemption."—*Heb.* ix. 12.

And of what worth would the blood of all goats or even of all men be, if they were sacrificed to obtain divine grace for us? It is only the blood of this Man-God which would merit for us pardon and eternal salvation. But if God himself had not devised this way to redeem us, as he did by dying to save us, who ever would have been able to think of it? His love alone designed it and executed it. Therefore holy Job did well to cry out to this God who loves man so much: *What is man, O Lord, that Thou dost so exalt him? why is Thy heart so intent upon loving him? what is man that Thou shouldst magnify him? or why dost Thou set Thy heart upon him?*[1] Ah, my Jesus, one heart is but little with which to love Thee; if I loved Thee even with the hearts of all men, it would be too little. What ingratitude, then, would it be if I were to divide my heart between Thee and creatures! No, my love, Thou wouldst have it all, and well dost Thou deserve it; I will give it all to Thee. If I do not know how to give it Thee as I ought, take it Thyself, and grant that I may be able to say to Thee with truth, *God of my heart*.[2] Ah, my Redeemer, by the merits of the abject and afflicted life that Thou hast willed to live for me, give me true humility, which will make me love contempt and an obscure life. May I lovingly embrace all infirmities, affronts, persecutions and interior sufferings, and all the crosses which may come to me from Thy hands. Let me love Thee, and then

---

[1] "Quid est homo, quia magnificas eum? aut quid apponis erga eum cor tuum?"—*Job*, vii. 17.

[2] "Deus cordis mei."—*Ps.* lxxii. 26.

dispose of me as Thou wilt. O loving heart of my Jesus! make me love Thee by discovering to me the immense good that Thou art. Make me all Thine before I die. I love Thee, my Jesus, who art worthy to be loved. I love Thee with all my heart, I love Thee with all my soul.

IV.

Benignitas et humanitas apparuit Salvatoris nostri Dei.
" The goodness and kindness of God our Saviour appeared."—*Tit.* iii. 4.

God has loved man from all eternity· *I have loved thee with an everlasting love.*[1] "But," says St. Bernard, "before the Incarnation of the Word the divine Power appeared in creating the world, and the divine Wisdom in governing it; but when the Son of God became man, then was made manifest the love which God had for men."[2] And, in fact, after seeing Jesus Christ go through so afflicted a life and so painful a death, we should be offering him an insult if we doubted the great love which he bears us. Yes, he does surely love us; and because he loves us, he wishes to be loved by us. *And Christ died for all, that they also who live may not now live to themselves, but for Him who died for them and rose again.*[3]

Ah, my Saviour, when shall I begin to understand the love which Thou hast had for me? Hitherto, instead of loving Thee, I have repaid Thee with offences and contempt of Thy graces, but since Thou art infinite in goodness I will not lose confidence. Thou hast promised to pardon him who repents; for Thy mercy's sake fulfil Thy promise to me. I have dishonored Thee by putting Thee aside to follow my own pleasures; but now I grieve for it from the bottom of my soul, and there is no sor-

---

[1] "In charitate perpetua dilexi te."—*Jer.* xxxi. 3.
[2] *In Nat. Domini*, s. 1.
[3] " Pro omnibus mortuus est Christus. ut et qui vivunt, jam non sibi vivant, sed ei qui pro ipsis mortuus est et resurrexit."—2 *Cor.* v. 15.

row that afflicts me more than the remembrance of having offended Thee, my Sovereign Good; pardon me and unite me entirely to Thee by an eternal bond of love, that I may not leave Thee any more, and that I may only live to love Thee and to obey Thee. Yes, my Jesus, for Thee alone will I live, Thee only will I love. Once I left Thee for creatures, now I leave all to give myself wholly to Thee. I love Thee, O God of my soul, I love Thee more than myself. O Mary, Mother of God, obtain for me the grace to be faithful to God till death.

V.

In hoc apparuit charitas Dei in nobis, quoniam Filium suum unigenitum misit Deus in mundum, ut vivamus per eum.

" By this hath the charity of God appeared toward us, because God hath sent His only-begotten Son into the world that we might live by Him."—1 *John*, iv. 9.

All men were dead by sin, and they would have remained dead if the eternal Father had not sent his Son to restore them to life by his death. But how? what is this? A God to die for man! A God! And who is this man? " Who am I?"[1] says St. Bonaventure. "O Lord, why hast Thou loved me so much?"[2] But it is in this that the infinite love of God shines forth. *By this hath the charity of God appeared*.[3] The Holy Church exclaims on Holy Saturday, "O wonderful condescension of Thy mercy toward us! O inestimable affection of charity! that Thou mightest redeem a slave, Thou didst deliver up Thy Son."[4] O immense compassion ! O prodigy! O excess of the love of God? to deliver a servant and a sinner from the death that he deserves, his innocent Son is condemned to die.

[1] " Quid sum ego ?"
[2] " Quare, Domine, cur me tam amasti ?"—*Stim. div. am.* p. 1, c. 13.
[3] " In hoc apparuit charitas Dei."—1 *John*, iv. 9.
[4] " O mira circa nos tuæ pietatis dignatio! O inæstimabilis dilectio charitatis ; ut servum redimeres, Filium tradidisti!"

Darts of Fire. 365

Thou, then, O my God, hast done this that we might live by Jesus Christ: *that we might live by Him*.[1] Yes, indeed, it is but meet that we should live for him, who has given all his blood and his life for us. My dear Redeemer, in the presence of Thy wounds and of the cross on which I see Thee dead for me, I consecrate to Thee my life and my whole will. Ah, make me all Thine, for from this day forward I seek and desire none but Thee. I love Thee, infinite Goodness; I love Thee, infinite Love; while I live may I always repeat, *My God, I love Thee, I love Thee;* let my last words in death be, *My God, I love Thee, I love Thee.*

VI.

Per viscera misericordiæ Dei nostri, in quibus visitavit nos Oriens ex alto.
." Through the bowels of the mercy of our God, in which the Orient from on high hath visited us."—*Luke,* i. 78.

Behold, the Son of God comes on earth to redeem us, and he comes stimulated alone by the bowels of his mercy. But, O God! if Thou hast compassion on lost man, is it not enough that Thou shouldst send an angel to redeem him? No, says the Eternal Word, I will come myself, that man may know how much I love him. St. Augustine writes: " For this reason chiefly did Jesus Christ come, that man should know how much God loves him."[2] But, my Jesus, even now that Thou hast come, how many men are there who truly love Thee? Wretch that I am, Thou knowest how I have hitherto loved Thee; Thou knowest what contempt I have had for Thy love. Oh that I might die of grief for it ! I repent, my dear Redeemer, of having so despised Thee. Ah, pardon me, and at the same time give me grace to love Thee. Let me no longer remain unmindful of that

[1] " Ut vivamus per eum."—1 *John,* iv. 9.
[2] " Maxime propterea Christus advenit, ut cognosceret homo quantum eum diligat Deus."—*De catech. rud.* c. 4.

great affection which Thou hast borne me. I love Thee now, but I love Thee but little. Thou dost merit an infinite love. Grant me at least that I may love Thee with all my strength. Ah, my Saviour, my joy, my life, my all, whom should I love if I love not Thee, the infinite Good? I consecrate all my wishes to Thy will; at the sight of the sufferings Thou hast undergone for me, I offer myself to suffer as much as it shall please Thee. *Lead us not into temptation, but deliver us from evil.*[1] Deliver me from sin, and then dispose of me as Thou wilt. I love Thee, infinite Good, and I am content to receive any punishment, even to be annihilated, rather than to live without loving Thee.

VII.

Et Verbum caro factum est.
"And the Word was made flesh."—*John*, i. 14.

God sent the Archangel Gabriel to ask Mary's consent that he should become her Son; Mary gives her consent, and behold the Word is made man. O wonderful prodigy! at which the heavens and all nature stand in astonishment! The Word made flesh! A God made man! What if we were to see a king become a worm, to save the life of a little worm of earth by his death?

So, then, my Jesus, Thou art my God, and not being able to die as God, Thou hast been pleased to become man capable of dying in order to give Thy life for me. My sweet Redeemer, how is it that, at the sight of such mercy and love Thou hast shown towards me, I do not die of grief? Thou didst come down from heaven to seek me, a lost sheep; and how many times have I not driven Thee away, preferring my miserable pleasures before Thee! But since Thou dost wish to have me, I leave all; I wish to be Thine, and I will have none other

[1] "Ne nos inducas ir tentationem, sed libera nos a malo."

but Thee. Thee do I choose for the only object of my affections. *My Beloved to me, and I to Him.*[1] Thou dost think of me, and I will think of none but Thee. Let me always love Thee, and may I never leave off loving Thee. Provided I can love Thee, I am content to be deprived of all sensible consolation, and even to suffer all torments. I see that Thou dost indeed wish me to be all Thine, and I wish to belong entirely to Thee. I know that everything in the world is a falsehood, a deceit, nothing but smoke, filth, and vanity. Thou alone art the true and only good; therefore Thou alone art sufficient for me. *My God, I wish for Thee alone, and nothing else;* God hear me, *for Thee alone do I wish, and nothing else.*

VIII.

Semetipsum exinanivit.
" He emptied Himself."—*Phil.* ii. 7.

Behold the only-begotton Son of God, omnipotent and true God, equal to the Father, born a little Infant in a stable. *He emptied Himself, taking the form of a servant, being made to the likeness of men.*[2] If any one would see a God annihilated, let him enter into the cave of Bethlehem, and he will find him as a little Infant, bound in swaddling-clothes, so that he cannot move, weeping and trembling with cold. Ah, holy faith, tell me whose Son is this poor child? Faith answers, he is the Son of God, and he is true God. And who has brought him to so miserable a condition? It was the love he had for men. And yet there are men to be found who do not love this God!

Thou, then, my Jesus, hast spent all Thy life amidst sorrows to make me understand the love Thou dost bear me, and I have spent my life in despising and displeasing

---

[1] " Dilectus meus mihi, et ego illi."—*Cant.* ii. 16.
[2] " Semetipsum exinanivit, formam servi accipiens, in similitudinem hominum factus."—*Phil.* ii. 7.

Thee by my sins! Ah, make me know the evil I have committed, and the love which Thou desirest to have. But since Thou hast borne with me till now, permit me not to give Thee any more cause for sorrow. Inflame me altogether with Thy love, and remind me always of all Thou hast suffered for me, that from this day forth I may forget everything, and think of nothing but loving and pleasing Thee. Thou didst come on earth to reign in our hearts; take, then, from my heart all that could prevent Thee from possessing it entirely! Make my will to be wholy conformed to Thy will; may Thine be mine, and may it be the rule of all my actions and desires.

IX.

Parvulus natus est nobis, et Filius datus est nobis.
"For a child is born to us, and a Son is given to us."--*Isa.* ix. 6.

Behold the end for which the Son of God will be born an Infant, to give himself to us from his childhood, and thus to draw to himself our love. Why (writes St. Francis de Sales) does Jesus take the sweet and tender form of an Infant, if it be not to stimulate us to love him and to confide in him? St. Peter Chrysologus had said before, "Thus he willed to be born, because he wished to be loved."[1]

Oh, dear child Jesus, my Saviour! I love Thee, in Thee do I trust, Thou art all my hope and all my love. What would have become of me if Thou hadst not come down from heaven to save me? I know the hell which would have awaited me for the offences I have offered Thee. Blessed be Thy mercy, because Thou art ever ready to pardon me if I repent of my sins. Yes, I repent with all my heart, my Jesus, of having despised Thee. Receive me into Thy favor, and make me die to myself to live only to Thee, my only good. Destroy in me, O thou

[1] "Sic nasci voluit, qui voluit amari."—*Serm.* 158.

consuming fire, everything that is displeasing in Thine eyes, and draw all my affections to Thee. I love Thee, O God of my soul, I love Thee, my treasure, my life, my all. I love Thee, and I wish to die saying, my God, I love Thee; and begin then to love Thee with a perfect love which shall have no end.

X.

Rorate, cœli, desuper, et nubes pluant Justum.—Emitte Agnum, Domine, dominatorem terræ.—Salutare tuum da nobis.
" Drop down dew, O ye heavens, from above, and let the clouds rain the just."—
" Send forth the Lamb, the Ruler of the earth."—*Isa.* xlv. 8; xvi. 1.—
" Grant us Thy salvation."—*Ps.* lxxxiv. 8.

Thus did the holy Prophets desire for so many years the coming of the Saviour. The same prophet Isaias said: *Oh, that Thou wouldst send the heavens, and wouldst come down: the mountains would melt away at Thy presence, . . . the waters would burn with fire.*[1] Lord, he said, when men shall see that Thou hast come on earth out of love for them, the mountains shall be made smooth, that is, men in serving Thee will conquer all the difficulties that at first appeared to them insuperable obstacles. The waters would burn with fire, and the coldest hearts will feel themselves burning with Thy love, at the sight of Thee made man, and how well has this been verified in many happy souls!—in St. Teresa, in St. Philip Neri, St. Francis Xavier, who even in this life were consumed by this holy fire. But how many such are there? Alas! but too few.

Ah, my Jesus, amongst these few I wish also to be. How many years ought I not already be burning in hell, separated from Thee, hating and cursing Thee forever. But no, Thou hast borne with me with so much patience, that Thou mightest see me burn, not with that unhappy flame, but with the blessed fire of Thy love;

[1] "Utinam dirumperes cœlos et descenderes; a facie tua montes defluerent . . ., aquæ arderent igni."—*Isa.* lxiv. 1, 2.

for this end Thou hast given me so many illuminations, and hast so often wounded my heart while I was far from Thee; finally, Thou hast done so much that Thou hast forced me to love Thee by Thy sweet attractions. Behold, I am now Thine. I will be Thine always and altogether. It remains for Thee to make me faithful, and this I confidently hope from Thy goodness. O my God! who could ever have the heart to leave Thee again and to live even a moment without Thy love? I love Thee, my Jesus, above all things; but this is little. I love Thee more than myself, but this is little also; I love Thee with all my heart, and this also is little. My Jesus, hear me, give me more love, more love, more love. O Mary, pray to God for me.

XI.

Despectum, et novissimum virorum.
"Despised, and the most abject of men."—*Isa.* liii. 3.

Behold what was the life of the Son of God made man, the most abject of men. He was treated as the vilest, the least of men. To what extreme of meanness could the life of Christ be reduced greater than that of being born in a stable? of living as a servant in an unknown and despised shop? struck, treated as a mock king, having his face spit upon? and, finally, of dying condemned as a malefactor on an infamous gibbet?

St. Bernard exclaims, "Oh, lowest and highest!"[1] A God, Thou art the Lord of all, and how art Thou contented to be the most despised of all? And I, my Jesus, when I see Thee so humiliated for me, how can I wish to be esteemed and honored by all? A sinner to be proud! Ah, my despised Redeemer, may Thy example inspire me with love of contempt and of an obscure life; from this time forward I hope, with Thy help, to accept from

[1] "O novissimum et altissimum."—*S. de Passione.*

my heart all opprobrium that I may have to suffer for the love of Thee, who hast endured so much for the love of me. Pardon me the pride of my past life, and give me love in its place. I love Thee, my despised Jesus. Go before me with Thy cross. I will follow Thee with mine, and I will not leave Thee till I die crucified for Thee, as Thou didst die crucified for me. My Jesus, my despised Jesus, I embrace Thee; in Thy embrace will I live and die.

XII.

Virum dolorum.
" A man of sorrows."—*Isa.* liii. 3.

What was the life of Jesus Christ? A life of sorrows; a life of internal and external sorrows from the beginning to the end. But what most afflicted Jesus Christ during the course of his life was the sight of the sins and the ingratitude with which men repaid the pains he had suffered with so much love for us. This thought had made him the most afflicted amongst all men that had ever lived on the earth.

So, then, my Jesus, I also added to the affliction Thou didst suffer during the whole of Thy life by my sins. And why do I not also say, as did St. Margaret of Cortona, who, when exhorted by her confessor to calm her grief and not to weep any more because God had pardoned her, redoubled her tears and answered, " Ah, my Father, how can I leave off weeping when I know that my sins afflicted my Jesus through the whole of his life?" Oh that I could die of grief, my Jesus, whenever I think of all the bitter anguish I have caused Thee every day of my life! Alas, how many nights have I slept deprived of Thy grace! How many times hast Thou pardoned me, and I have again turned my back upon Thee! My dear Lord, I repent above all things for having offended Thee. I love Thee with all my heart; I love Thee with all my soul. "Ah, my sweet Jesus, permit me not to be separated any more from Thee."[1] Let me die rather than betray Thee afresh. O Mary, Mother of perseverance, obtain for me the gift of holy perseverance.

XIII.

Cum dilexisset suos, qui erant in mundo, in finem dilexit eos.
"Having loved his own who were in the world, He loved them unto the end."—*John*, xiii. 1.

The love of friends increases at the time of death, when they are on the point of being separated from those they love; and it is then, therefore, that they try more than ever, by some pledge of affection, to show the love they bear to them. Jesus during the whole of his life gave us marks of his affection, but when he came near the hour of his death he wished to give us a special proof of his love. For what greater proof could this loving Lord show us than by giving his blood and his life for each of us? And not content with this, he left this very same body, sacrificed for us upon the cross, to be our food, so that each one who should receive it should be wholly united to him, and thus love should mutually increase.

O infinite goodness! O infinite love! Ah, my enamoured Jesus, fill my heart with Thy love, so that I may forget the world and myself, to think of nothing but loving and pleasing Thee. I consecrate to Thee my body, my soul, my will, my liberty. Up to this time I have sought to gratify myself to Thy great displeasure; I am exceedingly sorry for it, my crucified love; henceforth I will seek nothing but Thee, my God and my all.[2] My God, Thou art my all, I wish for Thee alone and

[1] "Jesu dulcissime! ne permittas me separari a te, ne permittas me separari a te."
[2] "Deus meus et omnia."

nothing more. Oh that I could spend myself all for Thee, who hast spent Thyself all for me! I love Thee, my only good, my only love. I love Thee, and abandon myself entirely to Thy holy will. Make me love Thee, and then do with me what Thou wilt.

XIV.

Tristis est anima mea usque ad mortem.
"My soul is sorrowful even unto death."—*Matt.* xxvi. 38.

These were the words that proceeded from the sorrowful heart of Jesus Christ in the garden of Gethsemani, before he went to die. Alas, whence came this extreme grief of his, which was so great that it was enough to kill him? Perhaps it was on account of the torments that he saw he should have to suffer? No; for he had foreseen these torments from the time of his incarnation. He had foreseen them, and had accepted them of his own free will: *He was offered because it was His own will.*[1] His grief came from seeing the sins men would commit after his death. It was then, according to St. Bernardine of Sienna, that he saw clearly each particular sin of each one of us. He had regard to every individual sin.[2]

It was not, then, my Jesus, the sight of the scourges, of the thorns, and of the cross which so afflicted Thee in the garden of Gethsemani; it was the sight of my sins, each one of which so oppressed Thy heart with grief and sadness that it made Thee agonize and sweat blood. This is the recompense I have made Thee for the love Thou hast shown me by dying for me. Ah, let me share the grief Thou didst feel in the garden for my sins, so that the remembrance of it may make me sad

[1] "Oblatus est, quia ipse voluit."—*Isa.* liii. 7.
[2] "Ad quamlibet culpam singularem habuit aspectum."—*T.* ii, s. 56, a. 1.

for all my life. Ah, my sweet Redeemer, if I could but console Thee as much now by my grief and love as I then afflicted Thee! I repent, my Love, with all my heart for having preferred my own miserable satisfaction to Thee. I am sorry, and I love The above all things. Although I have despised Thee, yet I hear Thee ask for my love. Thou wouldst have me love Thee with all my heart: *Love the Lord thy God with all thy heart, and with all thy soul.*[1] Yes, my God, I love Thee with all my heart, I love Thee with all my soul. Do Thou give me the love Thou requirest of me. If I have hitherto sought myself, I will now seek none but Thee. And seeing that Thou hast loved me more than others, more than others will I love Thee. Draw me always more, my Jesus, to Thy love by the odor of Thy ointments, which are the loving attractions of Thy grace. Finally, give me strength to correspond to so much love which God has borne to an ungrateful worm and traitor. Mary, Mother of mercy, help me by thy prayers.

XV.

Comprehenderunt Jesum, et ligaverunt eum.
"They took Jesus and bound him."—*John*, xviii. 12.

A God taken and bound! What could the angels have said at seeing their king with his hands bound, led between soldiers through the streets of Jerusalem! And what ought we to say at the sight of our God, who is content for our sake to be bound as a thief, to be presented to the judge who is to condemn him to death? St. Bernard laments, saying, "What hast Thou to do with chains?"[2] What have malefactors and chains to do with Thee, O my Jesus, Thou who art infinite goodness and

---

[1] "Diliges Dominum Deum tuum ex toto corde tuo, et in tota anima tua."—*Matt.* xxii. 37.

[2] "Quid tibi et vinculis?"—*Lib. de Pass.* c. 4.

majesty? They should belong to us sinners, guilty of hell, and not to Thee who art innocent and the Holy of holies. St. Bernard goes on to say, on seeing Jesus guilty of death, "What hast Thou done, my innocent Saviour, that Thou shouldst be thus condemned?"[1] O my dear Saviour, Thou art innocence itself; for what crime hast Thou been thus condemned? Ah, I will tell Thee, he replies: the crime Thou hast committed is the too great love Thou hast borne to men. Thy sin is love.[2]

My beloved Jesus, I kiss the cords that bind Thee, for they have freed me from those eternal chains which I have deserved. Alas! how many times have I renounced Thy friendship and made myself a slave of Satan, dishonoring Thy infinite majesty! I grieve above all things for having so grievously insulted Thee. Ah, my God, bind my will to Thy feet with the sweet cords of Thy holy love, that it may wish for nothing but what is pleasing to Thee. May I take Thy will for the sole guide of my life. As Thou hast had so great care for my good, may I not care for anything but to love Thee. I love Thee, my sovereign Good; I love Thee, the only object of my affections. I know that Thou alone hast loved me truly, and Thee alone will I love. I renounce everything. Thou alone art sufficient for me.

XVI.

Ipse autem vulneratus est propter iniquitates nostras, attritus est propter scelera nostra.

"But He was wounded for our iniquities, He was bruised for our sins."—
Isa. liii. 5.

One single blow suffered by this Man-God was sufficient for the sins of the whole world; but Jesus Christ was not satisfied with that; he wished to be *wounded and*

---

[1] "Quid fecisti, innocentissime Salvator, quod sic condemnareris?"
—*Lib. de Pass.* c. 4.

[2] "Peccatum tuum amor tuus."

bruised[1] for our iniquities, which means to say, wounded and torn from head to foot, so that there should be no whole part remaining in his sacred body. Hence the same prophet beheld him full of sores like a leper. *And we have thought Him as it were a leper, and as one struck by God and afflicted.*[2]

O wounds of my sorrowful Jesus, you are all living evidences of the love which my Redeemer preserves for me; with tender words do you force me to love him for the many sufferings that he has undergone for the love of me. Ah, my sweet Jesus, when shall I give myself all to Thee, as Thou hast given Thyself all to me? I love Thee, my sovereign good. I love Thee, my God, lover of my soul. O God of love, give me love. By my love let me atone to Thee for the bitterness I have given Thee in times past. Help me to drive from my heart everything that does not tend to Thy love. Eternal Father, *look at the face of Thy Christ,*[3] look at the wounds of Thy Son, which seek pity for me, and for their sake pardon me the outrages that I have committed against Thee; take my heart entirely to Thyself, that it may not love, seek, nor sigh after any other but Thee. I say to Thee, with St. Ignatius, " Give me only love of Thee and Thy grace and I am rich enough."[4] Behold this is all I ask of Thee, O God of my soul; give me Thy love, together with Thy grace, and I desire nothing else. O Mary, Mother of God, intercede for me.

[1] " Vulneratus, attritus."
[2] " Et nos putavimus eum quasi leprosum, et percussum a Deo, et humiliatum."—*Isa.* liii. 4.
[3] " Respice in faciem Christi tui."—*Ps.* lxxxiii. 10.
[4] "Amorem tui solum cum gratia tua mihi dones, et dives sum satis."

XVII.

Ave, Rex Judæorum.
"Hail, King of the Jews."—*Matt.* xxvii. 29.

Thus was our Redeemer scornfully saluted by the Roman soldiers. After having treated him as a false king, and having crowned him with thorns, they knelt before him and called him king of the Jews, and then, rising up with loud cries and laughter, they struck him and spit in his face. St. Matthew writes: *And platting a crown of thorns, they put it on His head. . . . And bowing the knee before Him, they mocked Him, saying, Hail, King of the Jews; and spitting upon Him they took the reed and struck His head.* And St. John adds, *And they gave Him blows.*[1]

O my Jesus! this barbarous crown that encircles Thy head, this vile reed that Thou dost hold in Thy hand, this torn purple garment that covers Thee with ridicule, make Thee known indeed as a king, but a king of love. The Jews will not acknowledge Thee for their king, and they say to Pilate, *We have no King but Cæsar.*[2] My beloved Redeemer, if others will not have Thee for their king, I accept Thee, and desire that Thou shouldst be the only King of my soul. To Thee do I consecrate my whole self; dispose of me as Thou pleasest. For this end hast Thou endured contempt, so many sorrows, and death itself, to gain our hearts and to reign therein by Thy love. *For this end Christ died, . . . that he might be Lord both of the dead and of the living.*[3] Make Thyself, therefore, master of my heart, O my beloved King, and reign and

[1] "Et plectentes coronam de spinis, posuerunt super caput ejus, et arundinem in dextera ejus. Et genu flexo ante eum, illudebant ei dicentes: Ave, Rex Judæorum.—Et expuentes in eum, acceperunt arundinem, et percutiebant caput ejus."—*Matt.* xxvii. 29.—" Et dabant ei alapas."—*John*, xix. 3.

[2] "Non habemus regem, nisi Cæsarem."—*John*, xix. 15.

[3] "In hoc enim Christus mortuus est et resurrexit, ut et mortuorum et vivorum dominetur."—*Rom.* xiv. 9.

exercise Thy sway there forever. Formerly I refused Thee for my Lord, that I might serve my passions; now I will be all Thine and Thee alone will I serve. Ah, bind me to Thee by Thy love, and make me always remember the bitter death that Thou hast willed to suffer for me. Ah, my King, my God, my love, my all, what do I wish for if not for Thee alone!—*Thee, God of my heart, and my portion forever.*[1] O God of my heart! I love Thee; Thou art my portion, Thou art my only good.

XVIII.

Et bajulans sibi crucem, exivit in eum, qui dicitur Calvariæ, locum.

"And bearing His own Cross, He went forth to that place which is called Calvary."—*John*, xix. 17.

Behold the Saviour of the world has now set out on his journey with his cross on his shoulders, going forth to die in torments for the love of men. The divine Lamb allows himself to be led without complaining, to be sacrificed upon the cross for our salvation. Go thou, also, my soul, accompany and follow thy Jesus, who goes to suffer death for thy love, to satisfy for thy sins. Tell me, my Jesus and my God, what dost Thou expect from men by giving Thy life for their sake? St. Bernard answers, Thou dost expect nothing but to be loved by them: "When God loves, he wishes for nothing but to be loved in return."[2]

Is it, then, my Redeemer, at so great a cost that Thou hast desired to gain our love? And shall there be any among men who believe in Thee, and not love Thee? I comfort myself with the thought that Thou art the love of all the souls of the saints, the love of Mary, the love of Thy Father; but, O my God, how many are there who will not know Thee, and how many that know Thee

[1] "Deus cordis mei, et pars mea, Deus, in æternum."—*Ps.* lxxii. 26.

[2] "Cum amat Deus, non aliud vult, quam amari."—*In Cant.* s 83.

and yet will not love Thee! Infinite Love, make Thyself known, make Thyself loved. Ah, that I could by my blood and my death make Thee loved by all! But alas that I have lived so many years in the world while I knew Thee, but did not love Thee! But now at last Thou hast drawn me to love Thee by Thy so great goodness. At one time I was so unhappy as to lose Thy grace ; but the grief I now feel for it, the desire of being all Thine, and still more the death Thou hast suffered for me, give me a firm confidence, O my Love, that Thou hast already pardoned me, and that now Thou dost love me. Oh that I could die for Thee, my Jesus, as Thou hast died for me! Although no punishment awaited those who love Thee not, I would never leave off loving Thee, and I would do all I could to please Thee. Thou who givest me this good desire, give me strength to follow it out. My love, my hope, do not abandon me; make me correspond, during the remainder of my life to the especial love that Thou has borne me. Thou desirest to have me for Thine own, and I wish to be all for Thee. I love Thee, my God, my treasure, my all. I will live and die always repeating, I love Thee, I love Thee, I love Thee.

XIX.

Quasi agnus coram tondente se, obmutescet, et non aperiet os suum.

"And shall be dumb as a lamb before his shearer, and He shall not open his mouth."—*Is.* liii. 7.

This was precisely the passage which the eunuch of Queen Candace was reading; but not understanding of whom it was written, St. Philip, inspired by God, entered the carriage in which the eunuch was, and explained to him that these words referred to our Redeemer Jesus Christ. Jesus was called a lamb because he was dragged into the prætorium of Pilate, and then led to death just like an innocent lamb. Therefore the Baptist calls him a lamb. *Behold the Lamb of God, behold Him who taketh away the sins of the world.*[1] A lamb who suffers and dies a victim on the cross for our sins. *Surely he hath borne our infirmities and carried our sorrows.*[2] Miserable are those who do not love Jesus Christ during their life. In the last day the sight of this Lamb in his wrath will make them say to the mountains, *Fall upon us and hide us from the face of Him that sitteth upon the throne, and from the wrath of the Lamb.*[3]

No, my divine Lamb, if in times past I have not loved Thee, now I will love Thee forever. Before, I was blind; but now that thou hast enlightened me, and hast made me know the great evil I have done in turning my back upon Thee, and the infinite love which is due to Thee for Thy goodness and for the love Thou hast borne me, I repent with all my heart for having offended Thee, and I love Thee above all things. O wounds, O blood of my Redeemer, how many souls have you not inflamed with love! inflame my soul also. Ah, my Jesus, continually call to my remembrance Thy Passion and the pains and ignominies that Thou hast suffered for me, that I may detach my affections from earthly goods and place them all on Thee, my only and infinite good. I love Thee, Lamb of God, sacrificed and annihilated on the cross for my sake. Thou hast not refused to suffer for me; I will not refuse to suffer for Thee whatever Thou requirest. I will no longer complain of the crosses that Thou dost send me. I ought to have been in hell these many years; how, then, can I complain? Give me grace to love Thee, and then do with me what Thou wilt.

[1] "Ecce Agnus Dei, ecce qui tollit peccata mundi."—*John*, i. 29.
[2] "Vere languores nostros ipse tulit, et dolores nostros ipse portavit."—*Isa.* liii. 4.
[3] "Cadite super nos, et abscondite nos a facie sedentis super thronum, et ab ira Agni."—*Apoc.* vi. 16.

Darts of Fire.

Who shall separate me from the love of Christ?[1] Ah, my Jesus, sin alone can separate me from Thy love. Ah, let it not be; rather let me die a thousand times; this I beg of Thee by Thy sacred Passion. I beseech thee, O Mary, by thy sorrows deliver me from the death of sin.

XX.

Deus meus! Deus meus! ut quid dereliquisti me?
" My God, my God, why hast Thou forsaken me ?"—*Matt.* xxvii. 46.

O God ! who shall not compassionate the Son of God, who for love of men is dying of grief on a cross ? He is tormented externally in his body by the innumerable wounds, and internally he is so afflicted and sad that he seeks solace for his great sorrow from the Eternal Father; but his Father, in order to satisfy his divine justice, abandons him, and leaves him to die desolate and deprived of every consolation.

O desolate death of my dear Redeemer, Thou art my hope. O my abandoned Jesus, Thy merits make me hope that I shall not remain abandoned and separated from Thee forever in hell. I do not care to live in consolation on this earth; I embrace all the pains and desolations that Thou mayest send me. He is not worthy of consolation who by offending Thee has merited for himself eternal torments. It is enough for me to love Thee and to live in Thy grace. This alone do I beg of Thee, let me nevermore see myself deprived of Thy love. Let me be abandoned by all; do not Thou abandon me in this extremity. I love Thee, my Jesus, who didst die abandoned for me. I love Thee, my only good, my only hope, my only love.

[1] " Quis ergo nos separabit a charitate Christi ?"—*Rom.* viii. 35.

XXI.

Crucifixerunt eum, et cum eo alios duos hinc et hinc, medium autem Jesum.

"They crucified Him, and with Him two others, one on each side, and Jesus in the midst."—*John*, xix. 18.

The incarnate Word was called by the sacred spouse, *All lovely; such is my beloved.*[1] At whatever period of his life Jesus Christ presents himself to us, he appears altogether desirable and most worthy of love, whether we see him as an infant in the stable, as a boy in the shop of St. Joseph, as a solitary meditating in the desert, or bathed in sweat as he walked about preaching throughout Judea. But in no other form does he appear more loving than when he is nailed to the cross on which the immense love he bears us forced him to die. St. Francis de Sales has said, the Mount of Calvary is the hill of lovers. All love which does not take its rise from the Passion of the Saviour is weak. How miserable is the death where there is no love of the Redeemer! Let us stop, then, and consider that this man, nailed to the tree of shame, is our true God, and that he is here suffering and dying for nothing but for the love of us.

Ah, my Jesus, if all men would stand still and contemplate Thee on the cross, believing with a lively faith, that Thou art their God, and that Thou hast died for their salvation, how could they live far from Thee and without Thy love? And how could I, knowing all this, have displeased Thee so often? If others have offended Thee, they have at least sinned in darkness; but I have sinned in the light. But these pierced hands, this wounded side, this blood, these wounds which I see in Thee, make me hope for pardon and Thy grace. I am grieved, my Love, for having ever so despised Thee. But now I love Thee with all my heart; and my greatest

[1] "Totus desiderabilis, talis est Dilectus meus."—*Cant.* v. 16.

grief is the remembrance of my having despised Thee. This grief, however, which I feel, is a sign that Thou hast pardoned me. O burning heart of my Jesus, inflame my poor heart with Thy love. O my Jesus, dead, consumed with sorrow for me, make me die consumed with sorrow for having offended Thee, and with the love Thou dost merit, I sacrifice myself entirely to Thee, who hast sacrificed Thyself entirely for me. O sorrowful Mother Mary, make me faithful in loving Jesus!

XXII.

Et inclinato capite, tradidit spiritum.

"And bowing His head, He gave up the ghost."—*John*, xix. 30

Behold, my Redeemer, to what Thy love for men has brought Thee—even to die of sorrow on a cross, drowned in a sea of grief and ignominy; as David had predicted of Thee. *I am come into the depth of the sea, and a tempest hath overwhelmed me.*[1] St. Francis de Sales writes thus: "Let us contemplate this divine Saviour stretched on the cross, as upon the altar of his glory, on which he is dying of love for us. Ah, why, then, do we not in spirit throw ourselves upon him to die upon the cross with him who has chosen to die there for the love of us? I will hold him, we ought to say; I will never let him go. I will die with him, and will burn in the flames of his love; one and the same fire shall devour this divine Creator and his miserable creature. My Jesus is all mine, and I am all his. I will live and die on his bosom. Neither life nor death shall ever separate me from my Jesus."[2]

Yes, my dear Redeemer, I hold fast to Thy cross; I kiss Thy pierced feet, touched with compassion and con-

---

[1] "Veni in altitudinem maris, et tempestas demersit me."—*Ps.* lxviii. 3.
[2] *Love of God*, book vii., ch. 8.

founded at seeing the affection with which Thou hast died for me. Ah, accept me, and bind me to Thy feet, that I may no more depart from Thee, and may from this day forward converse with Thee alone, consult with Thee on all my thoughts ; in a word, may I henceforth direct all my affections so as to seek nothing but to love Thee and please Thee, always longing to leave this valley of dangers to come and love Thee face to face with all my strength in Thy kingdom, which is a kingdom of eternal love. In the mean time let me always live, grieving for the offences I have committed against Thee, and always burning with love for Thee, who for love of me hast given Thy life. I love Thee, my Jesus, who hast died for me; I love Thee, O infinite lover ; I love Thee, O infinite love ; I love Thee, infinite goodness. O Mary, Mother of beautiful love, pray to my Jesus for me.

XXIII.

Oblatus est, quia ipse voluit.

"He was offered because it was His own will."—*Isa.* liii. 7.

The incarnate Word, at the moment of his conception, saw before him all the souls that he was to redeem. Then thou also, my soul, wast presented with the guilt of all thy sins upon thee, and for thee did Jesus Christ accept all the pains that he suffered in life and death; and in doing so he obtained for thee thy pardon, and all the graces that thou hast received from God—the lights, the calls of his love, the helps to overcome temptations, the spiritual consolations, the tears, the compassionate feelings thou hast experienced when thinking of the love he had for thee, and the sentiments of sorrow in remembering how thou hast offended him.

Thou didst, then, my Jesus, from the very beginning of Thy life, take upon Thee all my sins, and didst offer Thyself to satisfy for them by Thy sufferings. By Thy death Thou hast delivered me from eternal death: *But Thou hast delivered my soul, that it should not perish; Thou hast cast all my sins behind Thy back.*[1] Thou, my love, instead of punishing me for the insults which I have added to those that Thou hadst already received, hast gone on adding to Thy favors and mercies towards me, in order to win my heart one day to Thyself. My Jesus, this day is come; I love Thee with all my soul. Who should love Thee if I do not? This is the first sin, my Jesus, that Thou hast to forgive me, that I have been so many years in the world without loving Thee. But for the future I will do all I can to please Thee. I feel by Thy grace a great desire to live to Thee alone, and to detach myself from all created things, I have also a great compunction for the displeasure that I have caused Thee. This desire and this sorrow, I see, my Jesus, are all Thy gift. Continue, then, my love, to keep me faithful in Thy love; for Thou knowest my weakness. Make me all Thine, as Thou hast made Thyself all mine. I love Thee, my only good; I love Thee, my only love; I love Thee, my treasure, my all; My Jesus, I love Thee, I love Thee, I love Thee. Help me, O Mother of God.

XXIV.

Deus Filium suum mittens in similitudinem carnis peccati, et de peccato damnavit peccatum in carne. Christus nos redemit de maledicto legis factus pro nobis maledictum, quia scriptum est: Maledictus omnis qui pendet in ligno.

"God sending his own Son in the likeness of sinful flesh, even of sin, hath condemned sin in the flesh."—*Rom.* viii. 3. "Christ hath redeemed us from the curse of the law, being made a curse for us, for it is written: Cursed is every one that hangeth on a tree."—*Gal.* iii. 13.

Hence we see that Jesus Christ willed to appear in the world as a guilty and an acused man, hanging on the cross to deliver us from eternal malediction.

---

[1] "Tu autem eruisti animam meam, ut non periret ; projecisti post tergum tuum omnia peccata mea."—*Isa.* xxxviii. 17.

O eternal Father, for the love of this Son so dear to Thee, have pity on me! And Thou, Jesus, my Redeemer, who by Thy death hast liberated me from the slavery of sin in which I was born, and of the sins that I have committed since my baptism, ah, change the miserable chains which once bound me a slave to Satan into chains of gold, which may bind me to Thee with a holy love. Arise and show forth in me the efficacy of Thy merits, by changing me, a sinner, into a saint. I have deserved to be burning in hell for many years past: but I hope by Thy infinite mercy, for the glory of Thy death, to burn with Thy love, and to be all Thine. I wish that my heart should love none but Thee. *Thy kingdom come.* Reign, my Jesus, reign over my whole soul. May it obey Thee alone, seek Thee alone, desire Thee alone. Away from my heart, ye earthly affections! and come, O ye flames of divine love; come and remain alone to possess and consume me for that God of love who didst die consumed for me. I love Thee, my Jesus; I love Thee, O infinite Sweetness and my true lover, I have no one who has loved me more than Thou; and therefore I give and consecrate myself to Thee, my treasure and my all.

XXV.

Dilexit nos, et lavit nos a peccatis nostris in sanguine suo.

"He hath loved us, and washed us from our sins in His own blood."—*Apoc.* i. 5.

So, then, my Jesus, in order to save my soul, Thou hast prepared a bath of Thine own blood wherein to cleanse it from the filth of its sins. If, then, our souls have been bought by Thy blood, *For you are bought with a great price,*[1] it is a sign that Thou lovest them much; and as Thou dost love them, let us pray thus to Thee: *We therefore pray Thee to help Thy servants, whom Thou*

[1] "Empti enim estis pretio magno."—1 *Cor.* vi. 20.

hast redeemed with Thy precious blood.[1] It is true that by my sins I have separated myself from Thee, and have knowingly lost Thee. But remember, my Jesus, that Thou hast bought me with Thy blood. Ah, may this blood not have been given in vain for me, which was shed with so much grief and so much love.

By my sins I have driven Thee, my God, from my soul, and have merited Thy hatred; but Thou hast said that Thou wouldst forget the crimes of a repentant sinner. *But if he do penance . . . I will not remember all his iniquities.*[2] Thou hast further said, *I love them that love me.*[3] I pray Thee, therefore, my Jesus, to forget all the injuries that I have offered Thee, and love me; whilst I also will now love Thee more than myself, and repent above all things for having offended Thee. Ah, my beloved Lord, for the sake of that blood which Thou hast shed for the love of me, hate me no longer, but love me. It is not enough for me that Thou shouldst only forgive me the chastisement I deserve, I desire to love Thee and to be loved by Thee. O God, who art all love, all goodness, unite me and bind me to Thyself, and permit not that I should ever be separated from Thee any more, and that thus I should deserve Thy hatred. No, my Jesus, my love, let it not be, I will be all Thine, and I desire that Thou shouldst be all mine.

XXVI.

Humiliavit semetipsum, factus obediens usque ad mortem, mortem autem crucis.
"He humbled Himself, becoming obedient unto death; even the death of the cross."—*Phil.* ii. 8.

What great thing is that the martyrs have done in giving their lives for God, while this God has humbled

[1] "Te ergo quæsumus, tuis famulis subveni, quos pretioso sanguine redemisti."
[2] "Si impius egerit pœnitentiam . . ., omnium iniquitatum ejus . . . non recordabor."—*Ezek.* xviii. 21.
[3] "Ego diligentes me diligo."—*Prov.* viii. 17.

himself to the death of the cross for their love? To render a just return for the death of a God, it would not be sufficient to sacrifice the lives of all men ; the death of another God for his love would alone compensate for it. O my Jesus! allow me, a poor sinner, to say to Thee, with Thy true lover St. Francis of Assissi, "May I die, O Lord, for the love of Thy love, as Thou didst deign to die for the love of my love." [1]

Is it true, my Redeemer, that hitherto, for the love of my own pleasures, unhappy that I am! I have renounced Thy love? Would that I had died before, and had never offended Thee! I thank Thee that Thou givest me time to love Thee in this life, that I may afterwards love Thee throughout all eternity. Ah, remind me continually, my Jesus, of the ignominious death that Thou hast suffered for me, that I may never forget to love Thee in consideration of the love that Thou hast borne me. I love Thee, infinite goodness; I love Thee, my supreme good; to Thee I give myself entirely, and by that love which caused Thee to die for me, do Thou accept my love, and let me die, destroy me, rather than ever permit me to leave off loving Thee. I will say to Thee, with St. Francis de Sales, "O eternal Love, my soul seeks Thee, and chooses Thee for all eternity. Come, O Holy Spirit, inflame our hearts with Thy love. Either to love or to die. To die to all other affections, to live only to the love of Jesus." [2]

XXVII.

Charitas enim Christi urget nos.

"The Charity of Christ presseth us."—2 *Cor.* v. 14.

How tender and full of unction are the words with which St. Francis de Sales comments on this passage in

[1] "Moriar, Domine, amore amoris tui, qui amore amoris mei dignatus es mori."

[2] *Love of God*, book xii. ch. 13,

his book of the divine love! "Hear Theotimus," he says; "nothing forces and presses the soul of man so much as love. If a man knows that he is loved by any one, he feels himself forced to love him; but if a peasant is loved by a lord, he is still more strongly forced; and if by a monarch, how much more so! Know, then, that Jesus, the true God, has loved us so far as to suffer death, even the death of the cross for us. Is not this to have our hearts put under a press, and to feel them squeezed and crushed so as to force out our love with a violence which is all the stronger for being so loving."

Ah, my Jesus, since Thou dost desire to be loved by me, remind me always of the love that Thou hast borne me, and of the pains Thou hast suffered to show me this love. May the remembrance of them be ever present in my mind and in the minds of all men, for it is impossible to believe what Thou hast suffered to oblige us to love, and yet not love Thee. Till now the cause of my negligent and wicked life has been, that I have not thought of the affection which Thou, my Jesus, hast had for me. All this time, however, I knew the great displeasure my sins gave Thee, and nevertheless I went on multiplying them. Every time I remember this I should wish to die of grief for it, and I should not now have courage to ask Thy pardon, if I did not know that Thou didst die to obtain forgiveness for me. Thou hast borne with me in order that at the sight of the wrong I have done Thee, and of the death that Thou hast suffered for me, my sorrow and love towards Thee should be increased. I repent, my dear Redeemer, with all my heart, for having offended Thee, and I love Thee with all my soul. After so many signs of Thy affection, and after the many mercies that Thou hast shown me, I promise Thee that I will love none but Thee. Thee will I love with all my strength; Thou art my Jesus, my love, my all. Thou art my love, because in Thee I have placed all my affections

Thou art my all, because I will have none other but Thee. Grant, then, that always, both in life and death and through all eternity, I may ever call Thee my God. my love, and my all.

XXVIII.

Charitas enim Christi urget nos.
" The charity of Christ presseth us."—2 *Cor.* v. 14.

Let us consider anew the force of these words. The Apostle means to say that it is not so much the thought of all that Christ has suffered for us that should constrain us to love him, as the thought of the love that he has shown us in wishing to suffer so much for us. This love made our Saviour say, while he was yet alive, that he was dying with the desire that the day of his death should draw near to make us know the boundless love that he had for us. *I have a baptism wherewith I am to be baptized, and how am I straitened till it be accomplished!*[1] And the same love made him say the last night of his life. *With desire, I have desired to eat this pasch with you before I suffer.*[2]

So great, then, my Jesus, was the desire that Thou hadst to be loved by us, that all through Thy life Thou didst desire nothing but to suffer and to die for us, and so to put us under the necessity of loving Thee at least out of gratitude for so much love. Dost Thou so thirst for our love? How is it, then, that we so little desire Thine. Alas, that I should have been up to this time so foolish! Not only have I not desired Thy love, but I have brought down upon myself Thy hatred by losing my respect for Thee. My dear Redeemer, I know the evil I have done, I detest it above all my other sins, and

---

[1] " Baptismo habeo baptizari; et quomodo coarctor, usquedum perficiatur!"—*Luke,* xii. 50.

[2] " Desiderio desideravi hoc pascha manducare vobiscum, antequam patiar."—*Ibid.* xxii. 15.

am sorry from the bottom of my heart. Now I desire Thy love more than all the goods of the world. My best and only treasure, I love Thee above all things, I love Thee more than myself, I love Thee with all my soul, and I desire nothing but to love Thee and to be loved by Thee. Forget, my Jesus, the offences that I have committed against Thee; do Thou also love me, and love me exceedingly, that I may exceedingly love Thee. Thou art my love, Thou art my hope, Thou knowest how weak I am; help me, Jesus, my love; help me, Jesus, my hope. Succor me also with thy prayers, O Mary, great Mother of God.

XXIX.

Majorem hac dilectionem nemo habet, ut animam suam ponat quis pro amicis suis.
"Greater love than this no man hath, that a man lay down his life for his friends."
—*John*, xv. 13.

What more, O my soul! could thy God do than to give his life in order to make thee love him? To give his life is the greatest mark of affection that a man can give to another man who is his friend. But what love must that have been which our Creator has shown to us, in choosing to die for us his creatures! This is what St. John was considering when he wrote: *In this we have known the charity of God, because He hath laid down His life for us.*[1] Indeed, if faith did not teach us that a God has willed to die to show us his love, who would ever have been able to believe it?

Ah, my Jesus, I believe that Thou hast died for me, and therefore I confess that I deserve a thousand hells for having repaid with insults and ingratitude the love that Thou hast borne me in giving Thy life for me. I thank Thy mercy, which nas promised to forgive those that repent. Trusting, then, in this sweet promise, I

---
[1] "In hoc cognovimus charitatem Dei, quoniam ille animam suam pro nobis posuit."—1 *John*, iii. 16.

hope for pardon from Thee, repenting, as I do, with all my heart for having so often despised Thy love. But since Thy love has not abandoned me, overcome by Thy love I consecrate myself all to Thee. Thou, my Jesus, hast finished Thy life by dying in agony on a cross; and what recompense can I, a miserable creature, make Thee? I consecrate to Thee my life, accepting with love all the sufferings that will come to me from Thy hand, both in life and in death. Softened and confounded at the great mercy that Thou hast used towards me, I hold fast Thy cross; at Thy feet will I thus live and die. Ah, my Redeemer, by the love that Thou hast borne me in dying for me, do not permit me ever to separate myself from Thee again. Make me always live and die in Thy embrace. My Jesus, my Jesus, I repeat, make me always live and die united with Thee.

XXX.

Et ego, si exaltatus fuero a terra, omnia traham ad me ipsum.

"I, if I be lifted up from the earth, will draw all things unto Myself."— *John*, xii. 32.

Thou hast said, then, my Saviour, that when hanging on the cross Thou wouldst draw all our hearts unto Thyself; why is it that for so many years my heart has gone far away from Thee? Ah, it is not Thy fault. How many times hast Thou called me to Thy love and I have turned a deaf ear? How many times too hast Thou pardoned me, and affectionately warned me by remorse of conscience not to offend Thee again, and I have repeated my offence? Ah, my Jesus, send me not to hell, because there I shall be cursing forever these graces which Thou hast given me; so that these graces, the illuminations Thou hast given me, Thy calls, Thy patience in bearing with me, the blood that Thou didst shed to save me, would be the most cruel of all the torments of hell. But now I hear Thee call me again, and Thou dost say to me, with the greatest love, as if I had never offended Thee: *Love the Lord Thy God with all thy heart.*[1] Thou dost command me to love Thee, and to love Thee with all my heart. But if Thou didst not command me, O Jesus! how could I live without loving Thee, after so many proofs of Thy love? Yes, I love Thee, my supreme good; I love Thee with all my heart. I love Thee because Thou dost command me to love Thee. I love Thee because Thou art worthy of infinite love. I love Thee, and desire nothing else but to love Thee, and nothing else do I fear except being separated from Thee, and living without Thy love. Ah, my crucified love, permit not that I ever leave off loving Thee. Ever call to my remembrance the death that Thou hast undergone for me. Remind me of the endearments that Thou hast used towards me, and may the remembrance of them incite me more and more to love Thee, and to spend myself for Thee, who hast spent Thyself as a victim of love on the cross for me.

XXXI.

Qui etiam proprio Filio suo non pepercit, sed pro nobis omnibus tradidit illum quomodo non etiam cum illo omnia nobis donavit?

"He that spared not His only Son, but delivered Him up for us all, how hath He not also . . . given us all things?—*Rom.* viii. 32.

What flames of love ought not these words enkindle in our hearts: *Delivered Him up for us all!*[2] Divine justice, offended by our sins, must be satisfied; what, therefore, does God do? To pardon us, he wills that his Son should be condemned to death, and should himself pay the penalty due from us: *He spared not His only Son.*[3]

---

[1] "Diliges Dominum Deum tuum ex toto corde tuo."—*Matt.* xxii. 37.

[2] "Pro nobis omnibus tradidit illum."—*Rom.* viii. 32.

[3] "Proprio Filio non pepercit."—*Rom.* viii. 32.

O God! if the eternal Father were capable of suffering, what grief would he not have experienced in condemning to death, for the sins of his servants, his well-beloved and innocent Son! Let us imagine that we see the eternal Father, with Jesus dead in his arms, and saying, *For the wickedness of My people have I struck Him.*[1] Rightly did St. Francis of Paula exclaim, in ecstasy of love, when meditating on the death of Jesus Christ, "O love! O love! O love!" On the other hand, with what confidence should not the following words inspire us: *How hath He not also, with Him, given us all things?*[2] And how, my God, should I fear that Thou shouldst not give me pardon, perseverance, Thy love, Thy Paradise, and all the graces that I can hope for, now that Thou hast given me that which is most dear to Thee, even Thine own Son? I know what I must do to obtain every good from Thee,—I must ask for it for the love of Jesus Christ; of this Jesus Christ himself assures me: *Amen, amen, I say to you, if you ask the Father anything in My name, He will give it you.*[3]

My supreme and eternal God, I have hitherto despised Thy majesty and goodness; now I love Thee above all things; and because I love Thee, I repent with all my heart of having offended Thee, and would rather accept any chastisement than evermore offend Thee. Pardon me, and grant me those graces which I now ask of Thee, confiding in the promise of Jesus Christ. In the name of Jesus Christ I beseech Thee to give me holy perseverance to death, give me a pure and perfect love towards Thee, give me an entire conformity to Thy holy will, give me finally Paradise. I ask for all, and hope for all, from

---

[1] "Propter scelus populi mei percussi eum."—*Isa.* liii. 8.

[2] "Quomodo non etiam cum illo omnia nobis donavit?"—*Rom.* viii. 32.

[3] "Amen, amen dico vobis: si quid petieritis Patrem in nomine meo, dabit vobis."—*John*, xvi. 23.

Thee through the merits of Jesus Christ. I deserve nothing; I am worthy of punishment, not of graces, but Thou dost deny nothing to those who pray to Thee for the love of Jesus Christ. Ah, my good God, I see that Thou dost wish me to be all Thine; I also wish to be Thine, and will not fear that my sins should prevent me from being all Thine,—Jesus Christ has already satisfied for them,—and Thou, besides, art ready, for the love of Jesus Christ, to give me all that I desire. This is my desire and my request; my God, hear me! I wish to love Thee, to love Thee exceedingly; and to be altogether Thine. Most holy Mary, help me.

XXXII.

Nos autem prædicamus Christum crucifixum, Judæis quidem scandalum, Gentibus autem stultitiam.

"But we preach Christ crucified, unto the Jews indeed a stumbling-block, and unto the Gentiles foolishness."—1 *Cor.* i. 23.

St. Paul assures us that the Gentiles, hearing it preached that the Son of God had been crucified for the salvation of mankind, reckoned it folly: *But unto the Gentiles foolishness;*[1] as if they said, Who can believe such folly, that a God should have willed to die for the love of his creatures! "It seems a foolish thing," says St. Gregory, "that a God should wish to die for the salvation of man."[2] St. Mary Magdalen of Pazzi, also rapt in love, exclaims in an ecstasy, Do you not know, my sisters, that my Jesus is nothing but love? rather he is mad with love. I say that Thou art mad with love, my Jesus, and I will always say so.

My beloved Redeemer, oh that I could possess the hearts of all men, and with them love Thee as Thou deservest to be loved! O God of love, why, after Thou

[1] "Gentibus autem stultitiam."—1 *Cor.* i. 23.
[2] "Stultum visum est ut pro hominibus Auctor vitæ moreretur."— *In Evang. hom.* 6.

hast shed all Thy blood in this world and given Thy life for the love of mankind,—why, I say, are there so few men who burn with Thy love? For this end didst Thou come, namely, to kindle in our hearts the fire of Thy love, and Thou desirest nothing but to see it enkindled. *I am come to cast fire on the earth, and what will I but that it be kindled?*[1] I pray, then, with the Holy Church, in my name and in the name of every one living, kindle in them the fire of Thy love; enkindle them, enkindle them, enkindle them! My God, Thou art all goodness, all love, all infinite sweetness, boundless in love; make Thyself known to all, make Thyself loved. I am not ashamed of praying thus to Thee, although up to this time I have been more guilty than others in despising Thy love,— because now, enlightened by Thy grace, and wounded by the many arrows of love Thou hast shot forth from Thy burning and loving heart into my soul, I am determined no longer to be ungrateful to Thee as I have hitherto been; but I will love Thee with all my strength, I desire to burn with Thy love, and this Thou hast to grant me. I look not for sensible consolations in loving Thee; I do not deserve them, neither do I ask for them; it is enough for me to love Thee. I love Thee, my sovereign good; I love Thee, my God and my all.

XXXIII.

Posuit Dominus in eo iniquitatem omnium nostrum. . . , et voluit conterere eum.

"The Lord hath laid on Him the iniquity of us all. . . . And the Lord hath pleased to bruise Him."—*Isa.* liii. 6, 10.

Behold the extent of divine love towards man! The eternal Father loads the shoulders of his Son with our sins; *And He was pleased to bruise Him.*[2] He willed that his own son should suffer with the utmost rigor all the

---

[1] "Ignem veni mittere in terram: et quid volo, nisi ut accendatur?" —*Luke*, xii. 49.

[2] "Et voluit conterere eum."

punishment due to us, making him die on an ignominious cross overwhelmed with torments. The apostle is just, then, when speaking of this love, to call it too much love to ordain that we should receive life through the death of his beloved Son. *For His exceeding charity wherewith He loved us, even when we were dead in sins, hath quickened us together in Christ.*[1]

Thou hast, then, my God, loved me too much, and I have been too ungrateful in offending Thee and turning my back upon Thee. Ah, eternal Father, look upon Thine only-begotten, mangled and dead upon that cross for me, and for the love of him pardon me and draw my heart wholly to Thyself to love Thee. *A contrite and humble heart, O God, thou wilt not despise.*[2] For the love of Jesus Christ who died for our sins, Thou canst not despise a soul that humbles itself and repents. I know myself to be deserving of a thousand hells, but I repent with my whole heart for having offended Thee, the supreme Good. Reject me not, but have pity on me. But I am not content with a simple pardon; I desire that Thou shouldst give me a great love towards Thee, that I may compensate for all the offences that I have committed against Thee. I love Thee, infinite Goodness, I love Thee, O God of love. It is but little if I should die and annihilate myself for Thy sake. I desire to know how to love Thee as Thou deservest. But Thou knowest I can do nothing; do Thou make me grateful for the immense love that Thou hast had for me. I beg this of Thee for the love of Jesus, Thy Son. Grant that I may overcome everything in this life to please Thee, and that in death I may expire entirely united to Thy will, and so come to love Thee face to face with a perfect and eternal love in Paradise.

---

[1] "Propter nimiam charitatem suam qua dilexit nos, et cum essemus mortui peccatis, convivificavit nos in Christo."—*Eph*. ii. 5.

[2] "Cor contritum et humiliatum, Deus, non despicies."—*Ps*. l. 19.

XXXIV.

Ego sum Pastor bonus. Bonus Pastor animam suam dat pro ovibus suis.
"I am the Good Shepherd. The good shepherd giveth his life for his sheep."—
John, x. 11.

My Jesus, what dost Thou say? What shepherd would ever give his life for his sheep? Thou alone, because Thou art a God of infinite love, canst say, *And I lay down My life for My sheep.*[1] Thou alone hast been able to show to the world this excess of love, that being our God and our supreme Lord, Thou hast yet willed to die for us. It was of this excess of love that Moses and Elias spoke on Mount Tabor: *They spoke of his decease that he should accomplish in Jerusalem.*[2] Hence St. John exhorts us to love a God who was the first to love us: *Let us therefore love God because God first hath loved us.*[3] As if he said, If we will not love this God for his infinite goodness, let us love him at least for the love that he has borne us in suffering willingly the pains that were due to us.

Remember, then, my Jesus, that I am one of those sheep for whom Thou hast given Thy life. Ah, cast on me one of those looks of pity with which Thou didst regard me once when Thou wast dying on the cross for me; look on me, change me, and save me. Thou hast called Thyself the loving Shepherd who, finding the lost sheep, takes it with joy and carries it on his shoulders, and then calls his friends to rejoice with him: *Rejoice with me, for I have found the sheep that was lost.*[4] Behold,

[1] " Et animam meam pono pro ovibus meis."—*John*, x. 15.
[2] " Dicebant excessum ejus, quem completurus erat in Jerusalem." —*Luke*, ix. 31.
[3] "Nos ergo diligamus eum, quoniam Deus prior dilexit nos."— 1 *John*, iv. 19.
[4] " Congratulamini mihi, quia inveni ovem meam quæ perierat."— *Luke*, xv. 6.

I am the lost sheep; seek me and find me: *I have gone astray like a sheep that is lost; seek Thy servant.*[1] If through my fault Thou hast not yet found me, take me now and unite me and bind me to Thee, that Thou mayest not lose me again. The bond must be that of Thy love; if Thou dost not bind me with this sweet chain Thou wilt again lose me. Ah, it is not Thou who hast been wanting in binding me by holy love; but I, an ungrateful wretch, who have continually fled from Thee. But now I pray Thee, by that infinite mercy which caused Thee to come down to the earth to find me. Ah, bind me; but bind me with a double chain of love, that Thou mayest not lose me again, and that I may no more lose Thee. I renounce all the goods and pleasures of the world, and offer myself to suffer every pain, every death, provided that I live and die always united to Thee. I love Thee, my sweet Jesus; I love Thee, my good Shepherd, who hast died for Thy lost sheep; but know that this sheep now loves Thee more than himself, and desires nothing but to love Thee and to be consumed by Thy love. Have pity on him, then, and permit him never again to be separated from Thee.

XXXV.

Ego pono animam meam.... Nemo tollit eam a me, sed ego pono eam a meipso.
"I lay down My life.... No one taketh it away from Me; but I lay it down of Myself."—*John*, x. 17, 18.

Behold, then, the Word Incarnate, urged alone by the love that he preserves towards us, accepts the death of the cross to give to man the life that he had lost. Behold, says St. Thomas, a God does for man more than he could have done if man had been (so to speak) his God, and as if God could never have been happy without man.

---

[1] "Erravi sicut ovis quæ periit; quære servum tuum."—*Ps.* cxviii. 176.

"As if," these are the words of the saint, "man had been God's god, as if God could not be happy without him."[1] We sinned, and by sinning merited eternal punishment; and what does Jesus do? He takes upon himself the obligation of satisfaction, and he pays for us by his sufferings and his death: *Surely he hath borne our infirmities and carried our sorrows.*[2]

Ah, my Jesus, since I have been the cause of all the bitterness and anguish that Thou didst suffer while living on this earth, I pray Thee make me share the grief that Thou didst feel for my sins, and give me confidence in Thy Passion. What would have become of me, my Lord, if Thou hadst not deigned to satisfy for me? O infinite Majesty, I repent with my whole heart for having outraged Thee; but I hope for pity from Thee, who art infinite Goodness. Arise, O Saviour of the world, and apply to my soul the fruit of Thy death, and from an ungrateful rebel make me become such a true son as to love Thee alone, and to fear nothing but to displease Thee. May that same love which made Thee die on the cross for me destroy in me all earthly affections. My Jesus, take my whole body to Thyself in such a way that it may only serve to obey Thee; take my heart, that it may desire nothing but Thy pleasure; take my whole will, that it may wish for nothing but what is according to Thy will. I embrace Thee and press Thee to my heart, my Redeemer. Ah, do not disdain to unite Thyself to me. I love Thee, O God of love. I love Thee, my only good. How could I have the heart to leave Thee again, now that Thou hast taught me how much Thou hast loved me, and how many mercies Thou hast shown me, changing the punishments that were due to

[1] "Quasi homo Dei Deus esset, quasi sine ipso beatus esse non posset."—*Opusc.* 63, c. 7.

[2] "Vere languores nostros ipse tulit, et dolores nostros ipse portavit."—*Isa.* liii. 4.

Darts of Fire. 401

me into graces and caresses? O holy Virgin, obtain for me the grace of being grateful to thy Son.

XXXVI.

Delens quod adversus nos erat chirographum decreti, quod erat contrarium nobis, et ipsum tulit de medio, affigens illud cruci.

"Blotting out the handwriting of the decree that was against us, which was contrary to us. And he hath taken the same out of the way, fastening it to the cross."—*Coloss.* ii. 14.

The sentence was already recorded against us that was to condemn us to eternal death, as rebels of the offended Majesty of God. And what has Jesus Christ done? With his blood he has cancelled the writing of the condemnation, and, to deliver us from all fear, he has fastened it to his own cross, on which he died to satisfy for us to the divine justice. My soul, behold the obligation that thou art under to thy Redeemer; and hear how the Holy Spirit now reminds thee: *Forget not the kindness of thy surety.*[1] Forget not the kindness of thy surety, who, taking upon himself thy debts, has paid them for thee; and behold, the pledge of the payment has been already fixed to the cross. When, therefore thou dost remember thy sins, look upon the cross, and have confidence; look on that sacred wood stained with the blood of the Lamb of God sacrificed for thy love, and hope in and love a God who has loved thee so much.

Yes, my Jesus, I hope everything from Thy infinite goodness. It is property of Thy divine nature to render good for evil to those who repent of their sins, are sorry for having committed them, and who love Thee. Yes, I am sorry above all things, my beloved Redeemer, for having so much despised Thy goodness, and, wounded by Thy love, I love Thee, and I ardently desire to please Thee in everything that is Thy will. Alas! when I was

---

[1] "Gratiam fidejussoris ne obliviscaris; dedit enim pro te animam suam."—*Ecclus.* xxix. 20.

in sin, I was the servant of the devil, and he was my master. Now that I hope to remain in Thy grace, Thou alone, my Jesus, art the only Lord of my heart, and my only Love. Take possession of me, then; keep me always, possess me entirely; for Thine only do I desire to be. No, nevermore will I forget the pains that Thou hast suffered for me; so shall I be more and more inflamed, and increase in Thy love. I love Thee, my most dear Redeemer; I love Thee, O Word Incarnate; my treasure, my all, I love Thee, I love Thee.

XXXVII.

Si quis peccaverit, advocatum habemus apud Patrem Jesum Christum justum, et ipse est propitiatio pro peccatis nostris.

"But if any man sin, we have an Advocate with the Father, Jesus Christ the Just, and he is the propitiation for our sins."—1 *John*, ii. 1.

Oh, what great confidence do these words give to penitent sinners! Jesus Christ is in heaven, advocating their cause, and he is certain to obtain pardon for them. The devil, when a sinner has escaped from his chains, tempts him to be diffident of obtaining pardon. But St. Paul encourages him, saying, *Who is He that shall condemn? Jesus Christ that died, . . . who also maketh intercession for us.*[1] The Apostle means to say, If we detest the sins that we have committed, why do we fear? Who is he who will condemn us? It is Jesus Christ, the same who died, that we might not be condemned, and who is now in heaven, where he is advocating our cause. He goes on to say, *Who then shall separate us from the love of Christ?*[2] As if he would say, But after we have been pardoned with so much love by Jesus Christ, and have been received into his grace, who could have the heart

---

[1] "Quis est qui condemnet? Christus Jesus, qui mortuus est . . . , qui etiam interpellat pro nobis."—*Rom.* viii. 34.

[2] "Quis ergo nos separabit a charitate Christi?"—*Rom.* viii. 35.

to turn his back upon him, and separate himself from his love?

No, my Jesus, I no longer rely upon myself so as to live separated from Thee and deprived of Thy love. I weep over the unhappy days when I lived without Thy grace. Now I hope that Thou hast pardoned me I love Thee, and Thou lovest me. But Thou dost love with a boundless love, and I love Thee so little; give me more love. Infinite Goodness, I repent above all things for having hitherto so ill-treated Thee; now I love Thee above all things, I love Thee more than myself; and I take more delight, my God, in knowing that Thou art infinitely blessed than in my own happiness, because I love Thee better—being, as Thou art, worthy of infinite love—than myself, who deserve nothing but hell. My Jesus, I wish for nothing from Thee, but Thyself.

XXXVIII.

Venite ad me omnes, qui laboratis et onerati estis, et ego reficiam vos.

"Come to Me, all you that labor, and are burdened, and I will refresh you."—
Matt. xi. 28.

Let us listen to Jesus Christ, who from the cross to which he is nailed, and from the altar where he dwells under the sacramental species, calls us poor afflicted sinners to console us and enrich us with his graces. Oh, what two great mysteries of hope and love to us are the Passion of Jesus Christ and the Sacrament of the Eucharist!—mysteries which, if faith did not make us certain of them, would be incredible. That God should deign to shed even the very last drop of his blood! (for this is the signification of *effundetur*). *This is My Blood*, . . . *which shall be shed for many*.[1] And why? To atone for our sins. But then to will to give his own body as

[1] "Hic est sanguis meus, qui pro multis effundetur."—*Matt.* xxvi. 28.

food for our souls,—that body which had already been sacrificed on the cross for our salvation! These sublime mysteries must surely soften the hardest hearts, and raise up the most desperate sinners. Finally, the Apostle says that in Jesus Christ we are enriched with every good, so that no grace is wanting to us: *In all things you are made rich in Him. . . . So that nothing is wanting to you in any grace.*[1] It is enough that we invoke this God for him to have mercy on us; and he will abound in grace to all who pray to him, as the same Apostle assures us: *Rich unto all who call upon Him.*[2]

If, then, my Saviour, I have reason to despair of pardon for the offences and treacheries that I have been guilty of towards Thee, I have still greater reason to trust in Thy goodness. My Father, I have forsaken Thee, like an ungrateful son; but I now return to Thy feet, full of sorrow and covered with confusion for the many mercies that Thou hast shown me; and I say with shame, *Father, I am not worthy to be called Thy son.*[3] Thou hast said that there is rejoicing in heaven when a sinner is converted: *There shall be joy in heaven upon one sinner that doth penance.*[4] Behold, I leave all and turn to Thee, my crucified Father; I repent with my whole heart for having treated Thee with such contempt as to turn my back upon Thee. Receive me again to Thy grace, and inflame with Thy holy love, so that I may never leave Thee again. Thou hast said, *I am come that they may have life, and may have it more abundantly.*[5] Wherefore I hope to receive from Thee, not only Thy grace as I enjoyed it be-

---

[1] "In omnibus divites facti estis in illo . . . ita ut nihil vobis desit in ulla gratia."—1 *Cor.* i. 5.

[2] "Dives in omnes qui invocant illum."—*Rom.* x. 12.

[3] "Pater, non sum dignus vocari filius tuus."—*Luke,* xv. 21.

[4] "Gaudium erit in cœlo super uno peccatore pœnitentiam agente." —*Luke,* xv. 7.

[5] "Veni ut vitam habeant, et abundantius habeant."—*John,* x. 10.

fore I offended Thee, but a grace more abundant, which shall make me become all on fire with Thy love. Oh that I could love Thee, my God, as Thou dost deserve to be loved! I love Thee above all things. I love Thee more than myself. I love Thee with all my heart; and I aspire after heaven, where I shall love Thee for all eternity. *What is there to me in heaven, and besides Thee what have I desired on earth? O God, God of my heart and my portion forever.*[1] Ah, God of my heart, take and keep possession of all my heart, and drive from it every affection that does not belong to Thee. Thou art my only treasure, my only love. I wish for Thee alone, and nothing more. O Mary, my hope, by thy prayers draw me all to God.

[1] "Quid enim mihi est in cœlo? et a te quid volui super terram? . . . Deus cordis mei, et pars mea, Deus, in æternum."—*Ps.* lxxii. 25.

HYMN.

The Soul sighing for Jesus.

This heart of mine is sighing,
    And yet I know not why;
Its sighs with love are laden,
    But whither do they fly?

My trembling heart, oh, tell me,
    Wherefore these burning sighs?
" I sigh for God, I languish
    For Jesus," it replies.

Sigh on, my heart, and cease not
    With sighs of love to swell;
Spend all thy life in loving
    Him who loves thee so well.

Sigh on, and let thy Jesus
    Alone possess thy breast,
And all thy hope in Mary
    With childlike spirit rest.

Send forth thy sighs like arrows
    To wound thy conqu'ror's heart,
Then hope for gifts the choicest
    His goodness can impart.

My trembling sighs, ah, hasten,
    To Jesus haste away;
Then at his feet take refuge,
    And there forever stay.

Say that a heart all burning
    With love has sent you there;
And ask what it shall bid you,
    For he will grant its prayer.

To love with all its being
    Is all the gift it sues;
Ask,—for to one that loves him
    No prayer can God refuse,

Pious Sentiments of a Soul that Desires to Belong Entirely to Jesus Christ.

I.

Sentiments of a Lively Faith.

O ye atheists, who believe not in God, fools that you are; if you do not believe that there is a God, tell me who created you? How can you imagine that there are creatures existing, without a previous power having created them? This world which you admire, governed as it is in so beautiful and constant an order,—could chance, which has neither order nor mind, ever have made it? Poor wretches! you try to persuade yourselves that the soul dies like the body; but, O God, what will you say, when in the next world you find that your souls are immortal, and that throughout eternity you will be unable to repair the ruin you have incurred?

But if you believe that there is a God, you must also believe that there is a true religion: and if you do not believe that the religion of the Roman Catholic Church is the true one, tell me which is the true one? Perhaps that of the Pagans, who admit many gods, and so destroy and deny all of them. Perhaps that of the Mahometans, which is a mixture of fables, of follies, and of contradictions; a religion invented by an infamous impostor, and framed rather for beasts than for men. Perhaps that of the Jews, who, indeed, had at one time the true faith; but because they rejected their expected Redeemer, who taught the new law of grace, they have lost their faith, their country, and all. Perhaps that of those heretics who, separating themselves from our Church, which was first founded by Jesus Christ, and to whom he promised that she should never fail, have confused all revealed dogmas in such a way that the belief of each one is contrary to that of his neighbor.

Ah! it is most evident that our faith is the only true one. Either there is faith, and then there can be no other true religion but ours; or there is no faith, and then all religions are false. But this cannot be; for if there is a God, there must be a true faith and a true religion.

But what much greater fools are those Christians who hold the true faith, and live as if they did not believe it! They believe that there is a God, a just Judge, that there is a paradise and an eternal hell; and yet they live as if there were no judgment, no heaven, no hell, no eternity, no God.

O God, how can Christians believe in Jesus Christ, believe in a God born in a stable, a God living obscurely in a shop for thirty years, working for his livelihood every day as a simple servant; in fine, how can they believe in a God nailed on a cross, and dying, consumed with grief; and not only not love him, but even make a mockery of him by their sins!

O holy faith, enlighten all those poor blind creatures who run to eternal perdition! But this light does ever shine forth and enlighten all men, both the faithful and unbelievers: *True light, which enlighteneth every man.*[1] How is it, then, that so many are lost? O cursed sin, thou dost blind the minds of so many poor souls, who open their eyes when they enter eternity; but then they can no more remedy their error!

How is it, my Jesus, that so many of Thy servants have shut themselves up in caves and deserts, to attend only to their salvation; so many nobles and even princes have retired to the cloister, in order to live in poverty and unknown to the world, to make sure of

[1] "Lux vera, quæ illuminat omnem hominem.—*John*, i. 9.

their eternal salvation ; so many martyrs have left all; so many tender virgins have renounced marriage with the highest nobles of the earth, and have embraced such torments as the rack, have braved the axe, the coat of mail, the red-hot gridirons, and the most cruel deaths, rather than lose Thy grace ; while so many others live in sins and far from Thee for months and years?

I thank Thee, my Jesus, for the light Thou givest me, by which Thou makest me know that the goods of this world are but smoke, filth, vanity, and deceit, and that Thou art the true and only good.

My God, I thank Thee that Thou hast given me this faith, and that Thou hast made it so clear to us by the fulfilment of prophecies, by the truth of miracles, by the constancy of martyrs, by the sanctity of the doctrine, and by the wonderful propagation of the same throughout all the world; so that if it were not true, it would be impossible not to say that Thou hadst deceived us, in proving it to us by the numerous testimonies that Thou hast given us of it.

I believe all that the Church teaches me to believe, because Thou hast revealed all to us. Nor do I pretend to comprehend intellectually those mysteries which are above my mind; it is enough that Thou hast said so. I pray Thee to increase Thy faith in me.[1]

II.
Sentiments of Confidence.

My Jesus, the sight of my sins makes me afraid; but the sight of Thee crucified animates and consoles me still more. Thou wilt not deny me pardon, since Thou hast given me Thy blood and Thy life. Wounds of Jesus, ye are my hope!

My dear Redeemer, at my death, in those last and

---

[1] "Adauge nobis fidem."—*Luke*, xvii. 5.

more vehement assaults which hell will make against me, Thou must be my consolation. I hope that by the bitter death Thou didst undergo for me, Thou wilt make me die in Thy grace and burning with love to Thee. And by those three hours of agony which Thou didst suffer on the cross, give me the grace to suffer with resignation and for Thy love all the pains of my agony. And thou, Mary, by that grief which thou didst feel when Jesus thy Son expired, obtain for me the grace that my soul may expire while making an act of the love of God; and may come and love him, together with thee, for all eternity in Paradise.

My Jesus, by Thy merits I hope for the pardon of all the outrages that I have committed against Thee. How can I, my crucified Love, fear to obtain forgiveness, if Thou hast died in order to pardon me? How can I doubt Thy mercy, whilst it is that which made Thee come down from heaven to seek after my soul? How can I fear that Thou wilt deny me grace to love Thee, if Thou hast suffered so much to gain my heart? How can I fear that the sins which I have committed, and of which I repent with all my heart, may deprive me of Thy grace, if Thou hast shed all Thy blood to wash me from my sins, and to enable me to regain Thy friendship? I see that Thou dost give me an abhorrence of the insults I have offered Thee, Thou givest me light to know the vanity of the things of the world, Thou makest me know the love that Thou hast borne me, Thou givest me the desire of being all Thine;—all these are signs that Thou dost desire to save me; and I desire to be saved, to come to heaven, where I shall praise Thy mercies forever.[1] May the grief that I feel for having offended Thee remain always present to my mind, and may the desire of loving Thee with all my heart be fixed there too!

[1] " Misericordias Domini in æternum cantabo."—*Ps.* lxxxviii. 2.

My beloved Redeemer, my Judge, when, at the point of death, I shall enter into Thy presence, ah, drive me not away from Thy face: *When Thou comest to judge, condemn me not.*[1] Send me not to hell, because in hell I cannot love Thee. Ah, let not those wounds which Thou bearest imprinted in Thee as signs of the love that Thou hast borne me, be an eternal torment to me! Pardon me, then, before the hour of judgment shall come. Grant that, the first time I see Thee, Thy look may be one of mercy, and not of anger; declare me then to be Thy chosen sheep, and not a lost goat.

> "Thou sufferedst upon the tree;
> Let not vain Thy labor be."

Let not Thy blood have been wasted in my regard.

I am a sinner, it is true; but Thou sayest Thou desirest not the death of the sinner: *I desire not the death of the wicked; but that the wicked turn from his way and live.*[2] I give up all, I renounce all the goods of this world,—pleasures, riches, dignities, honors. I see that they are all filth, lies, and poison; and I turn to Thee, my God. My crucified Jesus, Thee alone do I desire, and nothing more!

O God! Thou hast given Thy life, my dear Redeemer, to gain heaven for me; and I, by my accursed pleasures, have lost heaven, and Thee the Infinite Good. I am not worthy to come into that kingdom of saints; but Thy blood and Thy death encourage me to hope this. Yes, I hope and wish for heaven; I desire it, my Jesus, not in order to enjoy more, but to be able to love Thee better, and to be certain of loving Thee always.

When, my love and my all, shall I see myself embrac-

---
[1] "Cum veneris judicare, noli me condemnare."
[2] "Nolo mortem impii, sed ut convertatur . . . et vivat.—*Ezek.* xxxiii. 11.

ing Thy feet, and kissing those wounds which have been the pledge of Thy love, and the cause of my salvation ? I read, my Jesus, in my conscience, the sentence of death which I deserve for the offences that I have committed against Thee ; but I read also upon Thy cross the sentence of pardon which Thou hast obtained for me by Thy death : *In Thee, O Lord, have I hoped; I shall never be confounded*.[1]

My dear Saviour, I hope Thou hast pardoned me all the past. When I call to mind the many times I have betrayed Thee, I tremble for the future ; but this very fear increases my confidence, because, knowing my weakness, I see that I can no longer trust in myself nor in the resolutions I have taken, and therefore I hope in Thee alone to give me strength to be faithful.

I am terrified at the thought of not knowing whether I shall be saved or lost ; but seeing Thee, Jesus, my Beloved, expiring on the cross for my salvation, I am animated by a sweet hope, which consoles me, and tells me that I shall love Thee without ceasing both in this life and in the next ; it tells me that one day I shall find myself in the kingdom of love, where I shall be entirely and forever consumed with Thy love, without the fear of losing Thee again. At this moment I do not even know whether I am worthy of Thy love or Thy hatred ; but I feel a great hatred of sin, I am disposed to suffer any death rather than lose Thy grace, I have a great desire to love Thee and to be all Thine ; these are all Thy gifts, and they are signs that Thou lovest me. If, then, I have reason to fear on account of my sins, I have still greater reason to confide in Thy goodness through the mercies Thou dispensest to me. I abandon myself therefore into Thy hands,—those hands which were pierced and nailed to the Cross, to rescue me from hell :

[1] "In te, Domine, speravi ; non confundar in æternum."—*Ps.* xxx. 2.

Into Thy hands I commend my spirit: Thou hast redeemed me, O Lord, the God of truth.[1]

The Apostle says: *He that spared not even His own Son, but delivered Him up for us all, how hath He not also, with Him, given us all things?*[2] If, then, O my Jesus, Thy Father has given Thee to us, and has sent Thee to die for us, how can we fear that he will refuse us pardon, his grace, perseverance, his love, and paradise? *With Him all things, all things without exception, has He given us.* Yes, my Redeemer, I hope all from the Blood Thou hast shed for me: *Help Thy servants, whom Thou hast redeemed by Thy precious blood.*[3]

O Queen of Heaven! O Mother of God, our hope, and the refuge of sinners, have pity on us![4]

III.

Sentiments of Penitence.

My Jesus, by that hatred which Thou hadst for my sins in the garden of Gethsemani, give me a true sorrow for all the offences that I have committed against Thee. O my accursed sins, I hate and detest you; ye have made me lose the grace of my Lord. I repent, my Jesus, for having turned my back upon Thee. Would that I had suffered any evil, rather than ever have offended Thee!

Ah, my sweet Redeemer, when I remember all the displeasure that I have given Thee, I do not weep so much on account of the hell I have deserved, as on ac-

---

[1] "In manus tuas commendo spiritum meum; redemisti me, Domine, Deus veritatis."—*Ps.* xxx. 6.

[2] "Qui etiam proprio Filio suo non pepercit, sed pro nobis omnibus tradidit illum; quomodo non etiam cum illo omnia nobis donavit?" —*Rom.* viii. 32.

[3] "Tuis famulis subveni, quos pretioso sanguine redemisti."

[4] "Spes nostra! salve; Refugium peccatorum! ora pro nobis."

count of the love Thou hast borne me! Yes; because the fire of hell which I have deserved is not so great as the immense love that Thou hast shown me in Thy Passion. And how is it, O God, that, knowing that Thou, my Lord, didst allow Thyself to be bound for me, scourged for me, spit upon for me, hanged upon a cross to die for me,—how is it that I could have so often despised Thy grace, and turned my back upon Thee? I should wish to die of grief; I repent, and am sorry above all things.

I know the evil that I have done in separating myself from Thee, my Sovereign Good. I ought to have suffered any pain, any evil, any death, rather than to offend Thee; and what greater evil could I commit than that of voluntarily losing Thy grace? Ah, my Jesus, my greatest affliction is, that I have despised Thy infinite goodness!

I thank Thee, my Lord, for the sweet promise of pardon that Thou hast made to sinners, of forgetting the sins of those who repent of having offended Thee: *I will not remember any of their iniquities.*[1] It is all the fruit of Thy Passion. O sweet Passion! O sweet mercy! O sweet love of Jesus Christ! Thou art my hope. What would have become of me, my Jesus, if Thou hadst not died, and paid the debt of my sins?

O God, I thought of offending Thee, whilst Thou thoughtest of using mercy towards me! After my sin, I thought not of repenting; but Thou didst think to call me. Finally, I have done all in my power to procure my own damnation; and Thou, so to say, hast done all Thou couldst not to see me damned. Thou art, then, an Infinite Good, and I have despised Thee; Thou art my Lord, and I have lost the respect due to Thee; Thou art infinite goodness, and I have turned my back upon

---

[1] "Omnium iniquitatum ejus . . . non recordabor."—*Ezek.* xviii. 22.

Thee ; Thou art worthy of infinite love, and hast loved me so much, and I have denied Thee my love, and displeased Thee so often. But Thou hast said that Thou canst not despise a heart that humbles itself and repents. Behold, I embrace Thy cross as a penitent ; I repent with all my heart for having despised Thee. Receive me to Thy favor, for the sake of that blood which Thou hast shed for me.

O Mary, hope of sinners, do thou obtain pardon for me, perseverance, and the love of Jesus Christ!

IV.

Sentiments of Purpose of Amendment.

My Jesus, I love Thee, and firmly resolve to lose all rather than forfeit Thy grace. I am weak, but Thou art strong. Thy strength will make me strong against my enemies. This I hope through Thy Passion : *The Lord is my light and my salvation, whom shall I fear?*[1]

I am not afraid, my crucified Lord, of losing my possessions, my relatives, or even my life ; I fear only to lose Thy friendship and Thy love. I am afraid that I may displease Thee, and may so see myself deprived of Thy grace. I pray Thee to keep alive in me this holy love ; help me to conquer all, that I may please Thee in everything.

"Most sweet Jesus, never permit me to be separated from Thee." I am the work of Thy hands ; I have been redeemed by Thy Blood ; do not abandon me to the misfortune of losing Thy love, and of separating myself from Thee. Assist me always in the dangers which shall befall me, and make me ever have recourse to Thee in them. I have a great desire to be faithful to Thee, and to live alone for Thee during the remainder of my

---

[1] " Dominus illuminatio mea et salus mea ; quem timebo ?"—*Ps.* xxvi. 1.

life ; do Thou give me the necessary strength. This do I hope from Thee.

My Jesus, increase in me the fear of displeasing Thee. I am horrified at my former treachery to Thee. But Thy merits console me ; and the many graces that Thou hast given me, these make me hope that Thou wilt not abandon me, now that I love Thee, since Thou hast shown me so much mercy while I thought not of loving Thee. I do not trust in my own strength,—I know well how little it is worth,—I confide altogether in Thy goodness ; and I firmly hope nevermore to see myself separated from Thee.

Oh that I could be assured that I should never lose Thee again, and that I should always love Thee ! But I resign myself to Thy divine will, which so disposes and ordains everything for my good, that I should live always in this uncertainty till death, to make me strive after a closer union with Thee, and to pray always, " Permit me nevermore to be separated from Thee." Yes, my Jesus, I repeat it (and give me grace always to repeat it) : " Let me never be separated from Thee ! let me never be separated from Thee !"

My Redeemer, I will no more depart from Thee. If all men should leave Thee, I will not leave Thee, even if it should cost me my life. I protest that, even if there was neither a heaven nor a hell, I would not leave off loving Thee ; because Thou, my Love, art worthy of infinite love, though there should be no reward for those who love Thee, nor any punishment for those who love Thee not.

Oh, if the years of my past life were to return, I would spend them all in loving Thee ! But they will never return. I thank Thee for having waited for me, and for not having sent me to hell as I deserved. And since Thou hast waited for me, I consecrate the rest of my life to Thee : I wish that all my thoughts, my desires, and my affections should serve only to please Thee, and to fulfil Thy holy will.

My beloved Jesus, I will not wait till Thou shalt be given to me at the point of death to embrace Thee. I embrace Thee now, and press myself closely to Thy nailed feet. My crucified love, to obtain for me a good death, Thou hast condescended to die a most agonizing and sorrowful death. At that hour, when every one will abandon me, do not Thou abandon me, my Redeemer; permit me not to lose Thee, or to separate myself from Thee. Receive me into Thy sacred wounds; and may my soul there breathe itself out in loving sighs, that it may come where Thou art to love Thee forever.

V.

Sentiments of Love.

O most loving Pastor of Thy sheep! for Thou hast spent, not all Thy riches, but all Thy Blood for them. O the goodness! O the love! O the tenderness of a God for souls! Oh that I also, my Jesus, could give my blood and my life on a cross, or under the axe, for the love of Thee, who hast given Thy life on the cross for me! May all angels and men eternally praise Thy infinite charity towards men! Oh that by my death I could make all men love Thee! Graciously receive, my Lord, this my desire; and give me grace to suffer something for Thee before I die.

Ah, the martyrs have done but little, O Saviour of the world, in suffering torments, the rack, iron hooks, burning helmets, and in embracing the most cruel deaths for the love of Thee, their God, who didst die for the love of them. Thou hast died for me also; and what have I done as yet, during all my life, for Thy love? My Jesus, let me not die in this state. I love Thee; and I offer myself to suffer for Thee as much as Thou wilt.

Accept this my offer, and give me strength to put it in execution.

My crucified Jesus! from Thy cross Thou didst foresee the offences I should commit against Thee; and, at the same time, Thou were procuring my pardon. Thou didst foresee my destruction, and didst prepare the remedy. Thou didst foresee my ingratitude, and Thou didst prepare for me remorse, fear, lights of salvation, calls to repentance, spiritual consolations, the tenderness and all the endearments of Thy charity. Thou didst vie with me to see which should conquer,—I in offending Thee, or Thou in redoubling Thy graces to me; I in provoking Thee to punish me, or Thou in drawing me to Thy love. When, my God, shall I have overcome all things to please Thee, who hast given Thy life for me? When shall I see myself detached from all, to be united to Thee and to Thy holy will? I desire it, and wish to perform it; but Thou must enable me to do so. I have not the strength to put it in effect. Thou hast promised to hear those that pray to Thee; I beseech Thee, with all my heart, not to let me live and die ungrateful for so much goodness.

O Word Incarnate! O Man of sorrows, born to live a life full of woes! O first and last of men!—first, because Thou art God, Lord of all; last, because in this world Thou wast contented to be ill-treated like the vilest of men,—even to suffer blows, spitting, mockeries, and curses from the very scum of the people. O divine lamb! O Infinite love, and worthy of infinite love! who hast given Thy blood and Thy life for me, I love Thee, and I offer Thee my blood and my life; but what is the blood of a worm in comparison to the blood of a God? —the life of a sinner to the life of an Infinite Majesty?

My beloved Jesus, who, urged on by the bowels of Thy mercy, didst come on earth to seek us lost sheep, ah, do not cease to seek me in my misery till Thou hast found me! Remember that for me also Thou didst shed Thy blood.

O my Jesus! who for my love didst deign to be sacrificed on the cross, there to die consumed with grief, I love Thee; and I desire to sacrifice myself entirely to Thy love. Stretch forth one of Thy pierced hands, and raise me from the mire of my sins; heal the many wounds of my soul; burn, destroy in me all those affections which belong not to Thee. Thou canst do this; grant it, then, for the sake of Thy Passion. This do I hope.

Because Thou hast loved me, Thou hast not denied me Thy blood and Thy life: I, because I love Thee, will deny Thee nothing Thou dost require of me. Without reserve Thou hast given Thyself all to me in Thy Passion and in the Sacrament of the Altar; I, without reserve, give myself all to Thee. Tell me what Thou desirest of me, and by Thy help I will do it all.

O ye damned souls! speak, and say, from the prison in which you are, what torments you most in hell,—the fire that burns you, or the love which Jesus Christ has borne you? Ah, assuredly the hell of your hell is this: to see that a God came down from heaven to earth to save you, and you, shutting your eyes to the light, have chosen of your own free will to be lost, and to lose this infinite good, even your God, who will be yours no longer, nor will you ever be able to regain him.

Ah, my Jesus! my treasure, my life, my consolation, my love, my all! I thank Thee for the light that Thou givest me. I love Thee; and I fear nothing but to lose Thee, and to see myself deprived of the power to love Thee. Grant that I may love Thee, and then do with me what Thou wilt.

My crucified Jesus! ah, break the chains of my inordinate affections, which prevent me from being wholly united to Thee, and bind me by the golden links of Thy love; but bind me so tightly, that I shall never be able to loose myself from Thee. The artifices of love that Thou hast used towards me were sufficient to bind me ; but I do not see myself united to Thee as I would wish. Do Thou accomplish this; Thou alone canst do it. O love of my Jesus, Thou art my love and my hope ! My Jesus, I desire Thy pure love, free from all interest of my own; and I care not if I am deprived of all personal satisfaction. Make me love Thee, and that alone is sufficient for me. I know, my Lord, that Thou desirest my love. This is why Thou hast not sent me to hell, and why for so many years Thou hast drawn near to me, and hast made these words sound in my ears : " Love Me, love me with all thy heart." Tell me what I must do in order to please Thee fully. Behold me now; I give Thee my will, my liberty, my whole self: I know not what more to give Thee. In this world I desire neither pleasures nor honors; the only happiness and honor that I desire is to be all Thine. Do Thou accept me. Help me with Thy grace, and never abandon me : *Be Thou my helper; forsake me not. Do not Thou despise me, O God, my Saviour.*[1] My love and my Saviour, despise me not as I have deserved. Remember how much my soul has cost Thee, and save me. My salvation is to love Thee, and to love none but Thee."

My Jesus, I wish for none but Thee. Thou hast said that Thou lovest those that love Thee.[2] I love Thee; do Thou also love me. There was a time when I saw myself hated by Thee for my sins; but now I detest them more than any other evil, and I love Thee above all things. Do Thou also love me, and hate me no more. I fear Thy hatred more than all the pains of hell.

[1] "Adjutor meus esto; ne derelinquas me, neque despicias me, Deus salutaris meus."—*Ps.* xxvi. 9.

[2] "Ego diligentes me diligo."—*Prov.* viii. 17.

Pious Sentiments.

My beloved Redeemer, I will say to myself, with St. Teresa: "Since I must live, may I live only for Thee. Let our own interests be put an end to. What can be a greater gain than to please Thee?"

VI.
Sentiments of Conformity to the Will of God.

My Jesus, every time that I say "Blessed be God," or "May the divine will be done," I intend to accept all that Thou hast ordained for me both in time and in eternity.

I desire no other office, no other habitation, no other clothing, no other food, no other health, but what it shall please Thee to send me.

I wish for no other employment, no other talent, no other fortune than that which Thou hast destined for me.

If Thou dost will that I should not succeed in my affairs; that my undertakings should fail; that my lawsuits should be lost; that my possessions should be taken away from me,—this also is my will.

If Thou wishest me to be despised, looked upon with ill-will, that others should be preferred to me, that I should be defamed and ill-treated even by my dearest friends,—this is my will also.

If Thou dost will that I should be made poor in all things, that I should be an exile from my country, imprisoned in a dungeon, and should be forced to live in continual sorrow and affliction,—this also is my will.

If Thou willest that I should be always ill, full of wounds, lame, obliged to remain in my bed abandoned by all,—this I desire also.

May all be as Thou pleasest, and as long as Thou pleasest. I put my very life into Thy hands, and accept whatever death Thou hast destined for me; and I also accept the death of my relatives and friends, and all that Thou shalt ordain.

I also unite my will to Thine in all that regards my spiritual welfare. I desire to love Thee in this life with all my strength, and to attain paradise, that I may love Thee as the seraphim love Thee ; but I am content with that which Thou dost will for me. If Thou dost will to give me but one single degree of love, of grace, of glory, I wish for no more, because it is Thy will. I value more the fulfilment of Thy will than anything that I could gain for myself.

In fine, my God, dispose of me and of my affairs as it pleases Thee. Look not at my pleasure ; for I desire nothing but what is in conformity to Thy will. Whether Thy treatment of me be harsh or kind, pleasant or unpleasant to me, I accept and embrace it, because both the one and the other come to me from Thy hand.

My Jesus, I accept besides, in an especial manner, my death, with all the pains which shall accompany it, according to Thy will, where Thou wilt, and at the time Thou wilt. I unite them, my Saviour, with Thy death ; and I offer them to Thee in testimony of the love I bear Thee. I desire to die to please Thee, and to fulfil Thy holy will.

VII.
Diverse Affections.

Oh, the unhappy state of a soul that is in sin and that has lost God! It lives on in wretchedness, but lives without God. God sees it, but no longer loves it ; he hates and abhors it. There was then, my soul, a time when thou didst live without God. The sight of thee no longer rejoiced the heart of Jesus Christ, as it did when thou wast in his grace, but was hateful to him. The blessed Virgin regarded thee with compassion, but detested thy deformity. When hearing Mass thou didst see Jesus Christ in the consecrated Host, who had become thine enemy.

Ah, my God, despised and lost by me, pardon me, and let me again find Thee ! I wished to lose Thee, but Thou wouldst not abandon me. And if Thou hast not yet returned to me, I pray Thee to come to me now that I repent with all my heart for having offended Thee. Let me be sensible of Thy return to me, by feeling a great sorrow for my sins, and a great love towards Thee.

My beloved Lord, rather than see myself separated from Thee and deprived of Thy grace, I am content to suffer any punishment. Eternal Father, for the love of Jesus Christ, I pray Thee to give me grace nevermore to offend Thee till my death ; may I die rather than turn my back upon Thee afresh.

Ah, my crucified Jesus, look on me with the same love with which Thou didst look on me when dying on the cross for me ; look on me, and have pity on me ; give me a general pardon for all the displeasure I have given Thee ; give me holy perseverance ; give me Thy holy love ; give me a perfect conformity to Thy will ; give me paradise, that I may love Thee there forever. I deserve nothing; but Thy wounds encourage me to hope for every good from Thee. Ah, Jesus of my soul, by that love which made Thee die for me, give me Thy love. Take away from me all affection to creatures, give me resignation in tribulation, and make Thyself the object of all my affections, that from this day forward I may love none other but Thee.

Thou hast created me, Thou hast redeemed me, Thou hast made me a Christian, Thou hast preserved me whilst I was in sin, Thou hast pardoned me many times; above all, instead of chastisements Thou hast increased Thy favors to me; who should love Thee, if I do not ? Arise, **and let Thy mercy triumph** over me ; and may the fire of love with which I burn for Thee be as great as the fire which should have devoured me in hell, O my Jesus, my love, my treasure, my paradise, my all !

O Incarnation, O Redemption, O Passion of Jesus Christ! O Calvary, O scourges, O thorns, O nails, O cross that did torment my Lord! O sweet names, which remind me of the love which a God has had for me, never depart from my mind and my heart; remind me always of the pains which Jesus my Redeemer has willed to suffer for me ! O most sacred wounds, ye are the perpetual resting-place of my soul; ye are the blessed furnaces where it forever burns with divine love !

My beloved Jesus, I have deserved hell, and to be forever separated from Thee ; I refuse not the fire nor the other pains of hell, if Thou for my just punishment dost will to send me there ; but what I cannot consent to is, not to be able to love Thee any more. Let me love Thee, and then send me where Thou wilt. It is just that I should suffer for my sins; but it is not just that I should have to hate and curse him who has created me, who has redeemed me, and who has loved me so much : justice requires that I should love and bless Thee forever. I bless Thee, then, and love Thee, Jesus my Love; and I hope to love and bless Thee for all eternity.

My sweet Redeemer, I know that Thou dost wish me to be wholly Thine. Ah, permit not that, from this day forward, creatures should have any part in that love which belongs altogether to Thee. Thou alone dost deserve all my affections, Thou alone art infinitely beautiful, Thou alone hast truly loved me ; Thee alone, then, will I love, and I will do all that I can to please Thee. I renounce all,—pleasures, riches, honors, and all the creatures of the earth ; Thou alone, my Jesus, art sufficient for me. Away from me, all earthly affections! Once

Pious Sentiments. 425

upon a time you had a place in my heart; but then I was blind: now that God by his grace has enlightened me, and has made me know the vanity of this world and the love which he has borne me, and that he desires me to give him all my love, I will consecrate it to him alone. Yes, my Jesus, take possession of my whole heart; and if I know not how to give it to Thee entirely as Thou desirest, take it Thyself, and make it Thine own. I love Thee, my God, with all my heart; I love Thee more than myself; draw me,[1] my Lord, all to Thee, and destroy in me the love of all created things.

O Paradise, O country of loving souls, O kingdom of love, O sure haven where God is loved for all eternity, and where there is no more fear of losing him! when shall I pass thy threshold, and see myself free from this miserable body, and delivered from the many enemies which continually try to deceive me in order to deprive me of divine grace? Ah, my crucified Jesus, discover to me the immense riches that Thou hast prepared for the souls that love Thee. Give me a great desire of possessing Paradise, so that, forgetting this world, I may there make my continual abode; and whilst I live, may I have no other desire than to come to see Thee and love Thee face to face in thy kingdom. I do not deserve this, and I know that at one time my name was written amongst those who were condemned to hell; but now that I am, as I hope, in Thy grace, I beseech Thee by that blood which Thou didst shed for me on the cross, to write me in the Book of Life. Thou hast died to gain Paradise for me: I wish for this, I ardently desire it, and I hope to attain it through Thy merits, that I may there ascend, to be consumed with Thy love by loving Thee with all my strength. There, forgetting myself and everything else, I shall think only of loving Thee, I shall desire

---
[1] "Trahe me."—*Cant.* i. 3.

nothing but to love Thee, and I shall do nothing but love Thee. O my Jesus, when shall this be? O Mary, Mother of God, by thy prayers bring me to Paradise. " Turn, then, most gracious advocate, thy eyes of mercy towards us; and after this our exile show unto us the fruit of thy womb, Jesus." [1]

[1] " Eia ergo, Advocata nostra! . . . Jesum, benedictum Fructum ventris tui, nobis post hoc exsilium ostende."

Sighs of Love towards God.

I.

Lord, who am I, that Thou hast loved me so much, and that Thou shouldst so much desire to be loved by me?

O my God, worthy of infinite love! I love Thee, or rather, I should say, I love Thee not.

I love Thee above all things; more than my life, more than myself; but still I see that I love Thee too little.

O King of Heaven! make Thyself also King of my heart, possess me entirely.

II.

I leave all, and turn to Thee. I embrace Tnee, I press Thee to my soul; despise me not, immeasurable good; I love Thee.

Now that Thou hast united me to Thee, O my Jesus, how can I see myself separated from Thee? I love Thee, and will never cease to love Thee.

Unite Thyself to me, Lord; let not the corruption of my sins drive Thee away from me.

III.

O God, O God! whom shall I love, if I love not Thee, my life, my love, my all?

Chosen among thousands.[1] My God, Thee only, Thee alone do I choose for my love.

My Redeemer, I desire no other but Thee.

---

[1] " Electus ex millibus."—*Cant.* v. 10.

Oh that I might be wholly consumed for Thee, who wast entirely consumed for me!

Take possession, Lord, of my whole will, and do with me what Thou pleasest.

IV.

O God not known! O God not loved! he is a fool that loves Thee not.

O my God! when I sinned I well knew that I was greatly displeasing Thee: have I done so? could I do so?

If I had died then, I should no longer have been able to love Thee. Now that I can, I will love Thee.

Lord, after having given me so many graces, permit me not to betray Thee again. Let me sooner die.

Thou hast borne with me, that I might love Thee. Yes, I will love Thee.

My God, Thou hast conquered me; I will withstand Thee no longer, I surrender myself to Thee.

V.

O God! how many years have I not lost when I might have been loving Thee!

I consecrate to Thee, my God, the remainder of my life; and who can tell how long it may be?

VI.

What are riches? what are honors? what are pleasures? God, God, I desire God alone.

O King of hearts, reign in my heart. Ah, draw me all to Thee!

Bind me, O God, to Thee, in such a way that I shall never be able to loose myself from Thee.

Thou wilt not leave me, I will not leave Thee. Then we shall always love each other, O my God, O my God.

VII.

Ah, make me all Thine before I die, my Jesus, my love, my life, my treasure, my all.

Ah, my Jesus and my judge, the first time I see Thee may it be with a propitious countenance!

When shall I be able to say, "My God, my God, I cannot lose Thee any more?"

When, Lord, shall I see Thee as Thou art, and contemplate Thee face to face for all eternity with my whole strength?

Ah, my Infinite Good, as long as I live, then, do I stand in danger of losing Thee.

My Jesus, what hast Thou not done to oblige me to love Thee? Yes, I will love Thee. I love Thee, I love Thee, I love Thee.

VIII.

O Eternal Father! for the love of Jesus give me Thy love.

Permit one of the most ungrateful creatures that have ever lived on the earth to love Thee.

My God, I will love Thee exceedingly in this life, that I may love Thee exceedingly in the next.

IX.

O my Jesus! Thou hast given Thyself all to me; I will give myself all to Thee.

What greater pleasure can I have than to please Thee, my God?

My beloved Jesus, I desire to love Thee as much as I have offended Thee.

X.

I love Thee, Infinite Goodness; make me know the great good that I love.

My Jesus, Thou art the vine, I am one of Thy branches; keep me always united to Thee; never let me detach myself from Thee.

O my God, how much do I rejoice in that Thou art infinitely happy!

XI.

Ah, Lord, where art Thou? Art Thou with me or not? Am I in Thy grace or not? Thou knowest that I love Thee, I love Thee; I love Thee more than myself.

Give me, my Jesus, that love which Thou requirest of me.

Oh that I had always loved Thee!

Oh, if I did but love Thee, my God, if I did but love Thee! I love Thee, but I love Thee too little.

Help me, Lord, to love Thee much, and to overcome all things to please Thee.

XII.

I give Thee my will. I desire nothing but that which Thou desirest.

I seek not consolations from Thee; I desire only to please Thee, my God, my love, my all.

O infinite God! I am not worthy to love Thee; suffer me to love Thee.

I hope to love Thee forever, O Eternal God!

O my dear Jesus! Thou hast suffered so much for me; I desire to suffer for Thee as much as it shall please Thee.

O God of my soul! I can trust myself no longer to live without loving Thee.

O will of God, Thou art all my love.

XIII.

O Omnipotent God! make me a saint.

It will be for Thy glory, Lord, to make one who was Thine enemy become Thy loving servant.

Sighs of Love towards God.

Thou didst seek me, my God, while I was yet flying from Thee; Thou wilt not discard me now that I seek Thee.

My most loving Jesus, in order to pardon me Thou hast not pardoned Thyself.

I thank Thee for giving me time to love Thee. Yes, my God, I love Thee, I love Thee, I love Thee, and I will always love Thee.

O God worthy of infinite love, may I this day be entirely converted to Thee, my love, my all!

Chastise me as Thou wilt; but deprive me not of the power of loving Thee.

XIV.

Divine Father, Thou hast given me Thy Son; I, a miserable creature, give myself to Thee. Accept me, for pity's sake.

I desire, Lord, to make up for the offences I have committed against Thee, by doing all that I can to please Thee.

I desire to love Thee, my God, without interest, without ceasing, and without reserve.

XV.

My Jesus, despised for me, may I be despised for Thee!

My tormented Jesus, grant that I may suffer for the love of Thee all the pains of this life.

I should wish, my Redeemer, to die for Thee, who didst die for me.

I resolve this day to give myself all to Thee.

Oh that all would love Thee as Thou deservest!

Grant, Lord, that I may leave undone nothing which I know to be pleasing to Thee.

Happy shall I be if I lose all to gain Thee, my God, my all.

O Jesus! sacrificed for me, I sacrifice to Thee my whole will.
O my God! when shall I be all Thine?

XVI.

Lord, what wilt Thou have me to do?[1]
I will sing forever the mercies of the Lord.[2]
Who shall separate me from the love of Christ?[3]
O good Jesus! never permit me to be separated from Thee, never permit me to be separated from Thee![4]
What have I in heaven? and, besides Thee, what do I desire upon earth? Thou art the God of my heart, and the God that is my portion forever.[5]

XVII.

"May I die for the love of Thy love, who didst deign to die for the love of my love!"[6]
"My love is crucified."[7]
"Give me but Thy love and Thy grace, and I am rich enough."[8]
"Let me die, Lord, that I may see Thee."[9]

XVIII.

Ah, my Jesus, they who love Thee not do not know Thee!

---

[1] "Domine, quid me vis facere?'—*Acts*, ix. 6.

[2] "Misericordias Domini in æternum cantabo."—*Ps.* lxxxviii. 2.

[3] "Quis nos separabit a charitate Christi?"—*Rom.* viii. 35.

[4] "O bone Jesu! ne permittas me separari a te."

[5] "Quid enim mihi est in cœlo? et a te quid volui super terram? . . . Deus cordis mei, et pars mea, Deus in æternum."—*Ps.* lxxii. 25.

[6] "Amore amoris tui moriar, qui amore amoris mei dignatus es mori."—*St. Francis Assisi.*

[7] "Amor meus crucifixus est."—*St. Pasch.*

[8] "Amorem tui solum cum gratia tua mihi dones, et dives sum satis."—*St. Ignatius Loyola.*

[9] "Moriar, Domine, ut te videam."—*St. Augustine.*

I love Thy pleasure, Lord, more than all the pleasures of the world.

My crucified Jesus, how is it that all are not captivated by Thee?

Thou hast died for me; oh that I could die for Thee, my Jesus, my love, my treasure, my all!

Lord, what shall I render to Thee for all Thou hast suffered for me?

XIX.

Infinite Goodness, I esteem Thee above all things; I love Thee with all my heart; I give myself entirely to Thee. Accept my poor love, and give me more love. May I forget all, that I may remember only Thee, my love, my all

I would wish to love Thee worthily. Accept, O God, this my desire, and give me Thy love!

XX.

I have offended Thee enough; now I desire to love Thee.

O God! O God! I am Thine, and Thou art mine.

May all be lost; but let not God be lost.

Let it cost what it will to gain God, he can never be dearly bought.

Thou alone, my Jesus, Thou alone art sufficient for me.

XXI.

O Mary! look on me, and draw me all to God.

Most amiable mother, I love thee exceedingly.

O Mother! give me confidence in thee, and make me always to have recourse to thee.

O Mary! it is for thee to save me. Thou canst make me holy: this is my hope. Have pity on me.

Aspirations of Love to Jesus Christ.

I.

My Jesus, Thou alone art sufficient for me.

My love, do not permit me to separate myself from Thee. When shall I be able to say, " My God, I cannot lose Thee any more?"

II.

Lord, who am I, that Thou shouldst desire so much to be loved by me?

And whom shall I love, if I love not Thee, my Jesus? Here I am, Lord; dispose of me as Thou pleasest.

Give me Thy love; I ask nothing more.

Make me all Thine before I die.

III.

Eternal Father, for the love of Jesus Christ have pity on me.

My God, I wish for Thee alone, and nothing more.

IV.

O my Jesus! would that I could be entirely spent for Thee, as Thou didst spend Thyself entirely for me!

If I had died while I was in sin, I could no more have loved Thee; now that I can love Thee, I will love Thee as much as I can.

To Thee do I consecrate all the remainder of my life.

I wish only, and I wish in all things, that which Thou dost desire.

V.

When I see Thee for the first time, my Jesus, may it be with a look of mercy.

May I die rather than ever offend Thee again.

Thou wilt not leave me, I will not leave Thee; so shall our love endure in this world and in the next.

VI.

I should be too ungrateful, O my Jesus, if I loved Thee but little, after so many graces.

Thou didst give Thyself all to me; I give myself all to Thee.

Thou lovest those that love Thee. I love Thee; do Thou also love me. If I love Thee but little, give Thou me the love Thou requirest of me.

What hast Thou not done to oblige me to love Thee? Make me conquer all things to please Thee.

VII.

Accept the love of a soul which has offended Thee so deeply.

Show me the immense good Thou art, that I may love Thee exceedingly.

I desire to love Thee exceedingly in this life, that I may love Thee exceedingly in the next.

VIII.

I hope to love Thee for all eternity. O Eternal God! Oh that I had always loved Thee! Oh that I had died rather than have offended Thee!

I give Thee my will, my liberty; dispose of me as Thou pleasest.

May my only happiness be to please Thee, O Infinite Goodness.

O my God! I rejoice in that Thou art infinitely happy.

IX.

Thou art omnipotent; make me a saint.

Thou hast sought me while I was fleeing from Thee; Thou didst love me when I despised Thy love; abandon me not, now that I seek Thee and love Thee.

May I this day give myself wholly to Thee.

X.

Send me any chastisement, but deprive me not of the power of loving Thee.

I thank Thee that Thou givest me time to love Thee. I love Thee, my Jesus, I love Thee; and I hope to die repeating, " I love Thee, I love Thee."

XI.

I desire to love Thee without reserve, and to do all that I know to be pleasing to Thee.

I love Thy good pleasure more than all the pleasures of the world.

I accept all the troubles that may happen to me, provided I love Thee, O my God. O my Jesus! that I could die for Thee, as Thou didst die for me!

XII.

Oh that I could make all men love Thee as Thou deservest!

O will of God, thou art my love.

O God of love, give me love.

XIII.

O Mary, draw me all to God.

O my Mother, make me always have recourse to thee. It is for thee to make me a saint. This is my hope.

Maxims for the Direction of a Soul that Desires to Attain Perfection in the Love of Jesus Christ.

1. To desire ardently to increase in the love of Jesus Christ.
2. Often to make acts of love towards Jesus Christ. Immediately on waking, and before going to sleep, to make an act of love ; seeking always to unite your own will to the will of Jesus Christ.
3. Often to meditate on his Passion.
4. Always to ask Jesus Christ for his love.
5. To communicate often, and many times in the day to make spiritual Communions.
6. Often to visit the Most Holy Sacrament.
7. Every morning to receive from the hands of Jesus Christ himself your own cross.
8. To desire Paradise and death, in order to be able to love Jesus Christ perfectly and for all eternity.
9. Often to speak of the love of Jesus Christ.
10. To accept contradictions for the sake of Jesus Christ.
11. To rejoice in the happiness of God.
12. To do that which is most pleasing to Jesus Christ, and not to refuse him anything that is agreeable to him.
13. To desire and to endeavor that all should love Jesus Christ.
14. To pray always for sinners and for the souls in purgatory.
15. To drive from your heart every affection that does not belong to Jesus Christ.
16. Always to have recourse to the most holy Mary, that she may obtain for us the love of Jesus Christ.

17. To honor Mary in order to please Jesus Christ.
18. To seek to please Jesus Christ in all your actions.
19. To offer yourself to Jesus Christ to suffer any pain for his love.
20. To be always determined to die rather than commit a wilful venial sin.
21. To suffer crosses patiently, saying, "Thus it pleases Jesus Christ."
22. To renounce your own pleasures for the love of Jesus Christ.
23. To pray as much as possible.
24. To practise all the mortifications that obedience permits.
25. To do all your spiritual exercises as if it were for the last time.
26. To persevere in good works in the time of aridity.
27. Not to do nor yet to leave undone anything through human respect.
28. Not to complain in sickness.
29. To love solitude, to be able to converse alone with Jesus Christ.
30. To drive away melancholy.
31. Often to recommend yourself to those persons who love Jesus Christ.
32. In temptation, to have recourse to Jesus crucified, and to Mary in her sorrows.
33. To trust entirely in the Passion of Jesus Christ.
34. After committing a fault, not to be discouraged, but to repent and resolve to amend.
35. To do good to those who do evil.
36. To speak well of all, and to excuse the intention when you cannot defend the action.
37. To help your neighbor as much as you can.
38. Neither to say nor to do anything that might vex him. And if you have been wanting in charity, to ask his pardon and speak kindly to him.

Maxims for Attaining Perfection. 439

39. Always to speak with mildness and in a low tone.

40. To offer to Jesus Christ all the contempts and persecution that you meet with.

41. To look upon Superiors as the representatives of Jesus Christ.

42. To obey without answering and without repugnance, and not to seek your own satisfaction in anything.

43. To like the lowest employments.

44. To like the poorest things.

45. Not to speak either good or evil of yourself.

46. To humble yourself even towards inferiors.

47. Not to excuse yourself when you are reproved.

48. Not to defend yourself when found fault with.

49. To be silent when you are disquieted.

50. Always to renew your determination of becoming a saint, saying, "My Jesus, I desire to be all Thine, and Thou must be all mine."

Acts that the Christian should Perform Every Day.*

On Rising, after having made the Sign of the Cross.

My God! I adore Thee, I love Thee with my whole heart.

I thank Thee for all Thy benefits, especially for having preserved me during the past night.

I offer Thee all my actions and sufferings of this day, in union with the actions of Jesus and Mary; and I make the intention of gaining all the indulgences that I can gain.

I purpose, O Lord! to avoid offending Thee this day, especially. . . .

It is good to make a resolution, particularly about the fault into which we fall the oftenest.

I beg Thee, for the love of Jesus, to grant me the grace of perseverance.

I resolve to conform myself to Thy holy will, and particularly in those things that are contrary to my inclination, saying always, O Lord! Thy will be done. My Jesus, keep Thy hand over me this day! Most Holy Virgin Mary, take me beneath thy mantle. And do Thou, O Eternal Father, help me for the love of Jesus

---

* It is known that St. Alphonsus in his ascetical books took care frequently to remind his readers of the most essential practices of Christian life; hence the many admonitions and various formulas, now short, now long, which we distribute among the complete works as well as among the smaller separate works, conformably to the author's design.—ED.

and Mary! O my angel guardian and my holy patron saints, assist me.

Our Father, Hail Mary, Creed; three *Hail Marys* in honor of the purity of Mary.

At the Beginning of Work or Study.

O Lord! I offer Thee this work.

Before Meals.

O my God! bless this food and me, that I may commit no fault about it, and may all be for Thy glory.

After Meals.

I thank Thee, Lord, for having done good to one who was Thine enemy.

When the Clock strikes.

My Jesus, I love Thee; never permit me to offend Thee again, and let me never be separated from Thee.

In adverse circumstances.

O Lord! since Thou hast so willed it, I will it also.

In Time of Temptation.

Frequent invocation of the holy names of Jesus and Mary.

When conscious or doubtful of having sinned, say at once:

O my God! I repent of having offended Thee. O Infinite goodness! I will do so no more.

And if you should sin grievously, go to confession as soon as possible. Before going to rest in the evening thank God for all the favors you have received; then make an examination of conscience. Afterwards make the Christian acts in the following manner:—

Act of Faith.

O my God, who art infallible truth, because Thou hast revealed it to Thy Church, I believe all that she proposes to my belief! I believe that Thou art my God, the Creator of all things; that Thou dost reward the just with an eternal paradise, and dost punish the wicked in hell for all eternity. I believe that Thou art one in essence, and three in persons, namely, Father, Son, and Holy Ghost. I believe in the Incarnation and death of Jesus Christ. I believe, in fine, all that the Holy Church believes. I thank Thee for having made me a Christian; and I protest that I will live and die in this holy faith.

Act of Hope.

O my God, confiding in Thy promises, because Thou art powerful, faithful, and merciful, I hope through the merits of Jesus Christ to obtain pardon of my sins, final perseverance, and the glory of paradise.

Act of Love and Contrition.

O my God, because Thou art infinite goodness, worthy of infinite love, I love Thee with all my heart above all things; and for the love of Thee I love my neighbor also. I repent with all my heart, and am sorry above all things for all my sins, because by them I have offended Thy infinite goodness. I resolve, by the help of Thy grace, which I beseech Thee to grant me now and always, rather to die than ever to offend Thee again. I purpose, also, to receive the holy Sacraments during my life, and at the hour of my death.

These three acts have been enriched with indulgences.*

Other Acts.

I adore Thee, my God, I humble myself in the abyss of my nothingness to the will of Thy infinite majesty.

I firmly believe all that Thou hast deigned to make known to me by means of Thy holy Church; and I am ready to give my life a thousand times for this faith.

---

* See *Rule of Life*, vol. i., ch. 2, § 6.

I place all my hope in Thee. Whatever good I may have, either in this life or in the next, I hope for from Thee, through the merits of Jesus Christ.

I love Thee, Infinite Goodness, with all the affection of my heart and of my soul, because Thou dost merit all my love. I unite my imperfect love to that which all the saints, most holy Mary, and Jesus Christ bear to Thee. Because Thou art the supreme good, I am sorry and repent of all my sins, detesting them as much as possible above every other evil. I resolve for the future rather to die than to consent to anything that may give Thee the slightest displeasure.

I offer Thee now and forever my body, my soul, and all my senses and faculties. Do with me, Lord, and with all that belongs to me, what Thou pleasest. Give me Thy love and final perseverance, and grant that in all temptations I may always have recourse to Thee.

I resolve to employ myself entirely in those things which are pleasing to Thee, being ready to suffer any pain and labor in order to please Thee.

I desire that all should serve and love Thee. I recommend to Thee all the souls in purgatory, as also all sinners; enlighten and strengthen these unhappy creatures, that they may know and love Thee. I rejoice exceedingly that Thy happiness is infinite, and will never have an end.

I thank Thee for all the benefits that Thou hast bestowed upon mankind, but especially upon me, who have been more ungrateful than others.

My beloved Jesus, I take refuge within Thy sacred wounds; do Thou there defend me from all temptations, till Thou shall grant me to see Thee and love Thee eternally in paradise.

Prayer of St. Bonaventure to Jesus Christ, to obtain His Holy Love.

Most sweet Jesus, pierce the interior of my soul with the sweet wound of Thy love, that my soul may ever languish and be dissolved with Thy love and with the desire of possessing Thee, and long to quit this life, that it may come to be perfectly united to Thee in a blessed eternity. Grant that my soul may ever thirst after Thee, speak only to Thee, find Thee, and do all for Thy glory. Grant that my heart may be ever fixed on Thee who art my only hope, my riches, my peace, my refuge, my confidence, my treasure, and my inheritance.

A Short Prayer to Jesus Christ Crucified, to obtain a Happy Death.

My Lord Jesus Christ, through that bitterness which Thou didst suffer on the cross, when Thy blessed soul was separated from Thy sacred body, have pity on my sinful soul, when it shall depart from my miserable body, and shall enter into eternity.

Prayer to the Ever Blessed Virgin, to obtain the Love of Jesus and a Happy Death.

O Mary! thou who so much desirest to see Jesus loved, if thou lovest me this is the favor which I now ask of thee, to obtain for me a great love for Jesus Christ. Thou obtainest from thy Son whatever thou pleasest: pray, then, for me, and console me. Obtain for me a great love for thee, who of all creatures art the most loving and beloved of God. And through that grief which thou didst suffer on Calvary, when thou didst behold Jesus expire on the cross, obtain for me a happy death, that by loving Jesus and thee, my Mother, I may come to love thee forever in heaven.

Manner of Making Mental Prayer.

I.

In the PREPARATION the following acts may be made:

My God, I believe that Thou art here present, and I adore Thee with all my heart.

I deserve at this moment to be burning in hell for my sins; O my God, I am sorry for having offended Thee; pardon me.

Eternal Father, grant me light in this meditation, that I may profit by it.

Then say a *Hail Mary* to the divine Mother, and a *Glory be to the Father*, etc., in honor of St. Joseph, of your guardian angel, and of your holy patron.

II.

Then read the MEDITATION; yet whilst reading we should stop at those passages in which the soul finds that it is receiving nourishment; and we should try to produce acts of humility, of thanksgiving, especially of contrition and love, of resignation and self-offering. We should say:

O Lord! dispose of me as Thou pleasest; help me to know all that Thou requirest of me; I wish to please Thee in all things.

We should especially apply ourselves to making petitions, in asking God to grant us holy perseverance, his love, light, and strength, that we mostly need in order to do his holy will, and to pray always.

III.

The CONCLUSION is made thus: We make the resolution to avoid some particular sin into which we fall the oftenest. We should finish by saying an *Our Father* and a *Hail Mary*, and never forget, in meditation, to recommend to God the souls in Purgatory, and all poor sinners.

Short Ejaculatory Prayers

FOR THE TWELVE GREATEST SOLEMNITIES IN THE YEAR,—SEVEN OF OUR LORD AND FIVE OF THE BLESSED VIRGIN,—WHICH MAY BE USED AT ANY OTHER TIME AND ON ANY DAY, ACCORDING TO EACH ONE'S DEVOTION.

For the Feasts of our Lord.

1. For the Holy Nativity of our Lord.

Come, my Jesus, and be born in my heart!

2. For the Circumcision of our Lord.

May Thy name, O Jesus, be my joy!

3. For the Epiphany.

With Thy Magi, O Jesus, I adore Thee, and love Thee.

4. For Easter.

My Jesus, let me first suffer, and then rejoice with Thee.

5. For the Ascension of our Lord.

Take my heart also with Thee into heaven.

6. For Pentecost.

Holy Spirit, Light, Fervor, and Perseverance.

7. For the Feast of Corpus Christi.

Jesus, our food! Jesus, our sweetness! Jesus, our joy!

For the Feasts of the Blessed Virgin.

1. For the Immaculate Conception.

Most holy Virgin, free from sin, and full of grace, at the first moment of Thy existence may I be free from sin, and in the grace of God, at the last moment of my life!

2. For the Nativity of the Ever-blessed Virgin.

Thy birth, O Blessed Virgin, was holy; may my death be holy!

3. For the Annunciation.

O Virgin ever blessed, thou art raised to the sublime dignity of Mother of God; may I remain always faithful in his service!

4. For the Purification.

Most holy Virgin, purer than the angels after thou hadst brought forth thy Son, may I be purified at least after I have sinned!

5. For the Assumption.

Most holy Virgin, who didst die out of pure love, may I at least die with contrition!

Let all, all be devout to the most blessed Virgin; and, after God, let us honor the most holy Virgin.

Happy is the Christian who has the most blessed Virgin for him; and miserable is that Christian who has not the blessed Virgin on his side.

The most blessed Virgin can obtain everything from God, because she is his true Mother, and is so much beloved by him; and she will do everything for us, because she is our Mother also, and loves us so much.

Let us, therefore, always try to gain her friendship more and more; let us ingratiate ourselves with her more and more, by continually fostering in ourselves devotion towards her.

Every day let us say her Rosary.

Fast in her honor every Saturday.

Observe the novenas and the fast before all her principal feasts.

Practise some devotion also on all her smaller, even her smallest feasts,

And let us, besides, in all our necessities, in all our misfortunes, have recourse to her, have confidence in her; and through her security in life, security in death, security through all eternity.

It must be so; for do you know what takes place in heaven? The most blessed Virgin stands before her divine Son—*Mater stat ante Filium*—and she reminds him of the womb where he was enclosed for nine months, and the sacred breast at which she so often gave him suck. The Son places himself before his divine Father—*Filius stat ante Patrem*—and shows him his pierced side and those sacred wounds which he received for our sake—*et ostendit Patri latus et vulnera*. And at the sight of such sweet pledges of a Son's love, he can deny nothing to his divine Son,—all is obtained for us: *ibi nulla poterit esse repulsio, ubi sunt tot amoris insignia*—there can be no refusal where there are so many signs of love. It is thus that St. Bernard, himself so devout to the ever-blessed Virgin, encourages us.

But since the most blessed Virgin is also the Mother of fair love, as well as being true Mother of God—*Mater pulchræ dilectionis*—she obtains for us holy love; and through her means God himself fills our hearts with his holy love—*ignem sui amoris accendat Deus in cordibus nostris*.

Live, Jesus our love, and Mary our hope!

HYMN.

Aspirations to Jesus.

Jesus, my sweetest Lord!
Jesus, my sweetest Lord!
My Good, my Spouse adored!

My God, O goodness infinite,
  My life's true life art Thou;
Flame of my heart, my Spouse most sweet,
  My love to Thee I vow.
            Jesus, my sweetest Lord, etc.

Jesus, for Thee I pine away,
  My love, and my desire;
And, more enamoured day by day,
  I burn with heavenly fire.
            Jesus, my sweetest Lord, etc.

Ah, Jesus, I would ever weep
  That I offended Thee;
Mine was ingratitude too deep,
  And basest treachery.
            Jesus, my sweetest Lord, etc.

My Jesus, when I call to mind
  That such a wretch as I
Have crucified a God so kind,
  I fain of grief would die.
            Jesus, my sweetest Lord, etc.

Hymn.

O Thou my hope, make me remain
  Faithful for evermore :
Better to die than be again
  As I have been before.
    Jesus, my sweetest Lord, etc.

While night and day my foes allure,
  In Thee do I confide :
Take Thou and place my heart secure
  Within Thy piercèd side.
    Jesus, my sweetest Lord, etc.

With Thy sweet chains, O Jesus, bind
  My rebel heart to Thee
Till death; my safety I will find
  In such captivity.
    Jesus, my sweetest Lord!
    Jesus, my sweetest Lord!
    My Good, my Spouse adored!

Novena to the Holy Name of Jesus.*

FIRST DAY.

The Giving of the Glorious Name of Jesus.

Consider, devout soul, that the holy name of Jesus is not a name invented by man, but it comes from God, who wished it to be made known by the archangel Gabriel, as St. Luke testifies: *His name was called Jesus . . . by the angel.*[1] St. Bernard[2] also says that this name is not a simple figure of things, a shadow without reality, but it is a palpable truth. *Jesus* is a name that expresses perfectly the hypostatic union of the divine nature and of the human nature. The world could not have been saved by a pure God, because God is impassible, nor by a pure man, because man is limited and finite. This is the reason why the holy name *Jesus*, which signifies the same as Saviour, as the angel declares,[3] has been given to the Son of God, made man through Mary, in order to show that both as God and man he accomplished the redemption of mankind by delivering them from the slavery of sin at the same time. In short, *Jesus* is a name that comprises infinity, eternity, immensity, wisdom, justice, mercy, and all the adorable perfections of God. What happiness for us to be reconciled with the eternal Father through the merits of this divine Media-

[1] "Vocatum est nomen ejus Jesus . . . ab Angelo."—*Luke*, ii. 21.
[2] *In Circ.* s. 1.
[3] *Matt.* i. 21.

---

* This Novena and the Hymn that follows it remained unpublished till the year 1866. They were recently discovered at Rome among the writings of our holy author.—ED.

tor who has had the goodness to pay our debt at the cost of his precious blood!

Adorable Jesus! if Thou hast sacrificed Thyself to deliver Thy people from the hands of their enemies in order to acquire an eternal name, it would be but fair that this name should surpass and eclipse every other name, even that of the seraphim, as St. Paul says: *Being made so much better than the angels, as He hath inherited a more excellent name than they.*[1] And if the eternal Father has wished that this name should be that of his Son, mayest Thou grant that, having experienced on earth its happy effects, we may arrive at the complete happiness in heaven to praise Thee and to bless Thee for all eternity.

Our Father, Hail Mary, and Glory be to the Father, etc., nine times, in honor of the giving of the glorious name of Jesus. We finish with the following versicle and prayer:

Sit Nomen Domini benedictum!	Blessed be the Name of the Lord!
Ex hoc nunc et usque in sæculum!	From henceforth and for evermore!
Oremus.	Let us pray.
Deus, qui unigenitum Filium tuum constituisti humani generis Salvatorem, et Jesum vocari jussisti, concede propitius ut; cujus sanctum Nomen veneramur in terris, ejus quoque aspectu perfruamur in cælis. Per eumdem Christum Dominum nostrum. Amen.	God, who didst appoint Thine only-begotten Son Saviour of mankind, and didst command that he should be called Jesus, mercifully grant that we may enjoy the vision of him in heaven, whose holy Name we venerate on earth. Through the same Christ our Lord. Amen.

[1] "Tanto melior Angelis effectus, quanto differentius præ illis nomen hereditavit."—*Heb.* i. 4.

SECOND DAY.

Sweetness of the Name of Jesus.

Consider, devout soul, that there is no name in the world that is equal to the name of Jesus in sweetness. " Nothing is sweeter to chant," says St. Bernard, "nothing more agreeable to hear, nothing more charming to think of, than the name of Jesus, the Son of God."[1] To preach it, is to give light to the understanding, is to inflame the will; to think of it, is to feed the soul, is to excite its fervor; to call on it, is to win grace and unction. In fact, we see that if a Christian find himself weighed down by sadness, whether through the artifice of our common enemy or in consequence of some misfortune that has befallen him, as soon as the name of Jesus passes from his heart to his tongue, by the light of this divine name, darkness is dispersed, the mind becomes calm, the heart is strenghtened, the faculties brighten up, and everything returns to life. This is the reason why St. Paul, as soon as he received from the divine Word himself the commission to publish his glorious name, began to repeat it so often, not only in his discourses, but also in the Epistles that he addressed to the Corinthians, Galatians, Colossians, Hebrews, and to all other nations. He knew by experience how sweet is the name of Jesus, what is its virtue to dispel the darkness of error and bring back men to the happy paths of perfect belief. Oh, how happy shall we be if in all our trials, on all sorrowful occasions, we take care to invoke the glorious name of Jesus, and while invoking it with our lips to consecrate our hearts to it! Then our soul will taste an ineffable sweetness, which we can never find here below.

Most amiable Jesus, Thou art the master of the angels, the Creator of the world, the sovereign of the universe.

[1] *Office of the Holy Name.*

Thou art my Lord and my God.[1] I thank Thee for having wished to take this most holy name for our consolation, for our encouragement, and for our salvation; and as, in this valley of tears, we have recourse in our needs to Thy glorious name by sweetly invoking it, grant that we may finish our lives in peace while saying, Live Jesus! Live our Saviour!

Our Father, Hail Mary, and *Glory be to the Father,* etc., nine times, in honor of the sweetness of the name of Jesus; versicle and prayer as above.

THIRD DAY.

Salutary Operation of the Name of Jesus.

Consider, devout soul, that the name *Jesus* signifies nothing else than Saviour; and St. Peter[2] assures us that the Eternal Father has not given to men any other name by which they may be saved amidst the snares of this deceitful world, than the adorable name of Jesus. It is this name that makes the truth of faith shine everywhere, and that calls all men from the depths of darkness to the adorable light of the Gospel. It is by virtue of this adorable name that the Apostle gave light to the blind, made the lame walk, healed the sick, raised the dead to life, and filled the whole world with astonishment. And if the Angel at first announced that Jesus would bring life into the world by delivering it from the cruel slavery into which Adam had plunged it, this good Saviour confirmed this promise himself when he declared[3] that he had come so that his sheep might have life, and might have it more abundantly. By virtue of his name we see idolatry overthrown, to the great confusion of the pagan princes and priests, who did all in their power to

---

[1] "Dominus meus et Deus meus."—*John,* xx. 28.
[2] *Acts,* iv. 12.
[3] *John,* x. 10.

Novena to the Holy Name of Jesus. 455

maintain it. We see the Synagogue vanquished, to the shame of the Jews, who with threats of punishments had forbidden the Apostles[1] to preach and invoke this powerful name. Ah! since in this world there is no good that is not due to the efficiency of the name of Jesus, let us acknowledge with humility and with love the source of all these riches; and if in the past we have been unfaithful, let us once for all put an end to our ingratitude, and let us endeavor to repair all the wrong that we have done, and say:

O amiable and holy name of Jesus! may the seraphim of heaven give to Thee for me suitable thanks, and never cease to praise Thee by forever repeating that Thou dost merit all glory, all honor, and all power. My sweet Saviour, I hope to obtain, by virtue of Thy name, the salvation of my body and soul; I hope that with this glorious name in my heart and on my lips, victorious over the world and the flesh, I shall have the happiness to sing Thy praises and to bless the august Trinity for ever and ever.

Our Father, *Hail Mary*, and *Glory be to the Father*, etc., nine times, in honor of the salutary operation of the name of Jesus; versicle and prayer as above.

FOURTH DAY.

Efficacy of the Name of Jesus.

Consider, devout soul, the efficacy of the adorable name of Jesus for the purpose of offering prayers pleasing to God, and of obtaining all that we ask of him. This name opens for us the way to arrive promptly at the feet of the Most High, and to have our prayers heard at once. The Gospel also attests that the prayers of Jesus himself have always been heard by virtue of his great name, and that he authorizes us to say, when

[1] *Acts*, iv. 17.

speaking to God, "Our Father, who art in heaven." In consideration of the name of Jesus, God looks with a favorable eye upon our petition; he accepts it kindly and grants it, because he sees that it bears his seal, and is marked with the precious blood of the Lamb that was immolated for us. For this reason Jesus exhorted the Apostles, and exhorts all, that we should ask in his name all that we ask of his Father, in order to be sure that we shall obtain it: *If you ask the Father anything in My name, He will give it to you.*[1] It is enough for him to hear the petition, and he will bestow upon us the favors that have been asked of him in the name of his beloved Son, with whom he is well pleased, and who, in order to satisfy his offended justice, has shown himself obedient ever unto death. We should, then, know how to profit by the efficacious power of the holy name of Jesus; being sure that our prayers will be heard, we should, often, every hour of the day, repeat our prayers to the Eternal Father, and we shall advance in perfection on the road of the divine precepts, until we attain the happiness of seeing and possessing him for all eternity in heaven.

O Sweet Jesus, our love and our hope! since Thou hast deigned to assume mortal flesh, in order to open to us the gate of pardon, and to render our prayers efficacious by virtue of Thy glorious name, grant that, in order to obtain from the heavenly Father graces and gifts, our prayers for perseverance may be heard, so that, faithful to the divine law to the end of our lives, we may, with Thy holy name on our lips, pass from this valley of tears to the glory of paradise.

Our Father, Hail Mary, and *Glory be to the Father,* etc., nine times, in honor of the efficacy of the name of Jesus; versicle and prayer as above.

[1] "Si quid petieritis Patrem in nomine meo, dabit vobis."—*John,* xvi. 23.

FIFTH DAY.

Consolation afforded by the Name of Jesus.

Consider, devout soul, that those who love Jesus are, by his sweet name, so much sustained and consoled in their afflictions and in all other evils that it is for them a happiness to suffer in order to be able to participate in these ineffable consolations. This, says St. Bernard,[1] is the reason why the Spouse of the Canticles compares the name of Jesus to oil : *Thy name is as oil poured out;*[2] for as oil gives light, food, and a remedy, so is the name of Jesus a light, food, and a remedy. All spiritual food without the name of Jesus is insipid and dry. No writing, however charming and interesting it may be, can be sweet nourishment to the heart if it does not contain the name of Jesus. If in the sermons, discussions, and conversations, the name of Jesus is not mentioned, the soul tastes no sweetness. The name of Jesus is honey to the mouth, melody to the ear, joy to the heart. This name rendered sweet the pains and torments of the martyrs, of the virgins, and of all the saints, so that when reduced to the last extremity, while invoking the name of Jesus, they were comforted ; they forgot their sufferings. Why should we, then, be cast down in our tribulations, in the storms that arise against us to throw us, perhaps, into the abyss of despair, when the name of Jesus alone can lighten the weight that oppresses us, and can carry us to heaven? Have, therefore, recourse to Jesus, faithful soul ; attach thyself to Jesus ; he is a secure haven in which we need not fear to suffer shipwreck ; he is the morning-star that guides us through the darkness to the way of salvation ; he is the watchful sentinel that discovers the enemy and puts

[1] *In Circ. s.* 1.
[2] "Oleum effusum, nomen tuum."—*Cant.* i. 2.

him to flight; in a word, he renders easy and sweet to you the yoke of the evangelical law.

O amiable name of Jesus! Thy devoted servants invoke Thee, since Thou art so prompt in coming to console them in their necessities. For pity's sake, my good Master, come also to give consolation to my soul, which, though sorely pressed on account of its combat with redoubtable enemies, and which, because of bad conduct, is perhaps far away from Thee, yet like the prodigal son hopes to find in Thee the clemency of a Father, and dares to say to Thee, with St. Anselm, O my Saviour! save me; save me, Jesus, and do not permit me to perish.

Our Father, Hail Mary, and *Glory be to the Father*, etc., nine times, in honor of the consolation that is afforded by the name of Jesus; versicle and prayer as above.

SIXTH DAY.

Peace that is given us by the Name of Jesus.

Consider, devout soul, that Jesus being the King of peace, whose presence was sought throughout the earth, as the Church proclaims in the Office,[1] cannot but bring consolation to us. So, before his birth, in order to give a token that his coming was peaceful, his divine Providence wished that the whole world, under the reign of Cæsar Augustus, should be in perfect peace. And when he was born the voice of the angels chanted the heavenly song that was heard by the shepherds of Bethlehem: "Glory to God in the highest, and on earth peace to men of good will." On this passage of the Psalmist: *In His days shall justice spring up, and abundance appear*, Origen remarks that the coming of Jesus, our Saviour, brought peace to the whole world. In fact, he reconciled us with the Eternal Father, from whom original sin had separated

[1] *In Nat. D.* 1 *Vesp.*

Novena to the Holy Name of Jesus. 459

us; he also quieted in us the inferior powers which in consequence of the same sin had revolted against the spirit; so that, says St. Bernard, by virtue of the name of Jesus, the transports of passion are appeased, the movements of concupiscence are repressed, and the soul finds itself brought back to the state it would have enjoyed had it persevered in original justice. This being the case, let us imitate St. Teresa, who, when asked by Jesus himself about her name, answered, without knowing him, "My name is Teresa of Jesus." Let us also say that we belong to Jesus; in this way we shall enjoy a continual peace on earth, and while becoming peaceful, which quality makes us the chosen of God, we shall perpetuate it forever in heaven.

O amiable Jesus! Thou art truly the king of peace and of tranquillity; this we experience when we invoke Thee in our trials. In the midst of the sad vicissitudes that afflict and harass us in this valley of tears, it is only in Thy very holy name that we find calm, peace, and repose. Ah! grant that we may hereafter be more fervent in the practice of good works, and that by faithfully following in the footsteps of the good Shepherd, like humble and docile sheep, we may be delivered from the nocturnal incursions of the infernal wolves, and seek shelter and protection in the fold of Thy very sweet heart.

Our Father, Hail Mary, and *Glory be to the Father*, etc., nine times, in honor of the peace that is given by the name of Jesus; versicle and prayer as above.

SEVENTH DAY.

Strength of the Name of Jesus.

Consider, devout soul, that Jesus, impelled by the ardor of his infinite love towards mankind, without leaving the bosom of his Father, clothed himself in our flesh, and came into the world to deliver us from its chains; that like an irresistible warrior he attacked man's enemy, Satan, who had become the sole master of this world that groaned under his tyranny because of the transgression of the law of God; that, finally, he conquered it, crushed it, and snatched from its grasp, as he himself has said,[1] the arms in which it had trusted, and divided the spoils of the conquered among his children, to whom he gave as their armor the sacraments and the sign of the cross. This victory made him so formidable to the demons of hell that his name alone causes all the powers of the abyss to tremble, and fills them with terror, as the Apostle says: *In the name of Jesus every knee should bow, of those that are in heaven, on earth, and under the earth.*[2] When hearing this adorable name the angels of light prostrate themselves out of respect, to render homage and to testify their gratitude to their Redeemer; but the angels of darkness humble themselves by force, being compelled by virtue of the Most High to acknowledge their conqueror, notwithstanding the shame, the spite, and the rage that torment them. And as for ourselves, whom Jesus has principally redeemed, let us imitate the good angels in rendering on our knees due thanksgiving for the good he has done for us, and by remembering not only the profound veneration with which his glorious name should fill our hearts, but the firm hope he gives us to acquire by his merits a blessed life in eternity.

O Jesus! Thou who didst allow to shine forth the strength of Thy name, to deliver us from the servitude of sin and the slavery of the devil, deign now and always to preserve our souls from all unworthy subjection. Show that Thou art a perfect conqueror by preserving Thy conquest with vigilant care; protect it from the iniquitous robber, so that he may no longer attempt to take

---

[1] *Luke*, xi. 22.
[2] *Phil.* ii. 10.

Novena to the Holy Name of Jesus. 461

even partial possession of it. Grant that our souls may always be worthy of belonging entirely to Thee. We can do nothing of ourselves without the help of Thy grace; be Thou so good as to aid us, to protect us, and, prostrate at the feet of Thy throne, we shall gratefully sing forever of the strength of Thy glorious name.

Our Father, Hail Mary, and *Glory be to the Father,* etc., in honor of the strength of the name of Jesus; versicle and prayer as above.

EIGHTH DAY.

Power of the Name of Jesus.

Consider, devout soul, that the glorious name of Jesus is wonderful in what regards the divine mysteries of his Incarnation, birth, life, Passion, death, resurrection, and ascension; all of which comprise things so profound and so sublime that the angels themselves cannot comprehend them, and that the Apostle[1] has said that they are a scandal in the eyes of the Jews and folly in the eyes of the Gentiles, while we see in them a celestial light that shows us the wisdom and the love of God. Yet consider, also, that it is wonderful in regard to its power. Jesus is the Word of the Eternal Father, and as nothing has been done without him, says St. John,[2] so nothing is preserved, nothing is governed independently of his power. It is by virtue of his name that the barbarians renounced idolatry to embrace the Gospel, the Apostles producing these marvellous conversions by the prodigies and miracles that astonished nature. It is by virtue of his name that the sun is resplendent, that the moon reflects its light, that the stars shine, that the planets follow their course, that men live on the earth, that the monarchs reign, that the humble are exalted, that the proud are humbled, mountains are levelled, that

[1] 1 *Cor.* i. 23.
[2] *John,* i. 3.

valleys are filled up; for the Eternal Father has placed all things in the hands of his Son.¹ And which of us will not prostrate himself to adore this name that is so great, so majestic, that fills heaven and earth! Which of us will not render to him the homage that is due to him, when we know that it is owing to Jesus that we are Christians, and that in imitating him, we can aspire to the glory of paradise!

O Jesus, all-powerful and truly wonderful! If the eyes of our soul had not been opened and enlightened by the light of faith, which Thou hast taught us by Thy own mouth, how should we ever have been able to know Thy divine mysteries! Without this aid, we should have always been buried in the darkness of ignorance and in the shadows of death. May thanks be always given to our sweet Jesus, who has had compassion on us, and in opening to us the gates of heaven has constituted us heirs of the eternal kingdom! And if our heart is entirely filled with joy for having received so great gifts, may our tongue never cease to praise him who is the author of them.

Our Father, Hail Mary, and *Glory be to the Father,* etc., in honor of the power of the name of Jesus; versicle and prayer as above.

NINTH DAY.

Triumphs of the Name of Jesus.

Consider, devout soul, that the name of Jesus did not triumph only over death and sin by despoiling hell of its power, but it also expelled from the height of the cross the devil, who had usurped the dominion over this world by drawing all things to himself. He not only triumphed over the persecutor, as he did over Saul on the road to Damascus, but he confounded his adversaries in

¹ *John,* xiii. 3.

Rome by means of St. Bernardine of Sienna and St. John Capistran. He also triumphed over the enemies of the faith in Hungary and Belgrade, where a small number of the faithful struck with consternation and vanquished the grand armies of the Ottoman Empire. The children of St. Francis, animated by the spirit and the example of this seraphic patriarch, were the first to revive the triumphs of the name of Jesus by erecting to it the first altar at Auxerre, in France, till the coming of St. Bernardine, who was proclaimed the principal author of the renewal of this devotion by the declaration of Pope Eugene IV.: *Characterem nominis Jesu ipse Bernardinus de novo adorandum invenerat.* "Bernardine has himself discovered the value of the name of Jesus, so that it might be venerated anew." Finally, the office and the veneration of the holy name of Jesus were extended to the whole Catholic world; and if the Seraph of Assisi revived the fervor of souls towards the Passion of our Redeemer, the Saint of Sienna, his son, everywhere revived the devotion to the adorable name which was the origin of our redemption. To propagate this devotion Pope Sixtus V. granted an indulgence of a hundred days to those who salute each other with the words: " Praised be Jesus Christ," and answering, " Forever." Moreover, a plenary indulgence is granted to him who at the hour of death invokes the name of Jesus, if not with lips, at least in the heart. If, therefore, the glorious name of Jesus has done so much good for us, let us, after the example of St. Mechtilde, consecrate ourselves to him, —our heart, our faculties, our words, so that everything in them may breathe the sweetness of Jesus; and also our actions, that one may see shine in them the virtues that Jesus practised on earth—his humility, his patience, his charity, his zeal, his love. By this means we shall, after this life, be able to take part in the triumphs of Jesus in heaven.

Novena to the Holy Name of Jesus.

O very amiable and very sweet Jesus, our God, our Saviour, our Father! how can we, miserable creatures that we are, respond to the love that Thou hast shown and that Thou dost not cease to show us? It is certain that Thou alone as God canst justly compensate Thyself, since before Thee we are as if we were not. And then, what have we that is not a gift of Thy bounty? Yes, O supreme good! all that we have comes from Thee; and as such we render it to Thee, in offering to Thee, in this novena that we celebrate in honor of Thy name, all that we are. But, knowing that our love is agreeable to Thee, we give Thee specially our whole heart which is the source of this love. Deign to receive it as belonging to Thee; and if it is not worthy of Thee, purify it of its imperfections and of its defects, so that we may see shine in it the name of Jesus, that, it loves only Jesus; that it thinks only of Jesus; and that, the superabundance of its affections communicating itself to our tongue, Jesus may be praised and blessed through all ages. Amen.

Our Father, Hail Mary, and *Glory be to the Father,* etc., in honor of the triumphs of the name of Jesus; versicle and prayer as above.

HYMN*

To the Infant Jesus.

Fair Child, how beautiful Thou art!
No greater can Thy sweetness be.
Thou hast possession of my heart;
It burns with love alone for Thee.

Thy littleness, O tender Child!
Is like a dart of love divine
That pierces with Thy sweetness mild,
To-day, this hardened heart of mine.

My only Good! Thy tears I see,
And Thou art trembling now with cold,
My heart that has been charmed by Thee
Is sad as I Thy grief behold.

Oh, may my heart Thy home e'er be,
My Love, my Conqueror Thou art.
Oh, take the food I offer Thee,
The food of love within my heart.

* See note page 451. There is another hymn to the Infant Jesus, page 332.

INDEX.

A

ACTS that every Christian should make every day, 440.
ADVENT, Meditations for every day, 172, 286.
ANGEL, God could have sent an angel to redeem man, 87.

C

CHRISTMAS, Discourses for the novena, 13; for the feast, 140; Meditations for the novena, 214, 301; for the octave and the following days, 238. Indulgences, 347.
CIRCUMCISION, Meditation for the feast, 316.
CONFORMITY to the will of God, pious sentiments, 421.
CONTRITION and firm purpose, pious sentiments, 415.

D

DETACHMENT from pleasures, 98; — from riches, 113; — from honors, 126.

E

EPIPHANY, Meditations for the feast and the octave, 268, 318.

F

FAITH, pious sentiments, 407.

I

INCARNATION, grandeur of this mystery, 174. See *Jesus Christ;* confidence with which it should inspire us, 289.
INDULGENCES attached to the exercises of piety in honor of the Infant Jesus, 347.

J

JESUS CHRIST was the arrow chosen and reserved to pierce the hearts of men, 89. His goodness and love for men, 192, 201, 214, 225, 232, 287, 293, 301, 309, 362; he loves each one as he does all, 92.

To gain our love, he made himself like us, 13, and made himself ours, 85 ; he becomes little, 32, 206, 219, 240, 303, poor, 305, humble, 306, suffering, 308. His desire to suffer for us, 296 ; his sufferings, 194, 199, 217, 222, 227; his greatest affliction was the foreseeing of our ingratitude and of our sins, 104, 204, 229, 294. His birth, 140, 179, 238, 314. Hymn, 322; he is in swaddling-clothes, 243 ; taking milk, 246 ; lying on straw, 248 ; sleeping, 251, weeping, 253 ; his solitude in the stable, 258, his occupation, 261, his poverty, 263; adored by the Magi, 268, 316; presented in the Temple, 270; his exile in Egypt, 272, 274, 311, 312; his return, 277 ; his dwelling at Nazareth, 279, 281, 312; his loss in the Temple, 283. He became a servant to deliver us from slavery, 46 ; he wished to appear as a sinner to atone for our sins, 59, 187, 197; his compassion for sinners, 67 ; he made himself weak to communicate to us strength, 73 ; he made himself afflicted to teach us mortification, 98 ; he made himself poor to teach us detachment from terrestrial things, 113 ; he humbled himself to teach us humility, 126, 182. He obtained for us more than Adam made us lose, 53. Happiness in having been born after his coming, 55, 185, 291. He is the fountain of grace, 208, 212, 298 ; the physician of our souls, 210 ; virtue in the name of Jesus, 151, 255, 320, 451. We ought to give him our whole heart, 93 ; sentiments of love, 417 ; aspirations, 434. Hymns, 332, 406, 465. Maxims for attaining perfection in the love of Jesus Christ, 437. Examples or apparitions of the Infant Jesus, 164.

JOSEPH, St., goes with the Blessed Virgin to Bethlehem, where Jesus is born in a stable, 142, 235, 314 ; he addresses the divine child, hymn, 330. He goes with Mary to present Jesus in the Temple, 270. He conducts Jesus and Mary to Egypt, 272, 311; he supports them by his labor, 274; he brings them back to Palestine, 277 ; and goes to dwell at Nazareth, where Jesus works with him, obeys, and edifies him, 279, 281, 312. He loses Jesus and finds him again, 283.

M

MAGI, they come to adore the newly-born Saviour, 268, 316.
MARY goes to Bethlehem, 140, 235 ; there she gives birth in a cave to the divine Infant, 145 ; she wraps him in swaddling-clothes, 243 ; nourishes him with her milk, 246 ; lays him on straw, 248 ; contemplates him sleeping, hymn, 328 ; she receives the Magi, 268 ; she offers Jesus in the Temple, 270 ; she carries him to Egypt, 272, 311; weans and dresses him, 312 ; she returns to

Palestine, 277 ; she remains at Nazareth, where Jesus obeys and edifies her, 279, 281, 312 ; she loses Jesus and finds him again, 283. Happy he who is devoted to Mary, 447.

MENTAL PRAYER, manner of making it, 445.

MORTIFICATION, taught by the example of Jesus Christ, 98.

N

NOVENA, indulgenced for the feast of Christmas, 347 ; for every month, 348. Novena of the name of Jesus, 451.

S

SIN : the foreseeing of our sins was that which afflicted Jesus Christ most, 104.

SINNER, repentant, confidence that he ought to have in seeing Jesus an infant, 39, 209 ; in seeing him take the form of the sinner, 65 ; sentiments of confidence, of contrition, etc., 409.

T

TEMPTATIONS, two means to overcome them, sacraments and prayer, 78.

STANDARD CATHOLIC BOOKS

PUBLISHED BY

BENZIGER BROTHERS,

CINCINNATI: NEW YORK: CHICAGO:
343 Main St.   36 & 38 BARCLAY ST.   178 Monroe St.

ABANDONMENT ; or, Absolute Surrender of Self to Divine Providence. By Rev. J. P. CAUSSADE, S.J. 32mo,   *net*, 0 40
ANALYSIS OF THE GOSPELS of the Sundays of the Year. By Rev. L. A. LAMBERT, LL.D. 12mo,   *net*, 1 25
ART OF PROFITING BY OUR FAULTS, according to St. Francis de Sales. By Rev. J. TISSOT. 32mo,   *net*, 0 40
BIBLE, THE HOLY. With Annotations, References, and an Historical and Chronological Index. 12mo, cloth,   1 25
Also in finer bindings.
BIRTHDAY SOUVENIR, OR DIARY. With a Subject of Meditation for Every Day. By Mrs. A. E. BUCHANAN. 32mo,   0 50
BLESSED ONES OF 1888. By ELIZA A. DONNELLY. 16mo, illustrated,   0 50
BLIND FRIEND OF THE POOR: Reminiscences of the Life and Works of Mgr. de SEGUR. 16mo,   0 50
BROWNSON, ORESTES A., Literary, Scientific, and Political Views of. Selected from his works, by H. F. BROWNSON. 12mo,   *net*, 1 25
BUGG, LELIA HARDIN. The Correct Thing for Catholics. 16mo,   0 75
—— A Lady. Manners and Social Usages. 16mo,   1 00
CANONICAL PROCEDURE in Disciplinary and Criminal Cases of Clerics. By the Rev. FRANCIS DROSTE. Edited by the Right Rev. SEBASTIAN G. MESSMER, D.D. 12mo,   *net*, 1 50
CATECHISM OF FAMILIAR THINGS. Their History and the Events which led to their Discovery. 12mo, illustrated,   1 00
CATHOLIC BELIEF; or, A Short and Simple Exposition of Catholic Doctrine. By the Very Rev. JOSEPH FAÁ DI BRUNO, D.D. Author's American edition edited by Rev. LOUIS A. LAMBERT. 200th Thousand. 16mo.
Paper, 0.25 ; 25 copies, 4.25 ; 50 copies, 7.50 ; 100 copies,   12 50
Cloth, 0.50; 25 copies, 8.50; 50 copies, 15.00; 100 copies,   25 00

"When a book supplies, as does this one, a demand that necessitates the printing of one hundred thousand [now two hundred thousand] copies, its merits need no eulogizing."—*Ave Maria.*
"The amount of good accomplished by it can never be told."—*Catholic Union and Times.*

STANDARD CATHOLIC BOOKS.

CATHOLIC FAMILY LIBRARY. Composed of "The Christian Father," "The Christian Mother," "Sure Way to a Happy Marriage," "Instructions on the Commandments and Sacraments," and "Stories for First Communicants." 5 volumes in box, 2 00

CATHOLIC HOME ANNUAL. A Charming Annual for Catholics. 0 25

CATHOLIC HOME LIBRARY. 10 volumes. 12mo, each, 0 50
Per set, 3 00

CATHOLIC MEMOIRS OF VERMONT AND NEW HAMPSHIRE. 12mo, cloth, 1.00 ; paper, 0 50

CATHOLIC WORSHIP. The Sacraments, Ceremonies, and Festivals of the Church explained. BRENNAN. Paper, 0.15 ; per 100, 9.00. Cloth, 0.25 ; per 100, 15 00

CATHOLIC YOUNG MAN OF THE PRESENT DAY. By Right Rev. AUGUSTINE EGGER, D.D. 32mo, paper, 0.15 ; per 100, 9.00. Cloth, 0.25 ; per 100, 15 00

CHARITY THE ORIGIN OF EVERY BLESSING. 16mo, 0 75

CHRIST IN TYPE AND PROPHECY. By Rev. A. J. MAAS, S.J. 2 vols., 12mo, *net*, 4 00
"By far the most serviceable manual that has hitherto appeared in the English language on a most important subject."—*London Tablet.*

CHRISTIAN ANTHROPOLOGY. By Rev. J. THIJIN. 8vo, *net*, 2 50

CHRISTIAN FATHER, THE : what he should be, and what he should do. Paper, 0.25 ; per 100, 12.50. Cloth, 0.35 ; per 100, 21 00

CHRISTIAN MOTHER, THE : the Education of her Children and her Prayer. Paper, 0.25 ; per 100, 12.50. Cloth, 0.35 ; per 100, 21 00

CIRCUS-RIDER'S DAUGHTER, THE. A novel. By F. v. BRACKEL. 12mo, 1 25

CLARKE, REV. RICHARD F., S.J. The Devout Year. Short Meditations. 24mo, *net*, 0 60

COCHEM'S EXPLANATION OF THE MASS. With Preface by Rt. Rev. C. P. MAES, D.D. 12mo, cloth, 1 25

COMEDY OF ENGLISH PROTESTANTISM, THE. Edited by A. F. MARSHALL, B.A. Oxon. 12mo, *net*, 0 50

COMPENDIUM SACRAE LITURGIAE Juxta Ritum Romanum una cum Appendice De Jure Ecclesiastico Particulari in America Foederata Sept. vigente scripsit P. WAPELHORST, O.S.F. 8vo, *net*, 2 50

STANDARD CATHOLIC BOOKS. 3

CONNOR D'ARCY'S STRUGGLES. A novel. By Mrs. W. M. BERTHOLDS. 12mo, 1 25

COUNSELS OF A CATHOLIC MOTHER to Her Daughter, 16mo, 0 50

CROWN OF THORNS, THE ; or, The Little Breviary of the Holy Face. 32mo, 0 50

DATA OF MODERN ETHICS EXAMINED, THE. By Rev. JOHN J. MING, S.J. 12mo, *net*, 2 00

DE GOESBRIAND, RIGHT REV. L. Christ on the Altar. Instructions for the Sundays and Festivals of the Year. Quarto cloth, richly illustrated, gilt edges, 6 00

—— Jesus the Good Shepherd. 16mo, *net*, 0 75

—— The Labors of the Apostles : Their Teaching of the Nations. 12mo, *net*, 1 00

—— History of Confession; or, The Dogma of Confession Vindicated. 16mo, *net*, 0 75

EGAN, MAURICE F. The Vocation of Edward Conway. A novel. 12mo, 1 25

—— The Flower of the Flock, and the Badgers of Belmont. 12mo, 1 00

—— How They Worked Their Way, and Other Stories, 1 00

—— A Gentleman. 16mo, 0 75

ENGLISH READER. Edited by Rev. EDWARD CONNOLLY, S.J. 12mo, 1 25

EUCHARISTIC GEMS. A Thought about the Most Blessed Sacrament for Every Day. By Rev. L. C. COELENBIER. 16mo, 0 75

EXAMINATION OF CONSCIENCE for the use of Priests who are making a Retreat. By GADUEL. 32mo, *net*, 0 30

EXPLANATION OF THE BALTIMORE CATECHISM of Christian Doctrine. By Rev. THOMAS L. KINKEAD. 12mo, *net*, 1 00

EXPLANATION OF THE GOSPELS of the Sundays and Holydays. From the Italian, by Rev. L. A. LAMBERT, LL.D. With An Explanation of Catholic Worship. From the German, by Rev. RICHARD BRENNAN, LL.D. 24mo, illustrated.
Paper, 0.25; 25 copies, 4.25; 50 copies, 7.50; 100 copies, 12 50
Cloth, 0.50; 25 copies, 8.50; 50 copies, 15.00; 100 copies, 25 00

"It is with pleasure I recommend the 'Explanation of the Gospels and of Catholic Worship' to the clergy and the laity. It should have a very extensive sale ; lucid explanation, clear style, solid matter, beautiful illustrations. Everybody will learn from this little book."—ARCHBISHOP JANSSENS.

FABIOLA ; or, The Church of the Catacombs. By CARDINAL WISEMAN. Illustrated Edition. 12mo, 1 25
Edition de luxe, 6 00

STANDARD CATHOLIC BOOKS.

FINN, REV. FRANCIS J., S.J. Percy Wynn ; or, Making a Boy of Him. 12mo, 0 85
—— Tom Playfair; or, Making a Start. 12mo, 0 85
—— Harry Dee; or, Working it Out. 12mo, 0 85
—— Claude Lightfoot ; or, How the Problem was Solved. 12mo, 0 85
—— Ethelred Preston; or, The Adventures of a Newcomer. 12mo, 0 85
—— Mostly Boys. 16mo, 0 85

Father Finn's books are, in the opinion of the best critics, standard works in modern English literature ; they are full of fascinating interest, replete with stirring and amusing incidents of college life, and admirably adapted to the wants of our boys.

FIVE O'CLOCK STORIES ; or, The Old Tales Told Again. 16mo, 0 75

FLOWERS OF THE PASSION. Thoughts of St. Paul of the Cross. By Rev. LOUIS TH. DE JÉSUS-AGONISANT. 32mo, 0 5c

FOLLOWING OF CHRIST, THE. By THOMAS À KEMPIS. With reflections. Small 32mo, cloth, 0 50
Without reflections. Small 32mo, cloth, 0 45
Edition de luxe. Illustrated, from 1 50 up.

FRANCIS DE SALES, ST. Guide for Confession and Communion. Translated by Mrs. BENNETT-GLADSTONE. 32mo, 0 60
—— Maxims and Counsels for Every Day. 32mo, 0 50
—— New Year Greetings. 32mo, flexible cloth, 15 cents ; per 100, 10 00

GENERAL PRINCIPLES OF THE RELIGIOUS LIFE. By Very Rev. BONIFACE F. VERHEYEN, O.S.B. 32mo, *net*, 0 30

GLORIES OF DIVINE GRACE. From the German of Dr. M. JOS. SCHEEBEN, by a BENEDICTINE MONK. 12mo, *net*, 1 50

GOD KNOWABLE AND KNOWN. RONAYNE. 12mo, *net*, 1 25

GOFFINE'S DEVOUT INSTRUCTIONS on the Epistles and Gospels. With Preface by His Eminence Cardinal GIBBONS. Illustrated edition. 8vo, cloth, 1.00; 10 copies, 7.50 ; 25 copies, 17.50; 50 copies, 33 50

This is the best, the cheapest, and the most popular illustrated edition of Goffine's Instructions.

"GOLDEN SANDS," Books by the Author of :
Golden Sands. Third, Fourth, Fifth Series. 32mo, each, 0 60
Book of the Professed. 32mo.
Vol. I. ⎫ *net*, 0 75
Vol. II. ⎬ Each with a steel-plate Frontispiece. *net*, 0 60
Vol. III. ⎭ *net*, 0 60
Prayer. 32mo, *net*, 0 40
The Little Book of Superiors. 32mo, *net*, 0 60
Spiritual Direction. 32mo, *net*, 0 60
Little Month of May. 32mo, flexible cloth, 0 25
Little Month of the Poor Souls. 32mo, flexible cloth, 0 25

STANDARD CATHOLIC BOOKS. 5

GREETINGS TO THE CHRIST-CHILD. A Collection of Christmas Poems for the Young. 16mo, illustrated,   0 50

GROU, REV. J., S.J. The Characteristics of True Devotion. Translated from the French by the Rev. ALEXANDER CLINTON, S.J. A new edition, by Rev. SAMUEL H. FRISBEE, S.J. 16mo,   *net*, 0 75

——— The Interior of Jesus and Mary. Edited by Rev. SAMUEL H. FRISBEE, S.J. 16mo, 2 vols.,   *net*, 2 00

HAMON'S MEDITATIONS. See under MEDITATIONS. 5 vols. 16mo,   *net*, 5 00

HANDBOOK FOR ALTAR SOCIETIES, and Guide for Sacristans and others having charge of the Altar and Sanctuary. 16mo,   *net*, 0 75

HANDBOOK OF THE CHRISTIAN RELIGION. For the use of Advanced Students and the Educated Laity. By Rev. W. WILMERS, S.J. From the German. Edited by Rev. JAMES CONWAY, S.J. 12mo,   *net*, 1 50

HAPPY YEAR, A; or, The Year Sanctified by Meditating on the Maxims and Sayings of the Saints. By ABBÉ LASAUSSE. 12mo,   *net*, 1 00

HEART, THE, OF ST. JANE FRANCES DE CHANTAL. Thoughts and Prayers. 32mo,   *net*, 0 40

HIDDEN TREASURE; or, The Value and Excellence of the Holy Mass. By ST. LEONARD OF PORT-MAURICE. 32mo,   0 50

HISTORY OF THE CATHOLIC CHURCH. By Dr H. BRUECK. With Additions from the Writings of His Eminence Cardinal Hergenröther. Translated by Rev. E. PRUENTE. 2 vols., 8vo,   *net*, 3 00

HISTORY OF THE CATHOLIC CHURCH. Adapted by Rev. RICHARD BRENNAN, LL.D. With a History of the Church in America, by JOHN GILMARY SHEA, LL.D. With 90 Illustrations. 8vo,   2 00

HISTORY OF THE MASS and its Ceremonies in the Eastern and Western Church. By Rev. JOHN O'BRIEN, A.M. 12mo, *net*, 1 25

HOLY FACE OF JESUS, THE. A Series of Meditations on the Litany of the Holy Face. 32mo,   0 50

HOURS BEFORE THE ALTAR; or, Meditations on the Holy Eucharist. By Mgr. DE LA BOUILLERIE. 32mo,   0 50

HOW TO GET ON. By Rev. BERNARD FEENEY. 12mo, paper, 0 50; cloth,   1 00

HUNOLT'S SERMONS. Sermons by the Rev. FRANCIS HUNOLT, Priest of the Society of Jesus and Preacher in the Cathedral of

6 STANDARD CATHOLIC BOOKS.

Treves. Translated from the original German edition of Cologne, 1740, by the Rev. J. ALLEN, D.D. 12 vols., 8vo, 30 00
Per set of 2 vols.,   *net*, 5 00
Vols. 1, 2. The Christian State of Life.
Vols. 3, 4. The Bad Christian.
Vols. 5, 6. The Penitent Christian.
Vols. 7, 8. The Good Christian.
Vols. 9, 10. The Christian's Last End.
Vols. 11, 12. The Christian's Model.

His Eminence Cardinal Satolli, Pro-Delegate Apostolic: " . . . I believe that in it is found realized the desire of the Holy Father, who not long ago in an encyclical urged so strongly the return to the simple, unaffected, but earnest and eloquent preaching of the word of God. . . ."
His Eminence Cardinal Gibbons, Archbishop of Baltimore: . . . "Contain a fund of solid doctrine, presented in a clear and forcible style. These sermons should find a place in the library of every priest. . . ."
His Eminence Cardinal Vaughan, Archbishop of Westminster: " . . . I cannot praise it too highly, and I think it might find a place in every priest's library."
His Eminence Cardinal Logue, Archbishop of Armagh, Primate of all Ireland: " . . . What is of real service is some work in which the preacher can find sound, solid matter. I believe Father Hunolt's Sermons furnishes an inexhaustible treasure of such matter. . . ."

IDOLS; or, The Secret of the Rue Chaussée d'Antin. A novel. By RAOUL DE NAVERY. 12mo,   1 25
INSTRUCTIONS ON THE COMMANDMENTS and the Sacraments. By ST. LIGUORI. 32mo. Paper, 0.25 ; per 100, 12 50
Cloth, 0.35; per 100,   21 00
KONINGS, THEOLOGIA MORALIS. Novissimi Ecclesiæ Doctoris S. Alphonsi. In Compendium Redacta, et Usui Venerabilis Cleri Americani Accommodata, Auctore A. KONINGS, C.SS. R. Editio septima, auctior, et novis curis expolitior, curante HENRICO KUPER, C.SS.R. The two vols. in one, half morocco, *net*, 4 00
LEGENDS AND STORIES OF THE HOLY CHILD JESUS from Many Lands. Collected by A. FOWLER LUTZ. 16mo, 0 75
LEPER QUEEN, THE. A Story of the Thirteenth Century. 16mo,   0 50
LIBRARY OF THE RELIGIOUS LIFE. Composed of "Book of the Professed," by the author of "Golden Sands," 3 vols. ; "Spiritual Direction," by the author of "Golden Sands" ; and "Souvenir of the Novitiate." 5 vols., 32mo, in case,   3 25
LIFE AND ACTS OF LEO XIII. By Rev. JOSEPH E. KELLER, S.J. Fully and beautifully illustrated. 8vo,   2 00
LIFE OF ST. ALOYSIUS GONZAGA. From the Italian of Rev. Father CEPARI, S.J. Edited by Rev. F. GOLDIE, S.J. Edition de luxe, richly illustrated. 8vo,   *net*, 2 50
LIFE OF THE EVER-BLESSED VIRGIN. From Her Conception to Her Assumption. 12mo, imitation cloth,   0 30
LIFE OF FATHER CHARLES SIRE. By his brother, Rev. VITAL SIRE. 12mo,   *net*, 1 00
LIFE OF ST. CLARE OF MONTEFALCO. By Rev. JOSEPH A. LOCKE, O.S.A. 12mo,   *net*, 0 75

STANDARD CATHOLIC BOOKS. 7

LIFE OF THE VEN. MARY CRESCENTIA HÖSS.
12mo, *net*, 1 25
LIFE OF REV. MOTHER ST. JOHN FONTBONNE. By ABBÉ RIVAUX. 12mo, *net*, 1 25
LIFE OF ST. FRANCIS SOLANUS, APOSTLE OF PERU.
16mo, *net*, 0 50
LIFE OF ST. GERMAINE COUSIN. 16mo, 0 50
LIFE OF ST. IGNATIUS OF LOYOLA. By Father GENELLI.
12mo, *net*, 1 25
LIFE OF ST. CHANTAL. See under ST. CHANTAL. *net*, 4 00
(LIFE OF) MOST REV. JOHN HUGHES, First Archbishop of New York. By Rev. H. A. BRANN, D.D. 12mo, *net*, 0 75
LIFE OF FATHER JOGUES. By Father FELIX MARTIN, S.J. From the French by JOHN GILMARY SHEA. 12mo, *net*, 0 75
LIFE OF MLLE. LE GRAS. 12mo, *net*, 1 25
LIFE OF MARY FOR CHILDREN. By ANNE R. BENNETT, née GLADSTONE. 24mo, illustrated, *net*, 0 50
LIFE OF RIGHT REV. JOHN N. NEUMANN, D.D. By Rev. E. GRIMM, C.SS R. 12mo, *net*, 1 25
LIFE OF OUR LORD AND SAVIOUR JESUS CHRIST and of His blessed Mother. Adapted by Rev. RICHARD BRENNAN, LL.D. With nearly 600 illustrations. No. 1. Roan back, gold title, plain cloth sides, sprinkled edges, *net*, 5 00
No. 3. Morocco back and corners, cloth sides with gold stamp, gilt edges, *net*, 7 00
No. 4. Full morocco, richly gilt back, with large figure of Our Lord in gold on side, gilt edges, *net*, 9 00
No. 5. Full morocco, block-paneled sides, superbly gilt, gilt edges, *net*, 10 00
LIFE OF OUR BLESSED LORD. His Life, Death, Resurrection. 12mo, imitation cloth, 0 30
LIFE, POPULAR, OF ST. TERESA OF JESUS. By L'ABBÉ MARIE-JOSEPH. 12mo, *net*, 0 75
LIGUORI, ST. ALPHONSUS DE. Complete Ascetical Works of. Centenary Edition. Edited by Rev. EUGENE GRIMM, C.SS.R. Price, per volume, *net*, 1 25

Each book is complete in itself, and any volume will be sold separately. Volumes 1 to 22 are now ready.

Preparation for Death.
Way of Salvation and of Perfection.
Great Means of Salvation and Perfection.
Incarnation, Birth, and Infancy of Christ.
The Passion and Death of Christ.
The Holy Eucharist.
The Glories of Mary, 2 vols.
Victories of the Martyrs.
True Spouse of Christ, 2 vols.
Dignity and Duties of the Priest.
The Holy Mass.
The Divine Office.
Preaching.
Abridged Sermons for all the Sundays.
Miscellany.
Letters, 4 vols.
Letters and General Index.
Life of St. Alphonsus, 2 vols.

STANDARD CATHOLIC BOOKS.

LINKED LIVES. A novel. By Lady GERTRUDE DOUGLAS.
8vo, 1 50

LITTLE COMPLIMENTS OF THE SEASON. Simple Verses for Namedays, Birthdays, Christmas, New Year, and other festive and social occasions. By ELEANOR C. DONNELLY. 12mo, *net*, 0 50

LITTLE MANUAL OF ST. ANTHONY. Illustrated. 32mo, cloth, 0 60

LITTLE MANUAL OF THE SODALITY OF THE CHILD JESUS. 32mo, 0 20

LITTLE PICTORIAL LIVES OF THE SAINTS. With Reflections for Every Day in the Year. Edited by JOHN GILMARY SHEA, LL.D. With nearly 400 illustrations. 12mo, cloth, ink and gold side, 1 00
10 copies, 6.25; 25 copies, 15.00; 50 copies, 27.50; 100 copies, 50 00
The book has received the approbation of the following prelates: Archbishop Kenrick, Archbishop Grace, Archbishop Hennessy, Archbishop Salpointe, Archbishop Ryan, Archbishop Gross, Archbishop Duhamel, Archbishop Kain, Archbishop O'Brien, Archbishop Katzer, Bishop McCloskey, Bishop Grandin, Bishop O'Hara, Bishop Mullen, Bishop Marty, Bishop Ryan, of Buffalo; Bishop Fink, Bishop Seidenbush, Bishop Moreau, Bishop Racine, Bishop Spalding, Bishop Vertin, Bishop Junger, Bishop Naughten, Bishop Richter, Bishop Rademacher, Bishop Cosgrove, Bishop Curtis, and Bishop Glorieux.

LITTLE PRAYER BOOK OF THE SACRED HEART. Prayers and Practices of Blessed Margaret Mary. Sm. 32mo, cloth, 0 40
Also in finer bindings.

LITTLE SAINT OF NINE YEARS. From the French of Mgr. DE SÉGUR, by MARY McMAHON. 16mo, 0 50

LIVES, SHORT, OF THE SAINTS; or, Our Birthday Bouquet. By ELEANOR C. DONNELLY. 16mo, 1 00

LOURDES. Its Inhabitants, Its Pilgrims, Its Miracles. By R. F. CLARKE, S.J. 16mo, illustrated, 0 75

LUTHER'S OWN STATEMENTS Concerning his Teachings and its Results. By HENRY O'CONNOR, S.J. 12mo, paper, 0 15

MANIFESTATION OF CONSCIENCE. Confessions and Communions in Religious Communities. By Rev. PIE DE LANGOGNE, O.M.Cap. 32mo, *net*, 0 50

MANUAL OF THE HOLY FAMILY. Prayers and Instructions for Catholic Parents. 32mo, cloth, 0 60
Also in finer bindings.

MANUAL OF INDULGENCED PRAYERS. A Complete Prayer Book. Arranged and disposed for daily use by Rev. BONAVENTURE HAMMER, O.S.F. Small 32mo, cloth, 0 40
Also in finer bindings.

MARCELLA GRACE. A novel. By ROSA MULHOLLAND. With illustrations after original drawings. 12mo, 1 25

MARRIAGE. By Very Rev. PÈRE MONSABRÉ, O.P. From the French, by M. HOPPER. 12mo, *net*, 1 00

STANDARD CATHOLIC BOOKS. 9

MARRIAGE, Popular Instructions On. By Very Rev. F. GIRARDEY, C.SS.R. 32mo, paper, 0.25; per 100, 12.50; cloth, 0.35; per 100, 21 00

The instructions treat of the great dignity of matrimony, its indissolubility, the obstacles to it, the evils of mixed marriage, the manner of getting married, and the duties it imposes on the married between each other and in reference to their offspring.

MEANS OF GRACE, THE. A Complete Exposition of the Seven Sacraments, of the Sacramentals, and of Prayer, with a Comprehensive Explanation of the "Lord's Prayer" and the "Hail Mary." By Rev. RICHARD BRENNAN, LL.D. With 180 full-page and other illustrations. 8vo, cloth, 2.50; gilt edges, 3.00; Library edition, half levant, 3 50

"The best book for family use out."—BISHOP MULLEN.
"A work worthy of unstinted praise and heartiest commendation."—BISHOP RYAN, of Buffalo.
"The wealth of matter, the admirable arrangement, and the simplicity of language of this work will make it a valuable addition to the household library."—BISHOP BRADLEY.

MEDITATIONS (BAXTER) for Every Day in the Year. By Rev. ROGER BAXTER, S.J. Republished by Rev. P. NEALE, S.J. Small 12mo, *net*, 1 25

MEDITATIONS (HAMON'S) FOR ALL THE DAYS OF THE YEAR. For the use of Priests, Religious, and the Laity. By Rev. M. HAMON, SS., Pastor of St. Sulpice, Paris. From the French, by Mrs. ANNE R. BENNETT-GLADSTONE. With Alphabetic Index. 5 vols., 16mo, cloth, gilt top, each with a Steel Engraving, *net*, 5 00

"The five handsome volumes will form a very useful addition to the devotional library of every ecclesiastic."—HIS EMINENCE CARDINAL LOGUE.
"Hamon's doctrine is the unadulterated word of God, presented with unction, exquisite taste, and freed from that exaggerated and sickly sentimentalism which disgusts when it does not mislead."—MOST REV P. L. CHAPELLE, D.D.
"We are using them daily, and are delighted with them."—MOTHER M. BLANCHE, Mother House Sisters of Charity, Mt. St. Joseph, O.
"Having examined the 'Meditations' by M. Hamon, SS., we are pleased to recommend them not only as useful and practicable for religious, but also for those who in the world desire by means of mental prayer to advance in the spiritual life."—SISTERS OF ST. JOSEPH, Flushing, L. I.

MEDITATIONS (PERINALDO) on the Sufferings of Jesus Christ. From the Italian of Rev. FRANCIS DA PERINALDO, O.S.F. 12mo, *net*, 0 ·75

MEDITATIONS (VERCRUYSSE), for Every Day in the Year, on the Life of Our Lord Jesus Christ. By the Rev. Father BRUNO VERCRUYSSE, S.J. 2 vols., 4 00

MEDITATIONS ON THE PASSION OF OUR LORD. By a PASSIONIST FATHER. 32mo, 0 40

MISTRESS OF NOVICES, The, Instructed in her Duties. From the French of the ABBÉ LEGUAY, by Rev. IGNATIUS SISK. 12mo, cloth, *net*, 0 75

MOMENTS BEFORE THE TABERNACLE. By Rev. MATTHEW RUSSELL, S.J. 24mo, *net*, 0 40

STANDARD CATHOLIC BOOKS.

MONK'S PARDON. A Historical Romance of the Time of Philip IV. of Spain. By RAOUL DE NAVERY. 12mo, 1 25

MONTH OF THE DEAD. 32mo, 0 75

MONTH OF MAY. From the French of Father DEBUSSI, S.J., by ELLA MCMAHON. 32mo, 0 50

MONTH, NEW, OF MARY, St. Francis de Sales. 32mo, 0 40

MONTH, NEW, OF THE SACRED HEART, St. Francis de Sales. 32mo, 0 40

MONTH, NEW, OF ST. JOSEPH, St. Francis de Sales. 32mo, 0 40

MONTH, NEW, OF THE HOLY ANGELS, St. Francis de Sales. 32mo, 0 40

MR. BILLY BUTTONS. A novel. By Walter Lecky. 12mo, 1 25

MÜLLER, REV. MICHAEL, C.SS.R. God the Teacher of Mankind. A plain, comprehensive Explanation of Christian Doctrine. 9 vols., crown 8vo. Per set, *net*, 9 50
The Church and Her Enemies. *net*, 1 10
The Apostles' Creed. *net*, 1 10
The First and Greatest Commandment. *net*, 1 40
Explanation of the Commandments, continued. Precepts of the Church. *net*, 1 10
Dignity, Authority, and Duties of Parents, Ecclesiastical and Civil Powers. Their Enemies. *net*, 1 40
Grace and the Sacraments. *net*, 1 25
Holy Mass. *net*, 1 25
Eucharist and Penance. *net*, 1 10
Sacramentals—Prayer, etc. *net*, 1 00

—— Familiar Explanation of Catholic Doctrine. 12mo, 1 00

—— The Prodigal Son; or, The Sinner's Return to God. 8vo, *net*, 1 00

—— The Devotion of the Holy Rosary and the Five Scapulars. 8vo, *net*, 0 75

—— The Catholic Priesthood. 2 vols., 8vo, *net*, 3 00

MY FIRST COMMUNION: The Happiest Day of My Life. BRENNAN. 16mo, illustrated, 0 75

NAMES THAT LIVE IN CATHOLIC HEARTS. Cardinal Ximenes—Michael Angelo—Samuel de Champlain—Archbishop Plunkett—Charles Carroll—Henry Larochejacquelein—Simon de Montfort. By ANNA T. SADLIER. 12mo, 1 00

NATALIE NARISCHKIN, Sister of Charity of St. Vincent of Paul. By Lady G. FULLERTON. 12mo, *net*, 0 75

NEW TESTAMENT, THE. 32mo. Limp cloth, *net*, 0.20; levant, *net*, 1.00; French calf, red edges, *net*, 1 60

STANDARD CATHOLIC BOOKS. 11

OFFICE, COMPLETE, OF HOLY WEEK, according to the Roman Missal and Breviary, in Latin and English. New edition, revised and enlarged. 24mo, cloth, 0.50 ; cloth limp, gilt edges, 1 00
Also in finer bindings.

O'GRADY, ELEANOR. Aids to Correct and Effective Elocution. 12mo, 1 25
—— Select Recitations for Schools and Academies. 12mo, 1 00
—— Readings and Recitations for Juniors. 16mo, *net*, 0 50
—— Elocution Class. A Simplification of the Laws and Principles of Expression. 16mo, *net*, 0 50

ON CHRISTIAN ART. By EDITH HEALY. 16mo, 0 50

ON THE ROAD TO ROME, and How Two Brothers Got There. By WILLIAM RICHARDS. 16mo, *net*, 0 75

ONE AND THIRTY DAYS WITH BLESSED MARGARET MARY. 32mo, flexible cloth, 0 25

ONE ANGEL MORE IN HEAVEN. With Letters of Condolence by St. Francis de Sales and others. White mar., 0 50

OUR BIRTHDAY BOUQUET. Culled from the Shrines of Saints and the Gardens of Poets. By E. C. DONNELLY. 16mo, 1 00

OUR LADY OF GOOD COUNSEL IN GENAZZANO. By ANNE R. BENNETT, née GLADSTONE. 32mo, 0 75

OUR OWN WILL, and How to Detect it in Our Actions. By the Rev. JOHN ALLEN, D.D. 16mo, *net*, 0 75

OUR YOUNG FOLKS' LIBRARY. 10 volumes. 12mo. Each, 0 50 ; per set, 3 00

OUTLAW OF CAMARGUE, THE. A novel. By A. DE LAMOTHE. 12mo, 1 25

OUTLINES OF DOGMATIC THEOLOGY. By Rev. SYLVESTER J. HUNTER, S.J. 3 vols., 12mo, *net*, 4 50

PARADISE ON EARTH OPENED TO ALL ; or, A Religious Vocation the Surest Way in Life. 32mo, *net*, 0 40

PEARLS FROM FABER. Selected and arranged by MARION J. BRUNOWE. 32mo, 0 50

PETRONILLA, and other Stories. By E. C. DONNELLY. 12mo, 1 00

PHILOSOPHY, ENGLISH MANUALS OF CATHOLIC.
Logic. By RICHARD F. CLARKE, S.J. 12mo, *net*, 1 25
First Principles of Knowledge. By JOHN RICKABY, S.J. 12mo, *net*, 1 25
Moral Philosophy (Ethics and Natural Law). By JOSEPH RICKABY, S.J. 12mo, *net*, 1 25
Natural Theology. By BERNARD BOEDDER, S.J. 12mo, *net*, 1 50
Psychology. By MICHAEL MAHER, S.J. 12mo, *net*, 1 50
General Metaphysics. By JOHN RICKABY, S.J. 12mo, *net*, 1 25
A Manual of Political Economy. By C. S. DEVAS, Esq., M.A. 12mo, *net*, 1 50

STANDARD CATHOLIC BOOKS.

PICTORIAL LIVES OF THE SAINTS. With Reflections for Every Day in the Year. Edited by JOHN GILMARY SHEA, LL.D. 50th Thousand. 8vo, 2 00
5 copies, 6.65 ; 10 copies, 12.50 ; 25 copies, 27.50 ; 50 copies, 50 00

PRAYER-BOOK FOR LENT. Meditations and Prayers for Lent. 32mo, cloth, 0 50
Also in finer bindings.

PRAXIS SYNODALIS. Manuale Synodi Diocesanæ ac Provincialis Celebrandæ. 12mo, *net*, 0 60

PRIEST IN THE PULPIT, THE. A Manual of Homiletics and Catechetics. Adapted from the German of Rev. I. SCHUECH, O.S.B., by Rev. B. LUEBBERMANN. 8vo, *net*, 1 50

PRIMER FOR CONVERTS, A. By Rev. J. T. DURWARD. 32mo, flexible cloth, 0 25

PRINCIPLES OF ANTHROPOLOGY AND BIOLOGY. By Rev. THOMAS HUGHES, S.J. 16mo, *net*, 0 75

REASONABLENESS OF CATHOLIC CEREMONIES AND PRACTICES. By Rev. J. J. BURKE. 12mo, flexible cloth, 0 35

RELIGIOUS STATE, THE. With a Short Treatise on Vocation to the Priesthood. By ST. ALPHONSUS DE LIGUORI. 32mo, 0 50

REMINISCENCES OF RT. REV. EDGAR P. WADHAMS, D.D., First Bishop of Ogdensburg. By Rev. C. A. WALWORTH. 12mo, illustrated, *net*, 1 00

RIGHTS OF OUR LITTLE ONES ; or, First Principles on Education in Catechetical Form. By Rev. JAMES CONWAY, S.J. 32mo, paper, 0.15 ; per 100, 9.00 ; cloth, 0.25 ; per 100, 15 00

ROSARY, THE MOST HOLY, in Thirty-one Meditations, Prayers, and Examples. By Rev. EUGENE GRIMM, C.SS.R. 32mo, 0 50

RUSSO, N., S.J.—De Philosophia Morali Prælectiones in Collegio Georgiopolitano Soc. Jes. Anno 1889-90 Habitae, a Patre NICOLAO RUSSO. Editio altera. 8vo, half leather, *net*, 2 00

ST. CHANTAL AND THE FOUNDATION OF THE VISITATION. By Monseigneur BOUGAUD. 2 vols., 8vo, *net*, 4 00

ST. JOSEPH, THE ADVOCATE OF HOPELESS CASES. From the French of Rev. Father HUGUET. 24mo, 1 00

SACRAMENTALS OF THE HOLY CATHOLIC CHURCH, THE. By Rev. A. A. LAMBING, LL.D. Large Edition, 12mo, *net*, 1 25
Popular Edition, illustrated, 24mo.
Paper, 0.25 ; 25 copies, 4.25 ; 50 copies, 7.50 ; 100 copies, 12 50
Cloth, 0.50 ; 25 copies, 8.50 ; 50 copies, 15.00 ; 100 copies, 25 00
"Am glad you have issued so practical a work, in a shape in which it ought to reach every Catholic family."—CARDINAL SATOLLI, Delegate Apostolic.

STANDARD CATHOLIC BOOKS. 13

SACRED HEART, BOOKS ON THE.

Devotions to the Sacred Heart for the First Friday of Every Month. By P. HUGUET. 32mo, 0 40
213. Imitation Levant, limp, gilt centre, round corners, edges red under gold, 1 35
Imitation of the Sacred Heart of Jesus. By Rev. F. ARNOUDT, S.J. From the Latin by Rev. J. M. FASTRE, S.J. 16mo, cloth, 1 25
Month of the Sacred Heart of Jesus. From the French of Rev. Father HUGUET. 32mo, 0 75
New Month of the Sacred Heart, St. Francis de Sales. 32mo, 0 40
One and Thirty Days with Blessed Margaret Mary. From the French by a Visitandine of Baltimore. 32mo, flexible cloth, 0 25
Pearls from the Casket of the Sacred Heart of Jesus. A Collection of the Letters, Maxims, and Practices of the Blessed Margaret Mary Alacoque. Edited by ELEANOR C. DONNELLY. 32mo, 0 50
Month of the Sacred Heart for the Young Christian. By BROTHER PHILIPPE. From the French by E. A. MULLIGAN. 32mo, 0 50
Sacred Heart Studied in the Sacred Scriptures. By Rev. H. SAINTRAIN, C.SS.R. 8vo, *net*, 2 00
Revelations of the Sacred Heart to Blessed Margaret Mary; and the History of her Life. By Monseigneur BOUGAUD. 8vo, *net*, 1 50
Six Sermons on Devotion to the Sacred Heart of Jesus. From the German of Rev. Dr. E. BIERBAUM, by ELLA McMAHON. 16mo, *net*, 0 60
Year of the Sacred Heart. Drawn from the works of PÈRE DE LA COLOMBIÈRE, of Blessed Margaret Mary, and of others. 32mo, 0 50

SAINTS, THE NEW, OF 1888. By Rev. FRANCIS GOLDIE, S.J., and Rev. Father SCOLA, S.J. 16mo, illustrated, 0 50

SECRET OF SANCTITY, THE. According to ST. FRANCIS DE SALES and Father CRASSET, S.J. 12mo, *net*, 1 00

SERAPHIC GUIDE. A Manual for the Members of the Third Order of St. Francis. 0 60
Roan, red edges, 0 75
  The same in German at the same prices.

SERMONS, HUNOLT. See under HUNOLT.

SERMONS ON THE BLESSED VIRGIN. By Very Rev. D. I. McDERMOTT. 16mo, *net*, 0 75

SERMONS for the Sundays and Chief Festivals of the Ecclesiastical Year. With Two Courses of Lenten Sermons and a Triduum for the Forty Hours. By Rev. JULIUS PUTTGEISSER, S.J. From the German by Rev. JAMES CONWAY, S.J. 2 vols., 8vo, *net*, 2 50

STANDARD CATHOLIC BOOKS.

SERMONS, SHORT, FOR LOW MASSES. A complete, brief course of instruction on Christian Doctrine. By Rev. F. X. SCHOUPPE, S.J. 12mo, *net*, 1 25

SERMONS, SIX, on Devotion to the Sacred Heart of Jesus. From the German of Rev. Dr. E. BIERBAUM, by ELLA MCMAHON, 16mo, *net*, 0 60

SHORT CONFERENCES ON THE LITTLE OFFICE OF THE IMMACULATE CONCEPTION. By Very Rev. JOSEPH RAINER. With Prayers. 32mo, 0 50

SHORT STORIES ON CHRISTIAN DOCTRINE: A Collection of Examples illustrating the Catechism. From the French by MARY MCMAHON. 12mo, illustrated, *net*, 0 75

SMITH, Rev. S. B., D.D. Elements of Ecclesiastical Law.
Vol. I. Ecclesiastical Persons. 8vo, *net*, 2 50
Vol. II. Ecclesiastical Trials. 8vo, *net*, 2 50
Vol. III. Ecclesiastical Punishments. 8vo, *net*, 2 50
—— Compendium Juris Canonici, ad usum Cleri et Seminariorum hujus regionis accommodatum. 8vo, *net*, 2 00
—— The Marriage Process in the United States. 8vo, *net*, 2 50

SODALISTS' VADE MECUM. A Manual, Prayer Book, and Hymnal. 32mo, cloth, 0 50
Also in finer bindings.

SOUVENIR OF THE NOVITIATE. From the French by Rev. EDWARD I. TAYLOR. 32mo, *net*, 0 60

SPIRITUAL CRUMBS FOR HUNGRY LITTLE SOULS. To which are added Stories from the Bible. By MARY E. RICHARDSON. 16mo, 0 50

STORIES FOR FIRST COMMUNICANTS, for the Time before and after First Communion. By Rev. J. A. KELLER, D.D. 32mo, 0 50

STORY OF JESUS SIMPLY TOLD FOR THE YOUNG. By ROSA MULHOLLAND. 24mo, illustrated, 0 50

SURE WAY TO A HAPPY MARRIAGE. A Book of Instructions for those Betrothed and for Married People. From the German by Rev. EDWARD I. TAYLOR. Paper, 0.25; per 100, 12.50; cloth, 0.35; per 100, 21 00

TALES AND LEGENDS OF THE MIDDLE AGES. From the Spanish of F. DE P. CAPELLA. By HENRY WILSON. 16mo, 0 75

THINK WELL ON'T; or, Reflections on the Great Truths of the Christian Religion. By the Right Rev. R. CHALLONER, D.D. 32mo, flexible cloth, 0 20

THOUGHT FROM ST. ALPHONSUS, for Every Day of the Year. 32mo, 0 50

THOUGHT FROM BENEDICTINE SAINTS. 32mo, 0 50

STANDARD CATHOLIC BOOKS 15

THOUGHT FROM DOMINICAN SAINTS. 32mo, 0 50
THOUGHT FROM ST. FRANCIS ASSISI and his Saints. 32mo, 0 50
THOUGHT FROM ST. IGNATIUS. 32mo, 0 50
THOUGHT FROM ST. TERESA. 32mo, 0 50
THOUGHT FROM ST. VINCENT DE PAUL. 32mo, 0 50
TRUE SPOUSE OF CHRIST. By ST. ALPHONSUS LIGUORI. 2 vols., 12mo, *net*, 2.50 ; 1 vol., 12mo, 1 50
TRUTHS OF SALVATION. By Rev. J. PERGMAYR, S.J. From the German by a Father of the same Society. 16mo, *net*, 0 75
TWELVE VIRTUES, THE, of a Good Teacher. For Mothers, Instructors, etc. By Rev. H. POTTIER, S.J. 32mo, *net*, 0 30
VISIT TO EUROPE AND THE HOLY LAND. By Rev. H. F. FAIRBANKS. 12mo, illustrated, 1 50
VISITS TO THE MOST HOLY SACRAMENT and to the Blessed Virgin Mary. For Every Day of the Month. BY ST. ALPHONSUS DE LIGUORI. Edited by Rev. EUGENE GRIMM. 32mo, 0 50
WARD, REV. THOMAS F. Fifty-two Instructions on the Principal Truths of Our Holy Religion. 12mo, *net*, 0 75
——— Thirty-two Instructions for the Month of May and for the Feasts of the Blessed Virgin. 12mo, *net*, 0 75
——— Month of May at Mary's Altar. 12mo, *net*, 0 75
WAY OF INTERIOR PEACE. By Rev. FATHER DE LEHEN, S.J. From the German Version of Rev. J. BRUCKER, S.J. 12mo, *net*, 1 25
WENINGER'S SERMONS.
Original Short and Practical Sermons for Every Sunday of the Year. Three Sermons for every Sunday. 8vo, *net*, 2 00
Sermons for Every Feast of the Ecclesiastical Year. Three Sermons for Every Feast. 8vo, *net*, 2 00
Conferences specially addressed to Married and Unmarried Men. 8vo, *net*, 2 00
WHAT CATHOLICS HAVE DONE FOR SCIENCE, with Sketches of the Great Catholic Scientists. By Rev. MARTIN S. BRENNAN. 12mo, 1 00
WOMEN OF CATHOLICITY: Margaret O'Carroll—Isabella of Castile—Margaret Roper—Marie de l'Incarnation—Margaret Bourgeoys—Ethan Allen's Daughter. By ANNA T. SADLIER. 12mo, 1 00
WORDS OF JESUS CHRIST DURING HIS PASSION, explained in their Literal and Moral Sense. By Rev. F. X. SCHOUPPE, S.J. Flexible cloth, 0 25
WORDS OF WISDOM. A Concordance of the Sapiential Books. 12mo, *net*, 1 25
ZEAL IN THE WORK OF THE MINISTRY; or, The Means by which every Priest may render his Ministry Honorable and Fruitful. From the French of L'ABBÉ DUBOIS. 8vo, *net*, 1 50

THE BEST, THE CHEAPEST, THE MOST POPULAR
EDITION OF

GOFFINE'S DEVOUT INSTRUCTIONS

On the Epistles and Gospels for the Sundays and Holydays; with the Lives of many Saints of God, Explanations of Christian Faith and Duty, and of Church Ceremonies, a method of hearing Mass, Morning and Evening Prayers, and a Description of the Holy Land. With a Preface

BY HIS EMINENCE CARDINAL GIBBONS.

8vo, cloth, 704 pages, with nearly 150 illustrations. $1 00

As a work of spiritual reading and instruction "Goffine's Devout Instructions" stands in the foremost rank. In it the faithful will find explained in a plain, simple manner the doctrines of the Church, her sacraments and ceremonies, as set forth in the Epistles and Gospels of the Sundays and holydays.
A greatly improved edition of this work is now published, with large clear type and beautiful illustrations, at such a low price that every Catholic family may possess it.

| 25 Cents each in paper. | LIBRARY OF CATHOLIC INSTRUCTION. SPECIAL PRICES FOR QUANTITIES. | 50 Cents each in cloth. |

CHURCH CEREMONIES, and Explanation of the Ecclesiastical Year. From the French of the Abbé DURAND. 16mo, illustrated.

THE SACRAMENTALS of the Holy Catholic Church. By Rev. A. A. LAMBING. 16mo, illustrated.

EXPLANATION OF THE GOSPELS and of Catholic Worship. By Rev. L. A. LAMBERT and Rev. R. BRENNAN. 16mo, illustrated.

CATHOLIC BELIEF. By Very Rev. FÁA DI BRUNO. 16mo.

| 25 Cents each in paper. | CATHOLIC FAMILY LIBRARY. SPECIAL PRICES FOR QUANTITIES. | 35 Cents each in cloth. |

POPULAR INSTRUCTIONS ON MARRIAGE. By Very Rev. F. GIRARDEY, C.SS.R. 32mo.

INSTRUCTIONS ON THE COMMANDMENTS AND SACRAMENTS. By ST. ALPHONSUS LIGUORI. 32mo.

THE CHRISTIAN FATHER. What He should be, and what He should do. 32mo.

THE CHRISTIAN MOTHER. The Education of Her Children, and Her Prayer. 32mo.

A SURE WAY TO A HAPPY MARRIAGE. A book for those betrothed and for married people. 32mo.

www.ingramcontent.com/pod-product-compliance
Lightning Source LLC
Chambersburg PA
CBHW051844300426
44117CB00006B/259